MW01518207

A SEARCH FOR

Anne Konrad's *Red Quarter Moon* is the gripping account of her search for family members lost and disappeared within the Soviet Union. Konrad's ancestors, Mennonites, had settled the Ukrainian steppes in the late 1790s. An ethno-religious minority, they became special objects of Soviet persecution. Though her parents fled in 1929, many relatives remained in the USSR.

Konrad's search for these missing extended family members took place over twenty years, on five continents – across muddy roads and lonesome steppes, and in old letters, documents, or secret police archives. Her story emerges as both haunting and inspiring, filled with dramatically different accounts from survivors now scattered across the world. She aligns the voices of her subjects chronologically against the backdrop of Soviet policy, intertwining the historical context of the Terror Years with her own personal quest. *Red Quarter Moon* is an enthralling journey into the past that offers a unique look at the lives of ordinary families and individuals in the USSR.

(Tsarist and Soviet Mennonite Studies)

ANNE KONRAD is a writer living in Toronto.

ANNE KONRAD

Red Quarter Moon
A Search for Family in the Shadow of Stalin

Early in January I went outdoors and looked up at the moon. Strange, I thought, one quarter of the moon is red. I took a closer look. From under a cloud, dark as night, a fiery stake long as a hand emerged and seemed to hold back the moon. As the moon tried to move forward, fearsome to behold, half a hand pushed itself forward and appeared to threaten the moon, forcing it to stop. The whole drama was over in a moment, but as I continued to look, I saw a star and it also disappeared. What can this mean?

Agatha Wieler

UNIVERSITY OF TORONTO PRESS
Toronto Buffalo London

© University of Toronto Press 2012
Toronto Buffalo London
www.utppublishing.com
Printed in the U.S.A.

Reprinted 2013

ISBN 978-1-4426-4250-8 (cloth)
ISBN 978-1-4426-1139-9 (paper)

Printed on acid-free paper

Library and Archives Canada Cataloguing in Publication

Konrad, Anne
Red quarter moon : a search for family in the shadow of Stalin / Anne Konrad.

(Tsarist and Soviet Mennonite studies)
Includes bibliographical references and index.
ISBN 978-1-4426-4250-8 (bound). – ISBN 978-1-4426-1139-9 (pbk.)

1. Konrad family.   2. Braun family.   3. Mennonites – Soviet Union –
Biography.   4. Mennonites – Soviet Union – History – 20th century.
5. Persecution – Soviet Union – History – 20th century.   I. Title.   II. Series:
Tsarist and Soviet Mennonite studies

BX8119.S65K65 2012   289.7'470904   C2011-903096-9

University of Toronto Press acknowledges the financial assistance to
its publishing program of the Canada Council for the Arts and the
Ontario Arts Council.

University of Toronto Press acknowledges the financial support of the
Government of Canada through the Canada Book Fund for its publishing
activities.

For Harvey

And for the thousands of unknown Mennonites who suffered
Soviet oppression

Contents

Photo section follows page 170

Foreword

A former colleague of mine, the late Professor Ernest Gellner, often observed that while Soviet official life was uncompromisingly grey and boring, private Soviet life was quite the opposite: colourful, dramatic, tragic, even heroic. He was absolutely right. And there is reason for this.

In an extraordinarily inhuman way the Soviet government disregarded individuals and their needs and wishes. Daily survival was a desperate struggle. Basic foodstuffs such as bread and potatoes were always in short supply, and so were daily necessities such as soap, toilet paper, and toothpaste. In fact, consumer goods were often out of reach of ordinary citizens, and when they were available they were of inferior quality. People were forced to go to tremendous lengths to satisfy the most basic needs.

Worse, there was terror – arrest, exile, execution. Terror destroyed individuals, broke millions of marriages, orphaned untold numbers of children, drove people out of their homes, and scattered families all over the country. The private lives of people were always under watch by the feared secret police – their agents and informers were everywhere. Terror made individuals fear one another, but it also meant that the helpless turned to one another in private and often secretly. Personal treacheries may have been ubiquitous, but so were personal bonds. Many of those hurled into the Soviet meat grinder did not survive. Some who did (such as the well-known poet Anna Akhmatova, the Nobel Prize–winning writer Aleksandr Solzhenitsyn, and others, known and unknown) wrote subsequently about their lives. Others outlived the Soviet Union to speak freely about what they and others had endured or could not endure. Then the formerly closed Soviet archives began to open. In the deadly monotone of official language, the archival documents began to reveal long-held secrets about people who had disappeared. Their lives proved both tragic and heroic.

Anne Konrad describes precisely such extraordinary lives – the lives of her extended family. This is a gripping story of individuals caught in an inhuman world. A Mennonite family, originally from 'Russia' (meaning the Russian Empire and the Soviet Union), they were eventually scattered across the globe: today's Russia, Ukraine, Germany, Mongolia, China, North America, and Latin America. The Konrads and the Brauns, with Netherlandic, East Prussian, and Polish roots, were immigrants to Russia. When towards the end of the eighteenth century Russia's German-born Empress Catherine II ('Catherine the Great') conquered 'southern Russia,' or the northern Black Sea shores, from Ottoman Turkey, she encouraged people to come and settle this sparsely populated area. Among those who responded to Catherine's call were German-speaking Mennonites who were promised freedom from religious persecution and exemption from military duties. The Konrads and the Brauns were among those colonizers who immigrated to Russia in the eighteenth and nineteenth centuries. They were left relatively free from outside intervention in their self-government.

The twentieth century hurled the Russian Mennonite communities into great turmoil, however. During the First World War, when Russia and Germany fought against each other, the German-speaking Mennonites were treated as enemy aliens, even though they remained largely loyal to the Russian government. Many had their property confiscated. Still, the Mennonites manifested their pacifism, performing alternative service in place of military duties for the Russian government.

The Bolshevik October Revolution of 1917 and the subsequent Civil War fundamentally changed the lives of the Mennonite colonists. The new Marxist government was suspicious of the Mennonite communities, which were tightly organized and resistant to outside control. Their reputation for hard work and apparent wealth – at least greater wealth than that of their Slavic neighbours – now pointed to them as class enemies. They were suspect, to one degree or another, in the eyes of all the major political groups – the atheist Reds, the chauvinistic Whites, the anarchists, and the Ukrainian nationalists. The result was outbreaks of violence against them. Thousands disappeared in the Soviet prison system or were killed. Many fled abroad – to Germany, Canada, Brazil, Paraguay, and other countries. Some Mennonites, exiled to the Far East, escaped to Manchuria, from where they then immigrated to the Americas. The Konrads and the Brauns were scattered around the globe.

As Iosif Stalin's 'revolution from above' gathered momentum in the late 1920s, the remaining Mennonites, regarded as kulaks (rich peasants) inherently opposed to the collectivization of agriculture, were dispossessed and exiled. Many were forced to abandon their traditional lives of farming and flee to industrial centres such as Donetsk, Ukraine. Others, seeking to escape the inevitable destruction of their traditional lives, sought to emigrate abroad. The Soviet government, however, fearing the adverse publicity of people fleeing from a 'Soviet socialist paradise,' allowed only a few to leave the country. The plight of the Mennonites was further complicated by the tragic famine crisis of 1932–3, which cost millions of lives across the country.

It is difficult to ascertain whether the Mennonites suffered more than others (the ethnic Ukrainians, for instance), but, in any case, the famine proved devastating to them. While religious and other groups abroad tried to organize financial and material aid for the famished Germans, Mennonites, and others in the Soviet Union, particularly in Ukraine, by then the Soviet Union's relatively cordial relations with Weimar Germany had deteriorated considerably and any aid from Germany was regarded with suspicion. Adolf Hitler's ascension to power in January 1933, at the height of the famine in Ukraine, dramatically aggravated Soviet–German relations. The German consulates in Kyiv and Kharkiv in Ukraine were called 'Hitler consulates.' As a result, all German speakers in the Soviet Union came to appear, in the eyes of the Soviet government, as fascist candidates and potential spies for Nazi Germany. By 1935 the Soviet government had collected complete data on all ethnic Germans and Mennonites in the country as potential enemy aliens.

As the clouds of war gathered to the west and to the east, Stalin terrorized the nation, in 1937 and 1938 (the Great Terror) killing nearly one million Soviet citizens as enemies of the people – German, Polish, and Japanese 'spies.' Almost as many people were arrested and exiled or confined to labour camps in remote areas of the country – Siberia, Kazakhstan, and elsewhere. The ethnic Germans and the Mennonites were among the hardest hit by the Great Terror, and among them were the Konrads and the Brauns, as Anne Konrad has discovered.

The Great Terror decimated the Mennonite colonies in Ukraine. Those who survived the Great Terror were then subjected to nearly wholesale deportation at the beginning of the Second World War. Nevertheless, the invading German forces did find surviving ethnic Germans (*Volksdeutsche*) in Ukraine, among whom they included the Mennonites. As the German forces were rolled back by the Soviet Red Army later during the war, almost all ethnic Germans as well as many Mennonites went along with the German military and left Ukraine. At least twenty-thousand of these Mennonites were later forcibly repatriated and sent to Siberia. Thus ended a century and half of German and Mennonite presence in Ukraine.

With admirable persistence, Anne Konrad has managed to trace the lives of most of her relatives affected by these tragic times. She has scanned archives and collected testimonies in several continents, ranging from Canada to Ukraine, to Siberia, to Paraguay. Konrad offers a unique perspective on the personal costs of religion in Russia.

Hiroaki Kuromiya

Acknowledgments

I am grateful to my parents Luise Braun Konrad and Peter Jakob Konrad for their dedication to family and to their many relatives and others in a former homeland. Daily, before breakfast, my father would pray aloud, mentioning relatives and people experiencing oppression in many parts of the world. In this way we children learned that victims were once vibrant people, that refugees need support, and that family and community are not to be taken for granted. Relatives were important, but where were they? My father was the only one of his originally nine siblings who escaped to Canada.

As a child, living in then backwoods northern Alberta, at every Christmas, Easter, or other religious holiday, my parents (with some of their nine children) attended a church service and then 'visited' with similarly sized Mennonite families. At the home of a relative we shared a meal, and while the adults sat together and talked about 'Russia,' we children played outdoors or at board games. After my family moved to British Columbia, we siblings annually visited our Uncle Nick and Aunt Kay on Christmas Eve, sitting in front of their fireplace as our uncle joked and our aunt handed around icebox cookies. As teenagers, we joined friends from our church to go house to house at midnight singing Christmas carols at bedroom windows.

Sparing us the grim details of Soviet persecution and loss, my parents talked about days in tsarist Russia with longing and nostalgia. We ate Russian, Ukrainian, and Dutch foods. We listened to German-language sermons in spare church buildings. In choirs, singing a cappella, or in a congregation with a lay presenter, we sang many of the hymns and carols our parents knew 'from Russia.'

Most people in the small communities where I grew up were fellow immigrant Mennonite families who had arrived in Canada after the Bolshevik Revolution. There had been a social levelling after the Revolution, and formerly rich and poor were on a relatively equal economic footing. Most were struggling pioneer farmers in Alberta and emerging successful dairy, chicken, and berry farmers in BC. With traditions and skills brought from hundreds of years of living in self-sustaining communities, originally in the Netherlands and Germany, then Poland and tsarist Russia, soon after they reached Canada these Mennonites built schools and churches, organized cooperatives, and developed communities. As they improved their farms and began to create businesses, took up trades and joined professions, they sought to keep their Anabaptist principles, their established methods of providing for the less fortunate, a great love of music, and biblical as well as secular education. There were differences of opinion, but none forgot the communities from which they had come.

By the time my parents died I had long ago left the community where I grew up, but my mother's letters had kept me in touch with that world. After my parents' deaths, assessing their archive of hundreds of letters and photographs, many from relatives scattered across the globe, I began to compile a saga of my immediate family, tracing my ancestors back to 1790 when they arrived on the wide open steppes of present-day southern Ukraine. Genealogy itself was fine, but I wished to know more than names and 'begats.' I devoured histories, sought out archives, read old newspapers, and looked up people with stories. The sheer number of people and events I was encountering made me decide to write a family record, placing people into their settings and times, and a separate book about the people who were missing – my uncles and aunts and other people who had not escaped the Soviet Union, the ones my parents' generation said had been *'verschleppt.'* Why had so many of my uncles – indeed, half of all Soviet Mennonite males – perished?

In the over twenty years that it has taken to reach publication, many people have assisted me in my research and quest. Early on, I explored the Mennonite Heritage Centre in Winnipeg, photocopying letters from Mennonite newspapers from the 1920s and 1930s. I thank archivists Ken Reddig and his staff, present director Alf Redekop and archivist Conrad Stoesz for their generous assistance. The Conrad Grebel Library in Waterloo, Ontario, was another source of Mennonite journals and newspapers. Leona Gislason drew my attention to files on the Internet. Anda Sipolins lent me books on Latvian women in Soviet prisons. William Schroeder and Helmut T. Huebert (Winnipeg) generously permitted me to use maps from their *Mennonite Historical Atlas*. Weldon Hiebert (Winnipeg) drew maps for this volume. I thank the State Archive of the Kherson Region Ukraine and archivist Elena Igorevna Stukalovo for generous access to interrogation files. I also thank the State Archive of Donetsk Region, Donetsk, Ukraine, and archivist N.B. Metalnikova for assistance. Similarly I thank the State Security Service Ukraine in Donetsk for access to the files I requested. I also am indebted to the State Archive Zaporizhiia Region, Ukraine, and archivist Aleksandr Teedev. The library of the BC Mennonite Historical Society (Abbotsford, BC) contained German *Einwandererzentralstelle* (Immigration Centre) or EWZ Files, records of Mennonite obituaries, and other materials. The University of Toronto Library provided many books on Soviet and Russian history. The Mennonite Centre Library in Toronto (St Clair and O'Connor) and Harvey Dyck's private Mennonite history library were easily accessible.

Audrey Poetker and Turnstone Press (Winnipeg) generously allowed me to include two of Poetker's poems. A quotation from *Captain Corelli's Mandolin* by Louis de Bernières, published by Vintage, is used by permission of the Random House Group Ltd (London, UK).

I thank Jack Thiessen (New Bothwell, Manitoba), for his wit and for checking Plautdietsch expressions I use in my book. The interrogation records of Isaak Isakovich Braun found in the State Archive of Kherson and of Johannes Isakovich Braun from the State Archive of Donetsk were translated from Russian by Elena Davidova, Serge Markarov, and Harvey L. Dyck (Toronto). I acknowledge my interpreters, the late Maria Vasilevskaya and Ludmilla Kariaka (Zaporozhye, Ukraine), and Nelly Konrad (Göttingen, Germany), who was both interpreter and confidant. My sister Lillian Toews and Mennonite historian John B. Toews (Abbotsford, BC) encouraged me.

Many people shared their stories. I am grateful to my mother's former pupil Anna Wiens Reimer and her son Hank (Oakwood, Ontario), Jacob Gossen (Leamington, Ontario), Leo and Erika Thiessen (Toronto, Ontario), Selma Woelk Neudorf (Toronto), Kay Braun and Henry Brown (Abbotsford, BC), Peter Braun (Montreal), and Jutti Epp Goering (Vancouver, BC). In Germany, over a period of years, I met with émigrés from the USSR, including my Uncle Gerhard Konrad (Bremen), his daughter Nelly (Göttingen), son Ottomar and wife Ira (previously Tashkent and now Bremen). I visited Lena Wiebe (Neuwied), her sister Agatha Klassen (Marienheide), and sister-in-law Amalia Wiebe and her sons Viktor (Leipzig) and Peter (Berlin), as well as a cousin, Helene Blumenschein (Rheine). In Bonn, Greta and Viktor Braun and their children were more than welcoming. Jakob and Nina Wiebe (Cappeln) invited us to their daughter's wedding. My cousin Maria Liebe Reich and her daughter Anna Marie (Zurich) added to an understanding of the Konrad family. My Aunt Justina Epp's children and grandchildren in Curitiba and Witmarsum, Brazil, and in the Chaco and in East Paraguay told us their stories.

I thank all the people in the former USSR who shared food, sometimes accommodation, laughter, and tears with my husband and me on our many trips to Ukraine, Russia, Kazakhstan, Uzbekistan, and Kirghizia. In particular I am indebted to Alici Braun, her son Vanya, his wife Tanya and daughter Dasha, also her son Volodya and Nadia (Shakhty), Maria Braun and her sons Jura and wife Tanya, Andrei and wife Natasha and Volodya and wife Natasha (Slavgorod), Andrei and Maria Braun and their family (Konstantinovka on the Kulunda steppe) and Pavel (Ufa). In Davlekanova on the Bashkir steppe Director Ramzil of the Stroitelnii Tekhnikum drove us around in his white Lada, and Massar Z. Muchametzyanov, director of the Historical Museum, in a town without taxis, located an ancient Lincoln to help us find my mother's village. Pyotr Vibe, director of the Omsk State Museum of History and Regional Studies (Omsk) helped us find my father's village. Boris Trenin of Memorial showed us prison cells in Tomsk. Historian Andrei Savin (Novosibirsk) aided my research.

John Staples, chairperson and associate professor of history at SUNY Fredonia, Jamestown, New York, read my manuscript and saw it as an important contribution to an understanding of the social history of the Soviet period. I thank him and Professor Hiroaki Kuromiya, Indiana University, for their interest and generous support of this book. I also thank my supportive colleagues at West Toronto Collegiate (Toronto) who supported my writing. Sarah Dyck (Waterloo, Ontario) and Elma Schemenauer (Kamloops, BC) gave me editing suggestions. At the University of Toronto Press I wish to thank Jenna Germaine for her helpful assistance and Patricia Simoes for her concept of an evocative cover design. I am indebted to Ian MacKenzie (Toronto) for his meticulous attention in copyediting, and to Wayne Herrington and Richard Ratzlaff for cheerfulness under production stress.

It is always good if your children will read your books. Maria, Toozie, Alexander, and Stephanie have done this. My love and gratitude goes to my husband, Harvey. I ransacked his well-stocked library so frequently that he had to search my study for books on Russian history. He accompanied me on the many trips to look up contacts and relatives. We joked that my relatives scattered across the world provided him with historical sources and excuses to travel. Always unwilling to talk about my writing in advance (superstitious, perhaps), I refused to let him read my manuscript until I had my draft completed. He told me I had too many names but totally supported the project. Having met survivors, learned about their lives and deaths, we shared a strong sense that the thousands who were denied communities, family life, homes, health, religion, and freedom from fear – those who suffered in the shadow of Stalin – needed to be remembered. But as real people and with more than names.

For consistency, and true to the era the book covers, I have used Russian spelling for most place names.

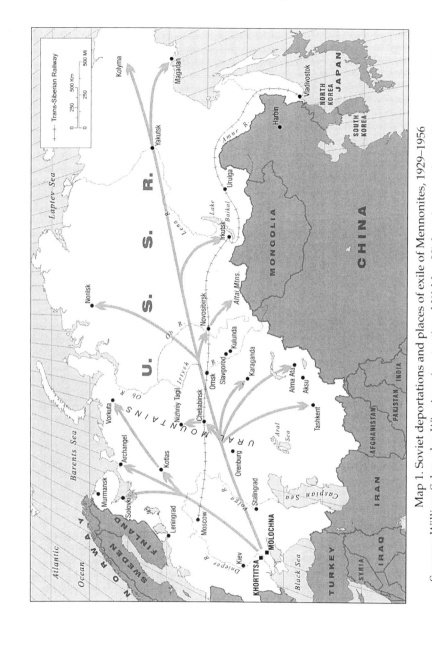

Map 1. Soviet deportations and places of exile of Mennonites, 1929–1956

Sources: William Schroeder, Winnipeg (content) and Weldon Hiebert (geographer and cartographer)

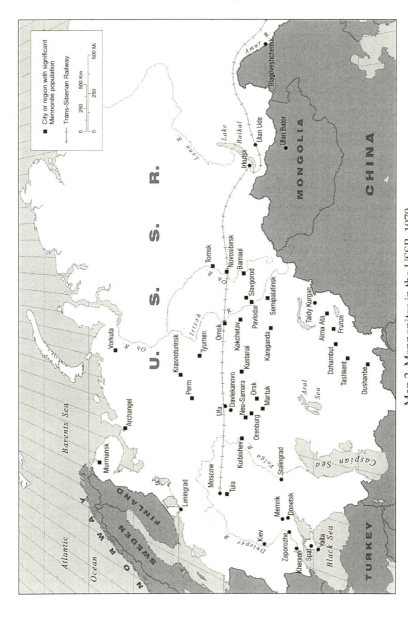

Map 2. Mennonites in the USSR, 1970

Sources: William Schroeder, Winnipeg (content) and Weldon Hiebert (geographer and cartographer)

KONRAD FAMILY*

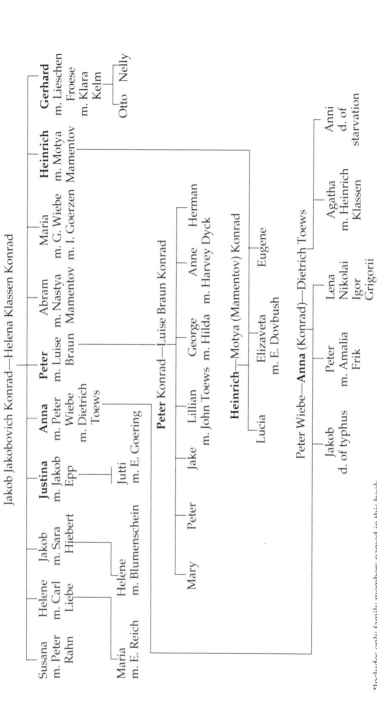

*Includes only family members named in this book

BRAUN FAMILY*

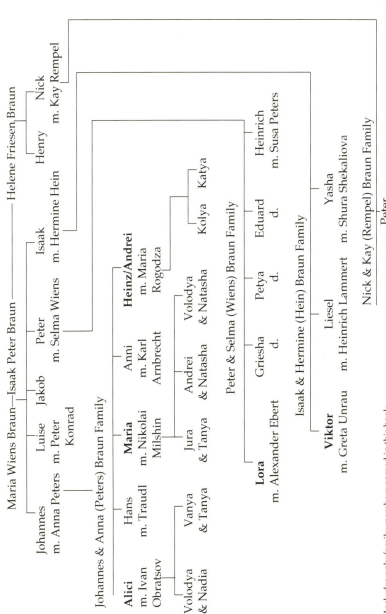

*Includes only family members named in this book

RED QUARTER MOON:
A SEARCH FOR FAMILY IN THE SHADOW OF STALIN

The ultimate truth is that history ought to consist only of the anecdotes of the little people who are caught up in it.

– Louis de Bernières

1

Secrets in a KGB Building

22 September 2007

The alarm rings at six a.m. The sky still is as dark grey and filled with smog as yesterday. Then, white tents and booths had mushroomed in the square below our hotel window, and orange, white, or blue flags fluttered as West-leaning and East-leaning supporters handed out pamphlets. Election Day in Ukraine is coming up, a democratic election in which people will choose free from threat. I have had a blinding migraine ever since we reached Zaporozhye, feel nauseated and can't eat, but we must do this thing. Now or never. People here say, 'We always have migraines. It's our air pressure.' The air is heavy with industrial pollution. We are in Ukraine to give talks at a conference in Dnepropetrovsk, organized by the university's history department on the topic of Soviet Germans, and have stopped in Zaporozhye for my husband, Harvey, to meet with city officials to discuss a memorial to Mennonite victims of Soviet oppression.

Today, Ludmilla, my endlessly genial interpreter from Intourist (I don't know Russian, and Harvey uses her for complicated negotiations in his regular research trips to Ukraine), is accompanying us as we catch an early local bus to Donetsk (now Dontes'k), a four-hour trip. We will try to see the interrogation records of two of my uncles, Johannes Braun and Heinrich Konrad. Both records are still in the archives of the SBU (the Ukrainian Security Service, formerly the KGB), rather than in the state archives. A few years ago when I had applied to the Donetsk state archive for the rehabilitation record of my mother's eldest brother, I was informed that it did not exist and I attributed the negative response to intransigence, to never admitting to past wrongs. In January 2002, when least expected, a letter arrived, mailed to my home from the Ukrainian consulate in Toronto, a one-page document stating my uncle was executed and posthumously rehabilitated. The information was kept not in the state archive, but in the former KGB archive, now the Ukrainian Security Service.

Since 1989, off and on, Harvey and I had searched for surviving relatives of my uncles and aunts, had gone to South America, Kazakhstan, Bashkiria, the Kulunda steppe in Siberia, and many parts of the globe, but mostly to the former USSR. The estimated population of Mennonites in tsarist Russia prior to the Russian Revolution was one hundred thousand. Of these, twenty-five thousand fled after experiencing the Russian Revolution and the Civil War of 1918 to 1921, most coming to Canada. Exit permits were stopped after 1926 and my parents escaped as refugees in 1929, but other members of their families remained. Before I began this trip to Donetsk I thought I had completed my book on the disappeared relatives, but this spring my historian husband was able to view interrogation records for a diary he was editing. His subject was a Mennonite arrested in the present Ukraine in 1933. The diarist, interrogated and sentenced to five years in the Gulag, survived and was able to get to Canada in 1948 to write a memoir describing what happened in prison. Unable to get these documents as a historian, but accompanied by the diarist's son, Harvey had seen the files. An infant at the time of his father's arrest, the son now lived in Ontario, and together he and Harvey were given access to the diarist's prison interrogation records. That was my door. A close relative had the right to see the documents, when coming in person. Now it is my turn.

It is still dark as our taxi stops in front of Ludmilla's five-storey apartment and as we drive through grey streets filled with minibuses hurtling people to work, she produces our bus tickets. I neither speak nor read Russian. At the terminal, early morning passengers huddle on benches, many smoking, others glum and shivering, but all silent. Cheerily, Harvey chats with Ludmilla about the name changes of Donetsk, from Yuzovka (or Hughesovka) to Stalino to the present Donets'k. Ludmilla is surprised that the place was originally named for a Welshman, J.J. Hughes, who started an ironworks here in 1870. In my grandparents' day in southeast Russia (now Ukraine), Yuzovka produced rails for their expanding railway system. All that changed in 1924. The Bolsheviks took over the plant in 1919, and from 1924 to 1961 the city was named Stalino. After Stalin's busts began to disappear from public view it became Donetsk. By then anyone related to my grandparents was long gone.

Ludmilla is doubtful the secret police will let us see anything. If only my head could clear and the roadway be less bumpy. We pass drab villages and stop at grim bus stations where no Western tourist would use the washroom sheds. We have our passports and copies of earlier correspondence with the archives, but we worry, since nothing is sure when dealing with the secret police.[1] Nobody wanted to make such arrangements for us, so we are coming unannounced.

Suddenly we are in Donetsk and the sun is out. The city is green, modern, and trendy, not at all the coal capital I had pictured. The former KGB building, which now houses the SBU, fills an entire block and has marble fittings on a square and modern front. In contrast to its grim purpose, a huge skylight floods the entrance with sunlight. In a lobby with several brown leather couches, a glass wall stretches across and partitions the space. In the centre of the glass wall an official slides open a glass wicket to speak to us. He tells Ludmilla to use the wall phone: 'State your business. Produce your documents.'

With me I have a letter sent to me by the Ukrainian consulate in Toronto, a document produced by the State Archive of the Donetsk Region (Oblast):

Donetsk Oblast State Administration
State Archive of the Donetsk Oblast
340086 City of Donetsk, Prospekt Lagutenko 12
Telephone (0622) 99-22-97, Fax (0622) 99-22-97
E-mail: donarc@abc.donbass.com
12 July 2001 No. 01/1-11/32

Archival Notice
Citizen Ivan Isaakovich Braun born on 14 January 1891 [sic] in the colony of Altonau of the former gubernia of Taurida, of German nationality, was, prior to his arrest, employed as an agronomist in the Solidovsk MTS of the Donetsk oblast and lived in the village of Kotlyarevka, Solidovsk rayon. According to a resolution of the NKVD of the USSR and of the Procuracy of the USSR dated 15 January 1938, he was charged with participating in a 'German counter-revolutionary diversionary organization' and engaging in sabotage in the collective farms served by the Solidovsk MTS. According to Article 54-2, 54-9, 54-11 of the Criminal Code of the USSR, he was sentenced to the ultimate pun-

ishment of execution by shooting, without confiscation of his property. This decision has not been changed.

There is no information regarding the date of execution of I.I. Braun, arrested on 23 December 1937.

By decision no. 3650-N-59 of the Court Collegium in Criminal Cases of the Supreme Court of the UkSSR of 16 April 1960, the resolution of the NKVD of the USSR and the Procuracy of the USSR dated 15 January 1938 regarding Ivan Isaakovich Braun born in 1891, is annulled and the case is closed for want of evidence.

In this case, citizen I.I. Braun is posthumously rehabilitated.

Base notice no. 17/10-11752-2F of 30 June 2001. Administration of the Security Service of Ukraine in the Donetsk Oblast
Director of the Archive
[signature and seal] N.B. Metalnikova[2]

When Harvey and I had visited a daughter of Johannes Braun in 1999, Alici, living in Shakhty, Russia, had begged me to find out what I could 'in the West' about her missing father. After receiving this letter, I was uncertain if I should share this news with her. Should that be the end of the story? Should hard-to-get records for fathers, brothers, and relatives be kept forever locked up, be stored in secret files? Or did they deserve better? Why was my uncle shot in 1938? Did he walk down a long tunnel to a KGB cellar? Who falsely accused him? What lay behind the accusation of belonging to a subversive group? Was this just for me to know or did Alici have a right to know? Should her two sons and grandchildren know? My father had said, 'Tell truth and shame the devil.' Voltaire had said, 'To the living we owe compassion, but to the dead we owe the truth.'

After I received the notice from the consulate, I sent Alici what I hoped was a compassionate letter and included a copy of the rehabilitation certificate.

She replied on 5 June 2002:

After I read the letter from the archive, I became ill. I kept hearing my father's voice. He was screaming, 'Shoot better!'

How gruesome, to be shot so soon after his arrest and then they wrote us otherwise. Why am I still alive to hear all the truth? I wept day and night.

After I read that, I rejected everything. Even the Bible was of no use to me.

Finally I read Psalms 41, 42, and 43, and it was as if I was hauled out of my grave.

I say to God, my rock, why hast thou forgotten me?

Why am I mourning because of the oppression of the enemy?

As with a deadly wound in my body, my adversaries taunt me,

While they say to me continually, 'Where is your God?'

Why are you cast down, O my soul? And why are you disquieted within me?

Hope in God, for I shall again praise him, my help and my God.

  Psalm 42: 9–11

I recovered and my son Vanya said, 'Now you again are our old mother.'[3]

Ludmilla tells us we are out of luck, that our request is denied, but we insist on going to a higher level. We point out that such records are now open to relatives, and am I not entitled, coming in person and being an immediate relative? As Canadians, historians, and writers in Ukraine for an international conference, we have little time. 'Wait,' says the voice of the wall phone.

After ten minutes an attractive blond young woman wearing a white, long-sleeved shirt and grey slacks beckons us through a turnstile into a separate room that's also glassed in. She explains that the rules insist we first present a written request and 'no access is granted until five days after a written official application is received.' Helpful, she assists in writing out the application but says she is not sure if the five-day rule can be waived. 'A higher-up official will decide. I will call you on your cellphone. Why not go see the city?'

Ludmilla gives her cell number.

We walk to a main street and find a bistro where Harvey and Ludmilla say the food is good. I do not eat. We wait for two hours and, no ring, decide to go back again. One block from the massive building, Ludmilla's cellphone jingles. 'You may come.'

As we enter the forbidding lobby, enclosed in glass, a young man walks towards us carrying a black suitcase – bigger than a computer and square. His hair and suit are black, and a stout middle-aged woman wearing crimson lipstick, also wearing black, is behind him. Without a word, the man motions us to follow him outside where the woman follows us. Nobody speaks, but the solemn quartet follows the man with the suitcase.

At the end of the street, reaching the back and older part of the former

KGB building, we enter a door, silently mount a stairway, and several stairway floors later are in a large room. A long table and several chairs fill one corner and, light years away, in an opposite corner is a desk with a telephone. Nothing else but a large window looking out to another part of the building, an alcove where the windows were barred.

Harvey asks if we may use his computer to take notes.

'No. And no photographs.'

The young man places the suitcase on the table and leaves. The 'guard' woman opens the suitcase and takes out three buff-coloured files. 'You may make notes.'

'May we photocopy?'

'No. These are criminal cases.'

2

Discovering

Who Is This Woman in Karaganda?

in the legends of my people
the rivers run red
with blood i wept
& dreaming i dreamt
i anointed new flowers
with clay from the grave
& with spittle
& her face was as strange as the flowers
& i said by the by
i am searching.

– Audrey Poetker[1]

The year 1989 was momentous: the Tiananmen Square massacre in China, despot Nicolae Ceausescu deposed in Romania, dissident Vaclav Havel ending Communist rule in Czechoslovakia, and Solidarity winning the election in Poland. And for me 1989 was the year I first met a daughter of the man whose interrogation records I finally saw in 2007. It was also the year my father died. Of his siblings, he was the only son who, sixty years ago, had escaped the Soviet Union in 1929.

Left behind in the communist state were my uncles, aunts, and other relatives. As a child I saw their faces on old stiff-backed photographs in a cardboard box, or sometimes glued between more current Kodak snapshots in my mother's photograph album. The people in the cardboard box and album had faces, but no personalities. Why had they disappeared and why were they important to my parents? Years later, sitting with my father in his room in the Tabor Home, we would look at the pictures and I would ask, 'Who is this?' or 'What happened to him or her?' and write the information on the back of the photo. (Who would know these people if my father died and there was no record?) He would say, 'This was my service buddy' or 'That is your aunt,' but often also, 'Who cares about these *alte Geschichten*?' Old stories, he said. He seemed to care. I knew this because for many years my parents had sent money and parcels of clothing, vitamins, small rugs (popular to hang on Soviet walls or to barter for food), and other dry goods to relatives in the USSR, also letters (in the 1960s) in which they inserted pages from daily devotional calendars. Letters were numbered, shared with other relatives, each answer recorded, and put into a cardboard box.

My father gone, in the distribution of our parents' possessions, I asked for their archive and became custodian of their 'Russian pictures and letters.' As I read through diaries, letters, and papers, I began to pair photographs with letters, and many questions arose, but now that I could ask better questions, where was my father? There were so many people whose stories I did not know. I felt it was now my duty to keep in touch with and to find those 'Russian relatives.' Surviving members of both my mother's and father's families, like chaff in the wind, had been blown across the USSR and beyond its borders. My parents knew their brothers were gone but never how or when they disappeared. Should nobody ever know what happened to them or thousands like them, families locked behind a cold wall? Should they be forgotten? Didn't my upbringing tell me we must remember those who suffered? As I would discover, some experienced collectivization, some tried to escape across borders or frozen rivers, some landed in prison, some were exiled to deserts or frozen tundras, some were sent to slave labour camps in the Ural Mountains or to German factories, and some survived through silence, luck, or military or political decisions. Not a child or adult was left untouched. They were the people I had to find.

For almost thirty years, my parents had heard nothing from or about their brothers or sisters left behind in the Soviet Union. After her death, in my mother's treadle sewing-machine drawer I had found a letter dated 1946 that had arrived when it was almost unheard of to get mail from the USSR. Coming from Siberia, the letter read, 'Your brother Johannes was taken.' My mother had kept this one in her machine, but many other letters, including ones from a Maria Braun, were in the cardboard box. None of the letters that eventually arrived after the 1960s dared to reveal details about life experiences – a dangerous topic when letters were regularly censored.

Maria Braun was a daughter of my mother's disappeared brother Johannes, the man whose records were in Donetsk. She might answer questions about her family, might know how her father disappeared. I met Maria on a hot Monday afternoon in August 1989, in the farthest corner of the Soviet republic of Kazakhstan. I was part of a Mennonite tour group, thirty of us visiting the Soviet Union to see where our parents, grandparents, and relatives had once lived or places to which our people had been deported. My husband, tour leader and historian, had organized the trip to commemorate the two hundredth anniversary of our ancestors settling in tsarist Russia. We had arrived in Moscow where in 1989 Soviet President Gorbachev was using words like *perestroika* (restructuring) and *glasnost* (openness) and, taking Lenin at his word, said, 'Glasnost is the sword that itself heals the wound it inflicts.' On a trip a year earlier, our jewellery had been inventoried to ensure it was taken out again, but a more relaxed climate was evident at the airport this time. We were pushed through customs without difficulty. This time our gifts to relatives we hoped to meet (jeans, cassettes, Walkmans) were left in unopened suitcases. Even airport customs control was less stomach wrenching. I slid my passport under a glass shield and stood silently, nervously waiting. A uniformed official fingered the passport and said nothing. Should I look him straight in the eye? Was he waiting for some signal? How long had it been now? Already ten minutes? What if he turned me back – as my mother feared? My mother had warned me, 'They'll know we escaped.'

Accompanied always by a Soviet guide from Intourist, we had travelled south into Soviet Ukraine, had seen the Dnieper River and Zaporozhye area where many of our great-grandparents and grandparents were born, had found my father's birthplace in Crimea, and had walked down the famous 192 steps of the Potemkin Stairs to the harbour in Odessa. We had been in Tashkent, Uzbekistan, in Frunze, Kirghizia, and in Alma Ata, Kazakhstan. At that time the Soviet travel company Intourist kept us on a tight leash, controlled stopping places with a stopwatch, and used guides who rarely deviated from their scripts. The names changed after the fall of the Soviet empire in 1991, and today Alma Ata is Almaty but still a place of apples – *alma* being 'apple' in Kazakh. Frunze is today's Bishkek, and Kirghizia and Kazakhstan are independent republics with American oil companies, stormy politics, and violence.

In Frunze, at the base of the snow-capped Tien Shan range, on a 'day off,' we had climbed though yellowed grass in the foothills and had gone up a mountain dotted with junipers till we reached the snowline. It was two weeks into our tour and we wanted to be free of any agenda, to breathe mountain air and drink from artesian springs. The guide's 'You have three hours' cautioned us not to climb too high or wander out of sight. Soon our bag lunches were dangling from bushes as we climbed higher. We met other groups of tourists, visitors from the German Democratic Republic, who envied us our freedom to travel.

Some members of our tour had met unknown and newly found relatives sent to Frunze, into exile. Back in the city we had shocked a small neighbourhood when our large Intourist bus wobbled onto a narrow street and stopped at a flower seller's house. The owner, a Mennonite widow with two adult children had built her house with sun-dried bricks. Her children had built a greenhouse with homemade plumbing. She was the daughter of Harvey's mother's foster sister (we were getting used to unravelling how people were related). A few of us also visited the apartment of a Heinrich Neumann, who lived with his in-laws Adolf and Raisa Schleicher in a tall, grey apartment building typical of the communist era. Although it was recently built, the place already looked old, with its crumbling stairwells, but inside the apartment residents had replaced state plumbing and heating with better materials salvaged from nobody said where and had closed in balconies to create just a little more living space.

In the safety of the apartment, behind a faux leather quilted door, Adolf Schleicher repeated the satirical Soviet magazine *Krokodil* joke about Soviet newspapers: 'In *Pravda* [truth] there is no truth and in *Izvestia* [news] there is no news.' Speaking in a soft south German dialect, he asked, 'When will they print what I saw?' and said he had dared to say a few things only in the last two years, since he still was unsure who would call him a Nazi, Fritzie, or Fascist.

Of Volga German descent (colonists invited by Catherine the Great two hundred years ago), he talked about the great famine brought on by Stalin's collectivization plan in the 1930s. Then seventeen, he had been in the Caucasus at the height of the famine and when he returned to his village it stank so much from the rotting dead that nobody would go near it. He had a wife and two children when he was arrested in 1938 and, sent into the Arctic Gulag to work off his ten-year sentence, his family starved to death, but he survived because he was the prison camp cook. He said that eleven camps had a thousand prisoners each, and every morning twenty-five bodies were removed from the barracks. Replacements arrived daily. 'Oh, there were piles of bodies five or six metres high in the spring, but nobody would believe it if I told them. I saw all of it. It is indescribable.' His second wife, Raisa, who had the same name as Gorbachov's wife, was Russian. He said he wanted his two granddaughters to speak German. He called to his six-year-old granddaughter, who folded her hands and, in a high voice, recited a childhood prayer in German.

In Alma Ata, under a clear blue sky our group walked the clean streets past water fountains to a square where Young Pioneers wearing red bandanas and white shirts solemnly marched around a patriotic flame. We paid special attention to an old Orthodox cathedral not destroyed by earthquakes or politics, and browsed an outdoor market where we tasted kumis, fermented mare's milk. Soon we crossed the tarmac and climbed into a small plane at the Alma Ata airport. Our destination was the city of Karaganda, in Kazakhstan's central coal-mining region, a city that we knew was built largely by prisoners and deported people, our fellow Mennonites among them. It seemed a troop carrier rather than a commercial airplane and, shifting our positions on a thin plastic cushions, we hoped the worn, metal seats would not collapse. The flight was just a short hop, but would the ancient Aeroflot plane be able to carry us to our destination?

Flying over the semi-desert, we were low enough to make out nomad yurts and to see flocks of sheep and shepherds on horseback – belonging to a collective farm. We saw a blue lake, then a barren airstrip loomed and we were in Karaganda (now Qaraghandy). Clambering into a waiting Intourist bus, slowly, over uneven pavement and potholes, we rode into town. Like elongated pythons, enormous dark grey pipes snaked beside the bus route and laced in and out of shanties and sunken empty lots. Oil? Gas? The new guide explained that the pipes were a heating system to centrally distribute hot water above ground in an eighteen-inch insulated pipeline.

All around were abandoned buildings, huts, and roads that had caved into sinkholes that stretched for blocks above old mine shafts. Built hastily to extract the ore, the underground tunnel supports had collapsed. Amid these ruins, someone pointed out a plain building without steeple, cross, or ecclesiastical symbol, which still stood on firm ground. The guide said it was a Mennonite church, and local believers told us later the building was held up by God's hand.

Karaganda had a two-storey Intourist Hotel of familiar undistinguished concrete. As we spilled out of the bus, Stan, the Intourist guide assigned in Moscow to accompany us from Day One, sat back and the local guide directed us to the hotel entrance. Suddenly a gaunt woman darted down the hotel steps and pushed aside the guide's restraining arm. In a black-and-white checked housedress, hair covered in a kerchief patterned with red roses, squinting through black-rimmed glasses, she inspected each tourist leaving the bus. She called out our names. 'There you are!' We stopped.

Who was she? Who were the persons standing behind her?

'We've been waiting for you for two days!' she chided, 'The hotel kept telling us you weren't here yet! Why are you late? I'm Maria Braun.'

The thirty members of our tour group filed past into the hotel as my brother, his wife, Harvey, and I absorbed Maria Braun. She pushed forward two young men who appeared to be in their late thirties and an equally young woman looking cheerful in curly brown hair, clinging patterned dress, white shoes, and black hose. All smiled hesitantly. 'This is my Volodya and his wife Natasha. This is my Andrusha and his daughter.' She pushed forward a blond child wearing an obligatory huge bow on top of her head, 'This is nine-year-old Vika.' Turning to us, 'What took you so long?'

It began to sink in. This rough-edged woman in cloth slippers and kerchief was the daughter of my mother's 'disappeared' brother Johannes. Scarecrow thin, in a defiant 'guardian of truth' pose, this Maria Braun provided the first details of 'what really happened' to my mother's brothers and other family members.

At the beginning of this tour, in Moscow we had sent Maria Braun a telegram (she had no phone) telling her when we would be in Karaganda, the city nearest her home in Slavgorod, Siberia, and here she was. Arriving by train, she found the only Intourist Hotel in the city, and, told she was not welcome, she had stayed with some of her acquaintances through the Baptist church ('the Brethren').

We invited Maria's group to stay with us, but American dollars had to pass through hands before they could occupy a room upstairs and join us in the dining room. As Maria's family came into the room for the evening meal – the first time that she had ever been in a hotel, let alone eaten in a hotel dining room – we asked if it bothered her that foreigners got preferred treatment, stayed in the best rooms, and had food that was not available in markets for Soviet citizens. She laughed, 'No! Did I know that foreign tourists got all these luxuries? I doubt that most of my fellow citizens know it either!' She covered her mouth and burst out laughing, '*We* get into a tourist hotel?' We smiled knowingly. Hadn't we noticed a burly doorkeeper at the entrance of every Intourist hotel we had visited – Moscow, Leningrad (St Petersburg), Odessa, Tashkent, or Frunze? Dressed like a Western doorman, his job was not to welcome people in but to keep people out. Often all it took for the doorkeeper to open the door was his look at our shoes. Guards also policed the Berioska Shop in Leningrad, a specialty state store that sold scarce goods (such as tea) for hard currency, but not roubles.

The rules bent, Maria and her sons were at our table. Excitedly, smiling, Maria looked around the room, watching our tourist group being served by waitresses in black dresses, wearing little white aprons. Her sons observed which spoon or fork we used, and Maria's granddaughter Vika eyed the pale sausages we tourists left untouched in a serving dish. Carefully she removed each limp sausage, rolled it into a small paper napkin and, with a shy smile at her Western relatives, pressed the elevator button and took the little gift into their room. This little shopper knew that people lined up in long cues for meat.

I kept looking at Maria Braun. Could she really be the daughter of that near movie star of my childhood, my mother's fabled brother Johannes? Bird-like, bony, slightly hunch-backed, in her mid-sixties, she looked twenty years older. Covered in that faded kerchief, her head bobbing, her bright eyes darting, she followed all comings and goings. Fluttering hands and gestures punctuated her sentences. Not shy, she approached our tour members in many conversations. 'Nice,' she would laugh, pointing at a tourist's shoes. Her own cloth slippers were worn and none of the shoes in our suitcases fit her. Sure enough, the next morning at breakfast two women grinned broadly as Maria tried on their leather loafers. Both fit. 'They're yours!' Amid hugging and laughter Maria had acquired two pairs of shoes, and a tourist was snapping pictures to show off in the United States.

My mother, Luise, had an elder brother, Johannes, and three younger brothers, Jakob, Peter, and Isaak. Their mother had died on a train en route to a hospital when my mother was eight years old. Her father had soon remarried, and three brothers and a sister (my Canadian uncles and aunt) were added to the family. Occasionally, when my family lived in northern Alberta, a box of apples arrived from one of them in BC. In the backwoods of northern Alberta where I was born and where we looked at the 'Russian pictures,' our mother used to tell us about her brother Johannes, that he had studied at the School of Commerce in the prosperous town of Halbstadt (now Molochansk) in present southern Ukraine, had attended university in St Petersburg, was a teacher, and later became an agronomist. In the family portrait he looked scholarly, certainly not like farmers in northern Alberta and not like his Canadian brothers who taught children to hoe long rows of strawberry plants in Abbotsford, BC, where we lived after the Second World War.

One photograph in my parents' collection showed Johannes in a long frock coat, white tie, and starched collar. One hand supported his infant daughter Alici, who was propped up on a park bench while his wife Anna, in her long skirt and white blouse, sat artfully (so I thought then) to make the triangle. Johannes had a small curling moustache, a very genteel one, and his hair was cut like Clark Gable's in *Gone with the Wind*, only he was not dark and charming – no, more an intellectual. Even my father spoke admiringly of his brother-in-law: *'Hans, der konnte singen!'* When Johannes Braun sang in that church in Siberia where my parents met, that rich bass voice had made the windows rattle. Not given to compliment easily, my father especially did not like soloists. To him they showed too much pride, like roosters crowing. But hearing Johannes, my father said, 'That man sings as well as Chaliapin,' the most famous Russian basso of the era.

But Johannes was *verschleppt*. He was one of many persons my parents, their friends, and relatives meant when they used the word to suggest disappeared or removed. To me it evoked the image of being dragged away by force. In the days before television and urbanization, my parents' friends, most of them fellow Mennonites who had emigrated from Russia in the 1920s, were homestead farmers in northern Alberta. On Sunday afternoons and religious holidays, a buggy or democrat would roll onto the yard, the visiting family would be fed at our kitchen table, and then, children sent outdoors to play Fox and Geese in the snow or tag around the straw stack, the adults would sit in the small parlour and talk about grain crops and Russia. In the fall, two or three families got together to butcher a pig, and even on that day, after the sausages were made and the hams were being smoked, seated on wooden benches around the large kitchen table for supper, the adults talked about Russia. We children listened. When we lived in BC they came by car and talked about berry crops or egg prices, but always also Russia. Over and over we would hear who was related to so-and-so or who had been *verschleppt*.

We children had found these 'Russia stories' a little tedious. If we bit into very strong pickled gherkins, we'd joke, 'Tastes like Russia.' Russia had become an evil place to our parents, but why to us? Who in the 1940s, the USSR being our war ally, printed letters or wrote stories about the Stalinist purges of the thirties, or slave labour camps? The word *Gulag* was not yet a part of everyday vocabulary. We youthful children of immigrants to Canada had other interests. We 'Canadians' read our England-based school materials and lived in the imaginary world of *The Wind in the Willows*, drank in gothic tales of Sir Walter Scott on moors and highlands. Nobody mentioned that there had been a Chief La Glace or Aboriginal people living on the shores of Rat Lake in our cow pasture. Nobody asked why our hamlet had a French name, La Glace, when it was populated by immigrant homesteaders from Norway, Britain, and since the nineteen twenties by German-speaking Mennonites from Russia. Exotic in our one-room school were tales of Grey Owl's two beavers and Indian love songs ('Oh, the moon shines tonight on pretty Redwing') magically turned on by a hand-cranked record player. Important people were Canada's Mounted Police in scarlet tunics and two dainty British princesses dressed in pastel coats. Their coloured photographs, along with those of decorated generals (so brave in a distant war), lined the top of the blackboard.

In Abbotsford, BC, we lived in what many years later I realized was a typical Russian Mennonite village. The long gravel road passing our house was lined with first-generation Mennonite farm families from Russia. Their berry fields, pastures, and chicken barns filled the long strips of land behind their houses. At every driveway stood a wooden milk stand (shiny metal cans waited for a Co-op truck pickup) and a metal mailbox that sometimes contained airmail letters from Paraguay, Brazil, Switzerland, Germany, and the USSR. The first years in Abbotsford, our back pasture (later a berry field) was cleared of giant stumps, some wide enough for half a dozen kids to stand on. Nearly all the families on our gravel road attended the Mennonite Brethren church, just a kilometre up the hill. The auditorium-gymnasium of the local Mennonite high school was the centre for countless community meetings.

It was after the end of the Second World War that Mennonites searched most hopefully for news of their relatives remaining in the USSR. During the dying days of the war, thousands of Soviet Germans, Baltic Germans, Latvians, Ukrainians, and other refugees from the USSR had flooded into Germany, Austria, Denmark – to 'the West.' After Germany's surrender, many were in refugee camps, at which

point Mennonites in Canada began to search for relatives and to negotiate to bring them to Canada. My parents appealed to the International
Red Cross, but Mennonites also sent personnel overseas to try to locate,
collect, and assist their refugees. That task was the responsibility of the
Mennonite Central Committee (MCC), an organization founded in the
early 1920s to provide relief during the famine following the Bolshevik
Revolution.

Home television was rare in our community after the war, so news
about 'our refugees' came as old and young flocked to the Mennonite
Educational Institute (MEI) auditorium to listen to MCC workers just
returned from overseas. Showing picture slides of the devastation in
Europe, they told about 'our brothers and sisters' spun into homeless-
ness. People at the meetings clamoured for information. Whom had
the MCC contacted? Had they brought back letters? What was being
done to 'find our people'? Fast action was needed. At a meeting in Yalta
before the end of the war, Britain, France, and the United States had
agreed to Stalin's demand that all refugees be repatriated to their country of origin. This meant that refugees in American, French, or British
spheres or zones in defeated Germany were in imminent danger of
being deported back to the Soviet Union. Fearing a return, refugees,
also known as 'displaced persons' (DPs), clamoured to remain in 'the
West' and to be reunited with relatives in Canada or the United States.
In Europe, MCC officials located and processed thousands of refugee
applications. Canadian and American church leaders appealed to their
governments to accept the DPs. Mennonites across Canada collected
monies to fund rescue operations.

Despite assistance of the Red Cross and MCC, none of my parents'
siblings were found, but other relatives surfaced. My Great-Uncle Ohm
Gheet, living just down the road, sponsored my mother's cousins – two
brothers with families from a refugee camp in Austria, Mennonite men
with Russian wives. Along came two of my mother's cousins, Tante
Agathe and her sister Tante Kathe. Tante Kathe wore a black dress,
white apron, and crisp white headdress, the uniform of a Mennonite
nursing order. To our home came my father's cousins, Margaret Konrad, a dour, dark-haired and heavyset woman, and her wan, fragile-
looking brother Abram with his timid wife Lena. We were a large
family with a small house. As an extra bedroom, my four brothers were
using a separate building under a dogwood tree on our yard. When our
'displaced persons' arrived, the boys took their blankets and moved
into the barn hayloft.

Our DP Konrads stayed all summer, earned money picking berries – first strawberries, then raspberries – did odd jobs and, winter approaching, moved to Vancouver to look for factory or household jobs. I have never forgotten the sight that fall of our DP guest Margaret. A stoic woman of few words, thick arms, and dark black hair wound tightly into a knot at the back of her head, she had placed a weathered black suitcase on the ground. Her arms had gone limp and she made no sound, but tears were streaming down her face, wetting her print dress with large flowers. Separated from all but one remaining member of her family, she was now again going out alone into an unknown world. A decision had been made that she (like many other DP women) was to take the Pacific Stage bus to Vancouver to find housework. Many years later I found out she came from a family of ten children, from which seven had been *verschleppt*.

As a girl living in the fertile Fraser Valley, I soon forgot about the endless *verschleppt* and refugee relatives. It was more interesting to wheedle parental permission to go roller-skating a few kilometres across the American border, or on dates to moonlight wiener roasts at Cultus Lake. Soon the refugees, lacking English, were employed in domestic or factory work in Vancouver or in local cannery plants or farms. Our preachers called urgent congregational meetings to decide if a 'widow' DP woman was permitted to remarry. Did she have proof her husband was dead? 'No? Well, then ...' Most preachers refused to marry such couples, even though spouses had been missing for a decade. Yet the many single refugee mothers with children proved to be a hardy set, and many of their children went on to highly successful careers in professions and especially in construction. Some became BC's wealthiest developers.

Encouraged by that one letter in 1946 from Omsk, Siberia, throughout the 1950s and 1960s Cold War, my parents persisted in searching for their relatives. Why had the woman written that my mother's brother Johannes Braun *was taken*, and, more puzzling, that his daughter Alici *went the way of her father*? How did she know and how did she dare to write? Twelve years after the end of the Second World War, in 1957, my father's youngest brother Gerhard wrote one cautious letter from Central Asia, and then nothing for another year. In 1961, Anna, wife of my mother's brother Johannes, wrote that she had last seen her husband in 1937, twenty years earlier. She wondered what had happened to her eldest son Hans, missing since he was drafted into the Red Army in the spring of 1939. She asked, 'Is he in America?'

When the first letters from the USSR arrived, written mostly by wom-
en, we did not know the risks these relatives took. I had long since left
the BC Mennonite community, but from my mother's letters to us over
many years in New York and then Toronto, I knew that she regularly
wrote to 'Russian relatives.' I did not comprehend the magnitude of
what she was spared. As my mother aged, unable to keep up her voluminous correspondence, her regular letters to seven children as well
as relatives in Canada, South America, and the USSR, my elder sister
took over letters to Maria Braun. She and Maria both had been born in
Siberia on the same frosty night in January 1924.

And here she was, the same Maria Braun.

As the rest of the tour group visited obligatory Soviet showplace kin-
dergartens and sites in Karaganda, in the hotel my brother, his wife,
and I listened as Maria Braun, sitting on the edge of the bed, declared
loudly, 'I'll say what I want even if the hotel room is bugged.' We suspected most were. She looked up at the ceiling light fixture, laughed
a fierce little laugh and shook her fist, 'What more can you do to me?'

Maria talked non-stop. She told us how comforting it had been for
her mother to correspond with our parents, how gifts of money had
saved her collapsing home. She complained that her brother Heinz
would not come to meet us, that he was stingy, sold produce at the
market, but never shared, had a mean wife. She had told him, 'Come,
the train fare is not expensive.' He wouldn't risk contact with people
from the West. All these years only she had risked a correspondence.
Oh yes, there was the risk of reprisals, but she hadn't cared. Now her
sister Alici was interested in us, but not Heinz, not him.

My brother and I spoke no Russian and Harvey was touring with
the group, but fortunately Maria remembered German so we com-
municated in our childhood language. Maria's sons were left out. Her
childhood language had become the language of the enemy, of Nazis,
Fascists, of reviled Germans (*Nemtsy*). Could she single them out for
ridicule? Besides, their father was Russian. In our hotel room (as I took
notes), Maria's deaf son Andrusha (Andrei) sat on the bed reading her
lips when she repeated something in Russian. Unable to follow, he soon
retreated with his daughter to their upstairs room. Maria's son Volodya
and his wife Natasha went downtown to look for a pair of shoes and for
a suitcase to carry back the goods we had brought. They left that evening
because soldier Volodya had just signed up for another five-year stint.

Some years previously, evangelical Baptists had converted Maria,
and with the zeal of a convert she now instructed us 'worldly Western-

ers.' First, she demanded we thank God for our meeting. Then, 'Don't you go down on your knees to pray?' Touched by the guilt of our freedom compared to her misfortune, we knelt on the bare boards of the hotel room floor. She looked critically at my hair and said, 'Women cover their heads before God.' My mother had called her headgear a *tuch* and wore it only while gardening, but here it meant something else. Since Baptist women had to wear dresses, I asked Maria how these dresses were acquired. 'Oh,' she explained, 'when any textile products come into town, we women line up for hours to buy whatever fabric has arrived and take it to a sewing factory. Then girls who do not like school and have taken a sewing course make the dresses in the factory. A large room stocks several patterns. You choose a pattern, have three fittings, and buy your dress.' (I would recall these sewing classes years later when we met Maria's granddaughter in Slavgorod.) She then told us why my sister's parcel of fabric had been returned. Receiving *fabric* was illegal, but machine stitching loose seams into fabric would make them 'curtains' or 'sheets' and legal to be sent.

Our group had arrived in Karaganda on a Monday, but once the local Mennonite church (on the 'island' among the sinking houses) discovered a North American tour group was in town, we were invited to conduct an evening service. At that time all Mennonite tour groups – there were several every year – automatically were invited to perform, the men to speak and women to sing. Of course Maria Braun wanted to attend. She observed the women in our group wearing sleeveless blouses, jewellery, make-up, short haircuts, and uncovered heads and turned to me in alarm, 'Are they Christians?' Earlier in our tour, we had visited Baptist churches (many Mennonites had joined the Baptists) and noticed that women over the age of fifteen wore head coverings, the younger ones gauzy pastel kerchiefs tied in a chic look. One member of our group felt a local parishioner touch her arm and as the woman dabbed at her face, the Canadian tourist thought, she's telling me what a hard life she's had. She stroked the woman's hand. No, no, the Baptist woman became more explicit. Rubbing her hand over her mouth, she wiped off imaginary lipstick. Next, she touched her earlobes, removing sinful earrings.

To emphasize their rejection of atheism, Soviet evangelicals had used a dress code. Women wore head coverings, long sleeves, and long dresses. As Baptist Christians saw it, the Soviets punished them for conducting services in private homes and sentenced honest leaders to years in prison. We in the free West, they said, had freedom of conscience and what did we do? We forgot the biblical injunctions on female modesty, became indistinguishable from unbelievers, and lost part of our souls. They wished wearing an outward symbol of religion could halt the process. The Soviets had viciously persecuted religion, had closed most churches, synagogues, mosques, and temples, and had torn them down or turned them into secular buildings. Evangelical Soviet believers who had held fast to their faith had felt a measure of relief as church life began to revive under Soviet President Brezhnev in the late 1960s, a period when official scrutiny was relaxed – and untrammelled corruption and alcoholism flourished. After repeated applications and frequent jailing of their religious leaders, the German-speaking Mennonites deported to Karaganda had received permission to be legally registered and to build a church in 1967.

As we left Karaganda, Maria embraced us and observed sadly, 'The difference between my children and you is that in 1929 my father wavered. Yours did not.'

Since I was teaching ten months of the year, finding my next 'missing relatives' took more than a dozen years with trips to Europe, the former USSR, and South America during summer holidays. In this quest I found myself in frequent discussions with many of my students. Most were recent immigrants, refugees from Vietnam, Ethiopia, Sri Lanka, and other countries who were trying to overcome the trauma of their experiences. They asked question, sought answers, and wrote journals revealing complex family histories, narrow escapes, expressions of great loss and pain. Irrevocably affected by totalitarian governments, they needed to tell their stories. What could I do for my 'disappeared'? Tell their stories.

Who We Are

Being unpopular with a government should have been familiar to Mennonites. As Anabaptists, persecuted by Catholics and Protestants, my Mennonite ancestors in the Netherlands fled to Poland in the 1500s and 1600s, settled in areas around Danzig (Gdansk), and learned Plautdietsch and High German. To retain their pacifist beliefs (and under economic pressure) they moved to Catherine's Russia in the late 1780s, where they pioneered in the southern steppes of today's Ukraine. Whenever I came to Ukraine I thought I should feel a connection to a homeland, a place where my grandparents, great-grandparents, and great-great-grandparents were born, a place full of stories of close communities, friendly villages, and hundreds of relatives, but that was a lost world, my parents' world.

My ancestors had come to a steppeland, planted forests and ploughed fields, built villages, churches, schools, windmills, flour mills, hospitals, and factories producing ploughs and harvesting machinery. They married and had large families, but almost no Mennonites now lived here. The first time I saw the city that my mother called Alexandrovsk, a place where as a young teacher she came on shopping trips with her Great-Aunt Wiens, it was called Zaporozhye. The Bolsheviks had removed imperial government and tsarist references and renamed administrative centres. Even a decade after the fall of the Party, Zaporozhye (now Zaporizhzhia) still seemed Soviet with its huge statues – Lenin on the waterfront, and Felik Dzerzhinsky (first head of the notorious secret police) – on the main boulevard. Not so the people on the main streets. Missing only the white gloves and perky hats, they reminded me of the 1950s, my teenage years when we dressed in our 'Sunday best,' men in suit jackets and women in high heels and dresses. I was told Ukrainian young women would go hungry to be in style.

From the Ukrainian steppe, Mennonites had spread out across the imperial empire to settlements as distant as Siberia and Central Asia, always replicating their organizations, building styles, foods, and even names. They married within the fold (practising endogamy), and family connections intertwined. Everyone seemed to be related to everyone else. There were crises; disputes and religious factions emerged, and large numbers of Mennonites immigrated to North America in the 1870s when faced with compulsory military service. Others stayed and negotiated a compromise, performing non-combatant service. They worked hard and a few built large estates, were factory owners and often philanthropists underwriting schools and hospitals, but most were farmers living in villages. By the early 1900s they also lived in cities. Then came the Diaspora.

The disparity between past and present, between image and reality was often a block or two away on a potholed side street. At an international conference on Mennonite themes held in 1999, sessions were held in banquet rooms brightly lit with sparkling chandeliers in the Intourist Hotel. Participants were served an abundance of food, whereas local people told us the average Zaporizhian subsisted on macaroni and bread. A conference attendee from Germany staying with a local family bought them food every day. The recent devaluation of the Ukrainian currency (grivna) had increased costs, and wages often went unpaid for months. The formally dressed people and handsome coaches of my parents' photographs now seemed unreal.

It seems human nature to want to present the best image. So it was no surprise that Zaporozhye officials pulled out all the stops for the international conference in 1999. Once they and provincial officials discovered that the Canadian ambassador and German cultural attaché were opening a museum exhibition and conference, a drawerful of grivna was opened. Not only were new curtains found for the museum, but also two sides of the Palace of Culture were painted pink (who sees the back?). This building had been a Mennonite church and two wall plaques were to be unveiled to commemorate that fact. Cobalt blue was fresh on the fence of a cemetery where a marker was erected to recognize the presence of ancestors, most in unmarked graves. Local people placed flowers at the new marker and at a Mennonite headstone that a villager had fished out of the nearby Dnieper River.

Public lectures were given in a university auditorium, and as a Ukrainian-Canadian and a Canadian Mennonite historian lectured, a woman beside me kept whispering, 'When is someone finally going to mention what happened to us? Are they ever going to acknowledge that we were exiled and had all our freedoms denied?' Now living in Germany, but originally exiled to Karaganda, Kazakhstan (her family had been deported from Soviet Ukraine in 1941), she wanted the facades to come down.

What kind of people were my ancestors, the 'Russian Mennonites'? Joseph Stalin had said people like my relatives were forgettable, at most a statistic among enemies to eliminate, but I was to discover how remarkable their lives were. Each deserved a life remembered, what my father had, a last ritual, and a personality.

In November 1989 my father had died.

5 January 1990 [excerpted from my journal][2]
Yesterday I unpacked the last box of my share of the parents' belongings and found a pink towel with ridiculous roses, worn through, but still smelling exactly like his room at the Tabor Home where he spent the last seven years. I folded the towel between two impersonal bed sheets and hid it in our linen closet. There was the clock too, loudly chiming just above his head to the very last minute of his life.

We were in his room. Dad had been in a morphine haze since about nine o'clock in the morning and lay on his bed breathing through an open mouth, a clear plastic oxygen tube lay either at his nostrils or on the bed near his face.

Yesterday he had wrestled it away, bunched and held the tubing clenched in his fist. 'Go away! I don't want it!' I thought he would yank the whole line out of the tank and hurl it across the room. My sister made soothing, withdrawing statements and said he might be hallucinating. That happens when the brain lacks oxygen. She had been a nurse. Today he hardly opened his eyes.

My brother George had arrived half an hour earlier, taken the chair beside Dad's bedside, but now was looking at the album of pictures of Spat, Crimea, that I had brought along. George and his wife had been in Spat with us in August. I had hoped to show Dad those pictures of his beloved boyhood home.

We watched his breathing. From time to time my sister Lill took his pulse and checked his feet. Feet get cold, she said, before someone dies. His feet were warm. I noticed his eyes had opened and Lillian had said how the pupils dry out when the eyelids don't blink, so I thought I'd better close his eyelids. His eyes were so pale – those deep blue eyes that all the women liked, as he used to joke – now seemed like fish eyes, vacant, shallow discs. As soon as I had closed his eyes he opened them again. And then it seemed his breathing was slower and I bent my face to his cheek and the breath was still slow and Lill jumped up from her chair, 'What's wrong, Anne?' 'His breathing is so slow,' I said, and she said, 'He's dying!"

She held his other hand and my brother Jake and his wife stood at the foot of the bed and George was right behind me and I kept my face to his cheek and couldn't say anything like they do in fiction, that last desperate 'I love you,' because I didn't want him to die, not just yet. But he wanted to die and there were pauses between the breaths and the thought flashed through my mind, would he have a sudden brightening, a shining 'seeing Jesus' expression on his face. There was just that heavy hand and the terribly cold brow and then Lill said, 'He's gone.' We sisters embraced and wept and then Lill said, 'Stop the clock.'

I missed the last conversations with him. I had seen him ten months ago and had planned to spend this weekend with him. Our son was flying in from San Francisco and I was coming from Toronto, taking a few days off work. We were going to 'visit Opa,' rent a car, take Dad out for drives in the Abbotsford hills, the Matsqui flats, as I had done on other visits, cheer him up before Christmas. Alexander had missed out on earlier visits to his grandfather, felt he really didn't know him and was looking forward to the weekend as well.

A high school and university friend was at our house that Sunday evening in Toronto. We were sitting at our dining room table, Harvey, she, and I at ten-thirty in the evening, laughing about teenage love pangs at our dear high school where we had been classmates those years in the late early 1950s when we all lived in Abbotsford. We didn't know yet that it would become a bedroom community for Vancouver. The telephone rang and Lill said, 'Dad is dying. The doctor gives him twenty-four hours. He has an infarct. It's like a blood clot. It will lodge.'

Vancouver airport was bright when Lill picked me up and we drove directly to Tabor Home. Dad had been very talkative all night, she said. Herman, our youngest brother, had arrived last night and when Lill said the doctor predicted Dad was dying, he had chuckled, 'We'll see.' Lill had asked, 'Should I call the children?' 'They likely could afford to come,' he had grinned. Herman came from Calgary, not that long a flight, and they had been sitting up all night. Dad had told stories, many stories about the Peace River Alberta days and about Siberia and the Crimea where he was born. He said his son Pete had been in Spat, and Pete had met people on the streets of Spat who had asked about the 'Old Konrad.' Imagine, those people in Spat remembered him! There had been brightness, spunk, and a playfulness that whole night. He had mixed up the stories about Spat because it was George who had told him about visiting Spat and there were no people on the streets of Spat that would possibly remember him, not when he was almost a hundred years. How he still yearned for his boyhood home.

The day before, he had talked about the day his own father died. He never talked about his parents to us children, never, unless we probed, and that was not often. I had tried to coax some details out of him. 'What kind of people were they, your brothers and sisters?' He asked, 'Who's interested in old stories?' In 1976 Dad's youngest brother Gerhard was finally permitted to leave the USSR and had come to Canada to visit. This brother had told me that Dad was very much like my grandfather. They had the same definitive tone, ending a conversation with, 'The truth of the matter is that ...' [Die Sache ist die ...]. I think Gerhard meant it as criticism, a baby brother complaint.

Was our grandfather just insistent or emotional too? Our father was insistent. He protected our mother. He disliked stupidity or meekness. He liked his children and grandchildren to take risks, to succeed. Yet he also had that vulnerability which made tears come to his eyes when he took his turn leading the prayer session at the beginning of a church service. How embarrassed we children were, sitting in the church pews. Men were not supposed to show strong emotion in public, unless they were preachers angry at sins or calling for repentance. Certainly men's eyes should not moist over a Bible passage extolling the goodness of God, or when singing a line of a hymn.

So he had talked about the day his father died when the family members were called in, one at a time, to say farewell. This was in 1928. A year before my parents fled Russia. The flight from Russia. He often talked about that.

Just in September, George, Hilda, Harvey, and I had come home full of our visit to the Crimean peninsula – those snapshots in my green photograph album, packed quickly. I was still hoping Dad would sit up and talk about the pictures. How memory would flood back and he'd say, 'This was the school. There stood the mill. Here we brothers played this trick.' Now we would never know. Was that Soviet clubhouse really the former Mennonite church? What were his brothers like?

During the day, Dad had been quiet, mostly sleeping uneasily. Once in a while he would rouse, sit bolt upright, push off the bedclothes, yank off the oxygen line, and announce, 'I have to go.' Lill wanted him to use the bedpan, but his legs came off the bed and the sweat poured off his face, cold sweat. Two people rushed to his washroom to get the portable commode chair and then two people struggled to raise him onto the commode, and when he had done, he would lie back, his whole frame gasping big shaking breaths as his chest heaved. The thick rasping gulps made us say, 'He can't go on like this. He'll die like this!' But still the man who loved horses determined his trousers would not be soiled.

Once or twice he reached down and checked that he was wearing pants, not pyjamas. Brown pyjamas. (They insisted he wear brown polyester trousers at Tabor Home – you can wash polyester, but woollen dress pants stink.) Herman had helped him to get dressed and Dad had insisted on wearing a proper shirt with pants. Hours after a wrenching urination session, he calmly inserted the oxygen tubing himself. 'That's the way it has to be done.' The pendulum clock above his bed kept chiming its loud clanging half hours and hours. In the afternoon my eldest brother, Pete, and his wife arrived. A tumour, a tennis ball in the middle of Pete's brain, had reduced Pete to this indomitable man with hooded eyes, sitting on that chair, looking at his father, loving past his strength as his father slept or lay speechless in pain.

Pete sat straight, facing Dad, willing him to wake up and recognize him. He kept declining suggestions that he rest. I knew, of all his children, Dad trusted Pete most.

Lill drove back to Vancouver and Herman and I decided to spell each other off, sit up with Dad all night. We found the couch in the Men's Lounge where a small artificial Christmas tree glowed in red and green lights and a silver-coloured coffee urn shone in a glow of plastic cheer. The staff night nurses checked in during the night and made a point of telling us how they liked our father, how he always had a little joke for them, that he was one of the few interesting men in the Home.

At seven in the morning Dad again called for the commode and Herman and I tried to follow the technique the night nurse had shown us. 'Dead weight,' Lill had said. What's dead weight? Herman and I lifted and again our father suffered. Such enormous pain and strain in the effort of self-sufficiency left Dad gasping, and I felt numb, just to watch him.

'Me be an angel?' Dad had asked on Monday. This was after the doctor had said, 'forty-eight hours to live.' How comical he would look, he had laughed. No, he couldn't quite see himself as an angel. Oh, he must have been bright, white light bright that day, and Lill was so lucky to share that lightness. The playfulness about his funeral. What especially would Dad like at his funeral, she had asked. Lill can come to the point like none of us ever dared, and he liked that about her. She and Dad had butted heads many times, but he liked that too. He liked spunk.

It had always been the sons-in-law who listened most attentively to my father's stories of Russia. When my young husband first studied Russian history, Dad would say to him, 'That's just book learning. You have to have lived there to understand. I lived there.' But Harvey persisted in learning and in listening to my father's stories, and they liked each other because they both could stand up for themselves. Lill's husband also patiently listened to Dad's stories and Dad had chosen him as the one to give his funeral sermon. John came from a long line of preachers. 'Well, I guess I won't be able to say anything at my funeral, will I?' Dad had said it like a small boy about to do mischief. Lill told us all these things as we sat in the room going over the same topics again and again. When the eight o'clock nurse suggested morphine, I wondered if we should agree. After the morphine Dad no longer roused himself and submitted to wearing a hospital gown.

Some things can only be understood when you know more about a person's background. I thought I knew our father a little better after the Russia trip. As if seeing Dad's boyhood home led to a greater connectedness to his missing family members. But when he died in his hospital gown with the strings tied at the back, a faint blue gown with a small-flecked design, I could imagine him in a Chagall painting. With wings, he'd be floating over the Tabor Home. Pale hospital gown, grey wavy hair, dear ancient head, thin bird's legs, he'd be wafting up into the clouds. Smiling.

We four children and a daughter-in-law sat with our father for several hours after he died. I had always thought this would be spooky, but when it happened, it seemed so natural. He lay on his maple twin bed, one of the pair he and Mother already owned on Centennial Street, and was covered by a pink quilt filled with the wool from Buttercup, grandson Walter's sheep. I was still stroking his forehead when Elisabeth, my sister-in-law, asked, 'Anne, how can you touch a dead person like that?' 'Oh, he's not a dead person,' I said, 'He's my Dad.' Then I noticed how the pockmarks, smallpox scars on his nose that had made young boys call him 'Strawberry Nose,' were beginning to disappear.

And then his nose became all smooth and quite handsome and I marvelled at that strange transformation. Then a young doctor took a quick look, and he declared our father officially dead.

We phoned everyone. It was important to our kids to participate in this funeral of their last grandparent. For our son it was the first close family funeral, a grandparent who had died in a Mennonite world where people knew each other. He was perhaps the last of his generation to have lived almost fifty years in the same community. Here he had belonged to a church with common traditions of burying, of sitting together after the coffin is laid into the earth. How strange I found that as a child. People should not sit and eat after a burial. Go home, I thought, show some respect. Now I know differently. You need people, want people to remember those funny, trite, or sad anecdotes, any reminiscence about your dear dead. Funeral receptions were always held in our church basements over raisin bread and coffee. Harvey had gone out and bought seven loaves because he guessed the modernized church might have cut out bread in favour of Danish pastries. We want to hang onto the old ways of our youthful memory. Raisin bread for funerals.

We planned the funeral for Saturday afternoon. Jake phoned the local funeral home director and the minister of the M.B. Mennonite church. In a community of hundreds of retired persons, Jake told us, 'You do that first, get the minister pinned down to make sure he doesn't have another funeral at the same time.' As it turned out there was another funeral about the same time, in another Mennonite church. A wedding was taking place at the same time in yet another Mennonite church.

So we divided up the who-would-do-what tasks. Thursday we selected the coffin. We all wanted Pete to have a role in the funeral. In our Dad's tradition, the eldest son was the one he called, but hidden by the brain tumour, the son was somewhere deep inside those half-closed eyes and silent thoughts. Sapped of strength, before his time.

We looked at the room of coffins. 'Which one do you think, Pete?' With funerals, and he attended hundreds, Dad never talked about 'expense'; he believed in a 'decent' funeral, not a stingy one or an extravagant one, but a 'proper' one. Pete stopped in front of a brown, solid, plain wooden coffin, 'How about this one? It's what I call the homestead model.'

Lill and I walked from Dad's empty room at Tabor Home to the small shopping mall. In late November, the shop had set out several pine wreaths in a pre-Christmas display. Pine wreaths on coffins was how it had been in a family snapshot taken beside the open coffin of my eldest sister Helen. Dad is holding my toddler brother and my sister Mary his twin sister. Mother is looking down at her fourteen-year-old daughter among the pine wreaths. We chose pine wreaths with some pale white freesia, and baby's breath, interlaced in the green boughs. In with white feathery chrysanthemums, Lill wanted lilies. Almost a hundred years ago our father had been born on an Easter Sunday in sunny Schöntal, Crimea.

It had been a day without rain and the mountains were out on that Friday, the day before the funeral. We had a rental car and Harvey decided to take our kids on an afternoon roundabout tour of the haunts of our youth, past the schools we had attended, the churches we had frequented, the places where we had lived, to the end of Emerson Road, as far as it goes. We could see the rose-tipped mountains and a deep valley, such a vista of Mount Baker that I had not seen all my years of growing up. We stopped at the cemetery where our Grandfather Braun, my mother's father, lay unvisited these many years. How tall the cypress trees had grown around the little old churchyard! When was I here last? When my six-year-old cousin was buried? Or was it when my high school teacher was buried the year I was in grade eleven? Now the dark green trees are a wall and the ancient wooden church with peeling white paint is owned by a struggling evangelical group. The Mennonite congregation that met here during the 1950s has built a modern structure with a giant overhead screen for singing choruses instead of the chorales we sang out of black hymnals. Everything points to the changing of a way of life. My father's death, the disappeared places of my youth, the call to return to this valley every year of my life. We want the freedom to change, but our parents, our homesteads, shouldn't they stay as they were?

There is a great crowd at the funeral on Saturday afternoon, many relatives, grandchildren, friends, and people who know the family. My father spent forty-three years attending Sunday morning services, weddings, funerals, Bible study sessions, prayer meetings, and congregational meetings. He never contemplated not going, even when he disagreed with the minister. They just had not studied the scriptures carefully enough or they would know what God said. Peter Konrad paid church dues without missing a tithe. He gave extra to missions and missionaries, but he was never a churchy phrasemaker and always kept a sceptical edge. I liked that about him. He smelled posturing.

In the ritual from the earliest funerals I can recall, after the burial comes a communal meal and time of sharing. In the church basement people sit at the long rows of tables, and elderly church members serve coffee or tea from shiny big kettles. People visit with others they have not seen in decades. George, master of ceremonies for the 'sharing' session, recalled a time when our father taught him not to go for revenge, to forgive another person's failings …

Why are you grateful that people attend? You think of your own demise and wonder, will it matter to anyone? You like the fact that your father touched *many lives, that this is still a community where people know each other, not only the person being buried, but also that person's children. You are with people who share a history, people whose parents shared your father's world. Did any of my father's missing brothers have this?*

The area where I grew up has changed. No more strings of farms along the gravelled roads, no milk cans on the stands beside the mailboxes, no berry crates being loaded or unloaded on your yard. The area is residential, has smart houses, blacktopped streets, apartment blocks and shopping malls. My dad's generation still farmed, but the next generation went into trades and professions, were urbanized. Many of the Mennonite children who grew up along our road have become highly evangelical. It's a 'Bible Belt.' Others have lost all contact with their roots. The neighbourhood no longer is homogeneously Mennonite. East Asian shops sit beside Funk's supermarket.

I won't describe the family gatherings after the funeral. It gets too complicated. It brings out all our places in the family. Families are endless threads, interwoven, knotted, quickly unravelled. Spouses aside, what do any of us have that holds us together, but our parents or our children? All our lives we try to find out who we are, what we want, or what makes us this way. We don't necessarily see the invisible strong family threads that cage us. Each has a set place and we re-enact our roles, especially at a parent's death.

3

Searching, 1926–1930

The Gates of Moscow

My parents had met in Siberia, she a refugee from west of the Urals and he returned from the Civil War. They began married life on a western plain in the small village of Maslianovka, twelve kilometres west of Omsk, near a trunk line of the Trans-Siberian Railway. It was a small village, twenty-five families living along a street of farmyards with log houses. Here rich black soil produced grain crops in fields dotted with islands of birch trees. Dirt roads that joined scattered villages were dusty in summer, and in rainy weather black gumbo sucked wagon wheels above their axles, forcing travellers to ride horseback or wait for roads to dry. In winter, snowdrifts closed roads, so it was small wonder my family used the railway as an all-weather route for short and long trips.

On a research trip in 1996, I had met Maria Reich, a cousin in Switzerland who, as a young teen in 1923, with her family had spent nine months in Maslianovka. Coming from Dresden, Germany, she had seen snow piled like whipped cream on rooftops, long icicles dripping down, prancing horses under Russian arched headgear and fur clothing. She had heard the scrunch of fresh snow underfoot and tasted milk warm from the cow. These things, with white birch trees and an endless blue sky, to her seemed romantic, a fairytale.[1] But the story of my father's family did not end happily ever after.

In the box of 'Russian pictures' was a large photograph of my grandparents' golden wedding anniversary, taken in Maslianovka in 1926. Many years later, in the early 1990s in Bremen, Germany, in the apartment of my father's 'lucky' brother Gerhard, I met Lena Wiebe, a cousin who recalled that the dirt street was lined with buggies, carriages, and wagons from three neighbouring villages, and that other people came on foot or by train to gather in the backyard.[2] Our six-year-old, Lena, black hair brushed and tied in a giant white ribbon, flouncing her white dress, dancing foot to foot, had run in and out among chairs and benches along the fence. 'So many people! So many chairs! So many children!' Flitting past women in long dark skirts, light-coloured, long-sleeved blouses or dresses, men suited up stiffly in Sunday clothes, some wearing white shirt and tie, others the 'comrade' cap, Lena looked for her two-years-older cousin Jutti Epp. 'Come,' she beckoned Jutti, and they ran past the adults through the crowded courtyard. Behind the house, squatting over grey ashes, were two large cast iron cauldrons filled with *Obstmoos*. How sweet this fruit compote smelled, made of just pails of raisins, prunes, and dried apple pieces. How heavenly delicious it must be! 'Oh, can we just taste it?'

'Off with you!' On they ran to the summer kitchen where Lena pointed out the layers of roasted chickens and ducks heaped in tubs and the mountain of golden brown, fresh and fluffy Zwieback buns, double-deckers, spread on a table.[3]

Grandmother Konrad, housemaids, her three married daughters, and three daughters-in-law had baked and cooked for days, and now everything was ready. Even real coffee beans had been procured and ground.

'I'll show you the cake. Tante Motya baked it. She calls it a *tablet*.'

Jutti's eyes widened when she saw the marvellous cake, a centrepiece on the table set for the reception. A meal would follow several sermons, much singing of hymns, poems, and prayers. Both girls turned towards the anniversary couple seated among their guests. Grandmother Konrad was wearing a traditional golden wreath as a crown on top of her lace black bonnet and Grandfather Konrad with his round belly looked proud. His thick hair that Lena liked to touch was almost white, his beard dark grey. Seeing Lena and Jutti edge in, his blue eyes brightened, but Grandmother's frown wrinkled her face.

Lena whispered to her cousin, 'See those fish on the cake, they're candy.'

Iridescent, they were on one side and gold on the other. Lena had watched her Tante Motya decorate the cake with the fish and flower confections. 'Opa, can I have a fish?' she whispered in the Plautdietsch Low German tongue used in the grandparent Konrad household. Grandmother looked very cross. 'Hush.' But a moment later Grandmother was greeting a guest, and as her Opa said, 'Hups!' a candy fish jumped and landed in Lena's mouth.

What nobody knew at the time was that this 1926 anniversary was the last happy family celebration of the large Konrad family. A permanent reminder of this event hung in the living room of our BC home where I grew up. In a simple wooden frame was a watercolour commissioned for the anniversary, a gift from their eight living children. The painting, which would have a journey to South America before it reached my parents' home, featured three leafy garlands linked together. The green foliage represented the 'green' wedding, the middle garland laden with fruits was the silver wedding, and the last one in autumn-coloured leaves, burnished red and bronze, the golden one. On the foreground a soft green swath bordered a pathway leading to a stone memorial marked *Ebenezer* and read, 'Hitherto hath the Lord helped us.'

I have a photograph of this event. Amazingly, the photographer had captured at least a hundred persons in his lens. Seated centrally were the grandparents. My grandfather in a three-piece Sunday suit, dark beard, full head of hair, had amused eyes and, under her black bonnet and almost invisible 'bridal crown,' my grandmother had a worried expression. Namesake grandchildren – nine Helenes (one, my eldest sister) and Jakobs – were clustered next to them, and others, altogether two dozen, knelt or sat on rugs laid out on the grass. Three daughters and three daughters-in-law with young children sat on Grandmother's side while bearded preachers and their wives sat on Grandfather's side. Three rows deep, nameless relatives and visitors were backed by tall poplar trees lining the street. When young, I looked at the photograph only to identify my parents and siblings. My mother held a white blur, my infant eldest brother. My father held dark-haired Mary, aged two. Now I tried to identify their *missing* brothers and sisters.

My grandparents' large house was built in traditional Mennonite style – house, barn, and carriage/storage shed under one roof – an architectural style going back to ancestors in the Netherlands. They had a large family, ten children. Next to the grandparents' yard was the smaller house of son Heinrich and his Russian wife Motya. Heinrich was one of the *disappeared*. Farther along was the home of my father's elder sister Anna and her second husband. Anna's three children from her first marriage (her husband had died of typhus) included Lena, our storyteller. In another house along the village street lived Dad's brother Abram, a veteran of the First World War married to Nastya, sister of Motya. My parents lived in a small cottage across the street.

Justina, one of my father's five sisters, her husband and family – including young Jutti – lived twenty kilometres away at Smolianovka. The eldest Konrad daughter Susana had died in childbirth when the family lived in Crimea, but her husband with a second wife came a hundred kilometres to Maslianovka to attend the celebration. They were extended family, calling my grandparents 'parents.' Dad's youngest brother, Gerhard, said he had not known until he was fourteen that the second wife, Susanna, was not his sister. The eldest Konrad son, a victim of the 1920 typhus epidemic, was represented by his six-year-old daughter and her mother. The only child not present was my father's elder sister Helene who, planning to be a missionary to India, had ended up marrying a German theologian in London in 1906 and moving to Dresden, Germany.

In the photograph I have three siblings, but another brother arrived in December and yet another was born in 1928. With five young children born close together, even under Communist law my mother had been allowed to hire a mother's helper, usually a local non-Mennonite young woman. Grandmother Konrad across the street had always had household help, and in a pre-mechanized farming era, Grandfather had routinely hired local farm workers for harvesting, spring seeding, or other farm work.

Before I actively researched the topic, I had asked my father about life under Communist law. 'At first the Reds did not seem so bad,' Dad had said. The Civil War had ended and, with some adjustments, the early Bolsheviks had allowed farmers to own private property. In 1921, to boost the economy after the end of the Civil War, Lenin had introduced what became known as the New Economic Policy (NEP).[4] To accommodate Soviet socialist policies, Dad had to join a cooperative. As he said, 'I could go along with the formation of local municipal committees made up of workers, rather than only rich landowners. We twenty-five families in Maslianovka pooled our marketing and purchasing of products and elected a board of three to run our cooperative.[5] I was elected chair of the board and it was a lot of work, getting permissions for everything, ordering supplies, buying and selling for the co-op. Often I had to take business trips to Omsk and I got tired of the hassle and red tape so I resigned.' My father paused. 'But then my successor was inept and they chose me again.' He carried on in this position until 1929.

But the golden wedding anniversary had coincided with a hardening of Communist policy. Anti-religious propaganda was increasing, preachers were disappearing, and many private businesses were being closed. Guests at the anniversary had discussed the tragedies of the recent Bolshevik Revolution and Civil War when relatives and friends from their former home in Soviet Ukraine had starved, been murdered, or become homeless, and much talk centred on the twenty thousand Mennonites who had left the Soviet state and immigrated to Canada between 1923 and 1926.

In a recorded interview with my parents in 1980, my brother Herman asked why they did not try to leave earlier.[6] My father explained, 'We wanted to leave in 1926, but the grain crop was very heavy in the fall, so I planned to leave after harvesting. I had already seen an eye doctor in Omsk to check for trachoma scars, a disease I had as a boy. Canadian immigration authorities would reject anyone with scars and fortunately I was declared healthy. October brought heavy rains to delay the harvesting, and after I finally got my crop done and we started on my father's fields, it snowed. I did not want to leave without threshing my father's fields and it got later and later. When I finally got to Omsk with our papers, applications were no longer being accepted.'

Some people did leave after 1926, and on the tape my father sighed. 'I should have reapplied. There was a list.'

'What would you have wanted to do here?' my mother asked. 'By then we already had something in Russia and here we had nothing.'

'Well, we could have had a better start. At that time Father-in-law Braun wrote they were getting seven dollars a day, and when we came we got one dollar a day. Father-in-law [Braun] worked six days and bought a cow for thirty dollars. You couldn't do that in Russia. I should have reapplied. There was a man. He found out who was responsible for issuing applications for exit visas. He made it his business to determine exactly where this government official lived and decided he'd give him a present. So, for twenty-five roubles he bought a gift and went to the back door, not the front door. The wife opened the door. He handed it to her saying, "This is a present from so-and-so." The next day he applied for papers and the official said, "Sure, right away."'

My mother demurred, 'W-e-l-l, if everyone had tried that ...' Her partner of sixty years was mildly reproachful: 'Everyone would not have tried it. It was dangerous for the person giving the gift, and for the person taking it, a dangerous business. But I ... well, I would have done it.'

My mother told the next story.

It was 28 April 1928, a cold, snowy morning in Maslianovka. Grandfather Konrad was ill. Next door, across the street, the mongrel dog started to howl. Outdoors, on his haunches, nose into the steel grey sky, he howled and howled. Son-in-law Dietrich Toews, Anna's second husband, ordered him to be quiet, but the howling continued. Dietrich was helping to nurse his father-in-law who was suffering from bladder or prostate disease. It was excruciating, being unable to void, and while a paramedic came regularly to drain his fluids, there was no help for him otherwise.

'Go,' Grandmother said when Dietrich entered the sickroom. 'Call all of them. He wants to say goodbye.'

Each child went into the sickroom individually and each said a last farewell. After Grandfather died they washed him and dressed him in his best suit and laid him out in a coffin in the unused summer room. All the little grandchildren filed by, tears streaming, calling out, '*Oba Opa, unsa Opa*' (Oh Grandpa, our Grandpa).[7]

Jakob J. Konrad, my grandfather, was seventy-three, considered old. His son Gerhard told me his father had died just in time and quoted the line '*Wer sterben soll, den Tod findet ihm*' (Whoever is meant to die, Death will find). Lucky to be dead.

After this, my parents moved into the larger house with Grandmother. Smarting from having lived with her in-laws for the first two years of her marriage, my mother was not too keen about the move, but her sisters were married and my father saw his duty. Grandmother kept to her room, my sister Mary recalled, only emerging in her black dresses to sigh and ask for quiet.

The same year my grandfather died, Stalin introduced his first Five-Year Plan, a plan designed to reverse the New Economic Policy free market system and to set quotas for production and development. The Soviets wished to create urban centres of industry, build railways and canals, subways, hydroelectric dams, and factories. To accomplish this, many more factory workers were required, and factory workers and growing cities required more grain and farm products. Further, to finance Stalin's building initiatives, the state was selling farm products abroad.[8] To meet all these demands, Stalin decided to change agriculture. Bolsheviks hated the 'Old World' thinking of private property and wanted to herd Russia's farmers into collective and state farms where their activities would be government controlled. Farmers would be forced to join collective (*kolkhozy*) and state (*sovkhozy*) farms instead of working private property. Socialism would move faster and more economically with larger operations, marketing would be more efficient, and of course the government would own the goods and grain produced. The problem? People still liked private ownership.

Stalin viewed Russia's peasants as relics of a bourgeois society, as class enemies who threatened the Bolshevik Revolution by controlling the food supply.[9] As he determined, and as his ministers Molotov and Kaganovich enforced the policy, in a communist socialist state, if private property owners did not wish to cooperate, they would be forced to comply. Farmers were placed in one of three levels or categories of wealthy, middle, or poor peasants. The most resistant to giving up their properties, well-to-do peasants, were labelled 'the hard-fisted ones' or kulaks. Remove them, Stalin said, and the poorer and middle peasants will be coerced to join the collective and state farms. Appeal to the bottom, the have-nots, let them think they will be the new local rulers. Sell the idea of a dictatorship of the proletariat. Talk about Lenin's promise of a 'radiant future,' of a Marxist property-less, market-less utopia, but enforce it through any means, including violence and terror. Use the tools Lenin had introduced – the secret police (Cheka), forced labour camps, fear, centralization of power, prohibition of free elections, and mass media propaganda.

In January 1928 Stalin visited Siberia to investigate a countrywide shortage of grain. He blamed the so-called kulaks (these 'enemies of the Revolution') for hoarding their produce.[10] To collect the 'hidden' supplies, Stalin urged local activists to show no mercy and introduced 'emergency measures' into the criminal code to arrest farmers and to confiscate their property. To accelerate his 'Five-Year Plan in Four,' the government began to impose exorbitant taxes and quotas of grain and meat for farmers and cooperatives to deliver to the state. Usually these quotas were greater than anything farmers produced. To fill a quota, farmers – as well as priests, clergy, and religious workers – might sell their livestock and even household possessions to buy enough grain at seven to eight times the market price to deliver to the government. That done, the state imposed additional duties or taxes and, with nothing left to sell and unable to buy more grain to deliver, they were then fined and told to pay, in cash, a penalty of five times the value of the original inflated quota. Now owing the government a large sum, they could see their property confiscated and sold for very low prices at auction, and next could be arrested and imprisoned.[11]

Slavgorod Mennonites felt the brunt of this new order. In this part of the Siberian steppe up to 18.2 per cent of Mennonite farmers were declared kulaks.[12] In October, celebrating the anniversary of 'Liberation from White Army Admiral Kolchak,' the Slavgorod Party secretary demanded that the quotas be filled completely. This resulted in a scene where a German farmer in Slavgorod with a pregnant wife was disenfranchised. Forced to move into an unheated shed, he had his belongings sold at auction. When the wife bought back a cradle, the Party officer tipped it over and resold it for five kopeks.[13]

Mennonites, like my Konrads (being pacifists), had a history of moving when in trouble with a government (from the Netherlands to Poland and Poland to Russia), but not surprisingly, other previously independent farmers resisted these measures in every way possible. In some parts of the USSR, rather than delivering meat to the state, desperate farmers killed their cattle.[14] Others burned buildings or murdered officials enforcing these harsh measures.[15] To escape arrest, many others abandoned their homes and moved.

The propaganda machine branded opponents of Stalinist policies as counter-revolutionaries, capitalists, bourgeoisie, vermin, parasites, subhuman kulaks, and exploiter landowners. The worst 'enemies' were factory owners, mill owners, the one-time gentry, and clerics. Propagandists shouted that 'land-grabbing, bloodsucker' bosses had abused and exploited workers for centuries for personal gain and these enemies should be removed ruthlessly – forgetting, my father said, that their harvests had fed Russia, and their agricultural improvements and implement factories were already industrializing the country. People were promised that in the new socialist state everything would be collectively owned, collectively worked, and collectively shared. Well, the Party people would need a little extra. Simon Sebag Montefiore's *Stalin* biography documents Bolshevik leaders spending holidays and going on hunting parties at expropriated Black Sea and Crimean resorts.

In this time of crisis, in the late summer of 1929, a Siberian Soviet inspector visited my parents' home to audit the books and collect revenues from the local cooperative my father chaired. On leaving, the official let drop the remark, 'Better if someone left soon.' Now my father knew he was on a list of kulaks, soon to be expropriated and disenfranchised, perhaps imprisoned or exiled.

That evening in Maslianovka, around a supper table set with cabbage borscht, fried sausage, and home-baked bread, my father's siblings assembled to discuss their dilemma. My father looked around the table. 'I think we should go to Moscow. Those Slavgorod Mennonites got out. If they can do it, we can. Get to Canada.'

All the family knew that my Braun grandparents with my mother's four youngest siblings had immigrated to Canada in 1924 and were now living in Steinbach, Manitoba, Canada. They knew about the

Slavgorod Mennonites from villages and isolated farms some distance east of Omsk on the Siberian plain. Seventy of them, denied exit visas locally, warned by their own leaders not to be reckless, had gone to Moscow and unexpectedly on 1 June 1929 had received permission to leave for Canada. In Moscow, another group of forty Siberian Mennonite families, including several preachers, had been allowed to leave on 5 August.

My father's younger brother Heinrich was reluctant. 'We can't go now. Motya is pregnant.' Then Nastya, the wife of my father's brother Abram, asked, 'Why leave for a strange country when Motya's and my family all are here?'

My father said, 'We're going. The Slavgorod ones got out and we'll try.'

The others just looked at him. That Peter always thought he knew best.

Like a match igniting a fuse, firing the hopes of thousands along its path, news of the successful Siberian emigrants who went to Moscow reverberated to the farthest corners of the Soviet Union where Mennonites or German speakers lived. Soon foreign photographers and journalists picked up the story of the flood of people arriving in Moscow and applying to leave. The stories dominated the international press. 'Workers in the Red Paradise' must not be happy if they were trying to flee. The topic especially captivated the German press and generated headlines. Heedless of a Soviet proviso that no further petitions to emigrate would be considered for the duration of Stalin's Five-Year Plan, people kept arriving in Moscow. All knew that some groups had left Moscow, and from Leningrad or Riga they were on their way to Canada. Wrote one Mennonite, 'Everyone wanted to grab the brass ring to get to Canada.'[16]

Word spread that people could even travel on credit, that Canadian Mennonites had made an arrangement with the Canadian Pacific Railway (CPR) for ocean transport and train travel in Canada, and refugees unable to pay their passage now could repay in Canada. Some recalled the story of Lot's family, where God's angels urged, 'Flee for your life; do not look back or stop anywhere in the valley; flee to the hills lest you be consumed.'[17] Communist Russia had become the biblical Sodom and Gomorrah.

Who was a kulak? Anyone who had ever employed more than three workers, owned mechanized machinery, a mill, a commercial building, a larger house, or several farm animals, or who had an annual income of more than 1,500 roubles was considered a kulak. Any registered church member, priest, rabbi, or preacher, or anyone who had tried to emigrate – all were 'kulaks,' 'enemies.' The categories would later change to include anyone the state wished to remove. Did my Siberian Konrads fit into the class of kulaks? My father had employed six workers. 'Three too many.' Of course, by definition Grandfather Jakob Jakobovich was the archetypal kulak with all the workers he hired and the lands he had owned, first on the Ukrainian steppe (Molochna Basin) where he grew up, then in Crimea where he had pioneered large tracts of land, or in Siberia where he had rented steppe fields and owned farmland in Maslianovka. His three sons Gerhard, Heinrich, and Abram had operated the gristmill, so that made those three brothers, what? Kulaks.

Many disadvantaged citizens and idealists, convinced they were ushering in a 'radiant future,' were eager to be part of a new system. Swept by communist promises, they saw anyone resisting the new religion of communism, anyone better dressed, better educated, any landowner who lived comfortably, and anyone religious as an 'enemy.' Marching through Omsk streets, young people, often members of the 25,000ers – the factory activists, workers, and Communist Party members sent out from Leningrad to the countryside to promote and carry out Bolshevik policies – carried banners shouting, 'Death to the Bourgeoisie.'[18] Urging the eviction of kulaks from their homes, farms, businesses, and mills, they sang the 1917 workers' 'Marseillaise.'

To the parasites, to the dogs, to the rich!
Yes and to the evil vampire tsar!
Kill and destroy them, the villainous swine!
Light up the dawn of a new and better life!

Grandfather Jakob J. Konrad escaped being named a kulak by dying, but others in his family were vulnerable. When in June 1929 Stalin ordered an intensification of the war on the kulaks (by December he would demand the liquidation of kulaks as a class), my father had guessed what lay ahead. Receiving the tip in September, he discreetly sold household belongings at a local bazaar. A small home auction sold a few more belongings at prices below value, and some things were given away. Two wicker trunks were packed with a few dishes, cutlery, clothing, family photographs, and my mother's large portrait of her (dead) mother. Feather pillows and duvets were stuffed into linen sacks (for years our family used goose down pillows brought from Russia), and pillowcases were filled with roasted Zwieback buns. Into another trunk went a smoked ham, smoked sausages, flour, and lard. A Primus burner commonly found in Russia and used when travelling by train took little room and could boil water or cook food in transit.

In October, sacks and trunks loaded onto a wagon, my mother, two months pregnant, a year-old child on her lap, and surrounded by four more young children climbed aboard. Which of my father's brothers (was it Abram or Heinrich?) drove the family to the Liubino train station I'll never know. As my mother wrote in her brief autobiography, when their train going west crossed the Urals and reached the town of Davlekanova in the Bashkir province, the family stepped off so she could revisit her parental home in the village of Gorchakovo. Her two brothers, Isaak and Peter Braun, lived with their families in the house abandoned by her father five years ago. My parents urged them, 'Come too. Let's try for exit visas.' As my mother with five children visited her old friends and neighbours and got acquainted with her brother's wives, Dad left for Moscow to find lodgings. After two weeks, having rented a room in a Moscow suburb, my father returned to Gorchakovo to fetch his family. My mother's brothers were in a quandary: stay or try to emigrate? They dithered. My parents left and never saw those brothers again.

Thousands of German-speaking families, Lutherans, Catholics, but the majority Mennonites from Siberia, were disembarking daily at Moscow's train stations. In the suburb Kliasma my father (and other men from hideaway areas) took the train into Moscow to stand on the main station platforms to watch for incoming families. My mother's Braun brothers failed to arrive, but from Siberia came Gerhard's family and his mother. The men from the dacha areas tried to get interviews and to pressure government officials to grant travel documents. Some tried to buy bread, but food ration cards were being denied to newcomers. Back in the rented rooms everyone feared a knock on the door by the secret police demanding, 'Who organized you? Why do you want to go?' 'Nobody organized us,' my father said. By November the numbers had risen to over thirteen thousand, with families filling every available rental space, largely in the pine-forested dacha village area surrounding Moscow.[19]

An effort to pressure the Soviet government to grant exit permits resulted in a massive demonstration including hundreds of women and infants who flooded Soviet President Kalinin's reception room. I don't know if my mother participated, but some women appealed to Lenin's widow Krupskaia and others to Russia's Tolstoyans who were sympathetic. A delegation appealed to the German consulate. The Soviets now faced a crisis. The ethnic German population of Russia was one and a quarter million and if more came to Moscow, the situation would become a colossal indictment of government policies. Whatever they did, Soviet–German relations might suffer. The secret police (now called the GPU) began to arrest and interrogate men they took for leaders of this insurrection. When arrests began, people in the dacha hideaways lay awake listening for the Black Raven police trucks. In Germany an organization called 'Our Brothers in Need' (*Brüder in Not*) began to collect funds to assist the Soviet-German refugees.[20] Embarrassing the Soviet government, the international press kept asking why thousands were trying to leave if communism, as the Soviets maintained, had created 'a land of happy people, a Red Paradise.'

Anxious to halt the refugee flood and stem the bad publicity, while urging applicants to be reasonable and return to their homes, the Soviet government began issuing exit permits. On 27 October the first group of refugees in Moscow left for Canada. On 30 October the Canadian government cited economic conditions and resistance to East European immigrants as reasons for closing its doors until spring. In response, Soviet officials immediately stopped processing applications. Though determined to keep good Soviet–German relations, the Soviets issued an ultimatum to the German government: 'Accept the half-starved and unemployed refugees or we'll send them east.'[21] Limited by its own dire economic state and the prospect of thousands of indigent refugees, the German government held off making a decision. Two trainloads of emigrants having successfully left Moscow for the West, the remaining families did not understand the sudden halt to procedures and did not believe that no country wanted to accept them. In mid-November Stalin returned to Moscow from his vacation and gave commands to clear all would-be emigrants out of Moscow. All in transit were to be stopped and turned back, and no more train tickets were to be sold to ethnic Germans. Guards posted at railway stations turned back my mother's younger brother Isaak Braun and his family coming from Gorchakovo.

Long before I began searching for my missing relatives, in a remote archive in Filadelfia, Paraguay, on a visit with Harvey to the Mennonite settlement in 1986, I unearthed a memoir to show my father, thinking he knew the people mentioned. Now this memoir and his son's letter in the Paraguayan Mennonite newspaper *Mennoblatt* caught my breath. Peter Rahn and his family were in hiding in the room next to my parents in the same small dacha at Kliasma. Rahn's gangly son Jash had a monthly train pass and was travelling to Moscow regularly. He was assigned to meet new Mennonite arrivals (easy for him to identify, he wrote) as they stepped off the train and conduct them to a travel bureau where four Mennonite men were registering, helping them to fill out papers and pay for exit visas.[22] The money was thrown into a sack hung on a nail on the interim office wall – everyone trusted the four men with their money.

Moscow streets were crowded with police and soldiers looking for arrivals. At the Kurskii station platform young Jash had identified an elderly Mennonite man with a handicapped wife who had collapsed. About to help her, he felt a hand on his shoulder. 'Follow me!' The soldier pushed him into a group of newly arrived passengers, herding them against the wall of the station. A Black Raven van drove up and forty to fifty new arrivals were locked into it and taken to Lubyanka prison.

Soldiers forced the remaining group to walk to the Butyrki prison near the railway station. There, put into a damp room, Jash was subjected to nightly interrogations and torture. Since he spoke Russian fluently and was well dressed, it was assumed he was a ringleader. He wrote that some men were tortured so badly that they could barely walk. Men in Lubyanka were stripped to their underwear, held in fetid and sweltering overcrowded jail cells one night and moved into ice-cold rooms the next, only to be returned to the overheated cell. Given no food and forced to find some space on a cement floor as they waited to be interrogated, many feared imminent death.[23] Jash remained two nights. A vehicle arrived to take him and others back to the train station, but near the station he saw his opportunity, jumped off, and dashed into the thick crowd. 'Urdai!' Stop! Lucky to get away, Jash made his way circuitously back to the hideaway dacha in Kliasma. Certain he was being hunted, he hid elsewhere for almost two weeks. But Jash had given the house number of the main dacha nearer to the road. As a consequence, the night following his arrest, the GPU showed up at that house and the people in it were taken away, imprisoned, or sent back.[24] Had the GPU searched the smaller dacha where my parents were hiding, I would never have written this story.

Almost six years old at the time, my sister Mary recalled sitting with her siblings in a darkened room, not daring to call, cry, or laugh. The windows covered with blankets, she remembered parents gathering in the room for prayer meetings. On their knees, adults were pleading for protection from the dreaded police. She recalled motors starting and stopping as Black Raven trucks prowled the streets. This trauma would contribute to her being fearful much of her later life.

My father's youngest brother, Gerhard, his wife, and her family, as well as Grandmother Konrad had arrived in Moscow a short time after my parents, and when Grandmother Konrad followed, Dad had hired a carter to take his mother and her luggage from the train station to the rental lodgings. As the loaded cart bumped along, in the distance the little group noticed a street patrol. Quickly the carter, followed by all the adults except Grandmother, dashed into hiding places under a little bridge, and there she sat like dowager Queen Victoria – black bonnet, black dress, amid a pile of baskets and bundles in an abandoned cart on a sidewalk. The police questioned her and she pretended not to understand. They shrugged and left the scolding babushka. This scene would be re-enacted.

Between 17 and 24 November, police trucks scoured the dacha areas, moving in an ever-widening circle through dacha villages Perlovka, Tarasovka, and Losinka, loading up families crowded into temporary shelter for weeks or months. By 25 November, of the estimated 13,000 attempting to emigrate, only 5,671, including my family, still cowered in their hiding places praying that the inevitable should not take place.[25] The international press, especially in Germany, was still printing heart-wrenching pictures of people being forced into cattle cars, of locked train doors, of children herded under police guard and women screaming. This publicity increased the public German outcry and added to the nationwide appeal for funds to help 'our Brothers in Need.' President Hindenburg contributed 200,000 marks.[26] The deportations in Moscow, combined with diplomatic pressure, decided the German government to agree to take the remaining 'Brothers in Need' into temporary refugee camps in Germany.

On Nov. 23 they had cleaned out Perlovka. That was Friday the 23rd of

November and it was said the next day they were to begin at Kliasma, but the next day nothing much happened and only towards evening the GPU slowly drove quietly along the streets.... We had barely fallen asleep when there was a knock on the door and they demanded entry. Again it was the terrifying GPU but this time they spoke in mild tones and were different. That night the GPU had been at many places where Mennonites lived, but instead of coming to arrest us, the GPU told us we had permission to leave for Germany. We should just organize ourselves because we were now allowed to leave.[27]

In this way, for 220 roubles each, the remaining 5,671 received exit visas, a red booklet with a hammer and sickle on its cover. From this group only 1,200 persons got to Canada.[28] From my parents' Omsk area, 340 families reached Moscow, but only 49 made it to Germany.[29] In Maslianovka and neighbouring Smolianovka, 101 farmers had sold properties or left them standing and gone to Moscow. Of these, only 12, including my parents, were successful in leaving.[30] Of 1,200 persons reaching Canada through Moscow, 7 were members of my family. What a slender thread.

My father said they left Moscow on 29 November 1929. Was it coincidence that on 29 November 1989, exactly sixty years later, at the age of ninety-nine, still sharp in mind and opinion, my dear father died? Was this a cycle completed, a life programmed to round out? A fortune-teller had told him he would live to be a hundred.

The refugees accepted by Germany on an interim basis were housed in three-storey army officer barracks from the First World War. Researching Mennonite newspapers from the 1930s,[31] I found lists of refugees in three camps, two of which, Hammerstein and Möln, were near Hamburg and one, Prenzlau, where my parents stayed, was near the Polish border. In the lists I found the names of my grandmother and of my parents.[32] Sponsors were also included in the lists. My parents were (nominally) sponsored by Grandfather Isaak Braun in Steinbach, Manitoba. Grandmother's sponsor was from Cullross, Manitoba, but she and many other refugees never made it to Canada.[33] Among those failing Canadian health inspections, many went to Paraguay or Brazil. Grandmother, almost eighty, would wait in limbo in Germany for two years and in 1932 join her daughter Justina and family, who were eventually accepted by Paraguay.

My mother was thirty-seven. I remember her only with grey hair and never considered that her experiences might have caused the early grey. She had told us her hair used to be 'awful,' auburn and naturally curling. She wanted 'straight hair and not red.' Her 'stateless' passport issued in Germany shows a haggard woman with 'straight' hair. Likely with grey strands too. My father's 'stateless' passport photo shows him with a shaven head, looking swarthy and grim. My elder siblings have shaved heads too. In the refugee barracks an epidemic of childhood diseases broke out, killing hundreds. One was my year-old brother. My father said two hundred children died and one family lost all its seven children.

What was it like to be a refugee? My parents did not dwell on this, but I know we grew up with the weight of this experience on our shoulders. We knew we were fortunate, that others were left behind. We knew our parents prayed for these siblings and other relatives in the USSR, but did not know if they were alive. We were not told to seek restitution or justice from the Soviets – nobody believed the USSR would crumble. In my family, we were not taught to hate; rather, it was our duty to help other refugees and oppressed persons, wherever they were.

In my community in Abbotsford, BC, there was an annual day of remembrance for Mennonite survivors of the 'Gates of Moscow' exodus. Initially they met at a campground near the brick plant. Refugee Remembrance Day later became a day for all Mennonite immigrants to thank God for their delivery from Soviet Russia. It included groups that left in the 1920s and those arriving after the Second World War. My parents were grateful to God, then to Germany for taking them in when no other country would have them. Also for many years they voted for the Liberal Party, the 'government of Mackenzie King,' which gave them a new life. They were grateful to the CPR that let them travel on credit and to Mennonite leaders in Germany and Canada who organized their rescue.

After three months in the German refugee camp, my parents and siblings travelled by train to Hamburg and boarded a boat to cross the English Channel to England. In Liverpool they boarded the *Minnedosa*, a two-funnel Canadian Pacific Line steamer, formerly a troopship of the First World War. In 1930 she carried 1,750 passengers – 550 cabin class and 1,200 refugees in third class. After an eight-day voyage, on 2 March 1930 the *Minnedosa* docked at the harbour of Saint John, New Brunswick.[34]

Arriving in Canada in the Great Depression was the worst time for a destitute immigrant family with four young children, but my mother always asked, what if her husband had been arrested, what if they had been sent back? And where were the others? Gerhard, his wife Lieschen, her parents and her deaf young brother, last seen in Moscow, did not reach a refugee camp in Germany. In Siberia there remained Dad's brothers Abram and Heinrich, his sisters Anna in Maslianovka and Justina in Smolianovka. Also left behind in the USSR were my mother's three brothers, Peter and Isaak Braun in Gorchakovo, Bashkiria province, and Johannes in Siberia.*

---

* Jakob escaped to Canada in 1929. To focus on members left in the USSR, his narrative will not be included except incidentally.

4

The Soviet State, 1930–1933

Gerhard Is Lucky

& i am a child, a child dancing
on this journey
in the beginning
all things begin
pawned to the grave
i close the gap with words
build altars of sound
strike every rock speechless.

– Audrey Poetker[1]

Twenty-eight years after they saw him in Moscow, my parents received a letter from the USSR and knew my father's brother Gerhard was alive. Stalin had died in 1953 and the fear that controlled Soviet citizens had been somewhat loosened by the speech of Communist leader Nikita Khrushchev on 24 February 1956, at the Twentieth Party Congress in which he denounced Stalin's crimes and his 'cult of personality.' It seems my parents had written to the woman in Siberia who had dared to write them one letter from Omsk in 1946 and she forwarded their letter to Gerhard. He replied,

Taldy Kurgan, Kazakhstan
6 January 1957
… Your letter lies in front of me and I read it again and again as one thought leaps over another and I don't know how to begin. I include a photograph so you will have an idea of the way we are now. We have a small photo of you that you sent Sara for Lena and Lena lent it to us to look at and return.

First I must tell you that my dear Lieschen died on 28 June 1942, in Aksu....[2]

Of my father's five siblings left behind in the USSR in 1929, Gerhard would be the only one he ever saw again. After his 1957 letter, Gerhard waited a year to write again and then, sporadically, his carefully crafted airmail letters found their way to our mailbox. Written in German, invariably he signed off with '*Aufwiedersehen*,' meaning, 'till we meet again' or 'we'll see you again.' For my parents this was the first direct information about a missing sibling (not counting the 1946 letter). Ten years after Gerhard's initial letter, the first member of our family to meet him was my husband, in 1967, on a research visit to the USSR. Harvey's parents used the occasion to look up his mother's long-lost foster sister (the flower seller in Frunze, Kirghizia – now Bishkek, Kyrgyzstan).

Since many Soviet cities and regions were closed to foreigners during the Cold War, they met in Alma Ata (Almaty), Kazakhstan. Gerhard lived about three hundred kilometres away in Taldy Kurgan, Kazakhstan, a town closed to foreigners, so with travel being cheap in Soviet days, Gerhard, his second wife Klara, and ten-year-old daughter Nelly flew to Alma Ata. Harvey's snapshots and stories about this meeting, as well as Gerhard's gifts to our three young children (Russian dolls wearing white aprons, black dresses, and braids) were my first impression of my father's youngest brother. Following Gerhard's advice – 'There are fewer ears in the bushes' – Harvey's conversations with Gerhard took place in public parks.

In 1977 Gerhard and his twenty-one-year-old daughter, Nelly, visited Canada, and when they met at the Vancouver airport, he and my father had not seen each other for forty-eight years. My family flew in from Toronto for this reunion. I saw in Gerhard Konrad a robust man, solidly built, a handsome man who wore an Uzbek embroidered skullcap at night to keep his thick grey hair flat. He impressed his relatives with his endless energy. Eager to go anywhere, do anything, he talked non-stop. I recall sitting for three hours straight on a hard dining room chair, not daring to interrupt while Gerhard reminisced with vivid detail, recalling numbers, dates, distances, weights – a personal computer long before we owned computers. Not in the habit of listening, whenever someone inserted a personal opinion or began a competing anecdote, his eyes became vacant or stole a look sideways, as he waited for a pause to jump in and say, 'That's exactly what happened to me when I was in …' Unable to speak openly for decades in the USSR, never having told his story even to his children, he was a geyser.

Since few Soviet relatives visited Canada in the 1970s and my parents lived in a predominantly Mennonite community, Gerhard's visit was a local sensation. Visitors poured into my parents' home to see 'our man from Russia' and to ask if he knew about his or her relatives behind the Iron Curtain.

At that time I was involved in raising a young family and teaching, not in finding *missing* relatives, but once I began my research, Gerhard was one of my early sources. How had he survived when most men his age disappeared? In the Russian Civil War (1918–21) White Army General Anton Denikin had noted that the Bolsheviks were intent on removing whole classes of people. I wondered if those 'classes' were economic or ethnic, if they included German-speakers, Mennonites. Martin Latsis, a Latvian secret police chief on the eastern front, one of the cruellest Bolshevik executioners, wrote,

In examining them [accused victims], do not search for material evidence that the accused has opposed the Soviets by word or deed. The first question to put is, what is his origin, his upbringing, education, or profession? The answer to these questions must determine the fate of the accused.[3]

Were my people persecuted more because of their ethnicity, their religion, or economic class? My parents looked only to understand the Soviet experience as part of God's plan; the fates of their brothers and sisters and other innocent victims were personal tragedies, but God would know the reasons. I wanted answers.

Gerhard's story came out in many meetings.

The baby of the Konrad family, a much-loved twelfth child,* Gerhard was born when his forty-five-year-old mother no doubt hoped that she was 'done,' menopause being the only constraint on the size of Mennonite families, or so it seemed. It was the turn of the century and my grandparents were living comfortably in the large Mennonite village of Spat in central Crimea. They were farmers. Living in the village, they also rented a vast tract of steppe land some fifteen kilometres away and their life revolved around church and agriculture. As he told us years later, Gerhard was born, *not* on 2 January 1900 as his birth certificate stated, but on *Silvesterabend*, New Year's Eve, 31 December 1899. That night most of the family had gone to church for the annual service of reflection and soul-searching, a part of Mennonite Brethren tradition,

---

* Two infants had died.

and when they returned to the pleasant house beside the giant wind-mill they found their mother in bed with a new baby. New Year's Day was an official holiday, and why the father did not register the child is a mystery to me, but Gerhard said an uncle registered the baby (him) the following day. 'Which date did you say?' asked his mother. 'Today, of course,' replied the uncle. His mother protested, 'But, but ...' The uncle just shrugged, 'So, what's the difference?' But what a difference it made. 'Saved me from being drafted,' Gerhard told us. 'Twice, it saved me. Put me into another century. I was always a year too young.'

Yes, born lucky. Who was he still to be alive when almost every male of his 'class' and generation in the USSR perished? When I asked about Gerhard, people invariably said, 'Oh, he was the lucky one. He was a fox.' Then, hinting, they would add, 'How did he do it?' Gerhard sur-vived sixty years of Communism. Men whose families had been land-owners, had employed workers, had owned mills, and were so-called kulaks were marked, yet Gerhard never was sent to a slave labour camp, was only briefly imprisoned, could easily have been sent to the Gulag, and sometimes he was just an eye blink away from it. A man who risked contact with his Western relatives in the 'evil West' during the Cold War (letter in 1957), a man who could not stop talking once he left the Soviet Union – clearly a book in himself – how did he do it?

We met Gerhard numerous times in Toronto and several times in Ger-many, where he lived after 1976. On one of his visits, Harvey captured Gerhard's stories on tape as they drove from Toronto across Canada in our orange VW camper en route to my parents' sixtieth wedding anni-versary celebration in BC.

Gerhard didn't say much about his life before 1929, but recalled the move from Crimea to newly opening lands and pioneering near Omsk, Siberia, in 1910. His father had bought farm buildings at a whistle-stop along the Trans-Siberian just west of Omsk. The station hamlet of Piket-noie had no local school so the two youngest Konrad children, Gerhard and Heinrich, were boarded with a Mennonite family in the village of Chunaievka nearer Omsk. Little three-year-old Lieschen Froese, who would become Gerhard's wife, sometimes sat on his knee. Gerhard, who loved machines, recalled accompanying his parents to an Interna-tional Agricultural Technology Trade Fair in Omsk in 1911; he remem-bered details about the family's steam-powered threshing machine in Crimea and their diesel threshing machine in Siberia. After completing grade school, he took courses in mill mechanics in Omsk and, even at the age of fourteen, said he could see that 'machines were the future.' It would prove fortunate for him after the Bolshevik Revolution that he had worker's papers and a diploma as a machinist. Gerhard was too young to be drafted in the First World War, and during the Civil War, when the White Army conscripted his brothers in Admiral Kolchak's campaign, he had not yet turned the military age of eighteen. Lucky. Gerhard was baptized as a young adult (Mennonites practise adult baptism) and sang in the church choir. At home, he helped run the family gristmill.

When Gerhard and Lieschen married, he twenty-seven and she twenty, they were still able to buy fifty-seven desiatinas of land near the Froese family in Chunaievka, twelve kilometres west of Omsk. Here, surrounded by birch forests along the Irtysh River, Gerhard sowed fields of wheat, barley, and oats, and was able to harvest one crop before the Soviet government began to levy its impossibly heavy duties. The 'extraordinary measures' to collect grain and taxes passed on 29 June 1929 had propelled my parents to leave and also affected Gerhard. His father had escaped being named a kulak by dying, but his father-in-law had not. Heinrich Froese was the chief miller and part owner of a grain mill employing thirty-six workers (who later tried to rescue him from exile) in Chunaievka, therefore just the 'exploiter, capitalist enemy, parasite kulak' the law was meant to catch. Summoned before a tribunal, his civil rights revoked, he was disenfranchised. Classifying him as a kulak, investigators made an inventory and confiscated all the family belongings. Put out on the street, the family could do nothing but leave.

Gerhard also was interrogated and disenfranchised, but not dispossessed of his home, so, when my father sent a telegram from Moscow in October 1929, as Gerhard said, 'We left everything standing and came.' Although not in the same quarters with my parents, his group experienced the same anxieties and night raids by the dreaded secret police in their Black Raven (*chornii voron*) trucks. In one of the raids, Gerhard and his father-in-law were caught and incarcerated in Moscow's infamous Lubyanka jail. 'Sign that you will go home and help build socialism in the Soviet Union. Sign that you don't wish to emigrate, that you promise to go home.' Gerhard signed and made his way to collect his wife and family members to return home.

At Moscow's main train station, soldiers crowded the unlucky asylum seekers into freight cars for their return to Siberia, and as Gerhard saw that there were no passenger cars, just empty coal cars without heat or amenities, he thought they would never survive the freezing trip back to Siberia. How could people be boarding those trains? As a train official was directing despondent would-be émigrés to various platforms, depending on their destination, quick-thinking Gerhard whisked out his birth certificate to show that he was born in Crimea. 'I'm a Crimean. Here's my passport.'

'So you are. What are you doing in this line-up? Get over to Track X.'

Gerhard said it was a kind of miracle that his father-in-law Froese, released from jail soon thereafter, found them. As Froese was asking directions, inquiring if anyone knew if his family had already debarked, a woman who had overheard Gerhard's exchange about belonging with the returnees to Crimea and being sent to Track X, told Froese that his family had gone south. Froese thought, Crimea is large. Where did they go? Quickly he boarded an express train and got off at a major terminal where he stood on the platform watching the trains go by, praying his family might see him. Sure enough, his son Willy seated at a window spied his father on the platform. As their train slowed to a halt, he opened the window. Reunited, the family group continued.

Gerhard's reputation for quick thinking, a fox smelling trouble, had begun. As far as the authorities knew, when he changed trains, he disappeared. Arrived in his boyhood home of Spat, Gerhard took the group to his uncle's house. 'To be in my boyhood village for Christmas, what a joy that was.' Little did Gerhard or anyone else know that this would be the last time for decades that Christmas Eve would be celebrated in that church. Gerhard knew that eventually he would have to register his presence in the village, but in the meantime the Froese group rented a house next door to the uncle.

To complete Gerhard's story, I looked up letters from the USSR sent to Canadian relatives and published in Mennonite newspapers in the 1930s (many anonymously). A writer in Minlertchik, the small Crimean village where my father and Gerhard had attended elementary school before the move to Siberia, told what happened the month after Gerhard's group arrived in Spat.

30 January 1930
Beat on all the doors over there! See if you can soften people's hearts to help us.... In order legally to enlarge the group of kulaks, more and more people are being disenfranchised. And if you are interested in knowing what they plan to do with us, to liquidate this class of people, buy Izvestia.... *The newspaper reports that special measures will be taken to evict and resettle these people in the North, in Siberian forests where they can cut trees. In our local newspaper yesterday there was the directive that the kulak class has to be cleaned up immediately. Today an inventory was taken at someone's house and everything was recorded, every handkerchief and so on, although there was no ostensible*

reason to proceed in this manner since the people targeted had so far complied with all regulations. What this tells us is clear. Anyone who does not wish to join a collective farm is treated like a kulak and driven out. You are not permitted to sell anything you own, no horse, cow, calf, nothing. What is happening now disrespects all human rights and emotions. Save us![4]

Another letter from the Crimea, written a month later by a Mennonite also unsuccessful in leaving the country, reported that practically everyone was being disenfranchised. Dispossessed, young and old alike were set out on the street without money, food, or clothing. Gold rings were taken and even gold teeth were being pulled out:

One woman was chased out in the middle of eating her dinner. She was not even permitted to finish her meal, but while the bandits sat down and ate her soup, she was driven out. Meanwhile her husband was being beaten up ... Without money, clothing, no husband, and in addition under strictest orders that nobody is permitted to take in such evicted ones under penalty of death.

Nobody is permitted to sell agricultural machinery or any farm inventory [animals or goods], not that anyone is able to buy. Anyone disenfranchised is not permitted to buy anything at the cooperative and the private stores have all been closed. Practically all their owners are imprisoned. All their money was taken from them. We could get back 150 roubles from the 200 we paid out in Moscow to get a passport, but if you ask for the money back, you'll be giving up any future possibility to emigrate, so hardly anyone is asking to get a refund, even those who had borrowed the whole sum in order to emigrate. Who wants to put a noose around your own neck?[5]

Gerhard and his father-in-law were told to report to a newly installed local *selsovet* (village council) in Spat. Separately, each was questioned: 'Name, former address, occupation? Have you ever owned property, been disenfranchised, and so on?'

Well, Father Froese went in first. He being a good Mennonite Christian and thinking you have to tell the unvarnished truth, when asked if he was disenfranchised, said yes. So it was my turn next. The government official was inexperienced, a new Komsomol, likely a recent factory worker from Simferopol, but a Red proletariat German-speaker. Here he was sitting in an office, head cocked like a bantam rooster. He asked me, 'Sind Sie stimmlos?' [He meant, 'Are you disenfranchised?' but Gerhard took the words verbatim. 'Are you without a voice?' – Stimme in German being 'voice.']

I replied, 'I can speak. I have a voice' [a pun on the word stimm-los].

The government official was exasperated, 'I asked, have you lost your franchise?'

'What do you mean?,' I asked. 'I can speak. I'm a worker. I have machinist papers. Can you take away the voice of a worker?'

The young official, knowing that it was workers who were to be heeded in the new order of things, was baffled, 'Well … no.'

'So?' I looked defiantly at the recent factory worker turned functionary.

'OK,' the man said and then barked, 'Go then!'

When I told my father-in-law Froese I had indicated 'no' when asked if I had been disenfranchised, Froese was aghast, 'But, Gerhard, that's a lie!' I said, 'The lie, dear Father, is that they say we are disenfranchised. That's the lie.'

Harvey, Gerhard, and I were sitting at our dining table in Toronto in 1980 when Gerhard told us this, and as he spoke his voice became agitated and emphatic.

I told myself, a Notlüge [a lie of necessity] is not a sin. You don't have to place yourself in front of a man with a loaded gun. When they took away our civil rights in 1929, I decided then and there that the Bible does not tell you that you have to obey the forces of evil. Our Mennonites wanted to be honest Christians. That's fine and good when you can help someone else, but when you can't help anyone else and when you are putting yourself in jeopardy, it's wrong.

Following this outburst there was a pause and then he chuckled, 'And besides, I had maintained my citizenship papers with my legal rights from my home village of Maslianovka where I lived before my marriage. These had not been annulled. Only in Chunaievka was I disenfranchised.'[6]

Then Gerhard told how he watched what happened in Spat. It began one Sunday on a mild day in February 1930 when Lieschen, her parents, and the Kroekers (the family of Gerhard's uncle) were all dressed in their Sunday best. They had just stepped out of the house to walk to church when a man they knew from the village rushed up to them and called out, 'The church is locked! They've put a huge lock on the door! No more church. It's state property, says the sign. It says, "This now is the Clubhouse!"'

Gerhard continued,

We stood in shock. Then we noticed several men, one a secret police GPU man but dressed in civvies, going to the preacher's house. Soon the preacher and his entire family of eleven children, including a nursing infant, came out of the house dressed in patched old clothes. Here it was Sunday and they had on the most worn-out clothes. As soon as they were all out of the house, the GPU man put a large lock on their door and announced loudly, 'This is not your house anymore. It now belongs to the state. You are enemies. Kulaks! Out! Be gone with you!' Then he turned towards us people on the street and shouted, 'And anyone who takes these vermin in, who helps them, you'll get the same fate!'

So how did he get the preacher's family to change from their Sunday attire into their oldest clothes? He had told the family that there was a shipment of grain at a railway station eight kilometres away and they were required to help unload it. What happened to them? They had to march off in the rain and mud to be loaded onto trains and sent to their deaths up North. Starved, many of them. Children died. Yes, that's how it was. They always took the preachers first.

We listened as Gerhard continued.

There is more. The main railway through the Crimean peninsula ran through Spat, and not long afterward word spread through the village that right here in Spat, halted at Sarabas Station and shunted to a siding, were cattle cars crammed full of newly declared kulaks. I had noticed a freight train rumbling through, boxcars filled with men and some holding entire families, but thought it an isolated phenomenon. Now I went to the station myself to peer at those cattle cars on a siding. Policemen kept us back, but soon a rumour began to circulate among those watching the stalled train: 'Psst, this train is bound for Germany.'

Gerhard shook his head.

To Moscow and then Germany like the lucky ones – your parents – of last November. That's what the people thought. How could anyone be so gullible? Do you know that soon people in Spat were clamouring to be allowed onto the cattle cars? I asked one old man hurrying towards the train, 'Who says they're going to Germany?' The answer was, 'Well, it's being said.' I said, 'Think, man, think! Look! The doors are barred. They're locked in. They're being sent to their deaths. To the North.'

By March 1930 Stalin's policy of disenfranchisement and dekulakization had rounded up a quarter of a million people in Soviet Ukraine and shipped these men, women, and children to so-called resettlement places in the far North or East. There were two categories for kulaks – 'hostiles' and 'non-hostiles.' 'Non-hostile' dekulakized Mennonite families in the older Molochna Mennonite settlement area, for instance, were able to relocate to nearby marginal farming areas to find shelter in sod dugouts or under the sky and to create new (struggling) villages named Oktoberfeld, Neuhof, and Krasnopil. Dekulakized 'hostile' persons were imprisoned, executed, or exiled.[7]

We asked Gerhard who had rounded up the unfortunate Mennonite so-called kulaks in the Crimean villages, since repressive regimes often made it a practice to get the oppressed to find their own people to do the dirty work. Gerhard said the ones doing the evicting were not fellow Mennonites, but eager young Komsomols, activists from Simferopol sent to the Crimean villages. Historian Colin Neufeld found that many of those carrying out the dekulakization orders for the Soviets were Ukrainians, Russians, Jews, and Germans, but some Mennonites also did so out of 'fear, intimidation and coercion' (a Mennonite who had been at such village council meetings said it happened with 'a gun to your head'[8]) or for economic or ideological reasons.[9]

In March 1930 Gerhard took the train to Simferopol to attend a fair where new machinery for state farms (*sovkhoz*) was being exhibited. As he told us, 'I was wearing a hat and someone said to me, "You must be a kulak. You're wearing a hat." Well, the director of a state farm wanted a mechanic, a tractorist, so I started work. Then someone told me, "You are condemning yourself working three times as hard as the others. They'll hate you for that." So I saw it was too dangerous, and after a week I left.'

Gerhard feared the local officials had found out that his father once lived in Spat and fitted the description of a kulak (isn't a son of a kulak a kulak?). It was time to disappear again. Considering where to move, Gerhard met 'a German-speaker from Siberia' (even telling us forty years later, he did not often name anyone) who told him about a cement plant in Donetsk where he could get a job right away. So he and Lieschen moved to the Donbas, an area where he hoped workers could go unnoticed, an area of metallurgical factories and collieries (in 1929 it was producing 77.3 per cent of the country's coal[10]). Years later I would read Hiroaki Kuromiya's *Freedom and Terror in the Donbas* to discover how common Gerhard's decision was, how thousands of other Soviet citizens were flocking to the Donbas, a traditional haven for outcasts fleeing persecution.[11]

At work Gerhard decided it was better not to associate with other German-speakers. 'You had to go where nobody knew you, or who your parents were, or what they had been. If you were German-speaking, pretty soon someone would ask, "Where are you from? Do you know so-and-so? Oh, I have a relative." Soon too many people would know who you were or where you lived and the authorities would find you.'

From Lieschen's parents in Spat he heard that soon after he left, someone had come to the house asking a lot of questions. Then he heard that the disenfranchised Froeses, Lieschen's parents and young brother Willy, were deported. A letter by a resident of Spat published in the *Mennonitische Rundschau* describes what happened:

Spat, Crimea, 29 March 1930
… Last Saturday, at four o'clock, Mama received the news from the village soviet that she should be ready [to be deported] at nine o'clock Sunday morning. She should pack bedding, clothing, underwear, only the most basic cookware, enough prepared food for seven days, provisions for three months, a hammer, axe, and saw. … Sunday the entire day there was baking and preparations…. Monday in the morning wagons carried away their belongings. All the people and baggage were locked up in the yard at Unruh's mill … The gate was heavily guarded and we were not permitted to approach closer than the middle of the street…. The young John. Dick has been imprisoned, but his wife, who is expected to give birth any minute, was loaded up too. Around four o'clock the door [of the mill yard] was opened and then it was off to Simferopol. More wagons loaded with similar 'state criminals' came from several Russian villages and Kangil. We [onlookers] started to sing the hymn 'Nur mit Jesu will ich Pilger wandern,' but it sounded so doleful. There was much crying on both sides. When the cavalcade of wagons had passed, we ran after it. We had to be very careful because the automobiles carrying the guards drove so close to us … The following night 120 wagons drove through here…. early in the morning a red train with bolted shut doors went by and the Walls were in it….

The disenfranchised families had been promised they would be reunited, but instead they were scattered even worse. The next morning the drivers of the wagons [taking the 'kulaks'] told us they had been loaded forty people to a wagon in the middle of the night. Such actions shun the light of day. Many chests had been taken back and their contents stuffed into sacks…. In their minds many will have said goodbye to their belongings … one of the wagons carried horse harness…. By Tuesday there was a fairly cold wind and many had not been loaded up at night. They had to stand on the wagons outside and freeze….

Agatchen and Hans were loaded onto the train the same evening. They had passed through here at night, as we discovered from a note tossed out [of the passing train].… They were very discouraged. Hans's words were, 'If God does not take pity on us, we're lost.' … Several children were said to have been run over.… Friday night the rest of the barracks were emptied out. There were many Tatars, Russians, and Lutherans.…

Of the flour we had kept back, there still were two sacks that we had to drop into the bottomless pit that is never filled [state requisition]. In the beginning three sacks seemed too little and now, the one that is left seems too little. And when it is gone we will have to accept that too.… Our garden plot is not ploughed and not one onion or potato is set. Many have planted just a little and others nothing at all. How can anyone have a desire to work when you do not know if you will be stolen away at night, loaded up like herrings and sent away?

It is now two weeks later.

… the disenfranchised ['non-hostiles' in resettlement areas] who have been working the whole time without payment, got a paper promise of money, but not a single kopek.… it is impossible to get most people to work. Instead they spend most of the time doing nothing, whereas previously at this time of year we would have been working day and night … Peter [husband] … went to church in the morning and likely will soon be dismissed for that reason. Kornelson and Enns preached; they are still here. Mart. Langemann, Abr. Klassen and Wiebe [preachers] have been sentenced to ten years but are still in jail … How long will this continue?[12]

People sent into exile in 1930 were still permitted to write to their families as well as to relatives abroad. I read many letters describing the fate of people like Gerhard's in-laws, sent to so-called resettlements in the arctic White Sea region around Arkhangelsk. A woman describes how the deportees were transferred:

We left at night. For five days and nights we drove with locked doors. There were two small windows in the car. We were not allowed to go out to relieve ourselves and we did not get enough water. How the children screamed for water! Then we were told, 'Take snow and let it thaw.' … We were under guard from when we left home until we arrived here. We were given soup three times a day, but what kind of soup you cannot imagine.

After five days and nights, the command came, 'Get out!' It was midnight. We were a train of fifty cattle cars, each containing forty to forty-eight persons. We had to stand outside under the open skies and freeze, each beside his belong-

ings. Finally they said, 'Walk to your quarters.' It was three versts [about three kilometres] to walk, cold, and about two feet of snow.

When we arrived at the barracks it was beyond our comprehension. I think not a single eye was dry.... Inside there were two feet of snow and it was dreadfully cold. It had all been built of such green wood that the water dripped. There are more than two hundred people in one barracks and ninety-four barracks have already been built ... we sleep with our clothes on or else we would freeze to death ... we see the stars through the roof.[13]

Witnessing the mass kulak deportations, the author of a letter written in the spring of 1931 suggests the remaining farmers in Spat – and this was true generally throughout the country – reluctantly joined the collective farms:

It is amazing how people deliver their last grain to the government elevators. They are chased away, arrested, imprisoned by the brigadiers ... yet it is called voluntary ... Join the collective? ... they say the documents are written in such a way to show that you entered the collective of your own free will.... They say when you have nothing left, logic itself will lead you into the collective. And when you are in the collective and do not want to be a godless one, you will be driven out, but without any means. Then you don't have anything. At your gate will be a black sign warning everybody not to associate with you, under penalty of death.... Here they call that boycotting. We call it killing.[14]

Lucky not to be in Spat, Gerhard had escaped deportation, but Lieschen's parents were in northern Arkhangelsk. Acquaintances in Spat had quickly taken in two young Froese grandchildren and written to Lieschen to come get them. Before her parents starved to death, Lieschen also was able to fetch her young brother from Arkhangelsk, but Gerhard's uncle from Spat (deported in 1932), had died.

The would-be emigrants in Moscow in 1929 who were sent back to Siberia fared hardly better. My father's brothers Abram and Heinrich watched the returnees, and although there were no letters from them in the family archive for that date, others wrote,

Siberia, April 1930
Yes, a lot has happened since you left. Many of those who looked for rescue with you in Moscow have been thrown back into misery. Likely you know the methods used to do this. It has become regular to liquidate all kulaks and

disenfranchised persons ... We live in constant fear also to be carried off.... There is not a single settlement left where one or the other one is not missing. Supposedly taken for two to three days, he has been behind bars for two to three months.... The plan is slowly to play us to death. If help doesn't arrive soon, we all are lost. Wherever you look you see pale, anxious faces and where you don't see.... And it is not about our earthly possessions – no, all have let go of these. Everyone is willing to leave everything where it is and to leave. The one who married you is in jail and the one who married us is in jail. Number 72 is full, full of martyrs [preachers].... Oh, if only all of you there and in Germany could see all the big and little hands, pale, impoverished, forsaken, stretching out to you to be rescued! ... Thousands are looking to the West for help ... Don't forget us![15]

Another correspondent records a dialogue with an activist, one of the 25,000ers:

QUESTION. *Why do you want to leave?*

ANSWER. *We want our religious freedom.*

QUESTION. *Religion isn't biting you. Pray as much as you like, day and night if you wish!*

ANSWER. *We can see that, but where are our preachers? They are all behind lock and key.*

QUESTION. *And what brought them there? Not their praying, but their agitation for emigration. We have sources everywhere that report to the G.P.U.*

ANSWER. *We don't wish to hand over our children to you.*

QUESTION. *Your children were born on Soviet territory and that makes them our children too. So we will do with them as we please. We cannot permit them to be inculcated with the stupidities of religion. They have to learn wholesome things.*

ANSWER. *What is wholesome for you communists? You teach that there is no God.*

QUESTION. *Industry, honesty, and non-aggression – that is our God.*

ANSWER. *If state and church are separate and the schools are supported by the state, then we can understand that religion should not be taught in the schools, but in a free country anti-religion should also not be taught in the school.*

QUESTION. *It has to be done. If the parents insist on indoctrinating their children, then the teacher has to talk that nonsense out of their heads.[16]*

While idealistic activists were dispossessing families and snatching their last food supplies in the countryside, city Bolsheviks were told that criminal saboteur farmers were denying the goals of the glorious Revolution by hoarding grain and meat products. Shops had empty shelves and there were line-ups for food because of those evil saboteurs, the kulaks. It was possible for young Soviets in Moscow to frequent restaurants, attend the ballet, go to the movies, drink in bars, and be totally unconcerned about what was happening to starving so-called kulaks and peasants.

In Donetsk, in a city choked with polluted air, a sky thick with smoke and coal dust, Gerhard, Lieschen, and the two rescued grandchildren had found a place to live, a place they would stay until August 1931. With his papers from Maslianovka and his 'worker' documents, Gerhard was hired as the chief machinist in a cement factory. But Donetsk was dangerous. Many specialists, foreign manufacturers, declared persona non grata bourgeoisie, had been arrested and, in a highly publicized 'Shakhty Affair' in 1928, technicians and engineers had been accused of sabotaging Soviet industry.[17] When anything went wrong with state output targets, the state looked for 'saboteurs.' By mid-1931 half the engineers and technicians in the Donbas had been arrested.[18] If machinery broke down, someone would be accused of deliberately sabotaging state property. Most Russian peasants, the new proletariats, not trained technologically, being catapulted into an industrial world, often lacked expertise. Anatoli Rybakov wrote that a peasant could be sentenced to ten years for being a 'wrecker' if he damaged a tractor. He would scratch his head and perhaps start to take more care, or, to avoid arrest, more likely give someone who knew a little about machinery a bottle to help him keep the tractor running. That was how the Soviets forced persons to look after property, through fear.[19]

Gerhard was watchful. As he told us in Canada, he was selective in questionnaires. He answered 'no' to 'Have you owned property?' or, 'Any relatives in foreign countries?' ('I always told myself that a *Notlüge*, a lie of necessity, is not a sin.') He did some interpreting from German into Russian or Ukrainian for fellow workers, but, since interpreters were soon arrested as traitors, he never had that on his record. Another danger he had discovered in Simferopol was that doing your work in half the time could get you into some dark corner with your head smashed. In the workers' 'Red Paradise,' contrary to official talk, no fellow worker really liked a browner, not in Simferopol, Crimea, and not in Donetsk.

One incident would trouble my Uncle Gerhard, even as an old man.

He, the Ancient Mariner, had his albatross. He told his tale at our Toronto house one evening in 1980.

It was a day shortly after I returned from a holiday. As the other workers were sitting and eating their lunches, a fellow worker whispered to me, 'Hey, Konrad. I'm not supposed to tell you this, but I warn you to leave.'

'How so?'

'The Komsomols working here have been talking about you behind your back and they are saying, "This Konrad is a kulak. His family used to own a mill. We're going to expose him." Now don't tell anyone that I told you, but just get out. Better leave today.'

I kept at my task adjusting a valve and asked who said that, but my fellow worker offered lightly and quickly, 'I can't tell you who's been saying that.'

No, no, I thought, he won't scare me that quickly. My co-worker faked a wide smile as he turned towards the lunchtime gang, but whispered again, 'Be careful! I'd be sorry to see you ...'

I nodded, 'It's fine. You'll see.'

Walking home, I mulled over my chances. I decided to return to work the next day, but to take along all of my documents, my citizenship papers, 'worker' and machinist papers. On entering the factory I walked up to my superior and said, 'I've worked for you for some time now and you've trusted me, isn't that right? Well, now I come back from my holiday and nobody will speak to me. Something is going on. I need you to have complete confidence in me or I'll have to leave. I'm not staying under a cloud.'

The superior, satisfied to have a genuine machinist among so many inexperienced young Komsomol workers, was taken aback. 'You have your papers, of course.'

'Of course. Right here.'

'Let's go to the director.'

At the director's office my superior explained that his best machinist was handing in a notice to leave because the workers under his supervision were mistrustful.

'Show your documents!' Upon perusing them, the director strode to the floor of the factory and called out, 'Apfelbaum!' He had identified the patsy. The man was dismissed on the spot.'

I kept my job at the cement factory and supported Lieschen and the two Langemann children and the summer wore on, one day as hot as the next."

Describing this incident to Harvey and me that evening, face flushed and both elbows leaning on the dining room table, Gerhard continued, defensively.

The cement factory was working night and day. One night I was awakened by a pounding on our door. 'Fire! The cement plant is on fire!' It was a night shift worker, someone from my floor. As I rushed into the plant, I could see one of the giant belts moving; the drive shaft was ablaze. It seemed that the night shift worker, whose job it was to grease the moving parts of the giant Braunschweig machinery, had left a can of grease standing opened near a moving belt. The greaser, newly hired and inexperienced, had also turned a valve incorrectly as he greased the moving parts. A belt, rubbed loose, had got caught in the machinery. Friction, spark, and conflagration.

I rushed onto the factory floor shouting orders to douse the flames with extinguishers. 'What have you done?' I roared at the greaser standing terrified near the scene of his mistake. The young man with the grease can pointed helplessly at the smoking machinery. 'Who hired you?' I bellowed again in the direction of the young greaser. 'Grab an extinguisher! You there, turn off the switch! Here!' I gave out orders. 'Turn that motor off too! Quickly, you there, lend a hand!'

With the help of the night shift crew, the fire was soon put out and I turned again to the unfortunate man with the grease can. 'Where do you come from? When were you hired? Who are you?'

The other workers stood and stared at the hapless greaser. Seemingly paralyzed with fear, he murmured the name of a sub-foreman who had recently hired him.

My mind raced. I knew it would be the fault of the person in charge and I was the chief machinist. Quickly I gave directions to remove the singed belts and heated parts of machinery. We substituted worn but not yet thrown-out belts to replace the scorched ones and cobbled things together to make the machinery wheels turn. One heavy beam had been especially damaged and needed to be replaced. This was a very delicate task, to fit an immense beam precisely into its place. I assigned eighteen men to help raise the beam, position it aloft, and on my command, to slowly lower it between the moving parts into its slot. One centimetre off and the machinery would malfunction.

The men raised the beam but did not seem to be coordinated. I watched, estimated, and shouted, 'Now!' The beam thundered down. As it smacked almost exactly into place, I felt a sudden stab, like a knife had cut through me. 'Air! Air!' I shouted and the men rushed to open a window.

What if the beam had miscarried? What if the men had not heard the young greaser name the incompetent sub-foreman who had hired him, but not given him adequate training? What if they found me responsible?

A medic rushed onto the floor, 'Where is the invalid?'

'What?' I asked angrily, 'You've called a medic? I'm not ill!'

'Oh, Konrad,' a night shift worker shook his head. 'You should have seen

yourself. You were as white as a corpse when you called for air. We thought you were a goner!'

This incident was far more serious than the hernia I had suffered. In the subsequent investigation into the accident, the sub-foreman who had hired the inexperienced greaser and the greaser were both arrested and shot.

Because of the hernia, I had to spend some time in hospital, and when I recovered I made my way back to the factory. En route I happened to meet a fellow worker who was dumbfounded to see me. 'What are you doing coming here?' the man stuttered, 'Don't you know your name is on the list of people being investigated for the fire?'

'Who, me?'

'Yes, they asked for Konrad. You were in hospital, but your name is on the list.'

'Thank you,' I told him. 'All is well.'

I made my way to the personnel department of the factory, picked up my documents, but instead of going onto the floor to my usual position, I turned and walked out of the factory. I kept my usual pace back to our lodgings.

'Quickly!,' I told Lieschen, 'We have to leave.' Within hours we were on a train bound for Mongolia.

This was the lesson of Stalin's new order. There were no accidents. Someone was responsible. There was no forgiveness. Could we, listening to this story, comprehend the complexity of Gerhard's situation? Had he said nothing and just taken control of the situation without looking for someone to blame, had he returned to work on the floor, he too would have been shot. Was he guilty?

After this experience Gerhard said he knew that henceforth he must always decline supervisory positions or workplace advancements. There was a reason for remaining anonymous, never being in charge, staying very briefly in any place. 'You had to move before the black spider found you in that cobweb.'

The cement factory incident of August 1931 taught Gerhard that Donbas was too close to Soviet eyes. If he ran, would they find him at the end of the world? His brother Abram had written Gerhard about escaping to Mongolia.

The train that Gerhard, Lieschen, and the two children quickly boarded in Donetsk after the cement factory incident moved east for nine days and nights across the width of the USSR empire, crossing the Siberian steppe into forested taiga, rounding Lake Baikal and reaching Ulan Ude. A lucky move.

Gerhard's brother Abram had not gone to Moscow, but neither did he sit and wait for the Party activists or the armed brigades to poke into his haystack, to ransack his cellar or chimney to gather up his last 'hidden grain.' He purchased railway fares for his family and by June 1930 was in Ulan Bator, Mongolia, a city ringed with yurts where cows and goats wandered about the streets and camels took riders on trails that passed for roads. Founded in 1649 as a Buddhist monastery (or lamasery), Ulan Bator had become the capital of Outer Mongolia in 1911. The Mongolian lama, chosen like Tibetan lamas, had lived in the temple at Ulan Bator until the Bolsheviks arrived. Revolutionary Mongolian forces helped by the Bolsheviks had defeated the retreating White Army in 1921, and since that time the Mongolian People's Party had formed the government. In 1924 the city was renamed Ulaanbaatar, meaning 'Red Hero,' but in 1930 the world's second communist country was still fairly independent of the Soviets.

Abram had found work with a shipping company, and, in the ancient Buddhist enclave of Ulan Ude, Gerhard found work with the same firm at company headquarters. Abram, hired as a mechanic supervisor, was at the Mongolian end in Ulan Bator. The cartage company conveyed goods between the USSR and Mongolia. As a chauffeur and truck driver, Gerhard made good money but, haunted by his recent mistake, was doubly cautious. In 1999, Gerhard's daughter Nelly in Göttingen, Germany, told me the following incident:

In Ulan Ude, one day in August 1933, Gerhard was summoned to the Department of Security. As he entered the local office, he noticed that the female Russian police official seated at a desk was fingering a letter with red and white striped edges, an airmail letter. Gerhard immediately recognized the handwriting but showed no surprise or emotion. The officer began to question him in a roundabout way.

'Parents?'

'My father is dead.'

'You have Western relatives?'

'No, no Western relatives.'

'No?'

The official looked hard at his face, 'No? We have a letter here addressed to you. From your mother.'

'My mother?'

'Yes, your mother.'

Gerhard was polite, but sceptical, 'If I may be so bold, where does this letter come from? My mother was in Moscow the last time I saw her.'

The official looked smug. 'From South America.'

'If a letter is supposed to be addressed to me, may I see who wrote it?'

The official handed over the letter. Written in German, it began, 'Ihr Lieben, Gerhard und Lieschen.'

He stopped reading, looked up, and dismissively handing the letter back, shook his head, 'Must be a mistake.' (Forget his mother atop that wheelbarrow with luggage in Moscow.) 'Don't know these people. It's not for me.'

'You won't accept it? You don't want to write a reply?'

'It's not for me.'

The official studied Gerhard's face. He did not colour. His voice was steady. He had not fingered the stamp or the return address. 'Hmmm,' the official pushed back her chair and tapped the letter on the desk, her eyes narrowing as they bored into Gerhard's impassive face. Nobody moved for what seemed like hours, but then she slapped the letter down and said curtly, 'Go then!' The drawer creaked as she took out a ledger and began to write.

Black eyes burning into his back, Gerhard did not turn around, but quietly opened the door, 'Thank you, Comrade' [Pozhalyista, Tovarishch], 'Goodbye' [Do svidaniya], and closed it. Later all he recalled were the officer's laser eyes and a disembodied brown GPU police uniform. Out of sight of the secret police office (OGPU), Gerhard quickened his pace. He booked his vacation time in the trucking office and went straight home where Lieschen, suffering from one of her many horrendous headaches, was lying on the bed. Usually Gerhard was solicitous, but today he whispered firmly, 'Pack! Everything! We have to leave immediately. They'll likely come tonight.'

Within an hour Lieschen, Gerhard, and the children had vanished without an address. They went west to Omsk, Siberia, where the father of the children (children rescued in Spat) had completed four years of his five-year sentence and had been released. He had recently married Suse, his dead wife's sister (also Lieschen's sister), and the children's aunt. The children were returned to them.

During a two-month vacation, Gerhard and Lieschen went to a labour camp to see the husband of yet another of Lieschen's sisters, Katya. When Gerhard and Lieschen arrived at the camp, Gerhard was wearing a greatcoat he had purchased in Ulan Ude. It was the kind you see on pictures of Stalin, cut in the style of the Soviet apparatchik, a long, double-breasted official's coat. In Gerhard's official coat and manner, he walked up to the camp gatekeeper: 'I'm looking for Mathies, the blacksmith.' The guard pointed to a nearby telephone booth, 'Go ask in the office.'

Gerhard placed a phone call and, sure enough, got Mathies on the line. He began to speak to him in their familiar Mennonite Plautdiet-sch when Mathies pleaded, 'Konrad, for heaven's sake, speak Russian! Please, just Russian!'

'Lieschen and I are on our way through. We want to see you.'

'Come tomorrow,' said Mathies. 'We're closed for tonight.'

Nobody intercepted the call. After all, wasn't this a Soviet officer?

'We have to be at work at 7:30 in the morning,' Mathies said.

'We'll be there before that,' Gerhard promised. 'We'll leave here at 4:00 a.m.'

'Be at the guardhouse,' advised Mathies. 'He's a Christian Orthodox. He's safe.'

The next morning before dawn, having given the gatekeeper a water-melon instead of a permit, Lieschen and the 'officer' Gerhard waited near the guardhouse.

Lieschen was afraid. 'Oh Gerhard, someone is coming out of the bushes!'

'It's okay, it will be Mathies.'

And it was.

They stayed three days, sleeping in the guardhouse with the 'safe' guard.

Later Gerhard helped Mathies's wife Katya get permission to be with her husband in the camp for three months. 'It was heaven for her to be with her husband,' Gerhard said when he told this story. 'They weren't allowed to write, so she never heard from him again.' Gerhard sighed, 'She never saw him again either.'

After visiting Mathies, Gerhard and Lieschen returned to Omsk, where Lieschen stayed while Gerhard headed back to Ulan Ude. He successfully collected his pay from the plant office and immediately returned to Omsk. Where now?

Mindful not to go places where anyone knew him, in October 1933 Gerhard and Lieschen took the train south to Semipalatinsk in East Kazakhstan. In the 1930s when Gerhard and Lieschen arrived, it was a steppe region where traditionally nomad Muslims, Kirghiz people, herded sheep. Important as a metal-mining and trade centre, it was a crossing point of trade routes between Russia, Central Asia, Mongolia, and China. Known today as Semey, Semipalatinsk is one of the most polluted areas as a result of a Soviet nuclear testing range where hun-dreds of aboveground and underground nuclear tests were made from the 1950s to 1990s. Developed after 1947, it is the world's largest nuclear testing site of the Cold War era.[20] Eighteen thousand square kilometres of land around the oblasts of Semipalatinsk, Pavlodar, and Karaganda were polluted. Generations were poisoned. But not in 1933.

It was the time of collectivization, and the Soviets had decided farms were needed in Semipalatinsk. Likely in defiance of Muslim religious beliefs, which they vowed to stamp out (but lucky for Gerhard), they decided on huge pig farms. The local Khirghiz peoples wanted nothing to do with swine, but the Soviets set up a state collective farm of seven thousand breeding sows. Not being a Party member should have precluded his getting work, but not here – Gerhard was immediately hired as a truck driver for the swine-production operation. A competent chauffeur and a mechanic who could repair trucks that broke down regularly on impossible roads, he was a huge asset. The swine farm had to fulfil its Soviet pork quota, and Gerhard – able to drive the truckloads of 'unclean' animals to market – was too useful to be arrested.

His daughter Nelly told me that while in Kazakhstan, Gerhard had once chauffeured Leningrad Soviet Party boss Sergei Kirov. I doubted the story since I knew Kirov was assassinated in December 1934. In my research I then discovered Stalin had sent Kirov to Kazakhstan to check the harvest in September 1934. It was possible.[21]

Swiftly escaping Soviet claws, zigzagging, disowning his relatives, keeping his mouth shut, and being an expert driver and mechanic, Gerhard was managing to stay alive in the early 1930s. If Lieschen got used to the desolate, endless steppe, the howling autumn windstorms, the freezing winters, whether they lived in barracks or huts, if Lieschen knitted, having bartered possessions for wool at a local market, I don't know.

Justina Crosses a River

Picture a spring morning in May 1908. Over the wide Crimean steppe a summer wind caresses tall grasses, wild tulips, and irises at the edge of a farmer's field. Startled by the snorting of horses, a pheasant flutters up over green wheat and then swoops low over the next field. A young woman in kerchief, print apron over a loose cotton skirt, and bare feet, digs her toes deeper into the warm earth. A basket at her feet is filled with fresh buns and a jar of *prips*, hot when she filled the jar in the kitchen, but now lukewarm, a coffee made of roasted barley whitened with cream. A team of horses pulling a harrow across the black field approaches. Walking behind the harrow, reining two horses and keeping the harrow pattern straight, the young man also is barefoot.

'*Hol aun!*' she calls out. '*Jeff mie dienje Lien.*' She grins as her one-year-younger brother stops beside her. '*Dee Tzarina well foahre.*' He sniffs, 'Tzarina! Well, take over for a few rounds.' He gives her the reins and reaches for a bun from her basket. Justina flicks the reins. '*Priamo!*'

Justina would rather be a farmwife than an empress, but a recent move from their home in the village of Spat into decidedly more humble workers' buildings on this steppe has changed her dress and work. Living on rental lands here at Kazanshi has also diminished her chances of meeting a desirable suitor. Justina's father had used his property in Spat as a guarantee on a loan to his brother-in-law for a business venture. That business collapsed and, having lost their lovely farm and home in Spat, the family moved into the five low buildings that made up the complex, the *khutor* or farm at Kazanshi.

Later that morning, the family maid, a young Tatar girl with long black braids, is hanging sheets on a wash line, and Justina's thirteen-year-old sister and her brothers, Peter (my father), twelve, Heinrich, ten, and Gerhard, eight, are just leaving the house to walk to school in Minlertchik when they see a cloud of dust on the road. Justina's mother looks through the door and orders son Peter, '*Schvind, hool Voda!*' (Quickly, fetch Father). As Peter dashes to the barn, a handsome covered carriage with a coachman rolls towards the farmyard. Soon Mother and Father Konrad recognize Frau Langemann, an elderly woman in a long-sleeved, high-necked, taffeta dress, and black lace bonnet. But who is the other guest, the slim, middle-aged and bearded man wearing a hat and Sunday suit?

The Konrads remember when a wealthy Widow Ediger came to Spat to become the second Frau Langemann after the tragic death of the first wife. Johann Langemann, a friend of Justina's parents, is a well-liked, well-to-do factory owner in Spat, and one of his daughters from the first wife has married a Konrad nephew. Unlike Justina's parents whose ancestors settled the southern steppes in the early 1800s, this Frau Langemann (then Frau Ediger) emigrated from Prussia years later and settled at Samara, along the Volga River. 'Latecomer. Uppity! Just speaks High German,' Justina's father had sniffed to his wife after first meeting the new Frau Langemann.

Seeing her visitors, Justina's mother begins her familiar lament, 'Oh dear, oh my, what will we do? If Frau Langemann had only let us know! If we only were still living in Spat! Before we were bankrupt, oh dear, oh dear ... How can we invite her into this poor parlour? We were such good friends with the Langemanns....'

'Oh, Mother,' Justina breaks in, 'Always "bankruptcy, bankruptcy." Can't we talk about anything else? Look, I'll quick grind some coffee.'

'If only we still had our nice house in Spat! Oh, to think she has to see us here....'

'Na, na Mutta,' Justina's father speaks soothingly. He gestures to son Peter, who is rooted to the spot, gawking. 'Show the coachman where to water and feed his horse.'

Gingerly Frau Langemann alights and introduces her companion. 'My son-in-law, Jakob Epp from Ufa. You remember? My daughter died ... my daughter, you know, some months ago, yes, God took her.' She sighs, 'His ways are not our ways. But we must trust the Lord. Left eight motherless children.'

'Yes, yes,' the Konrads recall the sad news. They invite their guests into the parlour and ask about the health of Herr Langemann. The Langemanns have recently returned from Vienna, where, Frau Langemann the Second reports, the famous Viennese surgeon Dr Eislett operated on her husband to remove a cancerous tumour. At first the operation seemed to have been successful, but now the news is grim again. No, factory owner Langemann is not doing too well. (He dies later that summer.)

Seated stiffly in the low-ceilinged parlour, Frau Langemann comes straight to the point. 'My son-in-law Jakob Epp is interested in your daughter Justina.'

All eyes turn to twenty-five-year old Justina serving the coffee. 'What?' She too looks up, startled. The visitor is a suitor? Why, he's almost the age of her father. In the doorway the eavesdropping younger siblings gasp. Suddenly aware of too many ears, Father Konrad thunders, 'To school with you! Do you want to be late?'

As they run off, Heinrich asks mischievously, 'Should I?' He points underneath the visitor's carriage.

'Better not,' advises Marichen (Maria). 'Justina is getting to be an old maid.'

'But Abram did last time.'

In the safety of the barn Justina's younger brothers had watched and laughed as her last suitor drove off their yard. A willow basket was tied under his buggy and, thumping away, it emphasized his rejection. Should a young miss of the house decline a proposal, tradition demanded her brothers made sure the unlucky suitor 'got the basket' [de Tjiepp jejäwt].

Inside the farmhouse Frau Langemann explains that she and her husband know Justina's reputation. Well, perhaps Justina is a little overshadowed by her strong-willed elder sister who left home to train as a medical missionary, but more to her credit. All in all, to Frau Langemann Justina appears capable of being a good wife and mother. As a church member and experienced housekeeper, she'll be a suitable match.

Justina's father says, 'Of course Justina will be the one who decides. In spite of the bankruptcy, we hope again to prosper, and the crops here at Kazanshi are good, but, well, Justina will be the one who decides, and in present circumstances there will not be a dowry.'

Jakob Epp smiles and says he is not in search of a dowry, but back in Ufa are his eight sons, the youngest, Kolya, is four and Yash, the eldest, is fifteen. He needs a mother for his children. As the Konrad parents turn their eyes on Justina, Frau Langemann takes in the harmonium, the ornate Kroeger wall clock, the fine dowry chest, all signs of an earlier prosperity, then nods and looks pointedly at the flushed young woman holding the coffee pot. Initially speechless, Justina almost stutters. *Hallo*, she thinks, this would be one way to escape the endless litany on 'bankruptcy.' He's not bad-looking, this Epp, a bit formal, but quite handsome really. Even if he admits he is in his late forties, no grey hair. His smile seems kind. They are all looking at her as she stammers, 'Ah, hum, eight boys?' Twice the number of her younger brothers. 'Eight?'

'The eldest is fifteen. Two are away at school. Of course we have household maids. We employ an entire Tatar family.'

Epp likes what he sees in Justina, her somewhat buxom build, her open face and merry eyes. 'You think it over,' he says earnestly. 'I'll come back in a week. We'll pray about it, shall we?'

'Yes, yes, of course,' Justina manages. 'Of course I'll pray about it. Of course.'

A few days later, even her parents are astounded when they ask Justina what she has decided and she tells them she is accepting Epp's offer.

'He's only six years younger than I am,' her mother protests, but her father says, 'Well, he has means. He's got two sons attending school, boarding in Halbstadt, and that's not cheap.'

Justina for once is not laughing, 'It seemed strange to me too, eight boys, but I feel it's my ordained way. I did pray and I have assurance it's my way.'

The wedding takes place on 15 June, a week later. A quiet wedding at the *khutor* with the preacher reading from Colossians 3: 12–23.

The new couple travels several days by rail back to Epp's home in Ufa where she meets the boys: Jakob (Yash), Peter, Johannes, Heinrich, David, Hermann, Wilhelm, Gerhard, and four-year old Nikolai (Kolya).

Did they stand in a row and salute like the von Trapp family children in *The Sound of Music*? Daughter Jutti wrote that Epp was known by his second family as a strong disciplinarian, someone whose sons obeyed on command.[22]

Before my research began, I knew Justina had survived. Every so often an airmail letter from Tante Justina, stamped Republica del Paraguay, addressed to Señor P.J. Konrad, arrived in our mailbox. Written in German Gothic script, her letters were a mystery to me. As a 'PAX boy,' my brother Herman had been an MCC volunteer on a Paraguay road construction crew for two years, met her, and said she was very like our father.[23] She was then living with her daughter Lena in Grossweide, a farm village in East Paraguay.[24] In 1986, Harvey and I visited the villages in Paraguay where Justina had lived and saw the farmhouse where she wrote her letters to my parents. A grandson and his family lived there now, and, as Justina had done, to prepare for Sunday visitors her grandson's wife raked the dirt pathways in their garden into intricate patterns every Saturday.

When I began Justina's story, her daughter Jutti lived in Vancouver and I was able to meet her and ask questions. On one particular evening over a long dinner of borscht and fondue in her Vancouver apartment, eighty-year-old Jutti told the story of her family's escape from Siberia. A storyteller of vivid detail, she confirmed that her mother was talkative, warm-hearted, joyful, and competent, someone who sang a lot with her children. Her father Jakob Epp took the Bible literally, disciplined his family physically, but was generous. 'Our workers ate at the family table.' He was knowledgeable, owned books, and was passionate about horses.

Shortly before his bride-hunting trip, Epp and his brother-in-law Ediger had scouted out settlement possibilities in western Siberia, where the government was offering cheap land near Omsk. So, a year after Justina and her new husband arrived at Ufa, they packed their boys, household goods, light machinery, and some livestock into freight cars and boarded the train to Siberia. Here, on a trunk line of the Trans-Siberian Railway west of Omsk, pioneers on a bare steppe, they built a sod house and swatted mosquitoes. The first year they had the help of the Tatar family from Ufa, but everyone worked hard. Epp's brother-in-law Ediger observed how deftly Justina managed the household and commented, 'Justina, you brought nothing into the marriage, but you're a good worker.' Smarting at this reminder of 'the bankruptcy,' Justina shook it off. What could you expect of a man with a pampered wife who wouldn't even wash her own hair? Imagine, she needed a maid!

Justina's first child unfortunately caught smallpox and died, but a second child, Helene (Lena), lived to become a frail little old woman whom Harvey and I met as Mrs Lena Janzen seventy years later in Friesland, Paraguay. Ironically all of Justina's six children born in frigid Siberia would find themselves spending most of their days in sweltering heat in the subtropics. Within a year in Siberia, three of the Epp boys died of tuberculosis and two others would be lost in the Civil War. Of Justina's stepsons only three survived: the eldest son, Jakob, and two younger sons.[25]

Four years after they had settled in Siberia, in 1913 a letter arrived from America offering to finance the emigration of one of Epp's sons. Coming from Ediger relatives (Epp's first wife) in California, this was a godsend. The eldest son, Jakob Epp Junior, aged twenty, showed no interest or skill in farming or milling and was a perfect candidate to climb the Californian 'Gold Mountain' and make his fortune. Mindful of an 'eldest son' status, both father and son thought it only proper that the Ediger relatives sent the young man a first-class steamship ticket for a luxury crossing in a state cabin. 'My father was shocked,' Jutti recalled, 'when his heir was subsequently asked to become a common worker, to do manual labour in America to repay his passage.' Very upsetting was a photograph of Epp Junior surrounded by a herd of black pigs. Years later the pig-keeper would pilot an airplane to South America to visit his siblings from his father's second marriage.

Fast forward to 1930.

First to be hit by the war on kulaks was Epp's second-eldest son. Married, with young children, he was accused of 'exploiting workers' for employing a babysitter and a stable boy. Disenfranchised and dispossessed of the family belongings, rather than risk being sent into a so-called resettlement camp, he and his family went into hiding. When his father was interrogated to elicit his son's whereabouts, he incautiously replied, 'Ask a rabbit where it runs when chased by a dog.' Not a good reply. Communist activists moved in and demanded Jakob Epp hand over horses and grain. Early in this year, Mennonites in the Slavgorod area were refusing to plant their crops and had handed in a petition to the German Embassy in Moscow that included four thousand names of persons wanting to emigrate.[26] At the same time a letter from the son in California advised them to leave via China. People coming through China were being admitted into the United States.[27]

This was not a new idea. Since the Trans-Siberian Railway linking Moscow to Vladivostok had been completed in 1916, Russians had regularly moved into and through China, and many had opened businesses in Harbin, the capital of Manchuria. Long associated with tsarist Russia, the city was filled with engineers, civil servants, administrators, merchants, and traders. Its architecture reminiscent of St Petersburg, Harbin was sometimes called the 'Moscow of the Orient.'

Prior to collectivization, to encourage settlement in the Amur region, the Soviets had offered reduced railway fares and certain grants. Several Mennonite groups had already moved east from their Siberian steppe lands into an area of fertile soil near the Russia-China border. Close to the Russian city of Blagoveshchensk on the Amur River, summer temperatures were pleasant, but winters extremely cold. In winter the river froze a metre deep so that even heavy trucks could cross for three months straight. The area in dispute since the Russo-Japanese War of 1904–5, people were crossing without Russian exit passports.[28]

In December 1928, a Siberian Mennonite family had successfully crossed into China over the frozen Amur River, and by 1929 so many were using the long river border to cross illegally into China that the Soviets ordered border officials to double efforts to arrest the escapees. Following the embarrassment of thousands of Soviet German-speaking citizens flocking to Moscow in 1929, Stalin's directives had made it illegal for Germans to buy train tickets or to travel near Russian borders. The conduit to Harbin across the Amur River was especially under surveillance, with trains regularly searched.[29]

In May 1930, hearing that seventy-seven Soviet Germans had reached Harbin, Justina and Jakob Epp took the risk and quickly sold what they could, gave things away, and invited an Adventist Russian family to move into their house. The Epps knew that sale of train tickets was forbidden unless permitted by the village council (*selsovet*), and officials in Omsk were suspicious of anyone asking to travel or to relocate to the Amur.[30] Spies, including some Mennonites, were widely distributed, but by July, Jakob Epp had persuaded a Mennonite working in the local council to give him a permit to purchase train tickets to Blagoveshchensk. He was warned, 'Don't speak German on the train.' Not telling their neighbours (you never knew who was an informer), Justina filled a trunk with sacks of roasted Zwieback, sausages, and bags of loose tea (hot water was available at train stations). Into another trunk went sheepskin coats and fur hats, feather pillows, comforters, and some clothes. Gold coins were sewn into dress hems and underpants.

For eight days and nights the train moved noisily across the vast steppe, snaking around Lake Baikal, through forests and mountains, and finally reached Blagoveshchensk. Trying to keep a low profile,

Jakob Epp looked for lodgings in a rundown inn that, as his daughter Jutti recalled, sheltered healthy bedbugs. In streets filled with Chinese, Mongolian, and other unfamiliar faces, they ran into a few German-speakers and were advised to get closer to their escape goal by working on a Soviet farm, a *sovkhoz*, near to the river border.

Crumpling a five-rouble note in his palm and giving a firm hand-shake to the right official allowed Epp to get a permit to reach the state farm. Accepted at the *sovkhoz*, the family was given one room of a house formerly owned by a family evicted as kulaks. Soon all worked. The elder Epp boys, eighteen and sixteen, drove tractors, their father super-vised farm operations, one daughter did farm work, another, aged fourteen, cooked for an engineering couple, and Jutti, twelve, crocheted a lace bedspread for the state collective farm manager's wife, who paid her with a large smoked fish. To heat and cook, Jutti scrounged fire-wood on the hills, picking up brush. She also trampled wheat sheaves in a primitive threshing method and was rewarded with an armload of straw, to use as fuel.

To mark the Lord's Day during that summer of 1930, the Epp fam-ily would sit on the grass in the local cemetery, gaze across the Amur River at the Chinese hills, and listen to their father read sermons. When the weather turned cold, *sovkhoz* workers put on warmer clothing, and out of their trunk came the Epps' Siberian sheepskin coats and hats. When the state collective farm secretary saw Epp and his sons, he said pointedly, 'You're kulaks. Look at your tailor-made coats, the fur hats your sons wear,' so Epp knew he had to advance his plans to escape. He needed horses and a sleigh, and he discovered that if you intend-ed to cut wood in winter, you were permitted to buy them. He then contracted with three other Mennonite families wishing to cross the frozen Amur River to hire a Chinese guide, a smuggler operating in Blagoveshchensk who charged two hundred roubles per person.

Of the three families, one named Wieler was desperately poor. On a bitterly cold November day Epp drove the twenty kilometres to the Wielers to discuss the escape plans and noticed Wieler had no win-ter coat. His daughter Jutti, telling the story, remarked with a tinge of bitterness, 'My father believed the Bible, where Jesus says, if anyone wants to enter the kingdom of heaven, let him sell what he has and give it to the poor. He who has two coats, let him share with him who has none. My father gave Wieler his *tulup* coat.'

Appropriate for Siberia, it was a long sheepskin overcoat, fur on the inside, without buttons or fasteners, but with a high collar that stood above the ears. Typically it was worn over another coat and fastened by a *bashlik* or hood with long wide ties that were pulled over a fur hat and fit over the collar of the *tulup*. The ties crossed at the chest and circled at the waist. In this way only the eyes of the wearer were exposed to the minus forty- to fifty-degree temperatures. With felt boots and rubber galoshes over the boots, the wearer kept warm in the Siberian winter. Snug in this outfit, Epp had driven to the Wielers, but when he arrived back at the collective farm, covered in hoarfrost and teeth chattering, Justina immediately noticed that he was not wearing the *tulup*. 'Jakob, what have you done?'

Epp took sick almost immediately. While his family cried, prayed, and spelled each other off sitting at his bedside, fourteen days went by without doctor or cure. Jutti recalled how she sat with her father and they would sing, '*Jesu, Heiland meiner Seele*,' a hymn they knew by heart. Feverish, alternately sweating or freezing, Epp repeatedly urged his wife, 'You must continue. When the guide says, go even without me. If I die, promise you'll go!' Then he'd look up at her and the children and whisper, 'But, please, don't leave me to die alone.' Jutti recalled how they wept, 'Oh, Father, we never would!'

On Saint Nicholas Day, 6 December 1930, Jakob Epp died. His boys made a rough coffin of wide barn boards, and daughter Lena, careful not to attract the attention, discovering that an elderly Russian woman had died the same day, saw a possibility to dig a grave with space for two. The less the *sovkhoz* knew of the death, the better their chances of escape. Wielding picks and shovels, two Mennonite men, neighbours from Smolianovka, helped the Epp children to chop out enough frozen earth to make a shallow grave. In the frigid dark of late afternoon, in the same cemetery where Epp had read from his book of sermons, his wife and children now stood silently. Justina said a prayer and Jakob Epp was buried.

While Epp lay dying, his partner had found a deserted house (recently used as a horse barn) only ten kilometres from the border and large enough to hold several families. There, ten days after Epp's death, the widowed Justina and her six children joined three other families: the Siemenses (Mrs Siemens due to deliver any minute), the impoverished Wielers, and a Neufeld family consisting of a peg-legged husband, wife, and children. At midnight the women and young children piled into sleighs, covering themselves with sheepskin rugs. The men and older boys rode or walked beside the sleighs. The temperature was forty below.

To prevent illegal crossings, border guards were stationed along the way, at the river, and on watchtowers along the shore. A gunshot cracked. A watchman? A frozen branch snapping off? The guide shouted, 'Turn!' and leaping forward, dangling the sleighs, the horses plunged into underbrush. Snorting, their flanks and faces scratched and bleeding, they struggled to pull the heavy loads that bobbed and surged. Frightened passengers clung to the sides, and the guide looked up, taking his direction from the stars.

Soon one of the Epp horses refused to move. While the Chinese guide cursed, the horse was cut loose and Epp passengers were redistributed onto other sleighs. Now Jutti was sent to stand on the back runners, holding for dear life onto the leading Neufeld sleigh. With the guide shouting threats, the sleighs jerked forward. Clothing began to freeze stiff and feet became numb, but slowly, over frozen streams, through open fields and brush, the four sleighs advanced towards the river.

Impatient with the slow progress, the guide smacked the Neufeld horses, and the lead sleigh soon was well ahead. Jutti recalled how she fell off and felt too numb to move. She remembered just wanting to sleep, but the guide wielded his whip, forcing her to get up and run after the sleigh. When Neufeld's horses, now bleeding from crashing through underbrush, refused to move farther, the guide shouted, 'Women! You on the sleigh (pointing at Jutti)! Get out and tramp down the snow!' The wooden-legged man was left to care for the children while his wife and Jutti, fearing the horsewhip and soon losing their rubbers over felt boots, tramped down a track. The other three sleighs were nowhere in sight.

Nine hours later, at the river, the guide halted to listen. When no alarm was sounded by armed guards along the riverbank, he slapped the reins. 'They'll follow our tracks. We can't wait for them to catch up.'

It was daylight now, a charred grey sky, but daylight. How could a loaded sleigh – no, three more sleighs – escape notice? Ahead was more than a kilometre of uneven ice. That was when what Jutti described as a miracle occurred. The steep bank, the frozen river, the fleeing sleigh, suddenly all were sheathed in heavy fog, a pillar of cloud that lowered itself to cover them like children of Israel fleeing Pharaoh's army over the Red Sea. So thick was the fog that, as it turned out, the border guards, sure that nobody would attempt to cross in zero visibility, left their watch positions for warmer quarters.

The sunlight returned as they reached the Chinese shore, where the guide walked the horses into his home village and stopped in front of a Chinese inn. 'I was terrified,' Jutti said. 'Greasy newspapers were pasted over its windows. Inside it stank of smoke, urine, sweat, and soiled clothing. In the acrid smoke shadows I could see glittering eyes staring at me. It was so dark, so dirty. People talked a strange language and I cried and cried for my mother. Mrs Neufeld tried to soothe me, but I continued to howl.'

Following the tracks of the lead sleigh, Justina, her children, and the other families had reached the frozen river. Scrambling to find sleigh marks, but also protected by the low-hanging cloud, they were lost until a rooster call directed them to the Chinese side. Two hours after the arrival of the guide with the Neufeld sleigh, having stumbled up the bank downstream from the first sleigh, they found their way to the same Chinese inn.

The Chinese guide took pregnant Mrs Siemens home to his Russian wife, and the following day Mrs Siemens delivered a baby boy. 'That,' stated Jutti Epp, who in later life had a career as a nurse-midwife, 'was another miracle.' Then she added, 'Being reunited with my mother was the best reunion I ever had in my entire life. The experience was also the most harrowing – and I lived through wartime in Germany. Nothing was as frightening as that trip and separation from my family.'

Contributing to the 'miracle,' unknown to each other, on that same night, 16 December 1930, the entire Mennonite village of Pribreshnoie, eighty-seven people located near the Chinese border, also crossed the frozen river and escaped in thirteen sleighs, guided by the 'pillar of cloud.'[31] For an entire village to escape was phenomenal. Then, 100 kilometres to the southeast, on the same day, an even larger group of fifty-four sleighs and 218 people from the two Mennonite villages of Shumanovka and Friedensfeld – without cloud or fog to hide them – crossed the frozen Amur River in bright daylight.[32]

But someone's gain is another's loss. Alarmed by these dramatic escapes, the Soviets ordered all villages bordering the Amur River to be relocated inland. Anyone caught attempting to escape was shot. Wherever possible, those already in China were to be forcefully repatriated.[33] Soviet military police came across the river, demanding that refugees huddled in Chinese inns be returned unless they could produce a passport. Illegal refugees were subject to heavy fines and in danger of being exposed by someone accepting a Soviet bribe.

The Epps sold their horses and sleighs to pay the Chinese guide and innkeepers but found that their Soviet currency was worthless in China. As the Soviet police were demanding that their Chinese innkeeper pay a large sum of money or hand them over, once more the inexplicable occurred. A Russian fur merchant from Harbin, happening to be at the border, paid their Chinese innkeeper the amount the Soviet militia demanded. Jutti later published the story of this 'angel in a bearskin coat' in a brief autobiography.[34]

The fugitives were using up more and more of their gold coins and, in extreme cases, possessions – pillows, watches, wedding rings – to pay for food and lodging as well residency permits. More money was needed for tickets to Harbin, and one memoir by an escapee said a family was forced to sell a daughter to a Chinese buyer.[35]

From the squalid border inns, the next leg of the Epp family's journey was by bus to Tsitsihar, from where the Chinese Eastern Railway would take them to Harbin. Justina had hidden several gold pieces in her undergarments, and these she sold in Tsitsihar to buy five tickets to Harbin. Her two eldest sons had to ride the rails. To buy food for the trip she sold her warm fur coat and, now destitute, she hoped Mennonites in Harbin would help. She also planned to write to her relatives abroad. On 12 February 1931, they reached Harbin. What a sight. A cosmopolitan city of golden-domed Russian Orthodox churches, of opera houses and bank buildings in classical Greek or Roman style, of Russian log houses and Chinese red-tiled roofs.

Hundreds of thousands of Russian émigrés and White Army personnel had found refuge in Harbin following Russia's 1917 Revolution and the Civil War. By 1930 the international metropolis had sixteen foreign consulates, as well as Western businesses, shops, theatres, banks, mills, factories, doctor and dentist offices, cultural facilities, and schools. Orthodox and other Christian churches mixed with Jewish synagogues, Chinese Buddhist temples, and Tatar mosques. People spoke varieties of Manchu-Tungus languages, Turkic, Korean, and Japanese, but mostly Russian or Mandarin. In 1931 in a city of 662,000, with half White Russians and half Mandarin Chinese, street signs were in both languages.[36] Most of the expatriate Russians and other refugees had no intention of remaining in Harbin and soon were pounding on consulate doors, begging to emigrate.

I recall a fellow university student in Vancouver telling me her White Russian parents, being wealthy, had smuggled gold out of the country by purchasing a hairdresser shop and filling the hollow hairdryer stands with melted gold. These they took into China as business equipment, financing their way to Canada. The Epps had no melted gold but planned to get to America, more particularly to California to be reunited with Epp's eldest son (no longer minding black pigs).

Justina's first task in Harbin was to find 'the MCC house.' To assist and house the growing number of Mennonite refugees fleeing across the Amur River, the Mennonite Central Committee (MCC) of North America had rented three houses in Harbin where refugees were crammed, up to five families sharing a room. Everyone slept, sat, and ate on the floor, cooking at a common wood-burning stove. No furnishing or bedding was provided, so Justina was overjoyed when a former employee at Epp's mill in Siberia gave her a bed. The three MCC houses provided shelter for 726 people, and 340 more lived in rented rooms or houses. A report to home churches in Canada and the United States described the severe hygiene problems of these houses. In one MCC house – a former Japanese institute – a pharmacy dispensed free medications, but even after being taken to Harbin hospitals, by October 1931, in one year, thirty-seven malnourished children had died, most from scarlet fever, and nine adults from typhus. Altogether, twenty-three Mennonite and twelve Lutheran babies were born and sixty-one children and seventeen adults died.[37] Mennonite ophthalmologist Johann Isaak, practising in Harbin since 1923, was mentioned time and again in refugee accounts as giving assistance and helping many of the first arrivals in Harbin to emigrate to the United States.[38]

Thinking her stepson in California would guarantee her entry, Justina immediately went to the American consulate to ask for immigration applications and received a jolt. 'Only sixteen refugees a month?' And no application forms handed out either?

My parents were in Canada, so Justina next tried the Canadian consulate and again she was told 'no.' It was the same at every consulate. 'We do not accept refugees with recent Chinese passports. No Russian passport? Sorry, no application forms to stateless people.' An MCC report of December 1931 listed 1,066 German-speaking refugees in Harbin: 550 Mennonites, 405 Lutherans, 50 Catholics, 44 Baptists, and 17 others. No country would grant them passports.[39]

Hoping to get help from her stepson in California, Justina meanwhile needed money. For the first two weeks she had received financial support from the MCC, but after that she was told, 'Get jobs. Anyone who can speak Russian should be able to find work.' Some refugees suddenly 'lost' their ability to speak Russian and stayed on the MCC dole, but not the honest Epps. Russian nobility, military officers living in exile, and international business persons all needed Russian-speaking maids, cleaners, carpenters, people to do odd jobs, even tutors for Russian or German. The streets of Harbin, crowded with rickshaws, cars, buggies, and streetcars, had thousands looking for work and too many jobseekers guaranteed low wages.

'At first, the taste of freedom was overwhelming,' Jutti said. 'You could laugh again, say what you wanted without worrying someone would report you. We looked at the cars freely driving the streets and none a Black Raven. See, we said, they have clothes in store windows! Not that we could purchase any.'

Women and girls supported their families as nursemaids, housekeepers, or cleaners, and Justina, aged forty-eight, cleaned windows for affluent expatriate Russian families. Her daughters were sleep-in domestics in Jewish households. Jutti, aged twelve, worked as a domestic in the home of a bank official, crossing the city at night to sleep on the basement room floor beside her mother. In the bitterly cold winter of 1930–1, the Songhua River (a tributary of the Amur) was frozen thick, and hoarfrost covered the basement windows of the three-story MCC house where Justina stayed with her youngest two children. Justina's sons were often unemployed. For a time one worked for a Chinese farmer outside the city, and the other became a live-in servant/handyman, washing floors or laundry, heating the stove, and so on. He also helped Justina do the family laundry, fetching her water.

On the other side of the world, the refugees in Harbin were not forgotten. In spite of repeated rejections in the United States and Canada, Mennonites, in particular Bishop David Toews of Rosthern, Saskatchewan, endlessly appealed to officials of provincial and federal governments to accept the Harbin refugees as immigrants. In Germany the foreign office, as well as the 'Mennonite Moses,' Professor Benjamin Unruh, looked for a country to accept the stateless Harbin refugees.

As the various agencies tried in vain to negotiate permission for Harbin refugees to immigrate to Canada, the United States or Mexico, Justina Epp's family remained in limbo for eighteen months, and during this time Japanese forces occupied Manchuria. Those who know the film *The Last Emperor* will recall that by February the Japanese had created a puppet kingdom Manchukuo and made (Henry) Pu Yi the last and deposed emperor of China, its puppet emperor. The new Manchukuo government demanded that refugees from Soviet Russia be removed, and threatened if they were not out by 31 March 1932, they would be returned to the Soviets.

This is where the League of Nations enters the story.

The 'Nansen Mission' (League of Nations Nansen International Office for Refugees) based in Geneva, Switzerland, was lobbying countries to admit refugees and assisted organizations in negotiating refugee resettlement with steamship lines and land companies. Fridtjof Nansen – Norwegian polar explorer, winner of the Nobel Peace Prize, and refugee advocate – had worked with the Red Cross to supply food aid in the famine following the Russian Civil War, but among his many efforts on behalf of war victims and refugees, Nansen was best known for creating the 'Nansen passport' – an identification certificate for stateless refugees allowing them to travel and settle in other countries.[40]

Carrying Nansen passports, the Harbin refugees were offered refuge by Brazil and Paraguay. The very day the Japanese seized Harbin (22 February 1932), the Epp family joined a group of almost four hundred Mennonite 'Harbiner' refugees eagerly crowded into eight fourth-class passenger cars of a poorly heated train. A representative of the Nansen Rescue Mission accompanied the group.[41] The train took them as far as Dalian, China, where they boarded a Japanese tanker for a four-day voyage over the Yellow Sea to reach Shanghai on 27 February, one day after the Japanese occupied that city. With little ceremony and hearing occasional cannon fire, the refugees boarded the *D'Artagnan*, a 24,000-tonne French steamer that would head, without stops, for Marseilles, France.

In Marseilles, French officials and representatives of the Red Cross and of French and Swiss Mennonite as well as international evangelical churches gave the refugees a strange and wonderful welcome. Following baths and medical check-ups, the 'Harbiners' were ushered into a special train that, twelve hours later, got them to Paris. Eighteen more hours by train brought them to the port of Le Havre on the English Channel, and there they remained three days, again met by international representatives. The Dutch Mennonites brought along trunks full of clothing to distribute on board the next ship that would take them to Asunción, Paraguay.

As the Harbin refugees waited in Le Havre, many meetings on their behalf were taking place. European Mennonite leaders such as Benjamin Unruh from Germany joined other aid administrators and the refugees to discuss their future. Mennonites in Russia were used to organizing themselves democratically and had done so for decades before the Bolshevik Revolution. They chose leaders, decided on village structures, and assigned responsibilities at village council meetings. A Harbin refugee wrote, 'We had town hall [*Schultebut*] meetings for two days non-stop.'[42] One major problem was that the European planning committee for resettling the refugees had counted on sixty families from Harbin and bought provisions for that many, but the actual number was eighty. A reapportioning took place before the ship left for South America. Sailing the last part by paddle-wheeler up the Paraguay River, they reached the heart of Paraguay in the Gran Chaco.

After hearing Jutti tell her mother's story, I happened upon Australian author Mara Moustafine's book *Secrets and Spies: The Harbin Files* describing many inhabitants of Harbin living in comfort and luxury and supporting the communist takeover of Russia. Moustafine discovered (as early as 1930) that some of her relatives in Harbin had worked as Soviet agents and spies. They were wary of émigré White Guards (White Russians), fearing they could destroy Bolshevism. Here was the contrast, on one hand my Soviet Mennonite farmers, Justina Epp and her children, fearing deportation to slave labour camps, were fleeing to Harbin cellars and working for a Harbin elite. On the other hand, Moustafine's relatives were buying Red Moscow perfume and spying to support the Soviet agenda. Some of Moustafine's spy relatives were happy to help build socialism, but others were dragged into Soviet machinations against their will.[43] The author at first assumed the choice to work as agents was 'patriotic duty.'[44] The opportunity to get a good education came with the assignment. But she discovered that even Soviet spies were arrested, tortured, and ultimately became Stalin's victims.

So Justina escaped into the 'green hell' of the tropics, from where her children would re-enter the story in Nazi Germany during the Second World War.

5

Years of Terror, 1935–1938

The Bread Baker

I could not think why my father never told us anything about this brother. Heinrich was fourteen, certainly old enough to be noticed before my father left home for his six years of non-combatant and military service.[1] Was Heinrich just 'that quiet kid he left behind'?

Visiting us in Canada in 1977, Gerhard brought Heinrich sharply to our attention. He called him by the nickname 'Drush' and told us Heinrich had been *verschleppt* – hinting darkly that a food package our father in Canada sent Heinrich in the 1930s caused his arrest. This was a stinging remark. Heinrich disappeared because of contacts with us? Gerhard said he himself had refused all money and packages from his wife's relatives in Canada. Had we sent Heinrich to his death? Were we unwitting executioners? During the worst years of collectivization, the years of famine in Soviet Ukraine, my father – although he found only odd jobs, lived in a sod-covered log house in the bush in northern Alberta, had eight children, and was virtually penniless in the Great Depression – had sent Heinrich five dollars. He had sent it via Germany where a company in Berlin, Fast und Brillant (run by Mennonite A.P. Fast), had Soviet permission to send food packages to relatives in the USSR. I remember being indignant, thinking how dare Gerhard suggest my father had damned his brother. And how foolish of Gerhard to refuse help.[2]

Bit by bit, over several years, I discovered more. In the era of perestroika and glasnost, a letter from the USSR arrived at the last address of my parents in British Columbia. The house had been sold ten years previously and both my parents had died more than a year earlier, but the present owners looked up my brother who lived nearby to deliver the letter. The text on the envelope was in Russian, a language my brother could not decipher. Translated, it was discovered the letter was from an Elizaveta Andreievna Dovbush. As her patronymic indicated, she was a daughter of Andrei, the Russian form of Heinrich, our father's brother Heinrich. Elizaveta thought her Canadian uncle and aunt were alive and was risking a contact. How she got their address was a mystery.

That summer my sister Lill and her husband were conducting a Mennonite tour group, and knowing when they would be in the city of Zaporozhye, Lill sent the recently discovered Elizaveta a telegram advising her when they would be at the Intourist Hotel. Elizaveta travelled seven hours by bus and got to the hotel where, helped by an interpreter, Lill met her briefly. After that contact, my extended family began to send Elizaveta financial support, which Harvey would deliver when he came on his yearly research trips. Elizaveta would stay in the city with her niece, Heinrich's only grandchild and daughter of his only son Eugene.

Heinrich was an enigma. His daughter knew little about his early life and Gerhard died before I could ask. I began with scraps. I knew both Gerhard and Heinrich had boarded with the Froese family to attend school, and on weekends or holidays they sat together on the train riding back and forth, home to school and back again. In her New Testament, Grandmother Konrad had entered Heinrich's birthday but not his marriage date or his wife's name (she also omitted the marriage date of her eldest daughter). Was she making a point? From my father's story I knew Heinrich was conscripted into Admiral Kolchak's White Army in 1919 and served as a medical orderly, but they were not in the same corps. At the end of the Civil War Heinrich helped his brothers Abram and Gerhard to operate the family gristmill. After his brother Abram married nineteen-year-old Anastasia Mamentov in a snowstorm in January 1921, Heinrich fell in love with her sister Motya, who Gerhard said was a young widow with a child.

My mother had told me these 'mixed marriages' happened very seldom. To this my father had added that it happened more frequently after the First World War as Mennonite men left their settlements and met more 'outsiders.' He and his brothers met many non-Mennonites and, previous to their move to Maslianovka in 1919, for almost ten years the family had lived in daily contact with German Lutherans, Russian Molokans, Orthodox Russians, and Muslim Kazakhs. Still, two

Konrad sons marrying 'outside' caused other Mennonites to say, 'What a shame. Konrad sons marrying Russians!' 'Who? Which Konrads?' 'The Russian Konrads.' 'Oh!'

More was at stake. In the pietistic Mennonite Brethren (MB) church my grandparents belonged to, marrying into any other (even Mennonite) religious group resulted in excommunication. Since neither of my father's two younger brothers was a church member (membership occurred upon adult baptism), they saved their parents that shame. Gerhard told me their wives, Molokan Russians, were well received. His mother had said, 'What can you do, when it's love?' The Molokan mother of the wives similarly had been very satisfied with her 'German' sons-in-law. 'Another son-in-law from that family would please me too,' she had told Gerhard, but, in love with Lieschen Froese, he took it as a compliment.

Heinrich and Motya lived on the same street with the other Konrads. When my parents left Siberia, Heinrich and Motya had two children born in quick succession: Lucia in 1926 and Elizaveta in 1927, but there was no record of Motya having a child from a previous marriage, as Gerhard had mentioned. The family kept a modestly furnished home where the samovar was always polished, the table covered in a fringed cloth, and the dishes of delicate porcelain. My cousin Jutti Epp told me that as a child she saw their gramophone and was astonished that a 'story and music came out of a box.' Another relative said Motya was fragile and sensitive and that Heinrich was gentle with her. This source said Motya did not want to risk emigration in 1929 since she thought, superstitiously, the baby she was expecting in November might then not be a hoped-for son.[3] In mid-November 1929, a son, Eugene, was born.

After my parents left, Heinrich and Motya heard rumours that the German agricultural attaché in Moscow, Otto Auhagan, had said it would again be possible to emigrate in the spring.[4] Twelve hundred Siberians believed the story and signed a paper listing their names. It was baked into a loaf of bread handed to the German consulate.[5] But as the hunt for kulaks intensified, activist 25,000ers arrived and Heinrich was obliged to hand over his 'extra' horses and cows. The family had a faithful old Russian servant called Ivan, and when the activists came to collect the last cow, which provided the only milk for three young children, Old Ivan lay down in front of the barn door and put up such resistance that the activists left in disgust. Soon afterwards Heinrich and Motya had to move out of their house and seek shelter in another village.

Heinrich could have witnessed the deportation of kulaks, seen the thousands of people at the nearby railway station of Issil' Kul sent to 'resettlement camps.' Letters to Canada reported that these deportees were taken into pathless wilds, told – with wolves howling nearby – to bed down under open skies. By morning many children and old people had frozen to death. Half of them dead after a trek of forty-five days and nights, the deportees reached a destination in the taiga, where they first had to construct log barracks. If they did not freeze or starve to death first, then surrounded by bogs in summer, swamp fever could claim them.[6]

Heinrich fled in March. One can picture the little family seated on hard wooden benches on the train, Motya, thirty-four, dark head bent over sleeping baby Eugene, and Heinrich whispering to the little girls, Elizaveta and Lucia. Wearing his comrade cap, he jumps down at station stops to get hot water and fresh bread. The train curves east through western Siberian steppe and enters taiga forests. Days and nights pass. After Irkutsk, the grade becomes steeper. The train twists in and out of mountain passes, follows the shoreline around the southern tip of Lake Baikal, the freshwater jewel of Siberia, and stops at Ulan Ude – where Gerhard would move after his Donetsk factory episode in August 1931.

In 1930 Ulan Ude was a town of small wooden houses (a huge Lenin statue on the central square and Soviet-style concrete buildings came later). Capital of the kidney-shaped Buryat Republic, Ulan Ude had once been the winter quarters of Cossack troops and was an important terminus for the Trans-Siberian Railway. Here the railway branched into three directions, one arm continuing across the Amur River to the Sea of Japan and ending at the Pacific port Vladivostok, another becoming the Trans-Manchurian Rail ending in Beijing, and the third, which Heinrich and family now took, the Trans-Mongolian Railway to Ulan Bator.

Passing through semi-desert, seared grass steppes, a vast treeless plain, the family looked out on endless sky, scrub, and rounded hills. Here and there on the rolling plains they saw herds of cattle and sheep and felt-lined white yurts. Near them, gaping at the belching train, nomad women and children wearing heavily padded clothing, and men and boys on stocky, thick-haired ponies were herding flocks of sheep. For generations Mongolian people had moved their herds and yurts following the grass. The train climbed a mountain range, and surrounded by the snow-capped Four Holy Peaks, it reached Mongolia's capital city Ulan Bator, the hiding place chosen by Heinrich's brother Abram.

In my parents' papers, I had found one letter from Heinrich. In Gothic script, written in purple ink on lined paper, without return address, the letter was postmarked 'Wernigerode, Germany.' Heinrich had mailed it to his mother (not accepted by Canadian immigration for health reasons, she had remained in Germany), who sent it to Canada.[7]

5 May 1930
Dear Geschwister in the great, great distance
Our best greetings to you. Today we received your most welcome letter of March 28, 1930 [my parents arrived in Canada in March] and we thank you very much for it. We are happy, thank God, that you arrived safely. Thank God, we all are well and alive, also Abram with his family, something we wish you from the bottom of our hearts too.

Since April 4 we have been living in the city together with Abram in the same lodgings. We couldn't stand it there [Siberia] any longer, first because of the economy – there was nothing to be bought anywhere – and then the life under those kinds of people. Now I am looking for work but still have no job. Abram works as a chauffeur and gets a good wage. So it's better here than in the village. Baked bread costs fifteen roubles a kilo here. We have had enough sugar every month for our family, three kilos and 700 grams. Meat is rationed to half a kilo every two days. On the market flour costs fourteen roubles per pud[8] in Siberia and twenty-five roubles per pud here. We haven't been able to hope for anything good so far.

The weather is nice here, often even hot, and often rain. Everything is green already. Here the winter is short and very changeable. Rain and snow and then frost, and that's the way it has been. Since the first of March it has been good weather. We still have enough to live and the Lord will of course help us further.

We have received three letters from Mama and we also got one from Gerhard not long ago. Now he is in Spat and is living together with his parents-in-law in the same house. They still have bread. He worked as a tractorist but is without work at the moment. He writes that they all are healthy and that they all want to go and look at the Crimea. There's nothing good to report from Yalta and Sevastopol. They are reported to have sent thirty thousand Russian families to the North, and they say also in our area. Well, let's hope things improve.

We received several letters from Justina too. They all are well too, thank God. As soon as we received your letter from the boat I wrote to your father-in-law [to sponsor Heinrich to come to Canada; Braun lived in Manitoba].

We received a letter from [illegible]. They also are well and alive. They sold everything in the fall in order to move away and now live in Baikal. They have bought themselves a little house and now have a horse and a cow. She writes nothing good about that place either. Many people from there are being exiled to [illegible] where they have to cut timber. They've sent Johann Loewen from Maslianovka there, but released him because of illness. They reinstated Jakob Huebner [re-enfranchised him] so maybe he'll return??? Gerhard's address is P.O. Spat, Crimea, c/o Johann Kroeker. Gerhard wants his letters there. Our address is Abram's address. We wait for a quick reply. Aufwiedersehen. Also greetings and kisses to your dear Geschwister.

Greet everyone who knows us. We wish you all the best.

M & H

PS Today is May 11 and I want to describe a little about what we are doing and to end the letter. Since April 8, 1930, I have worked as a shipping clerk [or warehouse worker] in the bakery 24 p. R [sic]. I get 75 roubles a month. The work is not too heavy and is fine. The bakery runs from 6 o'clock in the evening to 6 o'clock in the evening, around the clock. Today it is dirty weather again. It has rained all night, and yesterday I had to walk the whole way in the rain, from the centre of the city to our lodging, which is at least three verst.⁹ We hope soon to find quarters in the yard of the bakery; then it will be easier. We are all well. Abram is home now. They have not yet received their goods, that is the large trunk and the [illegible].

Write and tell us how you like it there and what would interest us if we could also come sometime. Where will you have to live? Or better said, be registered, and in what way? How will you have to pay for your expenses? Are you permitted to live where you like or where they send you? Please describe everything. We are far more curious than you can imagine. We hope for an early reply and good news.

We remain in greetings and kisses, your ever-loving Geschwister

Motja and Heinrich

PPS Dear Relatives,

I send you a greeting. Wish you God's blessings. Kisses to you and the children. God be with you in your new abode.

Motya¹⁰

By 1932 Bolshevism had reached Mongolia. The Konrad brothers watched silently as Buddhist temples and monasteries were confiscated, priests and monks were led out, imprisoned, or murdered. Nomad herds were forcibly collectivized, business shops expropriated, and resident Chinese traders expelled. As Gerhard told us in 1977, conveying goods between Mongolia and the USSR, Abram's truck was inspected at the border checkpoint each time, guards sticking bayonets through bales of grain or straw, checking for fugitives. Life seemed dangerous.

Motya's brothers were in the Donbas. Unemployment had almost disappeared here by 1930, creating a labour shortage.[11] When they wrote that jobs were available, after just two years in Mongolia, Heinrich announced he was moving south. Abram and Nastya protested, but Heinrich (perhaps Motya missed her mother, who was with her brothers in Donetsk) insisted he would be more invisible as a proletarian in an industrial centre. They all seemed to have the same hope, to become invisible.[12] So, reversing places, Heinrich left Ulan Bator for Donetsk, and Gerhard went from Donetsk to Ulan Ude.

Heinrich found lodgings in Snezhnoie (Snizhn'e), Ukraine, a town near the present Ukraine-Russian border, a site of many coal mines. He got a job in a bakery, and Motya's mother moved in with them. Elizaveta had told Harvey her father was kindly, devout, a practising Christian, as was her mother, that he loved and played with his children, and that he worked as an accountant or bookkeeper in the bakery. 'During school recess I used to go to the bakery, where I would sing or recite a verse, and my father rewarded me with a piece of pastry of my choice. He taught me to sing "Oh Susanna."'[13] In a letter to my sister Mary, Elizaveta wrote that a worker in the bakery also used to give her buns to share with the children in her class.[14]

In 1932 and 1933, the years of famine, Stalin introduced an internal passport preventing starving rural citizens from moving into cities. These were years when Hitler with his hatred of Bolsheviks was rising to power in Germany, while Stalin was looking for spies, 'enemies of the people,' and 'wreckers' in every factory. Heinrich's family was not doing well. The last time we saw Gerhard in 1991, when the USSR was crumbling, I asked him about my father's five-dollar gift to Heinrich, and he told me about Heinrich's refusal to leave the Donbas area. Gerhard had urged Heinrich to return to Ulan Ude. 'I told him it was dangerous in Donetsk.' (Remember the cement plant incident.) Heinrich had insisted, 'I've done nothing. Why would they arrest me?' And Motya, complaining about moving so many times, had said they had a roof over their heads, the girls were settled in school, and her mother lived with them – many reasons not to move.

In my parents' box of letters, I had found a yellowed scrap of paper written by Motya in purple ink in 1934 or 1935, thanking them for some money. Using his Russian name, Motya wrote that Andrusha's health was very poor and 'we live our lives as proletarians, no cow, no chickens, no bottle of milk a day for the children.' She closed by wishing my parents God's grace and love. Was this the money for which Heinrich was arrested, as Gerhard intimated on his visit to Canada?

I would discover that what Heinrich thought, and even the money itself, was irrelevant. Local Party officials following Stalin's directives were concerned only with Heinrich being a 'German,' a *Nemets*, who had accepted help from abroad. This help, in food packages or money, was demonized as 'fascist dollars' or 'Hitler's crumbs.'[15] Soviet Ukraine was still reeling from the recent mass starvation following collectivization and people were still sending letters abroad begging for help from relatives in Europe, Canada, the United States, Asia, and elsewhere. Religious leaders abroad wrote to the highest levels of their governments about the plight of their Soviet co-religionists, to no avail. When it seemed the world had closed its eyes to the plight of ordinary Soviet civilians, relatives abroad sent food packages or money that could legally be redeemed at Torgsin (the State Society for Trading with Foreigners) stores for food products. People within the USSR were bringing in their gold, silver, jewellery, crosses, and other valuables to Torgsin stores to trade for food or clothing – also to leave their names and addresses, later so useful for the secret police.

The Soviets were paranoid about non-Russian/Ukrainian ethnic groups with relatives abroad, particularly those living at the borderlands of capitalist countries: Poles and Germans on the west, and, in the east, Koreans and Japanese. They might want to attack the USSR. Terry Martin states that Ukrainian communists saw *all* Germans in the USSR as kulaks and particularly targeted those receiving help from Germany.[16] Suspicion accelerated after Hitler became chancellor in 1933. Now his spies were imagined to be everywhere. Indeed, by 1938 a head of Ukrainian police would say that all Germans and Poles in Soviet Ukraine were spies.[17] Convinced by Stalin's spin doctors that spies and terrorists were everywhere, citizens lived in constant fear.

This tense atmosphere was exacerbated after Stalin's potential rival and regional Bolshevik Party boss in Leningrad, Sergei Kirov, was assassinated in December 1934. Historians still argue whether or not Stalin ordered Kirov's assassination, but none dispute that, directly following the murder, Stalin signed an emergency law that resulted in the arrest and sentencing of millions of peoples. In a random reign of terror, thousands of older Bolshevik leaders, Soviet military officers, Party officials, and ordinary citizens – Poles and Germans in greater numbers – were arrested as terrorists, executed, or sent into concentration camps.

Responding to the anti-terrorism measures, local Party officials looked around to see how they could find more terrorists. Soon District Party committees were lobbying Moscow to take harsher measures. How about people requesting overseas support, especially coming 'from bourgeois and fascist organizations in Germany?' Shouldn't such 'disloyal, anti-Soviet' activity be severely punished?[18] Those who received 'Hitler's crumbs' should be expelled from the Party and 'purged from the collective farms.' Milkmaids, stablemen, pig-tenders, crop growers, former so-called kulaks and preachers, dismissed as class enemies, lost their farm jobs. Also expelled were people who gave aid to those who had been expelled. Village lists were kept of how many money vouchers and packages came in, how many persons accepted, and how many refused help from abroad.[19] The money obviously was seen as propaganda, and those who accepted help were 'fascist agents.'[20]

Alert people like Gerhard recognized this threat. But Mennonites abroad did not see that help sent to starving family members in the USSR – especially via Germany – confirmed Soviet views that the recipients would be sympathetic to Germany. Which Canadian relatives knew that receiving financial help was considered treason? Not my parents. An article in the *Bote* (a Mennonite newspaper widely circulated in Canada), written by a son-in-law of A.P. Fast (Fast and Brilliant Company already mentioned), located in Berlin, described how his parents (declared kulaks), with eight children, were exiled to Arkhangelsk. Starving, they wrote to him. The A.P. Fast Company was able to send them monthly food packages until one package arrived opened, its contents replaced with bricks. The family sold their clothes for food, but still his father starved to death. Thousands of packages like my father's were sent from Berlin.[21]

Yet accepting foreign currency was not illegal. Police records discuss a case in 1934 where a woman in Molochansk (formerly a Mennonite town named Halbstadt), was dismissed from her job for accepting financial help. She appealed to the director of Torgsin and received an official note on 4 September 1934 saying that having received transfers from abroad was no grounds for her dismissal from work, or for that of her daughter.[22] However, by 1936 Torgsin stores were closed.

The regional Communist Party committee in Molochansk took another tack. Already strongly critical of 'Germans,' especially Mennonites, for refusing to join the Party or to enrol their children in Pioneer and Komsomol programs, it added another 'crime.' Those people could still be found guilty of counter-revolutionary actions because they persisted in maintaining ties with 'fascist and bourgeois states' through letters. A resolution in December 1934 requested that such 'active counter-revolutionists be immediately expelled and isolated from the rest.'[23] Any correspondence between my parents and their siblings in the USSR was stopped.

There is no information on Heinrich's family between 1934 and 1938, but we know these were the purge years. Reading story after story about the climate of intimidation and fear, it seemed ironic to me that 1937–8 was also the Jazz Age, a time when in Moscow the new Metro subway with its chandeliers and cathedral marbles (taken from central Moscow's demolished Orthodox cathedral) struck the world as wonderful. The opulent Moskva Hotel was opened. In movie houses people watched documentaries of super-heroes, miners, and pilots performing Herculean feats. Children of the Bolshevik brass were excited and happy, believed in the 'radiant future' and the creation of the Soviet New Man, and (like Spiderman today) secret police NKVD boss Felix Dzerzhinsky was a children's hero.

It was 1938. Elizaveta was ten years old. She told the story.

I remember that a lot of snow had fallen in February in Snezhnoie. My father's boss at the bakery had told him, 'Andrusha, disappear for two weeks.'

'But I'm innocent,' my father insisted. 'They won't arrest me.'

I was home with my mother on February 28, the day men came with a sleigh and horses, uniformed men, secret police wearing blue hats. There were two shifts at school and I was in the morning shift, with my elder sister Lucia in the afternoon. They were three men. They turned everything upside down in our home and searched in all the corners. Then they told my father to come with them.

'Take your winter underwear!,' my mother screamed.

He had half an hour to pack. My mother was crying and one of the men turned to her: 'Stop your crying, woman. Your husband will soon be back.'

Suddenly, one man at each side, they roughly seized my father and marched him outside. We had no time to say farewells. Screaming, my mother ran behind the sleigh and I ran behind my mother.

'Father! Andrusha!'

We kept calling out as we ran behind the sleigh with my father, but he was not permitted to turn around or look at us. We ran behind that sleigh all the way to the NKVD building. People came out on the street to look at the spectacle, a hysterical wife and child without coats running after a sleigh with police officers.

The sleigh stopped. A man came out of the NKVD building and shouted at my mother, 'Shut up if you don't want your children to be orphans.'

Then Mother had to apologize to them.

Every day my mother came and stood outside of the building to keep watch. With many women whose men had been taken, she lined up at the door and tried to get information about father's charges or trial date. One time she did see my father being led to the bath. He recognized her and made a hand signal, putting his fingers to his mouth indicating that he was hungry. She never saw him again.

Do you know that the NKVD in the area won an award, a 'red badge' for having fulfilled the plan, arrested the required numbers – perhaps oversubscribed the quota – and the town was praised? If all the tears of the mothers and children could have been collected, there would have been enough to drown the town.'[24]

From jail Heinrich was able to release a document that allowed Motya to receive his last pay cheque, but after this the family was destitute. Who would employ the wife of an 'enemy of the state' when it was illegal to help her? With three children to support, Motya went on her knees to her landlady, who allowed them to stay. She gave them some produce from her garden, saying, 'I won't let you starve to death.' Motya found a job pushing coal cars at a mine head and sold their possessions, including her gold locket and a very expensive mattress made of camel hair. Elizaveta remembered pulling the hair out of the mattress, bit by bit, and selling it at the outdoor market.

What a relief when Motya found a cleaning job in a hospital, where she was permitted to take home some food from the hospital farm. As payment for looking after the hospital's pigs, she received two piglets, which she and her children raised and sold. They then were able to 'buy' a space next to the hospital kitchen in a kind of barracks, a roof over their heads. During this time, to earn some money, Elizaveta and her sister looked after other children. 'I was small for my age. When the child cried, I also cried.'

Elizaveta wrote an anecdote about Memorial Day, a Soviet substitute for Easter, when people visited cemeteries.

This is a special day on which we bring eggs, baking, and sweets for the poor who have to beg to survive. I remember my childhood when we lost our father. Mama worked in the hospital for twelve roubles a month, and together with Grandmother we were five people. At that time we were some of those children who went to the cemetery for the good things left on graves there. It was one day when we had enough to eat.

During the time, Mama used to hide us with pillows and say, 'Children, now pray the Lord's Prayer.' We had a two-hundred-year-old Bible from our Mamentov grandmother. Mama sang psalms for us in the years after Papa was taken, but saw no ray of light.[25]

Nobody would tell Motya where her husband was taken – I discovered that he ended up in Donetsk only when I asked for his file there in 2005 – and she assumed he was sent to a prison camp 'in the North.' Nobody was writing letters abroad anymore, but Heinrich's brother Gerhard, until then a truck driver on a swine farm in Semipalatinsk, did come to see Motya in 1939. Elizaveta remembered their visit. It was a year after her father disappeared and Gerhard brought a school knapsack for her brother Eugene. She was able to complete six years of school, her sister seven, but the boy with the new knapsack finished only four before events scrambled their lives once again.

Sensing 'the spider web was again being violently shaken,' Gerhard relocated in January 1938. By this time internal passports were required, and permission to travel was needed, so this being the time of the greatest number of arrests, how could he have accomplished that move? After a lifetime of carefully revealing very little, Gerhard merely said he worked for 'a Soviet official,' but he added pragmatically, 'Where better to hide than under the eyes of your pursuers? Find a place where they need you for their own comfort.' Perhaps some official at Semipalatinsk had him transferred to Alma Ata.

At the foot of the Ala-Tau ridge of the Tien Shan Mountains, Gerhard was a chauffeur for a 'Soviet official,' driving him back and forth to his business office. Again transparent, Gerhard had learned how to deny his past, to ingratiate himself, to be unseen and at the same time useful. As he told us, 'We were very careful never to make any friends in Alma Ata,' said Gerhard. 'Aware we could be arrested at any moment, that secret informers were everywhere, we never invited anyone, nor were we ever in a group of even five people. Whenever I filled out questionnaires, I continued to write "no" for "relatives abroad?"'[26]

Gerhard would see Motya again, but neither would ever again see Heinrich.

The Agronomist

Then there was the disappearance of Johannes, my mother's favourite brother. I wrote his story and my husband said, 'You're not capturing his personality. We know he was Maria Braun's father, that he had a powerful singing voice, and that he was handsome.' Does it add to his personality to know that in the few items she brought from Siberia, there was a postcard that he sent her as a girl? That his young son (seventy years later) recalled going with his father to fetch rye to thatch a roof? That my grandfather (his only entry about any of his children in his voluminous archive of mostly religious topics) boasted about Johannes graduating from the best Mennonite commercial institution with a gold medal? That he taught a year before he went on to university in Leningrad and was the only one of her family to attend my mother's wedding? My mother last saw her brother in Siberia. By then Johannes was married to Anna, the woman in the portrait in which he stands in his frock coat, tiny fingers of a baby girl curling tight in his hand.

On my next trip to BC after meeting Maria Braun in Karaganda, I interviewed my Aunt Kay, widow of my mother's youngest brother, Nick. She told me she knew a little about Johannes, mostly about his wife, Anna. She was a daughter of onetime prominent residents of Aunt Kay's village. Aunt Kay remembered seeing the young couple walking on the street of Nikolaipol, 'a smart-looking man, walking with our Anna Peters.' She dimly recalled being at their wedding held in a *Scheune*, a carriage shed. There being no banquet halls, a carriage house was a frequent site for festive gatherings. Aunt Kay was seven when she saw the courting couple and attended the wedding, but said,

I remember because of the Eichenfeld massacre. It was during the Revolution, I'm not sure, maybe 1919. My father had already been arrested, beaten, and put into prison. Revolutionaries discovered some hidden tsarist gold coins in our house. Two of my brothers had been harvesting in Eichenfeld and my mother must have been psychic because she sent word for them to come home. My brothers returned the night before eighty people, nearly all the men in Eichenfeld, were slaughtered in a single night.[27]

We asked each other how it was possible to have a big wedding in the middle of the Civil War. Memory often insubstantial as morning mist, how was I to know if Aunt Kay was right? I did know that Johannes and Anna were in Siberia when my parents married in 1920. They were still there when my parents left in 1929. Not much more. I was reading what (after we met her in Karaganda) Maria Braun had written my mother and came across a question she asked about some nuts my mother was drying. Maria wanted to know if the nuts were hazelnuts like her family had in Kotlyarevka. I had a place, Kotlyarevka. In a Mennonite atlas the village appeared in the Memrik settlement. Maria Braun had died before I could ask details, but I now knew where Johannes and his family lived after they left Siberia. Maria's brother Heinz would tell me years later that as a young boy he had helped his father to collect wagonloads of rye to thatch the roof of a house they had bought in Kotlyarevka. The house was cheap because it had been pushed in by the wind, but his father had put a rope of wires around the house and slowly pulled it ('the insides creaked') back to its original position and 'the thatch was so well placed, not a drop soaked through.'[28]

Before I met Heinz I visited his eldest sister Alici, the baby in the portrait of handsome Johannes. Alici lived in Shakhty, Russia, and by 1992 was corresponding with me. She was seventy-nine by the time I met her. Widowed, she lived in a mining town surrounded by black mountains, the slag heaps of a coal-producing industrial area now much depleted of resources and working mines. In 1999, following a conference in Zaporozhye, we hired a taxi to drive us eight hours to find her. To enter Russia we needed a visa, available in Canada upon a personal or professional invitation from a Russian source – or as tourists, a hotel booking. A personal invitation would have forced Alici to pay fees and fill out many forms – an impossible task for an aged woman housebound with rheumatoid arthritis. We paid for a hotel room in Rostov, one we had no intention of using, since Alici lived two hours out of the city. Intourist in Zaporozhye had warned us about hassles, high duties, taxes, and difficulties at the border, but our driver did the talking and money changed hands, so all went smoothly.

The mountains of slag at Shakhty were a dismal sight, but here and there, like green underskirts, trees had managed to root in the lower levels. Finding Alici's street was like negotiating a crater-pocked battlefield. The taxi swam through flooded muddy streets, inched over exposed pipes, and edged around potholes. Our driver kept asking for directions and once or twice we came to blind ends, abandoned pits now filled with weeds and the flotsam of plastic bags and bottles. The 'good times' following the collapse of Communism had missed Shakhty. Alici's street was lined with customary Soviet-style picket fences and one-storey small houses. Communists had outlawed two-storied homes as elitist.

Behind a high wooden gate we found a small red brick bungalow with green shutters, Alici's home for the last thirty-seven years. Her husband had died four years earlier, but her adult sons Volodya and Vanya and three granddaughters lived nearby. A pail and brush recently used to whitewash inside walls stood on the step of Alici's back door, the only entrance. She welcomed us, speaking calmly, softly. How different from her sister Maria in Karaganda, that woman of high-pitched voice.

As we stepped around piles of bricks stacked up in her yard, Alici apologized, saying her daughter-in-law got them as a salary. She was a bookkeeper at a brick factory, the only one still running in Shakhty. 'Terrible, the unemployment after the Fall. Terrible.'

People kept referring to the end of communism as 'the Fall.' Vanya, Alici's forty-five-year-old son was a director in a ceramics factory, and his wife, rather than be unemployed, worked for bricks. Harvey had visited Alici seven years earlier, when the ceramics factory still produced decorative vases, figurines, dishes, tea and coffee sets, all manner of creative pottery. Now it produced only tiles. 'Market,' Vanya said. 'All our buyer in Italy takes is tiles.'

Alici wore a well-used, green polyester dress and cloth shoes. She pointed to a long garden behind her house, 'Remember my plum trees?' she asked Harvey. 'A drought last summer and – no fruit.' Harvey had photographed Alici with a basin of blue Italian plums. I thought how much Alici reminded me of my mother, that 'Braun' nose, that slightly aloof lift of her chin, the fine bone structure of her face, those kind blue eyes, the curling wisps of pure white hair escaping from a pulled back hairstyle. My mother had always worn a chignon, but Alici's hair was bound in a ponytail, one she found incongruous too. 'I'd like to cut it. Ridiculous really, but my church forbids cut hair.' She paused, eyes twinkling, 'Maybe I'll do it anyway.'

'Would you like to freshen up?' She indicated the garden where we saw a washstand beside a tap and a 'one-seater' privy next to a wire cage-like henhouse and several other structures. The next day we discovered the garden included cherry trees and several tomato plants, recently watered. Alici had always grown her own potatoes, she told us, but the invasion of the Colorado potato beetle had ended that. 'Vanya will buy me a sack.'

As we washed up in the garden, Alici told us that she took a weekly shower every Saturday. Her son Vanya drove her to his factory to use the company facilities. Also, she used a hand basin. A coldwater tap in the kitchen had been installed since Harvey's visit seven years earlier. In 1992 he had written,

Alici is such a warm, open, loving person, who has looked forward so much to this first contact with her family abroad. Her life is stable and, as things go here, reliable. Her son Volodya (40s), his wife Natasha, and their two daughters Katya (16) and Lena (12) live two houses down the street. They are, according to Alici, busy with their own lives and needs, having less time and money for their mother than her favourite son Vanya with his wife Tanya and their daughter Dasha. A name like Dasha was used only in noble families, Alici, confides. Vanya lives downtown in a small two-room apartment that he has decked up nicely with tiles in the kitchen, pine door, the usual rug on the wall in the living room, and so on.

Alici's house is cut up into four roomettes, two halls, and a kitchen. The thick walls and a coal-burning pech make it warm and cosy. She feels herself better off than ever in her life. She has a large vegetable garden with ripe tomatoes, beets, carrots, and potatoes, apples, many plums, cherries, pears. Several outbuildings include a summer kitchen with a bath [banya], pens for a few hens and chicks, and a new garage where Vanya keeps his workbench and tools. There is no indoor running water or plumbing. Water is a hand-filled container over a sink, with a pail underneath, but she has an electric stove. The walls are whitewashed yearly and the floor is painted a traditional brown.[29]

Much had changed. The *banya* or sauna was gone and the locked garage contained only bricks. Since theft increased greatly after 'the Fall,' Alici's remaining three chickens were caged. The house of her son Volodya next door was now a weekend home. A younger woman, Nadia, had replaced former daughter-in-law Natasha, who lived with twenty-year-old daughter Lena in an apartment. The divorce troubled Alici.

In recent years, like her sister Maria, Alici had begun attending a conservative Baptist church erected after 'the Fall' with financial help from Baptists in Germany. In parts of the former communist empire, religion was making a comeback. Orthodox churches were being rebuilt, and where once only old women dared to be seen in churches, now people of all ages entered, kissed icons, crossed themselves, said prayers, and attended christenings and weddings. Baptists (of the strict denomination) seen as a sect, were still ridiculed as 'religious fanatics' for their focus on female appearance and prohibition of television, drinking, and smoking.

'I missed a church' Alici said, 'but I was terrified my sons would abandon me if I attended. I told them I needed it. My husband had died. He never believed. I waited till after "the Fall." My sons said, just go if I wanted to, so I've been attending. But now I can't walk, and I pay out a third of my monthly pension for this taxi service to church [a distance of perhaps four blocks up a steep hill, over a very potholed road]. A man picks me up and brings me back. Poor man, he has nine children and they always look hungry, so I bring a loaf of bread along and give it to them in the car. The children, tall thin youths and little ones, devour it in a few minutes.'

In the days of our visit, we had long discussions. When I asked about her father, Alici turned tables and asked what I knew. Ah, for her the unknown past, but for me my mother's memories. Alici kept returning to the topic of her parents' wedding. She thought her mother's parents had moved to Siberia after the area was flooded for the hydro dam built on the Dnieper at Zaporozhye. I knew from my reading that the flooding happened in 1927 and memoirists of Siberia mentioned that the Peters were in Siberia before the 1917 Revolution. With memory fallible and documents destroyed, how often we were left with more questions than answers. Why had Johannes and Anna married in 1919 in Nikolaipol, a village near the future hydroelectric dam, if Anna's family was already in Siberia and Johannes's family was in Bashkiria province? Alici recalled that her father had worked in a Mennonite mental hospital. I wondered if Johannes had opted for this work as his alternative non-combatant service. If so, he could have been in Nikolaipol in southeastern Ukraine during the Civil War. But wait, what brought (his wife) Anna Peters back to this area if her family was settled by 1917 in Siberia? Alici said her father was staying with his uncle, 'one with two musical daughters' when working in a psychiatric hospital.

I recalled that my Grandfather Braun had two brothers, but which one had two musical daughters? Or was it the other side of the family? A Mennonite mental hospital, Bethania, existed near the Dnieper River, near Nikolaipol, so perhaps that was the one. Where were all the records? Were they perhaps destroyed by the flooding for the dam or in the civil war? As Alici and I belaboured minute details, I realized how important it was for her to recover every possible scrap of her parent's life. Like an archaeologist, layer by layer, she sought to uncover events and images to recreate a fuller life for a man, a father whose final days were still unknown, for tears not wiped. Could tracing such small dots restore a life?

In 1919, during the typhus epidemic that accompanied the Civil War, before the appointed wedding date and after invitations had been sent out, Johannes became ill. Against the wishes of her parents, Anna, aged twenty-two, accompanied by a brother, had nursed her fiancé back to health. Was Anna a nurse? Had she been a nurse during the First World War? Again Alici and I had to speculate. Anna Peters came from a prosperous home so, after the family moved to Siberia, did she return to the South to attend one of the Mennonite girls' high schools? Did she stay on to train as a nurse? Mennonite nurses did volunteer during the First World War. It was possible. Once again I noted the loss of personal history. Alici's mother had shared little family history with her children. Even harmless details could incriminate. So much family history and culture had been stolen from children, and, now when it was possible to ask, nobody was alive to answer.

Ironically, in exploring the wedding topic with Alici, I gained an insight into the dynamics of my mother's childhood home. Alici told me her father had been adamant about refusing to return or ever to marry in his parental village. He could not bear his stepmother. Alici asked me, 'Why did he dislike her so much, do you know?' We speculated about a young stepmother's relationship with eleven-year-old Johannes – whose mother had died less than a year earlier. My mother was eight when she lost her mother, and I recalled that she had suggested an unhappy childhood. I discovered the degree of discord in that household only from another cousin in Kazakhstan. That took another few years.

Alici was more confident about details of her parents' life in Siberia where her father Johannes was a teacher in Issyl Kul and where she was born in 1920 (as I noted, three months before my parents' wedding). In 1921 Johannes and Anna Braun moved from Issyl Kul to Peterskhutor, a cluster of farms owned by five Peters families, where Alici's grandfather Johann Peters, a farmer and Mennonite preacher, had built a two-story home. Unusual for the time and atypical for a Mennonite house, memoirists had suggested the family was hoity-toity.[30] Johannes and Anna had five children: Alici born in 1920, Hans in 1921, Maria in 1924, Anni in 1926, and Heinz in 1928.

In answer to my question of why the family had not immigrated to Canada when the grandparents left in 1924, Alici said that Grandfather Braun had come to Siberia and urged them to leave. 'Mama wanted to, but not Papa.' My parents didn't consider immigration in 1924 either. As my father said, things seemed to be improving. ('At first the Reds didn't seem to be so bad.') Hadn't Lenin announced in 1921 that private ownership and enterprise would help rebuild the shattered Russian economy? Weren't law and order being restored? Mennonites in Russia had even established an organization to foster improvements in agriculture for those who saw a future in the USSR. For those not so optimistic, that same organization facilitated exit permissions. Assisted by travel loans from the Canadian Pacific Railway Company, in the three years before 1927, twenty thousand Mennonites, mostly those who suffered loss of property and family members during the Revolution and Civil War, had left for Canada.

But why did Johannes not come to Moscow in 1929 with my parents? At our Karaganda hotel meeting, Maria had said her father lacked the courage to leave, but later he began learning English and was eager to go. Alici recalled, packed, they were waiting for the wagon to take them to the railway station when they got word that people were being sent back from Moscow.

In December 1929 Stalin delivered his 'war on kulaks' speech outlining the collectivization of agriculture, and Alici recalled (was it 1930?) that one of her uncles at Peterskhutor, Franz Peters, was declared a kulak. The family's possessions confiscated, as pariahs the whole family was forced onto a wagon that drove them to the train where they were crammed into cattle cars, locked in, and sent to northern banishment. She was a girl of eleven and even though helping such 'enemies of the state' was forbidden, standing at the road watching her uncle's family hauled away, she had thrown a loaf of bread onto the moving wagon. This family 'sent into the snow' was in exile five years before surviving members returned to Omsk.

When Johannes was arrested (in 1931?) and kept in prison for several months, activist 'Reds' (the 25,000ers) tried also to take away Alici and her ten-year-old brother, Hans. They intended to place them in a Soviet orphanage to be re-educated, to be taught Soviet ideology and atheism. Their mother, Anna, pleaded to keep her children and the 'Reds' relented. Both Alici and Maria Braun, on separate occasions, told me about the day the activists came to take their cow, their only source of food while their father was in prison. The children all hung onto the cow's tail and cried. In Maria's telling, the activists let the rope fall and spared the cow. In Alici's memory the cow was taken in spite of tears.

Directly after his release from prison, Johannes Braun packed up his family and moved southwest to the Memrik Mennonite settlement in Stalino district in today's eastern Ukraine. They found lodgings in the village of Kotlyarevka, near the town of Selidovka. The Memrik settlement, consisting of eleven Mennonite villages, was one of the first so-called daughter colonies of the original 1804 Molochna Mennonite settlement. The sisters didn't know why they came here, but it may have been the call of a 'free Donbas,' a haven for persons fleeing dekulakization. Who knew that Stalin would make it a major target? The sisters knew as little about the history of Memrik as about their father's boyhood on the Bashkir plains near Ufa where he and my mother grew up. Alici called it a 'German' rather than Mennonite settlement, and both Maria and Alici thought their family moved in among strangers.

Yet their German-language school was full of children from surrounding traditionally Mennonite villages.

Russian Mennonites of my parents' generation belonged to a relatively small gene pool and loved discovering who was related to whom. Certainly before the Revolution the Braun family would immediately have participated in that parlour game: 'Oh, you must be related to Isaak I. Braun. He's my Aunt Tina's second cousin. She married Isaak Ediger and he was ...' Instantly the family would have found connections. But as Gerhard Konrad said, in the 1930s you hoped never to be recognized or to have relatives.

The village of Kotlyarevka, named for the nobleman Kotlyarevsky whose estate had once covered much of the territory, was situated in a shallow valley along a dry riverbed. Across the riverbed was its twin village, Michaelsheim, and both were near the large Ukrainian town of Selidovka.[31] The Soviets had introduced minority language schools in an attempt to win ethnic groups to adopt Communism, and Johannes and Anna may have chosen Kotlyarevka because only ten kilometres away was the ten-classroom residential intermediate German-language school, the Ebental Internat, where they enrolled their elder children.[32] These schools created a generation of children – German-speaking Mennonites, Volga and Black Sea Germans, Rumanians, and others – who knew less Ukrainian or Russian than their parents; Russian became mandatory after 1938.

The Great Famine in Ukraine came in 1932–3.[33] The 'artificial famine' resulted in the greatest number of deaths Ukraine would ever know.[34] As already noted, peasants balked when told to relinquish their land, animals, and produce to the state, or to join collective farms. Unable to pay exorbitant taxes, people cut down fruit trees or butchered animals. With hardly any grain sown or food produced, nothing could be delivered to the state and nothing was left to eat. What was worse, confiscated grain that was piled up at train stations, without proper storage, cover, or transportation, often rotted. Citizens were forbidden to glean or to touch one kernel from the state piles. A Mennonite mother who picked up fallen cobs of corn on a road was arrested for 'theft' and handed an eight-year prison sentence.[35]

This was the climate in which Johannes Braun's family lived in Kotlyarevka. People in Ukraine were starving, and posters and pamphlets were urging the eradication of 'bloodsucker, vermin, and subhuman kulaks.' Quotas of how many kulaks to arrest were set at Communist Party headquarters and each village cell was told to draw up its list and make arrests. In naming suspected 'enemies,' spying was encouraged: 'Haven't you overheard someone speak negatively about the Soviets?' When the prepared list was read out at a collective farm assembly, no one dared to vote against it. Could people follow Gerhard Konrad's plan, move if you thought your name was on the list? The internal passport now prevented anyone from moving without authorization.

Mennonite historian Peter Letkemann estimates that in Soviet Ukraine, 10–25 per cent of the Mennonite population was dekulakized: dispossessed, disenfranchised, and often deported to work camps. From 1933 to 1941 some ten thousand Mennonites were arrested – a figure at least four times higher than the national average.[36]

Johannes, knowing that intellectuals were targeted, decided to retool. He enrolled in the one-year course Soviets offered in nearby Lugansk to become an agronomist. Agronomists were schooled in the use of fertilizers (which were non-existent), operation and repair of tractors, depth of ploughing (directions that often disagreed with local farmers' knowledge of their soils), and so on. (Shallow or deep ploughing became a topic in his police file.) Alici told me that for the first ten months her father was in Lugansk (Voroshilovgrad) studying for his agronomist's certificate, the family was without a wage-earner. Asked what they lived on, she explained that her father had sold their piano, one from Siberia. Johannes loved his piano, but without funds, he sold it to a Jewish buyer.

Upon his return from Lugansk, Johannes became an agronomist at the state collective farm machine-tractor station headquarters in Kotlyarevka. Machine-tractor stations, *mashinno-traktornaya stantsiya*, MTS, were state-owned stations that rented out heavy agricultural machinery, tractors or combines, to the surrounding collective farms. They supplied agronomists and skilled personnel to operate and repair equipment and to advise on farming.[37]

Alici recalled several episodes. 'One day two years after we arrived, my father said, "Come Alici, let's go and visit our piano." We walked to the home of the buyer and, tired, I was invited to rest in an adjoining room while my father visited with the owners. I had fallen into a light sleep when I was roused by the sound of someone playing. I peeked through the slightly open door and saw my father, tears streaming down his face, playing his onetime piano.'

To help ends meet, Alici's mother, Anna, took in sewing and mending, earning a little money to buy food. Her mother also rented out a room to summer vacationers from Donetsk. Alici recalled how a Jewish mother and her children came regularly to Kotlyarevka for its country air and lakeside. This mother always fed her children a breakfast of raw eggs beaten with sugar called 'googily.' Once the mother was away and the vacationing children ate Anna's breakfast of fried potatoes, which they loved. 'Oh no,' their mother said when they clamoured for a repeat of Anna's fare. Back to the healthy googily.

By 1934 Grandfather Braun and his family had lived in Steinbach, Manitoba, for ten years and Alici, barefoot, dreamed of owning a pair of shoes. She wrote them asking for a pair of shoes and was thrilled, when in 1935 or 1936 (she recalled, sixty-three years later) Grandfather Braun sent five dollars. It was enough for her father to go to a Torgsin store, buy rice, sugar, flour, other necessities, and a pair of shoes. Telling her story in German, Alici used the diminutive *meine Schuchen*, caressing the words, 'my little shoes.' Alici had no idea that her letter would complicate her life years later.

At first Johannes and his family attended church in Kotlyarevka and Alici recalled that the MB church in the village was functioning when they first moved, but closed at Christmas 1934.[38] First the building was assessed with higher and higher biweekly taxes (fifty roubles per member). Then the local preacher was accused of 'leading the people astray.' He was arrested and sentenced to a ten-year banishment.[39] The building became the administration office for Kolkhoz-Thaelmann MTS, the machine-tractor station where Johannes worked as an agronomist. A story is told about the key to the church. Kept by a deacon who died not long after the church was confiscated, rumour had it that the key was interred with him. Party officials from Selidovka threatened to dig up the deacon, whereupon the deacon's daughter handed over the key to the militia.[40]

For five years, from 1932 to 1937, the Braun children studied in German-language schools, the two youngest in the village and the three older ones – Alici, Hans, and Maria Braun – boarding at the Ebental Internat ten kilometres away. They returned home infrequently, but sometimes, Alici said, their father came to school to see them. As I listened to Alici talk about the school, I experienced one of those eureka moments. Her school must be the same one a friend in Toronto had described to me the previous winter. We had known Leo for thirty years but never discussed his school. I didn't know yet that Johannes's children had been at Ebental but knew Leo came from Memrik. After meeting Alici, I asked Leo if he remembered the Brauns. 'Yes,' he replied, 'Alici was an unusual name. She was beautiful!' Leo could not recall

Alici's brother Hans who was in his class, but he recalled the following incident.[41]

Local authorities conducted a house-to-house census in each village, and one of their questions was, 'Are you a believer?' The official census-taker arriving at Leo's door was a relative. When given the question, Leo's father, a deacon in the Mennonite church, answered, 'Yes.' Now came Leo's turn. He saw his father's pained expression (it was forbidden to instruct children in religion), saw him turn sadly away, so Leo murmured quietly, 'Yes.' Quickly the census taker coughed and said, 'Step outside with me a minute. I have work to discuss.' Outside Leo was informed, 'It's not good for you, nor good for your relatives.' So then the census-taker marked Leo's answer as no.

To avoid the Sunday, traditionally a holy day, in the autumn of 1929 the Soviets introduced a revolutionary calendar with a 5-day cycle. Six weeks equalled a month, with seventy-two weeks in a year. The missing 5 days (out of 365 days a year) were state holidays. By 1931, a 6-day week allowed people to have the same free day or day off, and by the summer 1940 the calendar had returned to a seven-day week.

During the revolutionary calendar, Leo recalled, if the free day fell on a Sunday, the children of believers were forbidden to leave the yard ('It was to intimidate us'). One of the villagers, called Lazybones, a Mennonite who had become a Party man, now swaggered about brandishing a pistol. His job was to spy on villagers and help to identify kulaks. His son also put on airs, going by Leo's home on the 'free' Sundays and taunting, 'Ha ha, you have to be fenced in.'

As we know, following the death of Kirov, the years after 1934 were ones of real terror, the *chistka*, when Yagoda (Iagoda), then Yezhov (Ezhov), heads of the Soviet secret police, acted as Stalin's executioners. Suddenly the smallest slip or mistake, smile or frown, any gesture could mean people were plotting treason. It seemed saboteurs and traitors were spilling milk, hexing crops, sabotaging agricultural production, coal production, factory output, and more. Mass arrests of innocent people became normal.

I will never forget first reading Wolfgang Leonard's book describing the show trials beginning in 1936 where diehard Bolsheviks were arrested and, confessing publicly to crimes they never committed, were executed.[42] Communists, especially Old Bolsheviks, were condemned for associating with priests, kulaks, tsarists, Civil War deserters, disenfranchised persons, or old regime police, or for hiring the offspring of pre-revolutionary elites.[43] Thousands were killed for 'counter-revolutionary' and state 'crimes.' Charges ranged from misgovernment (violation of government directives and policies), corruption, sabotage, violation of Party regulations, pursuing Trotskyite policies, to treason, and having connections with 'enemies of the people.'

'Who is next?' As Gerhard had told us, since anything could be overheard and misinterpreted, nobody laughed or told jokes. Informers were everywhere. Workmates denounced one another. Denounce someone and save yourself. In the local village councils or cells, people voted to arrest a denounced person or were themselves arrested. This was the terror of 1937 and 1938. Invariably it happened at night, and people lay awake listening for the sound of heavy boots and the knock on the door. As the grey dawn seeped through, they'd think, 'Tonight we've escaped.' Altogether in the Memrik settlement alone, 240 Mennonite men were forcefully removed from their homes, most never to appear again.[44]

It was almost Christmas 1937. Officially nobody mentioned the day, but quietly at night, behind blanketed windows, families remembered days when Christmas brought small gifts and home baking. Alici and Hans were at the Ebental Internat, nine-year-old-Heinz and eleven-year-old Anni were in the village school, and only thirteen-year-old Maria was home with their mother. She told us the story.

'The day before Christmas Eve, 23 December 1937, my father had a premonition of his impending arrest. That morning, as he was going out to work and my mother was washing the family laundry by hand, he said to her, "Anna, pack a bundle of food and some clothes. I'll be next."'

Anna packed some Zwieback and warm socks and sat down to do her usual sewing, supplementing her husband's salary that hardly covered food and the children's tuition. Suddenly, at midday, Maria's father was home. 'Quickly,' he urged, 'My things!' Then they came in and took her father.

Immediately after her husband was arrested and marched out of the house, Anna Braun phoned the school at Ebental. 'All men over age eighteen are being taken! Hide!'

In our hotel room meeting in Karaganda, Maria had told us her father was put on the list by a colleague agronomist, a Ukrainian – 'a terrible man,' Maria said, 'a man hated secretly by many people because he regularly reported innocent people.' Not that it helped, but there was a kind of rough justice for the man who denounced her father. Said Maria, 'He was dealt with by his own people, found in a field one day – eviscerated.'

When no news came of where the police had taken her husband, Anna searched for him in all the nearby prisons. She tried the prison in Stalino (Donetsk), in Krasnoarmeisk, and at the secret police and local militia buildings, both in the same yard on Sovetskaya Street in the nearby town of Selidovka. A high fence of wood slabs surrounded the prison yard and here she came to stand in line to ask about her husband. A woman in Anna's same predicament described how wives and mothers or sisters tried to find out where their men were detained:

You can't believe how difficult it was for us to find out. For days and nights in the wintertime, we stood in long queues in front of the information office to get even a fingertip of news. Mostly we received a churlish or snappish answer, or none at all. Then we tried to get some small item to our men in prison, sometimes just to get the signature of the recipient. Just to get the signature! It had to be a very small item that we were permitted to hand in, a few pieces of underwear at most, no foodstuffs. But often the items stayed inside, or, after we had been standing there for two or three days, they were not accepted, not even the smallest token of life.

It was pitiful to observe the many women standing in front of the high prison walls. Totally silent, pressed against each other in the minus twenty-five- to thirty-five-degree cold or in blizzards, patiently waiting until it would please the officials to speak to them, or not to.

Several times the prison officials set large chained dogs free upon the freezing, hungry, and waiting women. Then we would run a few streets over and sit ourselves down behind some fence or in a ditch and wait for the morning in order to try our luck again. Mostly we then would not get to the front of the line until evening and usually, without having found out anything except perhaps for having delivered a small parcel, deeply depressed, we would have to walk back home in wind or rain.... That's how it was until January 11, 1938. Then the men were all gone! All the prisons needed to be emptied. But where to? To the North?! Since then we know nothing.[45]

Anna appealed to the police. 'My husband had a pawnshop ticket in his pocket that we absolutely need. We pawned both of our gold wedding rings to buy food for the children. Without the pawn stub, how will I ever retrieve those rings?' She was told, 'No, he's not here.' But one day mysteriously the pawnshop stub was returned and her heart raced. Now she would know where he was. 'Where?' she asked. 'Where did it come from?' Nobody knew. For years she hoped for one word from or about her husband. For years she prayed for his safety and health. No news came.

Families of 'criminals' were seen as traitors, and after their father's arrest the Brauns lived in daily fear of being evicted. When that didn't happen, they turned to the question of survival. Without the father's earnings there was no money for tuition or board at Ebental Internat, so the eldest two children – Alici, seventeen, and Hans, sixteen – looked for work. Alici told me she had hoped to be a telephone operator, but although she had the education and requirements, as the daughter of a 'criminal' she was 'a security risk.' She was lucky the collective farm accepted her and Hans as labourers.

For a brief time thirteen-year-old Maria stayed in school, but without money for her meals, her mother brought Maria a pot of soup that soon got sour as it sat under her bed. Exasperated, not long after her father's arrest, she arrived home and announced, 'That's it! I'm quitting. I can't stand going back to school and no food. I'm finding a job.'

Initially local Mennonite men had been the Kotlyarevka farm's administrators, but these jobs were now entrusted to Party members only. It was not certain they would accept Maria, but she boasted she could work like an adult in whatever brigade she was placed by the farm manager. Getting the job, she handled pitchforks, mucked out barns, and dug or hoed. Each worker was required to put in two hundred workdays a year, and wages came out of any profits the collective showed at the end of that year, depending on the crop yield and all expenses being paid first. During harvest time the workday could extend to twenty hours with even the crippled and blind called on to help. When everything was tallied at year's end, Maria had earned her own food, but little else.

Peter Disappeared in Bashkiria

In a formal portrait of my mother's family, four sons and my mother are lined up in the back row and my grandfather Braun's second family is in front. My mother, at eighteen, her hair drawn back in a pouffe, is serious and formal in a long-sleeved dark dress. Ranged by age and height, her four brothers look similarly solemn. Johannes, twenty, wears a double-breasted jacket with shiny buttons, his school of commerce (*Commerzs-chule*) uniform. Next in age is Jakob (who changed his name to Jake Brown in Canada), a handsome youth of sixteen in a starched collar and suit. He also escaped in 1929. Then comes Peter, thirteen, who 'disappeared.' Last in line, my mother's youngest brother, Isaak, aged ten, stands rigidly focusing on the camera. My mother had said, 'Isaak was *verschleppt* because he was a preacher,' but nothing about Peter.

Having completed high school, at the age of twenty-one, my mother began teaching on an estate near the Dnieper River. The Felsenburg estate, owned by her Great-Uncle Heinrich and Aunt Wiens, was part of a vast tract, three thousand acres of steppe land once owned by a Russian nobleman who fell on hard times. It had been divided among the children of the new owner, who had erected grand houses and farm buildings. They had planted orchards, woodlots, and avenues of trees, as well as formal gardens. With hired workers and farm managers, they raised sheep and grain. I had interviewed my mother about her teaching career and, after she died, interviewed her pupil Anna Wiens Reimer from the estate.[46]

Felsenburg, the Wiens family estate, was situated fifty kilometres from the nearest large town. Mail was collected at a Russian village four kilometres away and a private telephone line connected three neighbouring homes owned by the Wiens's siblings. It was a quiet life, like in a Jane Austen novel, with the family providing its own entertainment in the evenings, the father of the house reading aloud from a book, the children and adults singing hymns as a daughter accompanied them on the harmonium. On Sundays, in a house church, Mr Wiens read a sermon and the family sang hymns. There were walks along a small river meandering along the front of the estate, and at times, travelling by horse and carriage or by train, there were trips for shopping or to chaperon children to high schools in the city of Alexandrovsk (today Zaporozhye).

My mother's brother Peter was performing his military service in the *Forstei*.[47] His camp being located near Felsenburg, he visited his sister on his days off. The better he got to know the estate family, the more frequently he came. In his dress uniform, highly polished boots, and 'captain's' hat, to the young Wiens daughters Peter Braun looked quite dashing. Selma in particular couldn't wait for him to stride down their tree-lined driveway. Sauntering beside the little river flowing through the estate, past flowerbeds, lilies, and lilac bushes, Selma and Peter fell in love.

For the first months of war in 1914, my mother recalled, life on the estate kept its quiet routine as if nothing had happened. Perhaps, as a first-year teacher, she was deeply absorbed in preparing her lessons, but she would have noticed that widely distributed German-language newspapers and periodicals were discontinued. Mennonites in Russia were normally very conscious of latent anti-German sentiment among the larger population.[48] Being pacifists and a German-speaking minority group, not wanting to be seen as unpatriotic, Mennonites (at their own expense) responded quickly to show loyalty to tsar and country.

During the Crimean War, Mennonites had provided assistance by hauling food to troops at the front and bringing back wounded soldiers for medical treatment. In 1914 thousands of men, and women as well, joined corps of Red Cross, and ambulance and nursing brigades (my father was part of an ambulance corps). Mennonites established hospital facilities and also collected money to assist soldiers' families – efforts that may have helped protect them. Did Peter Braun become a medical orderly? It seems he remained at his *Forstei* camp and was within reach of the Wiens's estate during the traumatic events that followed.

Hatred created by the hardships of the war was resulting in fierce pogroms in which German shops, banks, and factories were looted or burned, and civilians were lynched. In August 1914 the German embassy in St Petersburg (to be renamed Petrograd) was stormed and vandalized by angry mobs. The Wiens household was alarmed to hear talk about 'that German woman' Tsarina Alexandra being kept under the spell of peasant shaman Rasputin. In December 1916, Rasputin was murdered by Prince Yusupov of the Russian nobility, but this did not solve the country's economic problems or reverse losses on the battlefront. Thousands of soldiers were deserting; strikes, demonstrations, and violent protests broke out as people demanded bread and land. As the army and even the Petrograd garrison guarding the empress mutinied, pressed by the parliament (Duma), Tsar Nicholas was forced to abdicate in March 1917. On the Wiens estate, the father of the house speculated that the tsar would flee to his cousin in England, but it never happened. In time a provisional government under Prime Minister Kerensky replaced the monarchy, but as we know, Lenin made the provisional government a short history.

I had grown up hearing that Mennonites in Russia had self-funded schools, hospitals, organizations to care for the deaf, the elderly, widows, and orphans, and funded the purchase of new land to develop daughter settlements for landless families, and also about reforms that the state had implemented following the 1905 Revolution. An elected parliament initiated land reforms to open up areas like Siberia for ownership, modernized industry, and improved education. But farmers were still subdividing land among their children and creating a huge landless population. Anti-Jewish pogroms continued, and poverty grew in cities. After the emancipation of the serfs, many peasants had moved to work in city factories under dreadful conditions – squalor described in books by Fyodor Dostoyevsky. Much of the population was still illiterate, and the state regularly, often brutally, suppressed liberal political views. Hundreds of unarmed strikers at a gold mine were shot for their appeals in 1912. So when the First World War broke out, there was much latent anger at the state. Initially it was suppressed by renewed Russian patriotism, but the bungling of military leaders and the incompetence of the tsar broke the people's confidence in its leaders. Revolution followed.

At the Felsenburg estate, the elder Wiens daughters began to wear red neck scarves to show their solidarity with the winds of change, the revolutionary goals of freedom, improved civil rights, and peace. As they learned bitterly, Bolshevik methods used to achieve 'equality and liberty' were not as expected. In June 1917 my mother left Felsenburg at the end of the school term to spend summer at home. The real Revolution came when my mother was back in the Bashkir province. Those 'ten days that shook the world' began on 7 November when the Bolsheviks overthrew the provisional government. My mother talked about the terrible time when the jails were thrown open, bandits raced through the land, and people were murdered. By December all presses were government property and anti-Bolshevik literature was silenced. The country was in a state of anarchy because laws and institutions had disappeared. With Lenin vowing to abolish private ownership and wipe out capitalists, peasants violently seized land and houses, while town workers attacked mills and factories. Banks were nationalized, the stock market was eradicated, and revolutionary tribunals replaced courts.

My father had joined a non-combatant ambulance corps at the outbreak of war and was at the Turkish front, then part of the Ottoman Empire (an ally of Germany and Austria-Hungary). After the failure of the British and French Allies to knock the Ottoman Empire (now Turkey) out of the war in the spring of 1915 and open the Dardanelles to send in supplies (remember Gallipoli), Russia was left to fight alone. My father was stationed at Kars when, in February 1918, Russia suddenly withdrew from the war. The new Bolshevik rulers, Lenin in charge, had signed a separate armistice with Germany at Brest Litovsk. My father said he never knew the terms of the peace treaty until years later. After Lenin signed the peace treaty, my father with the military men at the front had immediately loaded trains with armaments and wounded and withdrawn in a disorganized retreat.

The country was a state in chaos. By terms of Lenin's treaty, Russia had to pay Germany indemnities and allow German forces to remain in areas they had been occupying or had conquered, especially in parts of Soviet Ukraine. Eight months later, the defeat of Germany annulled the peace treaty, but by then Russia was in a civil war. It was Whites against Reds, with anti-Bolshevik Russian generals leading a volunteer White Army to fight the Bolsheviks' Red Army organized by Trotsky.[49]

During this period of anarchy, my mother's family in Bashkiria suffered a pogrom. As my mother told the story many times, one evening a Russian neighbour, a member of the gentry, arrived at their house in Gorchakovo and asked to be hidden till he could escape on the next train. Her father knew the man well, had discussed ideas and played chess with him, and so he did not hesitate to help. He hid the aristocrat and very early in the morning drove him to the train station in Davlekanova. In the eyes of the revolutionaries, this act, assisting a bourgeois, was counter-revolutionary and her father would pay for it.

As she herself witnessed from a neighbour's window, eighty sleighs descended onto their yard and loaded up everything transportable from house, barn, and storage. Farm animals and goods, including clothing, food, and furniture, disappeared. Worse, my grandfather and two sons, Isaak and Jakob, badly beaten, were left for dead. The men were nursed back to health and neighbours stepped in to provide food, clothing, and other necessities. The pogrom so terrified my grandfather that, once he recovered, fearing a new assault, he decided to flee to the provincial capital, Ufa. He moved his young wife and their children into a house he owned in the railway town of nearby Davlekanova and left his recuperated sons to look after the farm. He took my mother along, as she said, to cook and look after him, but also to protect her from wanton marauders. Bandits had previously tried to rape both her and her stepmother. Her stepmother had cleverly told them she had a sexual disease. Forced to carry a light into the sheepfold and told to undress, my mother had escaped by dropping a lantern and burrowing under and becoming indistinguishable from the sheep. Unable to find her, cursing, the ruffians had left.

Her father's plan was to wait in Ufa until things quieted down, but finding the city full of fleeing estate owners, he heard, 'The Reds are here. Keep moving.' Across the Ural Mountains by train, they reached the Mennonite settlements in western Siberia and stayed with relatives. My mother, with only the clothes she was wearing, was a refugee. That's when she met my father.

My mother had left her teaching position at Felsenburg just in time.

Back near the Dnieper River, anarchist bandit leaders with peasant armies were targeting estates, murdering and raping owners, looting and burning homes. Greatly feared was Ukrainian revolutionary firebrand Nestor Makhno. Makhno was a man every Russian Mennonite child in Canada knew was close to the devil. Makhno's army of peasants stole Mennonite and German Colonist horses and buggies to mount with machine guns (seen in museums in Ukraine). Galloping around the countryside waving black flags, vowing vengeance, anarchist bandits sliced people up with sabres.

When I met my mother's pupil Anna Wiens Reimer, now a widow in Kingsville, Ontario, she told me that at Felsenburg her parents were on friendly terms with their workers from the surrounding community, that her father's life was once spared because a local revolutionary recognized him as the landowner who had given free grain and straw to the wives of soldiers drafted in the world war. Also during a crop failure her grandfather had provided bread for a whole year for villages on his property.[50] She also told me that my mother's brother Peter Braun, concerned for his sweetheart Selma (Anna's elder sister), had rushed to Felsenburg after his camp was closed.[51]

A kilometre away from the Wiens's home was the estate of her Aunt and Uncle H. Neufeld. Another kilometre farther along the river lived her Aunt and Uncle Goosen, and behind them was the estate of her Aunt and Uncle G. Neufeld. On 26 August 1918 the G. Neufelds were entertaining visitors when revolutionary bandits attacked. Their one daughter was able to save herself by escaping the house and hiding in the orchard, but the Neufeld parents and visitors were shot dead and their farm manager, ordered to hitch horses to the carriage beforehand, was also shot. Gunshots whizzing over her, terror-stricken all night, the next morning the daughter discovered the bodies and telephoned her relatives. The Wiens family, including beau Peter Braun, attended the funeral, five coffins overflowing the house.

Tragedy struck again. On the adjoining estate, Selma's recently widowed Aunt Goosen, with her six children, had moved 150 kilometres south to a safer place. Only two weeks after her brother's murder, she and her driver, returning for some belongings, were discovered lying in a field not 10 kilometres from her home, shot through the head. This funeral was held at Felsenburg.

Estate owners were the first targets of the revolutionaries, but massacres also took place in villages. The men in the village were usually slaughtered with sabres or shot, the women raped and houses burned.

Many homeless and orphans roamed from village to village trying to find work, food, and lodgings. Overwhelmed by the atrocities and coached by German Army officers who occupied the region after the treaty of Brest Litovsk, Anna Wiens's brothers had armed themselves, but the amateur defenders with German weapons were no match for Makhno's larger peasant armies. The Wiens family was in panic and, with the daily and nightly attacks, in early September the family fled south to hide in villages near the city of Alexandrovsk, the family divided among relatives willing to harbour them.

Peter Braun accompanied them to the city. I asked myself, after he was standing near his sweetheart at the coffins of her murdered uncles, aunts, friends, and faithful retainers, what would a twenty-two-year-old suitor do? Volunteer to join the White Army to fight the revolutionary bandits? My mother thought Peter tried to join the White militia. Trotsky's Red Army finally had stopped anarchist gangs like those of Makhno and turned to fighting the White Army. Reds against Whites, the Civil War was intense and lasted for several years. In southern Ukraine, battles raged, with local inhabitants never knowing which army was in control.

Over a two-year period some villages were occupied alternately a dozen times. Each time armies demanded food to be cooked, horses to be given up, and wounded or sick soldiers to be nursed and billeted in homes. These ill-clad soldiers, forced to fight and live in unreliable and unsanitary conditions, were often covered with typhus-carrying lice. Also, poor local peasants often robbed clothing and arms from soldiers slain on the field, thereby infecting themselves. Thus typhus spread and killed thousands of civilians as well as soldiers.

At some point Peter Braun was captured by the Red Army, but in the confusion of civil war he escaped. He had lost touch with the Wiens family, who, homeless for two years, were moving from one relative to the next, surviving by sleeping on floors, hoeing, milking cows, anything to earn food. Anna Wiens Reimer said she owned 'absolutely nothing,' no thread to patch a piece of clothing, no shoes, and wore only a thin, home-sewn cap to cover hair clipped short to ward off lice. She told of eating bread made of dust swept from the corners of barns, mixed with water and baked.[52]

Then came more tragedy. In 1920 Mrs Wiens became ill with typhus and, when her younger daughter, Katya, still attending a girls' high school in town, received the news of her mother's illness (not knowing that her mother had already died), the seventeen-year-old schoolgirl and her fiancé caught a ride with a driver. They were on a road to Melitopol when the wagon was attacked and all three were murdered. Robbed of their vehicle, horses, money, and clothing, they were left naked on a field, fed on by birds of carrion.[53]

News of the famine in Russia made world headlines and international and American relief agencies responded. The American Relief Administration, spending twenty million dollars, headed by Herbert Hoover, brought in trainloads of corn for grits, rice, lard, sugar, bread, milk, and cocoa, and set up soup kitchens. Seed grain, tractors, and farm equipment were brought in to help farmers once again grow food.[54] On a smaller scale, the American Mennonite Relief agency (which would become the MCC in 1922) legally set up soup kitchens to bring food to save thousands of Mennonite and Ukrainian lives in Mennonite settlements. A Mennonite described the arrival ('from our Brothers in the U.S.A.') in the Molochna settlement of American Fordson tractors, seed grain, Hershey chocolates, and diesel oil (from Holland Mennonites) that helped his family. Using cows to plough and seed fields, farming began again.[55] Not everyone had access to soup kitchens or donated seeds and embarrassed Soviets did not help to spread the news of foreign help. Later the Soviets would say the purpose of the food help was espionage.

Some time during the famine, Peter Braun found his sweetheart Selma Wiens working in Alexandrovsk (Zaporozhye). Without means, they decided to be married on 28 August 1921.[56] Peter and Selma moved to the village of Gorchakovo in Bashkiria, into the Braun parental house. Anna Wiens Reimer had told me that my grandfather had 'enticed' Peter and Selma to come to the farm by writing them 'such a nice letter' after they married. He had *begged* them, promising them half the farm. Living in poverty in the city, they had finally agreed. In 1924 the senior Brauns, with their four children, immigrated to Canada, leaving behind Peter and his family, as well as son Isaak and his family.

Why did Selma and Peter Braun not emigrate in 1924? Not only Peter's father, but also Selma's father and six siblings left for Canada that year. I asked Anna Wiens Reimer why Selma and Peter Braun did not come with her Wiens family, and she said that her father had entered their names, but when her brother tried to pick up their papers he was told applications could only be done in person. 'The authorities said, "Unless they are here, ready to travel, we don't give them."'

And why did they not come to Moscow? She thought they would and wondered why they had not. She then went on to say that some of her siblings had settled in Manitoba, as did my Braun grandparents. Years later in Canada, a sister in Manitoba had asked my Grandfather Braun why Peter and Selma were left behind. He would not answer. Anna said, 'We could only surmise that Peter and Selma had no money of their own, and no way of getting to Moscow for their papers.'

How could I discover what lay behind my grandfather's refusal to answer and, worse, a refusal to give a son funds to travel? My Uncle Henry in Abbotsford, a son of the second wife, had told me Grandfather Braun had sold heavy farm machinery, which the bandits were unable to remove from the barn in the 1919 pogrom. It paid for their passage, and they even had cash left over when they reached Canada.[57]

Anna thought Selma and Peter were forced to join a collective farm and that Peter became the farm manager. She emphasized they should have emigrated, that it was still possible to get exit visas till 1926, and that 'Peter was unhappy, as it was very risky to be the manager of these farms.'[58] When I asked why they didn't come in 1929 after my father urged the Braun brothers to join him, she again shook her head, 'Yes, why not?'

The situation on the Braun farm was no better than anywhere else. A letter written in January 1932 from Gorchakovo reported a bread shortage and lack of clothing. It ended with, a plea: 'If you have a heart for such wounded people as we are, then please send something.'[59]

Many times I had read and reread my grandfather's papers, sifting through sermon notes and poems, looking for any personal information. I found a buried anecdote Grandfather Braun wrote to illustrate what he called 'God's providence.' In one of his devotional talks for young people's meetings, he read a letter his daughter-in-law Selma had written in which she said her husband Peter, the 'collective farm secretary,' was in hiding, for snares had been set out for him. She and her children were 'living desperate lives somewhere in the Volga region.'

I went into town and wanted to see if I could find any grits for food for my children and myself, but I found nothing and very sad, I wanted to return home. Then I thought to myself, you should go to the post office once more. You have gone in vain so many times, but perhaps there will be something for you. And there it was, a letter from my sister in Grunthal, Manitoba, and a dollar inside, and from my brother in Ontario came five dollars. I don't know how I got out of the postal station, but suddenly I was on the street weeping tears of joy. And what did I do next? For a dollar I bought flour and I went home and baked, first for the children and then for myself, each a small loaf of bread.[60]

Since Torgsin shops (where Selma exchanged her hard currency for food) were closed by 1936, Selma's letter likely was sent around 1934 or 1935. For the next thirty years nobody knew if Peter, Selma, or their children were dead or alive, had been arrested, exiled, or killed.

The Preacher

Another missing brother was Isaak. How my mother knew her brother Isaak was arrested remains unknown. In searching through my parents' 'Russian letters,' I came across some from a Liesel Braun. Liesel, Liesel, who was Liesel? Liesel was Isaak's daughter. There they were in the 'Russian Letters' box, nineteen Soviet-stamped airmail letters from Liesel Braun. Coming from the Soviet Republic of Kazakhstan, they covered 1965 to 1982, written in German, in Gothic or Latin script. Liesel never revealed details about her father Isaak. Nothing in Grandfather Braun's papers either. No letters saved. You might think letters would flow during the Second World War when the Soviets were our allies. Not so. The Soviets had no intention of letting the world know what was happening in their forced labour camps, and who here wished to question our faith in 'Uncle Joe'? Even my Canadian uncle seemed proud of him. I was a passenger in my Uncle Henry's car just after the end of the Second World War. As we crossed the border from British Columbia into Washington State, Uncle Henry answered the customs control officer's 'Where were you born?' with 'Born in Russia. You know, Uncle Joe.' It sounded strange to me. The man my parents feared, that Joseph Stalin was Uncle Joe?

Liesel's first letter, dated 15 January 1965, with an address in the Alma Ata region, lamented the death of her mother and mentioned two brothers.

15 January 1965
My dear Tante Luise, it has long been my intention to send you a token to show we are alive. We wish you all much success and happiness in the New Year and good health. We also are healthy, except for my youngest little daughter who has the measles and was very ill for four days.... Since I have been left alone with the children, we often feel lonely and forsaken. Soon it will be two years since my husband deserted us and soon afterwards my mother died. Now I

have nobody to share sorrows and joys with me except my three dear children. Leni, the eldest, is fifteen. Kolya is eleven years old, and little Lieschen is eight. We live distant from my brother Viktor, five kilometres away. Yasha lives in the Urals. We have been without our Papa for a long time. 'Oh, my Papa!'

Please write back right away. If this little note reaches your hands safely, I will write more. My dear ones, I think of you so often.

PS This song is so precious to me, 'God does not forsake His own.'
I enclose three pictures of Mama's funeral.

In Liesel's letters after 1965, invariably one or another family member was ill and she constantly called upon God to help in her difficult situation. She was overjoyed when parcels with clothing arrived from Canada. After she received a large velour carpet, a rug typically hung on the wall, she had a photograph taken. Over the years, always poor, she wrote that her children finished school, went to work, and married. Her eldest daughter married a Volga German, and by 1982 they had three children. Her son Kolya spent two years in compulsory military service and was imprisoned for five years for engaging in religious activity. Liesel began to call him Nikolai when he married. Soon he had children. In poor health, Liesel retired from her job of bookkeeper at the age of fifty-two, three years before she was eligible for a pension. She had put in the required number of working years to be eligible for retirement, but after several illnesses and without a pension, her finances shaky, she asked for help. Eventually she moved in with her married daughter. By 1977 she had unsuccessfully applied three times to immigrate to Germany. In 1978 and 1979 she again failed to get Soviet permission to leave.

Among the letters from Kazakhstan, one letter was from Liesel's sister-in-law, wife of her brother Viktor, a thank-you letter for a parcel received. Viktor's family enjoyed music and both he and his wife had retired early for health reasons. When word came that Viktor was immigrating to Germany, my parents asked my father's brother Gerhard (in Germany since 1976) to keep a lookout for a Viktor Braun. One Sunday in 1980, visiting fellow *Umsiedler* (as the immigrants from the USSR were then called) at an Evangelical Baptist church built by the new arrivals in Bonn, Gerhard heard Viktor Braun's daughters singing a duet in the church. He reported that the family was in temporary accommodations and that two married daughters remained in the Soviet Union.

Viktor did not reply to a letter Gerhard sent after the Bonn meeting. After reading Gerhard's account of his meeting with Viktor's family in Bonn, I wrote to Viktor's last address in Bonn. The letter was returned, address unknown. Once more going through the letters in 1995, I noticed in a postcard of the church that Uncle Gerhard had visited in Bonn, the *Baptisten Brüdergemeinde* (Baptist Brethren). Someone in this church might know the Brauns. I wrote to the church asking that my enclosed letter to the Brauns be conveyed, and several months later a letter arrived from Viktor. They had received my letter and were interested in establishing ties. In this convoluted way a son of my mother's brother Isaak was rediscovered in July 1996. How much faster the process would have been with telephone cards, the Internet, and e-mail.

Journal, 18 July 1996
We have met Viktor and Greta Braun. We phoned from Amsterdam, where I had waited in the airport to meet up with Harvey arriving from Ukraine. We collected our rental car, phoned again to say we'd be late, and headed south at the amazing speeds of the Autobahn. 11:30 at night and we are checking our directions as we exit the superhighway at Bonn. Voilà, waving from the embankment at the turnout road, we see a young couple beside a parked car, 'We're the Brauns!' The granddaughter of my verschleppt *Uncle Isaak Braun and her husband pilot us to her parents' apartment.*

'We've been waiting for you!' The woman sounds like our Maria Braun. Grey hair pulled back tightly in the typical Mennonite chignon, wearing a print housedress and broadly smiling, Greta sweeps us up a few stairs into their second-floor apartment. A somewhat bent, older man with a white pompadour and an uncanny resemblance to my eldest brother emerges from a bedroom – my cousin Viktor. We will stay with the Brauns four nights.

Viktor and Greta live in a planned community of low-rise apartment houses built for ethnic German emigrants from Russia fifteen years earlier. Viktor and Greta Braun moved to this complex after they left temporary housing. Viktor uses a cane, but on Sunday morning we walk with him and Greta the short distance to their church – the same Baptisten Brüdergemeinde Uncle Gerhard attended in 1980. The congregation is made up of what Germans call Russlands' Deutsche or Aussiedler. Many, like the Brauns, have lived in Germany for over a decade, and their church music has acquired a German pop music or Schlager beat. Otherwise the service is similar to Mennonite church services I knew as a child. There was always an opening session devoted to spontaneous prayers, both women and men taking turns, emotional prayers giving thanks or making pleas. The missionary reports and German sermon also were similar. As I remembered, here too women sit on one side of the aisle and men on the other. A few younger families break that pattern. The front rows are filled with blond, neatly dressed children. There is a baby's crying room at the side of the church and a balcony at the back seats the teenaged youth.

After lunch the children and grandchildren arrive. Before and after a traditional Sunday mid-afternoon meal (in Mennonite culture called Faspah) of cold cuts, pastries, and sweets, we talk about each other's lives. We ask countless questions about their life in the USSR and feel an immediate kinship. Viktor has some difficulty speaking because of his paralysis, but he and I spend most of Monday discussing his father's and his own life. Greta is the more colourful storyteller, but everyone feels it is very important for Viktor to tell his story himself. We are his first 'Braun' relatives from the West. The children add details about their life in Central Asia, about growing up labelled Fascists. They say their grandmother raised them because their parents came home exhausted from working all day on the collective farm vineyards. They mention a son agitating for the Helsinki Accord's promised freedoms and having to bury all the evidence of his activities to prevent his father from being arrested. They explain the frequent house searches. 'We were always "different" because we did not join Young Pioneers or Komsomols.' They lived in constant fear of discrimination and arrest.

The Soviet-born children of my cousin Viktor say they are in a no-man's land; no place is 'home.' In the USSR they were the Nemtsy, the hated Germans, and were discriminated against, and they longed to go 'home' to Germany. But when they got here, they were told they were Russians, unwelcome immigrants. They know little about Mennonites, do not distinguish between their ancestors and the Colonists, the German (Catholic, Lutheran) settlers of Imperial Russia. 'We were all just Germans.' I wonder when this happened, as my parents had always distinguished between our Dutch-background Mennonites [Menniste] and ethnic Germans [Dietsche].

We discuss present-day German class-consciousness. The children of Greta and Viktor Braun who have lived in Germany almost fifteen years want to be 'real Germans.' They stress that they were returning to the 'homeland.' Most have an accent-free speech. One daughter has pointedly joined a non-immigrant church, and another speaks no Russian with her children. To me these sentiments are foreign. Although raised speaking German, my family never viewed Germany as our 'homeland.' When I think on it, my generation acculturated slowly. In Abbotsford, in that somewhat transplanted Russian Mennonite village, we had our own school, German, then English-language churches and social groups made up almost entirely of Mennonites. My generation married fellow Mennonites. The next generation assimilated – forgot German, attended non-Mennonite churches, were non-church-goers, and most often married non-Mennonites. Innumerable immigrant groups had followed this model, had allowed grandparents to associate with neighbours who spoke their language while their grandchildren grew up in the local culture. For the Brauns, scattered in the city, acculturation was meant to accelerate.

Living under Communism, the Brauns still had the church and home traditions of pre-revolutionary Russian Mennonites. Not knowing their Mennonite past, they used generic words like Christian traditions. But they seemed like people we had grown up with in Canada in our immigrant Russian Mennonite communities. We thought they had our Russian Mennonite ways, our sense of humour. Being away from 'Mennonite influence' for almost seventy years of Communism, we ask, how is that? Oh, it was their mothers, they say, Viktor's mother Hermine, as well as his mother-in-law, Agatha Unrau, the grandmothers raised in Mennonite homes before the Revolution had influenced the children. These grandmothers had kept their traditions and religion (clandestinely), had instilled the beliefs and influenced the habits of their grandchildren. These women gave them a moral yardstick, a sense of responsibility for a wider world, a way of meeting adversity. We nodded. It sounded familiar. The Brauns seemed to have a strong sense of themselves. Perhaps the Braun mothers' faith provided easy answers: God has a plan. Your suffering is for some reason beyond your comprehension, but the Higher Being has a purpose for you. You believe this and learn to separate yourself from the destroying hate, anger, and cynicism into which a totalitarian state could lead. You preserve your humanity.

Viktor shows us a small family photograph of our Braun grandparents he has photocopied from a book written by a German Mennonite historian. He points to a family portrait that I recognize as the same one in my mother's collection.

'That's my father Isaak, that shorn boy at the end of the row. But that young woman in the back, who is she? And that man in the uniform, how did he get in there?'

I am surprised. The 'young woman' is my mother, his father's sister. The 'man in the uniform' is his father's eldest brother, our Uncle Johannes. How doesn't he know?

'I got the photograph from a book.'

Viktor was two when our Grandfather Braun emigrated to Canada and six when my parents left. He never saw his Uncle Johannes. Did his mother burn incriminating family documents and photographs, knowing it would be too easy for a child inadvertently to let out a confidence that a grandparent was a so-called kulak? That a parent had a 'capitalist' sister abroad? That a father attended a bourgeois school?

I asked Viktor what he knew about our other uncle, the Peter Braun whose family had also lived in the Gorchakovo house and whom he should remember. 'Our Uncle Peter was a mayor and a communist. That's why he escaped.'

'Communist? Mayor? Escaped? When? Where? The charges seemed implausible, but what did I know about Peter Braun? My mother thought her brother Peter had been in the White Army. Being a communist seemed unlikely, but who knew how people survived?'

We moved to another topic. At one point Greta said, 'Stop. Play something, Viktor.' He stood up holding a six-key harmonica in shaking hands and played a hymn.

The following day the family took us on a boat excursion up the Rhine. On the deck of the long riverboat gliding past ancient castles and towns or hills combed with green grapevines, Viktor continued his story. He wanted someone 'in America' to be interested. All those years when they lived in Kazakhstan they had thought about those relatives lucky enough to emigrate before 1930. They had dreamed of one day perhaps meeting them, or someone who would remember his father. And we were the fortunate ones, the ones to whom he gave this gift, his life story.

And so I learned about Isaak Braun. Isaak had been beaten up with his father and brother when the anarchist bandits plundered their farm and left the men for dead. A year later, Isaak's thoughts had turned to romance. A Dietrich Hein family owned a store in town as well as a farm in an outlying Mennonite village. Prominent in church and community affairs, the family also boasted seven lovely daughters. Isaak fell in love with Hermine, third-youngest of the daughters. Viktor said his parents had told their children nothing about their growing up or courtship, but I had a book of memoirs written by Mennonites who had emigrated from the area where my mother grew up, my *Ufa* book that included photographs. One picture was of the Hein children in the Davlekanova Mennonite High School orchestra. Viktor said his father played several instruments and sang in the church choir. Who knows how long he had his eye on her – perhaps already in school where she sang in the choir, or as a young actress in a literary evening drama production. Following the Civil War, in 1921, Isaak and Hermine married, she twenty, he two years older. My Uncle Henry in Canada recalled the young couple moving in with the Braun parents in the home in Gorchakovo, taking over the spare or summer room. Henry remembered Isaak saying, 'She's an angel. He was so in love!' Then he added, 'One day Hermine's sister came to collect the young wife after a falling out.

Did Isaak ever have his share of making amends with his angel!' Having met my step-grandmother and Hermine's mother-in-law, I could imagine a few difficulties, a few tempests.[61]

Viktor did not know why his father stayed on the farm when Grandfather and his second family immigrated. I asked if perhaps it was that during the more relaxed period of NEP, a theological preacher-training school and a new Bible school had opened in Davlekanova. A postcard Isaak had written my father (in my parents' papers) indicated that Isaak Braun might have been enrolled in this school. The postcard stated Isaak had paid teacher (*Lehrer*) Karl Friedrichsen fifty roubles and would pay a further fifteen roubles. Karl Friedrichsen was the director of the Davlekanova Bible School operating 1923 to 1926 and graduating three men. Was Isaak one of the students at the school and did my father help pay his tuition?[62] Viktor did not know.

Viktor was proud that his father graduated from the Davlekanova High School. Built by Mennonites, progressive for its day, the school Harvey and I would see in 2001 on our trans-Siberian trip was co-educational and offered academic and religious subjects as well as the arts. Asked about the attempt to go to Moscow, Viktor said they (as well as his mother's two sisters) were stopped and turned back, but that an uncle, Jakob Hein, made it. The uncle, arrested, was taken to the notorious Lubyanka and then the fearsome Butyrki prison where prisoners were tortured to force them to promise to return home. The uncle returned, but seen as an agitator for emigration, was rearrested and tortured to death in August 1931.[63]

When Isaak's family was turned back, they dared not go to rural Gorchakovo to be declared kulaks. 'Get out!' [*Skoro davai!*] Isaak found an office job in Davlekanova where (my uncle Henry in Abbotsford stated) Grandfather Braun had owned a stone house. Like others, Isaak Braun hoped a reversal of policy would allow them to emigrate. Viktor chuckled recalling an aunt running up excitedly, 'Have you heard the news? They're letting us go! They've promised! On 32 May we can go! Isn't it wonderful?'

In my red *Ufa* book a memoirist stated that a thousand people in cattle cars left the Davlekanova station, headed for exile in 1931. The victims were singing all verses of 'Nearer My God to Thee.'[64] Viktor did not know if his parents witnessed the kulak deportation trains, but to escape that fate, his father decided to move south to Samara (Kuibyshev, Russia) along the Volga River. Here Isaak was a caretaker of a technical school.

One day when his father was out of town (Viktor was in grade two), suddenly his mother Hermine noticed a cloud of dense black smoke rising from the technical school. Not long afterward, the police were at her rooms demanding, 'Where is your husband?"

'He went to buy supplies today.'

'Aha. Well, you are all under house arrest. Don't leave.'

Viktor recalled his mother praying anxiously, mother and children waiting for Isaak's return, and when he arrived late at night all cheerful, they knew the police had not yet spoken to him. Upon hearing news of the fire, Isaak made a fast decision.

'Pack! I think I know what this is. I'd never get a fair hearing. Quickly, Hermine, we can still catch the last train. Children, get dressed. We're walking.'

The train took them south towards the Ukrainian steppe where they hoped to disappear as newly important proletariats, *workers*. This move took them deep into the cradle of Mennonite settlements where Braun ancestors and co-religionists had pioneered. We know it was an area of the worst famine that the country had known, but it also was the area of Stalin's hydroelectrical dream of greatness. Central to Soviet industrialization was the Dneprostroi dam being built across the Dnieper River at the city of Zaporozhye (formerly Alexandrovsk).

Our Braun family left the train before they reached the mighty dam, deciding to look for work in the village of New York along the banks of the Krivoy Torets River. Named by Count Ignatieff's American wife, New York was one of seven Mennonite villages of a settlement, established on land bought by the Old or Khortitsa Mennonite Colony from Count Ignatieff in 1888. In this daughter settlement, Mennonite industrialists had built factories and steam mills employing hundreds of workers before the Revolution.[65] Here Isaak found work as a bookkeeper and the children attended school.

Gertrud Penner, a child in New York in the 1930s, possibly one of Viktor and Liesel's playmates, described the two large factories built by Mennonite industrialists Niebuhr and Unger. Located next to a forest, the Unger factory produced bricks and the J.G. Niebuhr factory manufactured farm implements (hay mowers, threshing machines, steam engines, etc.). The Brauns may have lived in the row housing Niebuhr had built for his workers. A brick sidewalk ran beside the wall of the Niebuhr factory leading to the living quarters where each home was equipped with a stall for the workers' cow or coal supply and a cellar for potatoes. Everyone fetched water from a tap at the centre of the village, the pipe insulated in winter by horse manure to keep it from freezing. Children played in a common courtyard and in summer gathered at the pond (*dreng*), a stream choked with grasses and scum, full of beetles and dragonflies, mud oozing between toes. In winter they slid down a long hill.[66] In 2009 we found a cemetery at the top of this hill.

Even in New York, Isaak Braun felt unsafe. He decided living in a large city ensured greater anonymity and moved his family to the outskirts of Zaporozhye, where thousands of foreigners from around the world – Americans, Germans, and other foreign experts – were still building and being shown the mighty hydroelectrical power station Dneprostroi. Then the largest dam in the world, it was built with the help of master American dam-builder Colonel Hugh L. Cooper (a detail not often mentioned in Soviet histories). Begun in 1927, the completion of the dam was celebrated on 10 October 1932 when four thousand foreigners were brought in to marvel at this Soviet achievement.

Mennonites living in the area wrote to relatives in Canada that the city had been transformed into a Potemkin village with stores suddenly stocked with food and goods nobody had seen for years. 'There was meat, sugar and white bread etc., plentiful supplies of everything,' but available only for the guests. In horse-drawn wagons filled with straw, school children were sent from over one hundred kilometres away to see the magnificent dam. Little schoolgirls were in awe, seeing stylish foreign women in high-heeled boots and fur coats. One little Frieda remembered years later that she had received a precious box picturing Prince Albert and a towel so soft she could feel it almost to this day.[67] At the same time other letters reported what the international press did not see, a family's poverty so great, they feared, if no help arrived, parents and six children would starve. A dollar could buy thirty pounds of grits and some flour. Could relatives please help? 'Mama has gone gleaning again, finding nests where mice have collected barley and she has collected several pud…. When two or three people get together, all they talk about is food.'[68]

The Brauns moved to Kichkas, formerly the Mennonite village of Einlage, a suburb of Zaporozhye. Many foreign engineers stayed on to supervise the operation of the dam, and local people could find work, women in households and men in construction and operation of the dam or in factories and related industrial projects, anything having to do with the massive facility. The Brauns may have moved here because there were many jobs, but also because it still had an active Mennonite church and a group of fellow believers – including the former Davlekanova Bible School teacher Karl Friedrichsen.[69] Isaak again became a bookkeeper. Likely it was Viktor who had to get up early and rush to stand in line at the bakery to get any bread, to race past the blacksmith shop and old factories that produced carriages, buggies, and wagons before the Revolution, factories once owned by Mennonites Braun and Unger.

During the worst of the famine (1932–3), like other skinny children, the Brauns hunted field mice and waited for spring when tender shoots of weeds emerged. Perhaps they robbed bird nests and climbed acacia trees to eat blossoms to reduce their hunger. Everywhere people were trying to hide food. Possibly Isaak's family received money from Canada. At that time the Soviets tolerated foreign money coming in, not because it saved lives but because it helped the state to buy products abroad. Through the Torgsin stores, where people bartered their valuables for food, the Soviets made a profit of 6 million roubles in 1931, 49.2 million roubles in 1932, and 106.3 million roubles in 1933.[70]

By 1935 harvests had improved and, with Isaak's salary, Hermine could buy a kitchen pot. In 1936 came another good harvest and the Soviets introduced Father Frost (similar to Santa Claus) with a trimmed tree as a New Year's celebration to substitute for Christmas. Isaak's family did not adopt Father Frost, but secretly, with several other Mennonite Brethren families in Kichkas, met for church services where Isaak preached. By day he worked downtown in an office and felt somewhat safer because (his son Viktor stated) people assumed from his name 'Isaak' and his appearance that he was a Jew. Many early Bolsheviks and Stalin's closest associates were Jews. Also the Soviets did not see Jews as 'counter-revolutionary enemies' at that time, nor were Jews specifically targeted like Poles and Germans during the Great Terror of 1937 and 1938.[71]

But to be a preacher was to be a marked man. By 1935 churches had been turned into recreation centres, dance halls, or grain warehouses. Preachers, priests, rabbis, mullahs, deacons, choir leaders, and religious workers of all faiths had disappeared in great numbers. Church members were being registered and preachers, named 'cultural servants,' were disenfranchised and deprived of a food ration card. In order to keep food ration cards, many preachers resigned their positions, wives of clerics divorced their husbands, and children 'divorced' their parents.[72] Benjamin Pinkus documented that 1936 was a time when the Soviets embarked on a defamation campaign against *German* clergy particularly – Mennonite, Protestant, and Catholic.[73] Your religion and ethnic classification (German) decided your fate. All contacts between Soviet Germans and the outside were stopped – newspapers, journals, or letters abroad.

After hearing Viktor's story, I read a memoir describing an arrest in Kichkas. Johann Rempel, a Mennonite, former schoolteacher, and teacher, disenfranchised because he preached, was arrested in 1934 but released after three weeks and warned not to preach again. With the agreement of his family, when requested to perform weddings or funerals, he nevertheless went to the surrounding villages and met with local Mennonites in the barn of an elderly couple. On Easter Monday, 1935, he spoke in the Mennonite church in a village across the Dneprostroi dam and saw the police sitting at the back. They followed him home. The police told the wife and children to stand against the wall, made a cursory search of the house, and read out a warrant for Rempel's arrest. Turning to the elder sons they asked, 'Do you agree with your father?' When the boys said they did, the police warned, 'Then you'll end up like him. We have the power to determine your fate. Your God can do nothing about it.' As the police had predicted, Rempel's four sons were arrested in subsequent years, in 1937, 1938, and 1941.

Rempel's wife was allowed to pack some underwear, a cup, dish, and spoon, with a bit of money into a bundle, and the 'criminal' was escorted outside. Nobody slept after their father's arrest, but son Hans had to be at work at a locksmith's early in the morning. He walked the five kilometres to the locksmith's workshop and arrived before anyone else at six. The shop boss, a Bolshevik Party man, sat down beside him on the bench. 'They took your father last night?'

'Yes.' The boy was surprised he knew.

'Do you know why he was arrested?'

The boy shook his head.

'Well,' said the boss, 'your family is German and you're Christians. We know that you are not criminals. You cannot do anything about the fact that you are Germans, but it's a different case with your religion.'

This boss then protected the son and other Mennonite young people in the workshop as best he could, allowing them to continue their jobs even though children of a criminal often were denied the right to work.[74]

Franz Wall, former director of the Mennonite hospital in Muntau (in present Molochansk and still functioning in 2009), was the first person in Isaak's church group to be arrested, on 6 April 1936.[75] Isaak Braun was arrested in the fall of the same year. With six other men from their home church he was charged with illegally counselling children not to join Pioneer and Komsomol clubs. Why did his children not wear the red Pioneer scarf? Atypically, Viktor's father, Isaak Braun, was able to tell about his trial in 1936. After Isaak's arrest, a troika panel had interrogated him and six other men accused of participating in anti-socialist activities. Night after night the prisoners were interrogated to get them to confess to false charges. Thrown into a cell, up to sixty men had to stand day and night in the foul damp as their feet swelled. One uncovered and overflowing latrine bucket sat in a corner. Sleeping during the day was forbidden and food consisted of perhaps a cupful of watery soup or slop and a tiny chunk of bread. Almost always at night, separately, prisoners were called out and questioned in a spare room under strong lights. Those who did not confess were threatened with harm to their families or with being taken downstairs to Room 00, the torture room. Sometimes fingers were broken, fingernails pulled off, and with every denial after countless questions came the interrogator's 'Ready to sign now?'[76]

Pressured to sign a blank piece of paper, a person could discover the space above his signature had later been filled in and he had confessed that all spirituality was a swindle, that all religion was a fable, and that he as a priest, cleric, or preacher had been lying to his parishioners. Often, when he saw what was signed, a man was driven half crazy with remorse and grief. Or a man could faint, be dragged out, and wake to see his signature on a confession.[77] Daniel Siemens, a preacher from Michaelsburg (a village where Isaak's family lived after Kichkas) survived this treatment to describe his ordeal. Was my uncle the Braun he mentioned?

We were all taken into an examination room and told that we had to fill a page describing how we had plotted to overthrow the Soviet government and to name the people who had been in the conspiracy with us. Anyone who refused to obey was beaten with a metal rod, the kind that is used as a wagon rod. It was rolled up in paper. One colleague was beaten so badly that his back was all blue. On the third day, blood gushing out of his mouth and nose, he died.

I myself filled several pages and made a huge list of names of fellow conspirators and handed in the papers. As a result I was not beaten but was declared to be a political criminal. Another colleague, Braun, was so upset by the whole process that he went mad and had to be taken to the mental institution and then disappeared. The government wrote to the village officials and told them how many criminals they were obliged to arrest in each village, and if the local officials did not meet the quota, they themselves were arrested. In this way several villagers disappeared every night.[78]

A Mennonite from Gnadenfeld, a Molochna village, charged with belonging to a counter-revolutionary organization working to assist Hitler, over a lengthy period of interrogations and threats was asked to name fellow conspirators.[79] One torture method was to place prisoners in cubicles so small that they were unable to sit or move, but stood, often on gravel or corn kernels, with arms at their sides until, legs hugely swollen, they became unconscious or agreed to sign untrue confessions.

Not knowing what was transpiring inside the prison, Isaak Braun's family waited for six months for a trial date. Then aged fourteen, Viktor recalled what his father had told them. Each arrested man was allowed one goodman, a type of lawyer, to speak for him. A witness had to appear in person to testify against the prisoner. One by one, his father's friends stood before a table covered in a red cloth where the three judges read out charges.

'Jakob Klassen, under Article 56, section 10, you are charged with counter-revolutionary activity … Article 56, section 11 … Article 54, section 10 …'

Prison sentences of two, three, five, and eight years were handed out before it was Isaak's turn. The procurator or judge turned to a German-speaking witness and asked him, 'Can you identify the prisoner?'

'Yes, I can.'

'Tell us who he is.'

'His name is Wall.'

'Wall? This man standing before you is Comrade Wall?'

'Yes.'

The procurator threw up his hands, 'Let him go! That man,' he said, pointing to Isaak Braun and looking at the witness, 'is not Wall!'

Isaak collapsed. And when he returned home, his family gasped but thanked God.

But Isaak was not the same man. This thirty-seven-year-old was a broken man whose eyes darted to the door with the slightest noise. His children watched in silent dread as he paced up and down the room, repeatedly went to the washbasin and began washing his hands, first with cold water, then with hot water, and then paced the floor.

Arrests continued. Isaak Braun was freed but lived in daily fear of rearrest. A knock on the door at night could be the feared secret police, but sometimes the knock on the window was, 'Come quickly. The store is receiving some fabric. Let's get in line.'

The family had to eat. Viktor said God answered their prayers when an old friend from New York village, Martens, suggested, 'Let's work on a collective farm. That will be better for you in your nervous condition.'

The two men walked the 120 kilometres downstream on the east side (or left bank) of the Dnieper River to the village of Mikhailovka (formerly Michaelsburg), an area accessible only by boat or on foot. The village was named after Russian Grand Duke Michael in a district (then called Fürstenland) of Taurida province. Here six Mennonite villages had emerged, Michaelsburg being the largest. Many early settlers in Fürstenland (those renting land) had immigrated to North America in the 1870s. A thousand had found homes on the West Reserve of Manitoba. In the early 1920s, a further exodus to Canada removed most of the remaining Fürstenland Mennonites, so that in the spring of 1937, when Isaak Braun and Martens arrived at the Engels Collective Farm, only fourteen Mennonite families were among the mainly Polish-Germans from Volynia.

The existing collective members had to vote on their applications. Martens appeared before the assembly first. A burly man, he looked a strong worker. 'I can work. My wife can help. We have three preschool children.' They voted yes. Isaak was anxious. He looked frail. What if they wouldn't want him?

'My name is Braun and I can work. My wife can work. My son is as tall as I am and my daughter is almost as tall as my wife. Our youngest boy goes to school.'

They voted yes.

Returning to Kichkas, the men collected their families, bundled their few possessions, and took the riverboat down the Dnieper, walking the last part. When they arrived, carrying their belongings, the farm manager said they could ask if anyone would share a house or rooms with them. Down the village row they went until they got to a mud-brick hut of two rooms inhabited by a Widow Unrau and her two children. She had compassion for this family from the city. 'Come in. I'll give you one of my rooms.'

The widow's daughter Greta Unrau later married Viktor Braun and at our Bonn meeting she confided her mother had misgivings, thinking the Brauns were a higher class: 'Listen to them talking High German to each other. And we're Plautdietsch. They might look down on us.' Soon, however, Widow Unrau had sifted flour and baked the traditional scones or biscuits (*Schnettje*) to feed the hungry Brauns. She even sent her dark-haired daughter Greta to fetch a sack of dried fruits from the rafters.

'We had no clothes then,' Greta recalled. 'Everything was ragged and worn out. When your dress was washed, you had to stay indoors till it dried because you had nothing else to wear. We all went barefoot.'

To provide some clothing for winter, after a long day on the farm, a mother would card and spin wool and, allowed to keep a third of her finished product, she might knit socks, stockings, caps, or sweaters – if she had needles. Then too she might try to sell these items for food, as collective farm wages were paid only at the end of a year.

The Braun children – Viktor fourteen, Liesel thirteen, and Yasha eleven – attended school but during school holidays worked with their mother, Hermine, in the fields. There was hoeing and weeding, and especially at harvest time all were required to work from sunup to sundown, the six-day week. They were happy when school began in September. I doubt if these children dared to challenge authorities, as told in some accounts. When Mennonite children got to the second verse of the 'International' and were supposed to sing, '*Kein Gott, kein Kaiser, kein Tribun*' (no God, no kaiser, no tribune) they remained silent or sang '*Ein (a) Gott*' instead of '*Kein Gott.*'[80]

Schoolchildren were solicited to inform on their parents or anyone else who said anything anti-Soviet. The Soviet child's martyr hero was eleven-year-old Pavel Morozov who turned in his father for saving some food for his pregnant mother. Pavel was killed by his neighbours. Innocently, children could betray parents. Such was the case of Nina. The teacher in nine-year-old Nina's school was describing Nazi Germany's starving children, comparing them to the evil tsarist days when only the nobility had sugar. Repeating this statement at home, Nina's mother laughed, saying there was so much sugar in the tsarist times that she had to be careful not to get too fat. Nina challenged the teacher, repeating her mother's words, and immediately her mother was pulled in for cross-examination. A bloody face, missing two front teeth, she was fortunate to come home at all.[81]

Isaak had kept his children out of the communist children's clubs. As I read through memoir accounts in Mennonite newspapers, I wondered if other Mennonite children joined the Octobrists (ages six to ten), Pioneers (ages ten to fifteen), and Komsomols (over fifteen years of age). Pioneer clubs had replaced the discredited Boy and Girl Scout organizations. Not only had Scoutmasters and Scouts fought in the White

Army against the Bolsheviks, but also the club taught Christian principles. The movement had been eradicated, but the communist organizations followed Scout methods, using rules, pledges, badges of merit and rank, awards, flag ceremonies, songs, sports, games, field trips, bonfires, festivals, marches, and moral education. Young Octobrists wore scarves pinned with a tiny gold picture of baby Vladimir Lenin on a ruby oval, and the older children wore red scarves tied like cowboy bandanas over white Pioneer blouses or shirts. Membership was optional, yet most children in the Soviet Union joined the clubs, and some Mennonites who attended Soviet schools in the 1930s and immigrated to Canada after the Second World War said they had begged to become Pioneers. All remembered – like Viktor and Greta Braun – being barefoot and being given food in school only if they were Pioneers.

Would I find Mennonite children wearing red neckerchiefs among the school group pictures printed in Mennonite newspapers? In photos of the Mennonite village of Osterwick, near Zaporozhye, I saw a dark photograph taken in 1932 or 1933, showing a grade one class, the children barefoot and boys wearing caps. One student remembered that the teacher was 'strict and taught manners besides reading and writing. He taught us to greet adults politely and to take off our hats.'[82] Another photo of an Osterwick kindergarten class in 1937 showed four female teachers and thirty-eight children (two toddlers on teachers' laps) neatly dressed, but barefoot. None wore scarves.[83] Another photo from 1937 showed an older class of seven- to eight-year-olds. Out of twenty-one pupils, two girls seated on the ground wore shoes, but the ones on a bench and standing behind were barefoot. No Pioneer ties.[84]

In 1938 (same teacher, Katya Ivanovna Kasdorf, and same group, with some additions), thirteen out of twenty-six wore sailor suits, but no Octobrist or Pioneer scarves. In that photograph many children held flowers – traditionally brought to a teacher on the first day of school in September. Why the sailor suits? These were not Octobrist or Pioneer outfits, so perhaps a shipment of 'clothes' arrived and the mothers lined up early to buy whatever came in. Rempel wrote that of these twenty-eight children, eighteen were repatriated to the USSR in 1945 – presumably having trekked to Germany with the occupation army in 1943 – 'and who knows if they are still alive.'[85] In a grade six class of thirty-one students in the Mennonite village of Liebenau, in May 1939, nine Pioneer scarves are visible – on almost a quarter of the class. Were Pioneers becoming accepted, or had non-Mennonites moved into traditional Mennonite villages (seven names are non-Mennonite)?[86] A photo of a school outing of a grade six Osterwick class in May 1941 (prior to the German occupation) shows twenty girls and four boys (why so few?) with no scarves visible. The writer suggests that Mennonite and Ukrainian children got along well. She writes, 'It was not right that my good Russian friend [Ukrainian?] Daria Litvinova (in the photo) was not able to attend school [after the occupation]. She was a good student and many of us were friends with her.'[87]

As the Braun children attended school at the Engels Collective Farm in Michailovka, Isaak Braun had become the bookkeeper. The farm cultivated grains, barley, and wheat, as well as cotton, and large patches of watermelons to sell at the Dnieper harbour. It also boasted an oil extraction plant. As was standard in a collective farm organization, a farm manager assigned work brigades: one worker brigade to hoe the fields, so many rows to be done each day; a milkmaid brigade to look after the calves, yet another to tend the chickens or pigs. Woe to any child looking after animals if a pig or calf escaped its pen.

The only holidays were the November Anniversary of the Revolution and May Day, with its bands and parades. On all other days, one hour was allowed for lunch, when Hermine would rush home to prepare something for supper or look after household chores. Men and women worked at different jobs and the family rarely had time together except at night when they worked their small garden plots, if they had a plot. The farm administration granted the Brauns a building plot and, after long hours in the sun on the cotton field, they hand-made mud bricks that formed walls of their new home. Brick by brick, a small two-room building took shape. Rafters supported a roof, and straw was laid over the rafters. The Braun family had a home.

But this was 1937. On 4 November a Mennonite neighbour from Kichkas, Franz Thiessen, aged forty-five, manager of the Soviet butter factory Insnab (a store selling food products only to foreign workers in the hydroelectrical industry), was arrested as a spy. His eighteen-year-old son (who survived to tell the story) was arrested as an 'agitator for a counter-revolutionary organization' in the Engels Factory School, accused of spreading propaganda against the state. A house search found two letters from Thiessen's sister in America (the Brauns also had corresponded with relatives in Canada). In prison, father and son were beaten and taken to the torture chamber. Falling unconscious, the son was dragged upstairs and signed a document. Sentenced to ten years in a remote prison camp, before his removal, he noticed that the portrait of secret police head Yezhov (Ezhov) had been removed from the prison wall. Since his signature was obtained under duress, he requested a new hearing and a new judge granted him a reprieve. He collected his personal effects coupon, got his clothes from the disinfect-ant chamber, signed a paper that he would not reveal what he saw or heard in prison, and left on 29 January 1939.[88] Of 295 persons arrested in Kichkas, only 5 ever returned home.[89]

The three-ton Black Raven truck arrived in Mikhailovka on 8 March 1938. Viktor told this story in Bonn in 1995. The Braun family had recently moved into their mud-brick house – where the walls smelled like wet earth and the floor of packed clay, smoothed and shined up by a slurry of cow manure to give a hard finish. Isaak had built a wooden table around which the family was seated. It was the end of a long day's work and his wife, Hermine, was dishing out fried potatoes when they heard a roar up the street. A trio of activist young Komsomol officials were shoving their way into houses and hauling out men. By the time the youths wearing the red star reached the Braun hut, twenty hand-cuffed men, heads down, silently marched ahead of them.

Bang, knock, crash, 'Open up!'

'We're looking for weapons! Any weapons?'

'No, we have no weapons.'

Hermine tried not to look at the attic where rough boards laid across the rafters hid the Bibles and hymnals brought from Kichkas. Isaak tried not to show his jittery nerves. Weapons? Pacifists carry no weap-ons. But sixteen-year old Viktor turned pale, for what his parents did not know, what nobody knew, was that he – skilled mechanically as well as musically, out of a burning hatred for what the Communists did to his father in prison, with a bit of metal here, a rod there – had secretly fashioned a gun that now was hidden behind a chest of drawers.

The men turned over beds, sliced through feather pillows, slit open the straw tick mattresses, dumped drawers, and poked into the stove. One pulled out a drawer in the kitchen table and held aloft a butchering knife, a fine knife with a wooden handle from the house in Gorchakovo. 'Aha! You have no weapons, you say? What's this?'

Tucking the 'weapon' under his belt as evidence, the newly recruited 'officer' roughly pushed Isaak towards the door. Another youth tied his hands behind his back. 'March!' There was no time for goodbye, no time to take along a jacket or coat, no time to take a piece of bread, no time to look back at his family, no hand free to wave a final greeting. Out of the door to join the column.

The horrified children looked at one another and found no words.

Viktor thought, at least they didn't find my gun. Maybe his father would get off, like last time. Liesel hurried to get her mother a cup of water, and Yasha, aged thirteen, stared at the footprints of fried potatoes on the floor.

The next day nobody on the collective farm asked why Isaak didn't come to work. Nobody asked what happened to the other men. Communicating with a raised eyebrow or slight nod, people went about their normal work and said nothing. To express an opinion was to be against the government.

The family thought Isaak must have been taken to prison in Kherson but never heard a word from him again. Perhaps he was summarily shot. Perhaps he was still alive, sent to a Siberian labour camp, or a prison, or en route to some prison. Perhaps they'd get a letter from him one day. Always they lived in fear, hope, and regret. Nobody had been able to say goodbye. Nobody was able to show sorrow or grief. Nobody could publicly mention his name. It was as if he had never existed.

Sixty years later, when his son finished telling the story, his body shook.

6

Second World War, 1939–1945

Isaak's Family Farms Collectively

When Isaak Braun was arrested, his family was grateful their house was more or less completed and that they were able to keep their work on the farm. Soviet propaganda was relentlessly denigrating Germans. In the 'Red Corner' at Engels Collective, farm workers watched Soviet filmmaker Sergei Eisenstein's anti-German and patriotic film *Alexander Nevsky*. With loudspeakers reporting that Hitler would soon attack the homeland, it came as a shock and relief when the Hitler-Stalin non-aggression pact was signed in 1939. As Greta Braun told Harvey and me in Bonn, it seemed unbelievable that Germans no longer were denounced as enemies. The Eisenstein film was quietly removed. Two years went by without a word from Isaak.

Once a year for May Day, after the usual speeches praising communism, Isaak's youngest son, schoolboy Yasha, received a celebratory piece of bread, a meatball, and potato. Viktor had quit school to work on the farm and his workdays, added together with his mother's, gave them more food at the end of the year. The women coped. Soap was not to be bought or made (no extra fat to boil with lye), so cooking pots were scoured with sand or ashes. Water was softened by pouring through ashes or straw. Stores were empty, but if any goods came in, line-ups formed overnight to buy rationed lengths of cloth. Allowed to keep a few hens, people paid with eggs. After a long day in the fields, a tallow candle for light, Hermine sat at a spinning wheel to turn wool into yarn. Permitted to keep a third of the yarn for her labour, she knitted stockings, sweaters, and headscarves. Used wool was unravelled bit by bit from worn-out sweaters or socks, tied together, and knitted again. Pieces of wood were whittled to make wooden shoes called *Holzpantofel*.

Viktor told us the collective farm manager offered to send him to school in Tokmak to take an accounting course before appointing him the farm bookkeeper. He looked at his sister doing heavy farm work and suggested, 'Send my sister Liesel. She is as smart at school as I am. She'll be a good accountant.' So they did. While Liesel went off for a year to Tokmak, Viktor kept his eye on pretty Greta Unrau with her thick, long, black braids, plotting to be on the same work brigade, hoping to be assigned to drive wagons with loads of watermelons to sell at the Dnieper River.

As she told us, Greta was a fun-loving girl, even reckless. 'I loved holding the reins, loved racing my wagonload of ripe watermelons the twelve kilometres to the river. I was fearless, quite so. I didn't bother with brakes, just galloped down those hills and never had an accident. The older men were aghast. I'd sell my load to the riverboat passengers – money all went to the collective farm – and in no time I was finished. Oh, we also sold watermelons along the Konskaia River near the farm.'

On one visit to Bonn, I brought her a book by a Mennonite folk artist who painted village scenes from Mennonite life in Russia before the Revolution. Scanning these brightly painted pages, Greta began to recall happier memories. She told how young people on the farm took moonlight boat rides after work. Gliding under the overhanging branches lining the river, they sang in harmony. She remembered fishing for pike. 'Oh, and making watermelon syrup! There were only two evaporating pans in the whole village, so we had to book them, take turns. Was that pink syrup ever good! Of course everything belonged to the state, not to us.'

Life without men had become the norm. Morning and evening, women and girls milked cows, fed pigs, shovelled manure, and worked in the fields. In the evening the village loudspeaker called youth to come to a meeting, dance, or club. Posters depicting beaming faces of workers who had over-subscribed their quotas of work, local heroes, were plastered on billboards. Red banners proclaiming, 'Life is better and happier!' were festooned on schools and public buildings.

For two years, in hot summer cotton fields, on long rows, the human spirit rising above all, the women and girls sang in four-part harmony. When threshing time came, they pitched sheaves onto hay wagons. Greta grimaced as she recalled 'those stubble fields and our bare feet! We had to tie the sheaves by hand and each had a quota to fill. We liked doing the tying after sundown when the dew had fallen – it softened the stubble. But cut hands and bloody feet – no matter, as we worked, we sang!' After work, the 'German' teenagers, Viktor with his harmonica, Greta with a song sheet, gathered in the Red Corner reading room, ignored the books on Marxism, the Communist pamphlets, and the slogans on the walls of the clubhouse, and sang. Mostly they sang secular Russian songs, but sometimes they quietly risked singing a German folk song.

Religion was never discussed openly. On Christmas Eve all parents and students were required to attend a large anti-religion meeting in the school where a teacher gave a talk about how Christmas was an evil invention of the church. Then, to obliterate any lingering memories of St Nicholas, the Soviet look-a-like Father Frost (at New Year's) brought gifts – perhaps a handmade toy. In schools pupils recited pro-Soviet poems and chorused, 'Thank you Comrade Stalin for giving us a happy childhood.'[1] But in her home, Hermine covered the windows and softly sang hymns with her children. Looking into the vast starry sky on sleepless nights, lonely Hermine thanked God for her children and pleaded for the return of Isaak.

Liesel was back from her year of school in Tokmak and had begun to keep the collective farm books when, on 22 June 1941, house to house and onto fields, the collective chairman (*pred*) ran, calling out breathlessly, 'Everyone! Everyone to the loudspeaker! Promptly! Minister Molotov will speak!'

It was Sunday, a day when in 1941 many collective farms had a rest day. What could Minister Molotov have to say that was important enough to halt activities? Hurriedly leaving her tasks, Hermine joined other women in faded kerchiefs and bare feet at the street corner loudspeaker. In his office the *pred* turned on the switch and the radio crackled a few times before an announcer's voice came on. 'Attention! Attention! Citizens of the great Soviet Union, attention! … a message from Comrade Vacheslav Molotov [foreign minister].'

'Comrades, citizens of our peaceful Soviet socialist nation, it is with deep sorrow and regret that I have to inform you that Germany has broken its non-aggression pact and has attacked the Soviet Union.'

With fascist enemy bombers attacking Soviet cities, he urged citizens to beware of saboteurs, deserters, or fascist sympathizers, to treat them without mercy. In this war to save the great motherland, young and old alike should ferret out collaborators and enemies. The Red Army would fight to the last man, remove every last Nazi soldier from its sacred soil. 'Our cause is just. The enemy will be crushed. Victory will be ours.'[2]

The women listened, speechless, stared at one another, and slunk back to their work. A handicapped man, Jakob Neufeld, working as a bookkeeper on another collective farm heard Molotov's Sunday noon hour radio announcement and later wrote that the news hit him like a blow to the head. He prayed it wasn't true. How would Germany risk taking on this giant empire, he asked, and what would happen to the *Nemtsy* now?

How many brutalities, humiliations, arrests, and persecutions will we have to face now? What will they permit themselves to do to us Germans now, us with our wives and children?

My fellow sufferers, seen as criminals, as traitors in the Soviet state, who already are on a black list and being watched, certainly we will experience this strife and be singled out first as scapegoats. Have we, our whole people, not tasted enough of this misery and tribulation? Great God, have pity on us or we will succumb under the weight of these trials.[3]

That evening a meeting took place. An agitated Party leader mentioned heavy German casualties and promised the Red Army would protect them. Even though the order of the day did not change in the first days of the war, the *Nemtsy* in Mikhailovka were terrified. A few began to be arrested for reportedly having made pro-German statements. The farm workers resolved to work extra hard to prevent Party leaders from finding fault with them, accusing them of sabotage. At the same time, women and old men prayed the Germans would deliver them from Communist oppression.

As described by eye witness Jakob Martens (who survived to immigrate to Paraguay after the Second World War), preparations for harvesting began in July and everyone worked long hours to bring in produce urgently needed by the Soviet military. People feared the Nazis. The loudspeaker radio reported high German casualties and praise for the Red Army. Teachers appeared in the fields to instruct workers on the use of gas masks and to warn them that German parachutists would be dropping poison in Soviet wells and streams, be dynamiting bridges. Farm workers were assigned night duty to guard telephone and electrical stations to prevent German saboteurs. Rumours spread. Someone had seen a downed plane and a Nazi in the cornfield. Immediately search parties were sent out, but came home hours later having found nothing.[4]

By August, many Jews and Roma (Gypsies) were heading east. While reports about Soviet victories were still glowing, young men and able-bodied women were abruptly called together. Ordered to pack food for ten days and take a spade, a brigade of trench-diggers was sent to dig tank traps to halt oncoming Germans. The Brauns wondered how the Germans could warrant tank traps when the radio was still reporting the invasion hundreds of kilometres away. Yet wagons were loaded with tents, provision, shovels, and diggers, and off they went – girls Greta and Liesel, their mothers Agatha Unrau and Hermine Braun, other *Nemtsy*, Ukrainian and Bulgarian neighbours. The platoon crossed the Dnieper River, passed Zaporozhye, and continued farther west. Nobody knew how far.

As Greta explained, a trench had to be dug three metres deep and eight metres wide. As she dug, she heard distant cannon shots, and soon leaflets resembling white feathers fluttered down from low-flying German planes. Citizens had been warned not to pick up the leaflets.[5] Sensing confusion among their guards, Greta said, 'We watched, then ran to pick them up. In Russian, in bright colours on paper not seen locally for a decade, we read, 'Stop digging your little holes. They can't stop our tanks. Go home to Mama. We'll be there to rescue you soon.'

Back at the farm, nineteen-year-old Viktor and other young men were ordered to collect the farm animals (cattle, horses, goats, sheep) and to keep them out of the grip of the Germans, to move them east. Little did he know how fortunate he was to have this task. In early September the (returned) German-speaking male trench-diggers, men and boys aged sixteen and over, were ordered to prepare warm clothing and food for ten days and be ready to depart in a day. Quickly 'German' mothers scrounged together underwear and socks, spent the night cooking potatoes and baking bread, all to go into a gunny sack that her last remaining son, or her husband, or grandfather threw over his shoulder as he stood at the dusty road early the next morning. As conscripts marched under police guard reached a house, the men fell in. Mothers, sisters, relatives, and sweethearts stood at the roadside weeping or ran beside the column, waving goodbye. People thought the men were destined for the Red Army. Not so.

With youths away on digging and herding tasks and able males marched off, the collective farm workload doubled for the remaining crippled, sick, and old men, for bewildered women and children. The Soviet bosses stayed. Since draft animals had been sent away, workers were told to use scythes, rakes, and other ancient hand tools like threshing stones to collect the harvest. At night, they guarded against sabotage.

Unknown to the villagers, on the west side of the Dnieper River, German tanks had crossed Polish-Soviet borders and were rolling over the steppes of Ukraine. Not reported on the village loudspeakers, the Red Army was in retreat. In clouds of dust on clogged roads, Soviet military vehicles, wagons loaded with equipment, as well as Roma and Jews were fleeing east. In 1999, at a conference in Zaporozhye, Alexander Prusin, an American academic born in Ukraine, told us his Jewish grandparents had stayed back, trusting their Soviet German neighbours. They thought talk about Nazi anti-Semitism was Soviet propaganda. Similarly, other Jews reasoned that Germany was a 'civilized nation.' Alas, their good opinion was misplaced.[6]

A witness wrote that weeks of denying that the Germans had advanced deep into Ukraine changed when Soviet administrators on collective farms suddenly put out 'all alert' signals and disappeared. Soviet soldiers were seen changing into civilian clothes and going east. Waiting for the inevitable, nobody worked in the fields and nothing moved, not animal or person. In the sky, Russian planes fought Stuka dive-bombing German fighter planes. Bombs dropped on highways and railways. Long trails of black smoke marked the falling planes and flames shot up as buildings or train cars exploded. Windows shattered and shrapnel sprayed onto streets.[7]

As the battle neared Zaporozhye, without warning, the Red Army blew up the mighty bridge across the Dnieper River, killing fleeing refugees, herders, and animals on the bridge. Exploding the Dneprostroi hydroelectric dam released a wave of water that killed many more refugees and animals waiting to cross the river ahead of the Germans. Bridge gone, the Wehrmacht was forced to a halt at Zaporozhye. Stalled on the western bank, a continuous battle took place. The standoff at the Dnieper River lasted over a month and gave the Soviets on the east bank time to pursue a scorched earth policy, leaving no food or help for an advancing enemy. Harvest fields were burned, factories were dismantled and shipped east, mines were flooded, and railways were dynamited. And local Soviet Germans and other 'potential collaborators' were systematically deported.

Before the bridge exploded, in roundabout ways, trench-diggers Liesel Braun, her mother Hermine, and the Unrau women had managed to return home when their Soviet guards abandoned their brigade. They did not know that Soviet administrators had drawn up plans to deport them. Cattle-herder Viktor had escaped the Soviet round-up of males prior to the German Army's crossing of the Dnieper River. As he recounted, with a comrade, police guards, veterinarians, and even milkmaids (who also cooked meals), he had been on back roads clogged with animals, usually a hundred cattle to a herd, as well as horses. Forced to move day after day, cows, often bawling for water, had begun to sicken and miscarry. It was a disorganized affair, with herders and guards shouting at wayward animals straying from the herd, horses bolting upon sudden gunshot explosions, and many animals dying. Rest stops had to be called. At night scouting parties searched for safe side roads. The Red Army was in retreat on the main roads.

As the herders watched dogfights between German and Soviet planes, rumours spread. How close were the Germans? Viktor said that he, with other German-speaking and Ukrainian herders, hoped the German army would liberate them. Already one month on the cattle run, Viktor and his friend Daniel Siemens, planning to be overtaken by the German army, began driving their cattle in big circles. Many animals, numbered before leaving the farms, had died, and herders worried how to account for the losses. Better the Wehrmacht come than to be forced to explain 'missing state property.' Better also, when stopped at frequent road checks and asked for papers, to say they were searching for runaway calves.

As Viktor told this story these many years later, he thought his pal Daniel must have been 'too cheeky in his answers.' Caught circling, Viktor's friend was arrested by Soviet police assigned to look for deserters. Taken to a Melitopol jail, he was shot. Viktor somehow saw his own name on a list of suspected saboteurs and went AWOL. Abandoning his cows, he surreptitiously made his way back home and arrived just one and a half days after the Red Army retreated from Mikhailovka. Sister Liesel, with other women, ordered to carry away farm food products, had hidden herself among the stranded farm machinery and tractors abandoned by their drivers along the side roads. Hearing rumours of a swift Wehrmacht advance, she also had returned home.

Between 4 and 6 September in a renewed offensive, the German army crossed the river to find two-thirds of the population of 'potential fifth columnists' on the east side of the river had been deported. The physically handicapped man, Jakob Neufeld, recorded how he, his wife, and two children waited for six days under open skies in a field at a railway station. No trains stopped. Suddenly their guards withdrew, the German army arrived, and he was told to return to his village. He wrote,

The next day I was astonished to see how the German militiamen, our saving angels, calmly, without the slightest timidity, worked ... greeted several people with 'Heil Hitler.' For us that was a totally new and astonishing greeting, something we had not yet heard. I asked myself, is it Hitler that inspires the soldiers, is responsible for their advance, their deportment, self-confidence, and assurance of an imminent victory for the Germans?

And is all of this to change in one blow?... Everything that we have lost, also our loved ones ... Unbelievable! ... And should we no longer live in fear, be able to go about our business ... able to live our lives without worry that what we had accumulated, our knowledge and skills or our Christian faith would put us in peril and lead to our destruction?[8]

Here was an anomaly: thousands of Soviet 'enemies' (Germans, Tatars) felt liberated, and thousands of Nazi 'enemies' (Jews, Roma) feared annihilation.[9] Quickly the Soviets emptied their prisons, killing thousands. Historian Magosci estimated the Nazis killed 850,000 to 900,000 Ukrainian Jews.[10] In their rapid advance the Germans captured millions of Soviet soldiers and these prisoners of war were largely allowed to starve to death. About three million Red Army POWs were killed.[11] Others were used as slave labour. Later a million German POWs died in Soviet hands.

Exiled to Siberia

Isaak Braun's family escaped deportation, but not so the family of Johannes and Anna Braun in Kotlyarevka. A Soviet decree of 28 August 1941 had ordered all 'diversionists and spies' to be deported on short notice. At our meeting in 1989 in Karaganda, Maria Braun had mentioned their deportation, but final details came out only after a trans-Siberian trip in 2001 when we met Heinz, her youngest brother.

In June 1941, of her five children, Anna Braun had kept daughters Maria and Anni, and young son Heinz. During the hiatus of the Molotov/Ribbentrop Pact of 1939, daughter Alici had gone to Omsk, and eldest son Hans had been conscripted into the Red Army. His mother had no word about his whereabouts. Was he deployed to the Finnish front to fight German Stuka dive-bombers with handguns? In a foxhole in a marshy plain, not daring to pop out his head? Had he been overtaken by German ground troops? Like thousands of Red Army soldiers, did he become a POW?[12]

With the German army stalled on the west side of the Dnieper River, the first group the Soviets rounded up (as on the west side) was *Nemet-skie* or 'German' males aged sixteen and over. On 6 September 1941, from police headquarters in Selidovka, the men and boys were marched away, they thought to join the Red Army, but actually to forced work camps. Mennonite Elder Jakob Tiessen lived in Kalinovo, a village near the Kotlyarevka home of Anna Braun and her children (in the Memrik settlement). One of the men conscripted, he described what happened:

In the morning enough ladder wagons from the surrounding Russian collective farms were brought out and we were taken to the railway junction Yasika-vataia ... loaded into coal cars, with locked doors.... On 23 September we were unloaded in Krasno-Tuurinsk and put up in a third camp consisting of eight barracks, one new, built of wet wood. German men from the industrial centres of Stalino [Donetsk], Voroshilovgrad [Lugansk] ... had also been brought here by train, several thousand men, many intellectuals, engineers, and specialists in various trades. An aluminium plant was supposed to be built here. The foundations were still to be dug out of the frozen ground, the water system to be laid, and trees to be cut for use as timber. The trees were to be carried by hand onto the worksite.

All of this in heavy frost, whereas everyone had been rounded up in the great heat of September, totally unprepared for winter.... People were wearing sandals and light caps and no gloves. With frostbitten limbs, the work norms could not be met, and subsequently food rations got smaller every month. A great dying took place.... By January 1942 more than half who had arrived in September 1941 had died.[13]

By September the NKVD was supervising centrally planned, enforced deportations of hundreds of thousands of Soviet citizens to Siberia, Kazakhstan, and Central Asia. By January 1942 deported 'unreliables' included soldiers in the Red Army and by 1943 whole national groups were exiled. No need to interrogate individuals, just look at origin and off to a prisoner boxcar you go under police guard. Historian Fleischauer points out the questionable legality of these deportations.[14] Besides *Nemtsy*, 'unreliable ethnic minorities' included Chechens, Crimean Tatars, Italians, Greeks, Iranians, Finns, Romanians, the Ingush, the Karachi, the Balkars, the Kalmyks, the Kurds, and Koreans.

I puzzled how the Soviets were able to separate out their villagers so quickly, 'Germans go' and 'Ukrainians stay.' Evidence from a Moscow jurist, cited by historian Fleischhauer, states that secret lists had been drawn up as early as 1934, after Hitler came to power in Germany, listing every German individual and family member born in the country or employed in Soviet industry.[15] Other lists named persons who had availed themselves of Torgsin stores. Long before computers, the lists used by the Communist Central Committee called up precise detail on numbers and occupations of all Germans in the USSR.

Anna Braun and her children were on a list among fifteen thousand Mennonites from the Memrik, Molochna, Borissovo, and Ignatievo settlements who were deported to Kazakhstan, Kyrgyzstan, and Tajikistan.[16] Thousands more were deported from Crimea, the Caucasus, and Volga areas. Canadian historian Peter Letkemann, who has collected the names of thousands of Russian Mennonite victims, states that twenty-five thousand Mennonites were deported and that by October 1941, from the Ukrainian area east of the Dnieper River, one hundred thousand Soviet Germans were deported.[17] Thirty per cent of Letkemann's list, mostly the sick, elderly, and children, died in transit.

When deportation began, Anna Braun was given two days' notice. She boiled recently dug potatoes, quickly killed her few chickens, and preserved the meat in lard. Next came baking and roasting bread. Told to pack only what could be carried, no more than 100 pounds, she rolled up bedding, a frying pan, and a few dishes and put everything into sacks, a pillowcase full for each child to carry. Any clothes they owned, one thing over another, was pulled on, even though outside it was a warm September day. Having supported herself by sewing, Anna also took her portable sewing machine.

When trucks drove up, unbaked bread stayed in the oven, barn doors were flung open, cows were left unmilked and pigs unfed. Half the animals in these villages died, and shocked Ukrainian neighbours took in the rest. Furniture stayed, and, as we would discover in a visit to Memrik in 2001, officials and others selected furniture from vacant houses. Crowded onto a flatbed pulled by a tractor, wondering how her husband would ever know where she was being sent, Anna Braun took one last look at the house Johannes had repaired. At the Zhelanaia train station (a station I saw in 2001), about five thousand persons of all ages stood waiting under armed guard.[18] Night came and still train after train loaded with dismantled factories or military equipment passed through. Armies had priority. Overhead, flying low, bombers met fighter airplanes. Amid the crying of children came the boom of cannons. A bomb hit one of the slow-moving trains. Frantically, rail workers moved to clear the tracks. Under a red night there was nowhere to sleep.

As morning came, children cried with hunger and mothers opened sacks and took out a potato, an onion, some dry beans, and scrounged for twigs and dried grass to build small fires to heat a bit of water. Water, water, where could you get water? Another day passed. A pregnant woman screamed in pain. A grandfather prayed. Camping at the station without toilets or water, deportees huddled together. Another night came. Some Ukrainian neighbours brought bread for their friends. Suddenly a woman called out, 'Let's sing.' She began a German hymn, *'Kommt stimmet alle jubelnd an, Gott hat uns lieb'* (Come let us all unite and sing). With hymns they had not dared to sing for years, they kept up their courage. Guards circled, guns ready.

After three days a train stopped. Once people were loaded inside the cattle cars, the doors were bolted. Those remaining at the station sang, but as one group after another left, the singing became thinner and thinner. Finally Anna, her sewing machine, and her children were locked in. A steam blast, and the train lurched forward.

For days and nights the train stopped, was shunted aside for military transports, started again, and stopped. Inside the crowded space people cried out for water. 'Eat snow!' The dreaded truth had soon been passed along, 'We're going north.' People who died en route were unloaded at train stops and dead children often were tossed out of the train. An ethnic German woman from Memrik told me it took twenty days and nights until guards began to drop off the 'freight,' some here, some there. She ended up in the Altaiskiy Krai, an area of forests and Altai Mountains bordering Eastern Kazakhstan.[19] From what Maria Braun had told me in Karaganda, I knew Anna Braun and her children were dumped off in deep snow, but not where.

Historian Peter Letkemann wrote that the deportation of 28,000 Mennonites to Central Asia or remote Siberia in 1941 was the 'final step in the removal of Soviet Germans from European Russia begun with the arrests and dekulakization of the 1930s' and continued in 1945 when 23,000 Mennonites were repatriated. It was an ethnic cleansing.[20]

The German Occupation

Let's explore the possibility that families like those of Anna or Hermine Braun were justifiably deported as potential collaborators or fifth columnists. The last news these families had from the outside world dated from the mid-1930s. It was illegal to listen to foreign radio stations or to own a radio, and persons I interviewed said it was a crime even to think about a foreign country. Perhaps the odd person dared to build a crystal set and listened to BBC news late at night, but mostly inhabitants lived with rumours and the propaganda on Soviet loudspeakers. Israeli researcher Meir Buchsweiler described Soviet Germans as 'astoundingly uninformed' about situations in pre-war Germany or even about Soviet policies and military preparation. Given their treatment by the Soviets, they had reason to oppose rather than support the Soviets whom they feared.[21] They had done nothing to warrant being seen as a fifth column threat.[22]

In defining a collaborator, Buchsweiler advised the reader to consider the difference between appearance and actual deeds. Did being anti-Soviet mean being pro-Nazi? No. Was wanting to leave the Soviet Union (provided you were not relaying secret information) or wishing to contact relatives on the enemy side, treason? No.[23] Could you expect people treated as enemies to feel loyalty to that state? Patriotism is a useful tool. It can be dug up, burnished bright for political objectives, especially wars; it can be used as a knife. Traitor! Sharper than a guillotine. But to be a traitor, isn't it necessary to be a citizen? What if the country where your ancestors were born, based on religion, or language, disenfranchises you and declares you an enemy?

I asked an eyewitness Mennonite woman, 'Did you run out to meet the Germans, "Welcome! We speak German?"'

'Oh no,' she replied, 'At first we hid. We were so afraid. We had been flooded with Communist propaganda, told that they were poisoning the drinking water. My little brother and I were hiding in a Ukrainian neighbour's house when we saw motorcycles. The Ukrainians begged us to go out, "You speak German." So we went. The first soldiers seemed friendly but didn't stay long. In no time they were off again, chasing the retreating Red Army.'[24]

What impressed another contact was how clean and well-dressed the invading army was. 'We all were in rags. German soldiers had leather gloves. We had never seen those. And leather boots. We wore wooden sandals or were barefoot. Those shiny boots, my, it was something. We didn't have uniforms like that. The Red Army wore rags.'[25]

In many villages the onrushing Wehrmacht army was welcomed by Ukrainian women carrying traditional bread and salt. In Stalin's drive to dekulakize and collectivize agriculture, Ukrainians had been driven to starvation and cannibalism, and those who were left in the villages – mostly women and children – watched the incoming German army with hope. Hope that the German invasion would rid the eastern countries of Bolshevism, of collective farms, would restore land ownership,

civil rights, and religious freedom. Perhaps even discover their disappeared men or, faint hope, allow for a 'free' Ukraine. Two Ukrainian
military units (code-named Nachtigall and Roland) even marched with
the German army in the June invasion. Expecting that the Germans
were 'liberators,' on 30 June 1941 Stepan Bandera, leader of a Ukrainian national movement in western Soviet Ukraine, proclaimed an independent Ukrainian state.

Since the Bolshevik Revolution, of all of the Dnieper Ukraine's peoples, the experience of Poles, Soviet Germans, and especially religious
citizens had been one of intimidation. Survival lay in saying nothing,
being inconspicuous, fearing anyone in authority, and obeying commands. The invading German soldiers were shocked to find such a
totally cowed population. Remarking on the drab and colourless people, one German soldier described the residents as 'ants destined to be
workers and nothing else.'

*Every individual initiative in them has been killed or stifled, because to be an
individual is to be suspect, in danger of being reported. They hesitate to express
any private opinions, fearing the GPU will return or that NKVD spies are
still at work. They seek to discover what the official view is and then adopt it
as their own. The elderly faces reveal that they have been living in constant
fear and suspicion. Surely with their supine attitude, any powerful ruler can
manipulate them.*[26]

The inability of 'ants' to speak out is seen in an anecdote recorded by
a Hans Rempel, who visited the village of Rosental and found a young
Mennonite man – hands in his pockets, wearing a threadbare dirty shirt
and trousers so short, pieced together and shapeless, that they hardly
resembled pants – leaning against a barn door.

QUESTION. 'Whose house is this?'
ANSWER. 'It belongs to the collective.'
QUESTION. 'What are you doing here?'
ANSWER. 'I'm a worker on the collective.'
*I asked if I could enter the barn, since the farmhouse had an exceptionally
large barn, a collective barn. The man moved over enough to permit me to pass.
Immediately I noticed the well cared for, purebred horses. 'What wonderful
horses you have!'*
*Now the man came to life. My praise of his horses had achieved this. Yes,
he assured me, the horses had been skinny, but were receiving better feed now.*

But these were by far not the best horses because those, rightly so, had been requisitioned for the war.[27]

The German army arrived in three distinct groups: the first waves were Wehrmacht soldiers, conscripted men and officers who fought the battles and were welcomed by the people of Ukraine, the 'liberators.' A woman now living in Canada told me that she had washed German soldiers' clothes and cooked meals for the first army wave to arrive. Then came huge Belgian horses that pulled the cannons and wagons of the Wehrmacht war arsenal over rutted Ukrainian roads. The next group was the military administration that organized local governments and sent many Ukrainians into slave labour as eastern workers (*Ostarbeiter*) to work in German factories. Last was the infamous Gestapo (*Einsatzgruppen*), SS storm troopers who carried out the killings of Jews, Roma, and others.

The captured territories were administered by the conquerors as foreign colonies. By 20 August 1941, the occupying Germans had established the *Reichskommissariat Ukraine*, an administration guided by the same rules as the German Reich. At first the German administrators were willing to work with moderate Ukrainian leaders and permitted Ukrainians their own schools, the reopening of churches and cultural societies, the printing of newspapers, and other freedoms, but, since Hitler viewed Ukrainians as subhuman (*Untermenschen*), schools did not last long. Then the occupying army began requisitioning foodstuffs in areas they passed through, often taking the last food, the last cow, burning homes and murdering civilians. Denied access to food, city dwellers in occupied areas, especially where it was thought many partisans hid, starved in great numbers. Captured partisans were shot or hanged.

I wanted to know how Mennonites responded when they were introduced to Nazi policies on Jews. I had read that Mennonites and Jews got along amiably, and my father had always spoken admiringly about Jews he knew. He had encouraged us children in mental math. '*Aber ein Jüdischer Kopf*' he would say about an ability to mentally compute numbers quickly. Mennonite villages in southern Ukraine usually had Jewish stores, and many Jewish tailors came to Mennonite homes, so they got to know each other. The tsarist government had even established a *Judenplan* to encourage Jewish agriculture where Mennonites and Jews had shared a village.[28] Writing about his Mennonite boyhood in the period immediately prior to and during the Bolshevik Revolution, Californian historian David G. Rempel wrote that anti-Semitism was 'common throughout southern Russia, and even Mennonites were not free of this disease,' but within his experience, 'during pogroms Jewish residents from nearby cities often found asylum in local Mennonite homes.'[29] Rempel grew up in the present Zaporozhye area, where his father was a grain dealer with regular business contacts with Jewish grain merchants.

Twenty years later, how would Mennonites on collective farms respond to Hitler's policy to exterminate Jews, or massacres in captured cities like Kiev? Did they know that back in Germany Nazis got rid of 'undesirables,' that there were ghettos and concentration camps in the Third Reich? That a 'Final Solution' decision was made to kill Jews in the spring of 1941?

They didn't know at first, Mennonite survivors wrote. There was a blackout of information about the rest of the world, and with the lack of personal radios, there was little they dared to ask. They found out when it happened in their neighbourhoods. In his memoir, Mennonite Jakob Martens writes, 'What Russian propaganda had been spouting to their own credit for a long time, and what most of us didn't believe actually came to pass. It was so crushingly depressing that it totally overwhelmed us all. My pen fights against repeating the horrors that were here perpetrated.'[30]

Occasionally I came across a Mennonite who resisted German commands. In Zaporozhye, German commissar Rehm ordered the Mennonite Johann Epp, head of the German Khortitsa district on the west side of the Dnieper, to force farm workers to harvest on Sunday. Epp resisted.

Rehm. 'Work or I'll shoot you.'

Epp. 'What would you rather have, my head or a harvest delivered?'

Rehm (grudgingly). 'Fine. If it's not delivered, that's your head.'[31]

Against Nazi regulations, Epp later reintroduced religion into Khortitsa schools.[32] Perhaps Epp got away with this because the Nazis considered Mennonites and German Colonists to be one of them – not as high in culture as the *Reichsdeutsche*, mind you, but renamed *Volksdeutsche*, to be given better treatment than Ukrainians.

When Nazi ideologist Alfred Rosenberg, Reichsminister for Occupied Eastern Lands, visited the area to inspect the repair of the hydroelectric dam at Dneprostroi, as demanded by custom, he was welcomed with bread and salt in Ukrainian villages. And in Khortitsa, a Mennonite teacher had her students put on an exhibition of handicrafts and Bibles. Rosenberg had attacked Judeo-Christianity.[33]

The occupation forces allowed German-speaking farm workers improved salaries, and youths, herders, or anti-tank diggers (who had escaped the 1941 Soviet round-up of males over the age sixteen) were invited to work for them. Ukrainians were employed to repair the Dneprostroi dam or the airport, as household help and as members of a police force. German-speakers, male and female, became office workers, interpreters, and so on.

Armies have to be fed, and Viktor Braun had told us that the first thing he did after returning from herding was to help harvest and thresh the grain. The ex-herders and trench diggers collected farm machinery from abandoned roadways, and caught horses, cows, and other animals left stranded. Shortages continued in raw materials, machinery parts, and gasoline, but grain, meat, and vegetables were delivered to the new rulers.

While Liesel Braun kept her job as the farm accountant, Viktor was asked to be an agricultural director, a *Landwirtschaftsführer*, and wear a uniform. He did not want to wear a uniform but accepted a job as interpreter offered in November 1941. 'It was because of the pay; a hundred roubles a month was good.' Soon he had to travel with army officers. Actually it was illegal to compel Soviet citizens to join the Wehrmacht, to conscript them, but few occupied Soviet *Volksdeutsche* knew that. Later, when they retreated with the German army in 1943 and got into occupied Poland, the *Volksdeutsche* refugees were quickly given German citizenship and then were promptly put into Waffen SS uniforms.

While Viktor was interpreting, life took a better turn for his mother Hermine, sister, and brother, as well as his future wife, Greta, and her mother. They had enough to eat, and permission was given to reclaim church buildings and to introduce work-free Sundays. Viktor told us his mother and sister helped to clean the former church. Churches, but not Jewish synagogues, that had been turned into clubhouses, dance halls, or granaries were restored as places of worship. Orthodox Russian churches reopened, and priests that had been swineherds could come out of hiding and resume their former roles. Church bells rang again from onion-domed cathedrals, and buried candles and chalices were exhumed to shine inside.

In Mikhailovka, Hermine Braun took her hymnal out of hiding, again attended church, and sang in a choir. On harmonica or guitar, her children openly accompanied hymns their father Isaak had sung. An infirm or elderly Mennonite preacher who escaped arrest could visit, preach a sermon, and pray. Still, mothers like Hermine Braun were disappointed at the lack of Christian faith in the occupying soldiers and teachers sent from Germany.[34]

The experiences of Mennonites under Nazi occupation are politically sensitive, and persons who eventually escaped the USSR and came to Canada have been reluctant to discuss this topic for fear of being stereotyped as 'collaborators.' Couldn't he have joined the Allies, someone once asked an acquaintance who found it impossible to discuss his escape. The man smiled, 'The Soviets were the Allies.' Become a partisan? This was a choice made by some of those denigrated as subhumans (*Untermenschen*) – Poles, White Russians, Ukrainians, Roma, and Jews. Treated brutally or liquidated, the numbers of partisans multiplied. But if treated better, would you object? The question of collaborators is murky. Were those who assisted Stalin in his brutal policies, people who benefited from that system, collaborators? One knows everyone feared Stalin, a man who did not hesitate to kill his friends, even wives of friends.

In German-speaking villages, the occupation government installed mayors who were accountable to an *Oberbürgermeister* (who oversaw four villages), who in turn was accountable to a district administrator (*Sonderführer*). The first disappointment for my witnesses was that the occupation government did not redistribute and privatize land. The collective farms remained, but for two years the collective farm was called a 'community farm.' The Nazi administrators seemed fairly benevolent. The Soviet Germans received a cow, a pig, and several hens from returned herded animals. For the first time in years the families had meat, eggs, and milk.[35] No longer despised *Nemtsy*, but *Volksdeutsche*, when the occupying civil administrators hired staff, *they* were employed in better-paying jobs as cooks, clerks, translators, and interpreters. Meir Buchsweiler did not think this strange, nor the fact that orders came down to do so.[36] German military, seeing the poverty and need among people of their own language, preferred to give them the jobs. 'It was in the nature of things.' The Brauns felt they were liberated. At last they were not despised as dregs of society. Somebody liked them.

Slowly they realized the mentality of their saviours. Hitler, through Heinrich Himmler, gave directives to 'Germanize' the Soviet Germans as quickly as possible. *Volksdeutsche* population lists were drawn up and citizens were encouraged to use the Hitler greeting [*Willst du ein echter Deutsche sein/So soll dein Gruss 'Heil Hilter' sein*]. Mennonites had always used Old Testament names. Now people with 'Jewish' names like Sarah, Isaak, or David were told to change them to Selma, Edwin, Dirk, etc. An old Mennonite named David Isaak (a double Jewish name!) refused to change his name to 'something German.'[37]

The Nazis began an ethnographic study of the occupied population of Ukraine. From 1941 to 1943 Karl Stumpp, an émigré academic living in Germany, with an eighty-man cohort from Germany, the *Sonderkommando Stumpp*, went village-to-village collecting and classifying information on hundreds of villages and settlements. The cultural and racial survey detailed how many Soviet Germans had been arrested, sentenced, deported, or murdered, or had died of hunger. It listed names of villages, personal backgrounds, numbers of males, females, children, languages spoken, numbers of mixed marriages, numbers of Jews, births, deaths, school reports – a voluminous record.[38] Confiscated by the Allies, Stumpp's data were deposited in the Library of Congress and are used by Mennonite genealogists to research family connections.

Teachers and young people, including Viktor's younger brother Yasha Braun, were sent to Germany to be indoctrinated in National Socialism. Others were sent to German teacher training schools in Prishib and Kiev, where they received good clothing, enough food, even music lessons. Medical staff and professionals, including teachers, arrived from Germany. If mothers could tell their children drilled in Communist ideology that God existed, then surely God had sent the Germans. But why did the Germans forbid the teaching of religion in schools? And why did they ask for the 'Heil Hitler' salute? Why was Christmas a winter solstice event with dancing around bonfires? And why did Germans discriminate against Ukrainian neighbours and kill Jews?

Memoirists write about the arrival of the Gestapo henchmen, when villagers were called in for questioning. 'How and when did you lose your husband, your son? Who did it?' If someone was fingered as having betrayed fellow villagers – had put names on a list of people to be kulakized or exiled – that person was executed. A Mennonite couple described how the guilty had to dig their own graves, into which they were summarily shot by the SS men. People in the village who heard the shots from the cemetery were shocked. Not even widows or orphaned children who had experienced hardship and humiliation agreed with this punishment.[39] Horst Gerlach cited a woman refusing to betray the name of the person who had falsely accused her husband in 1937. A small number of Mennonite men who were accused or confessed to naming persons were shot.[40]

In a Canadian Mennonite newspaper, a memoirist from the village of Felsenbach in the Borosenko settlement (east of Mikhailovka) witnessed a brutal slaughter. Aged fifteen, he and two friends saw ninety-two Roma lined up in a Mennonite cemetery in broad daylight in May 1942. He described how occupying Nazi administrators later unsuccessfully attempted to distribute their clothing among the horrified German-speaking Felsenbach villagers.[41] I checked for letters to the editor commenting on this graphic description of the massacre and found none. Buchsweiler wrote that 137 trucks were filled with the clothes of Babi Yar victims, and these were distributed mostly among Soviet *Volksdeutsche*. He cites an I. Thiessen as confessing in the Mennonite newspaper *Der Bote*, in 1979, that he received some Jewish goods from the German occupation officers – an action that he now regretted.[42] A boy at the time, another Mennonite said he had never understood until much later why his father forbade him from ever accepting clothing available at the occupation administration office in his village.[43]

When Nazi 'sanitation' police reached a Jewish village, they rounded up young and old, forced them to dig a huge pit, lined them up at the edge, and shot them. None were spared. Some Mennonites from surrounding villages went to see what had happened, or were ordered to help shovel dirt on the pit. They saw the bloody earth, or perhaps some even saw the empty village that had housed a thousand people. My husband visited a village in 1995 and saw the site of a covered pit. 'Three hundred people,' a local witness said. 'The covered pit moved for days.' Harvey asked the inhabitants if local Mennonites had participated in the massacres and they said no. Although many Jewish villagers had fled across the Dnieper River before the German army arrived, most did not. *Volksdeutsche* often were moved into emptied Jewish houses. Mennonite memoirists report that with the murdering of Jews they got a new insight into their German 'liberators.'

Writing in retrospect, some Mennonite survivors stated that, as objects of Nazi propaganda and favourable treatment, they did not know where to turn. Shaken and confused by the brutality of their 'protectors from Bolshevism,' many sought comfort by turning to religion. In some Mennonite villages there were religious revivals where people experienced conversions or renewals of faith and requested traditional adult baptism. Viktor and Liesel Braun, as well as Greta Unrau, were baptized.[44] Jakob Neufeld wrote about the difficulty of finding pews as well as church workers. Feeble old preachers still tried to pay calls to reopened churches. Neufeld was pleased that twenty girls and women and a few young men were baptized in Gnadenfeld in June 1943.[45] Mennonite elder Heinrich Winter, again active as a preacher, found many people being baptized in the Old Colony [Khortitsa settlement] – thirty-nine persons in Osterwick in 1943.'[46] Preacher Nic. Enns reported a baptism of 1,500 persons, 'especially among Russians' (Orthodox? Baptists?) in the Dnieper River. He wrote that altogether in Ekaterinoslav province three thousand were baptized on Pentecost Sunday, 6 June 1943, in Dnepropetrovsk.[47] Historian Karel Berkhoff wrote that in some regions there were rumours that unbaptized children would be shot (were they Jews?) and local authorities made the baptism of (Orthodox) children up to the age of twelve mandatory.[48] Yet in the sixty villages of the large Molochna settlement, as Jakob Neufeld lamented, no real return to religion occurred. Neufeld felt the German occupiers did not really support the growth of religion, and in fact discouraged it. Also the time (of the occupation) was too short to train enough church workers.[49] Most preachers and young men had been taken away in successive Soviet sweeps.

Volksdeutsche teenaged boys were urged to form military brigades. To young Mennonite boys denied religious instruction or the teaching of pacifism for a dozen years, the sight of smart uniforms was tempting. Passing himself off as sixteen in order to be a soldier, a memoirist had told his mother, 'German uniforms have "God with us" [*Gott mit uns*] stamped on their belt buckles.'[50] The Wehrmacht had employed fashion designers and tailors to produce their uniforms. Seen now in movies, the field-grey or mouse-grey tunics fitted well and were enhanced with insignia and medals. Battle helmets, steel with leather Y-straps, sported badges of valour. A Nazi chaplain had a silver Christian cross on his peaked cap.

The Mennonite newspaper *Der Bote* published a photograph taken 1 November 1942 of Mennonite youths in Molochansk (former Halbstadt), some wearing swastika armbands, marching past Heinrich Himmler.[51] Though their mothers disapproved, with fathers, grandfathers, or uncles taken away by the Soviets, many recently, a number of Mennonite youths in the Molochna area volunteered to join a 'self-defence' unit, the *Reiter Schwadron*.[52] I was shocked to read a memoir by a Mennonite who voluntarily joined that cavalry unit (members were later inducted into the Waffen SS), wore the Nazi uniform, made the Hitler salute, and on furlough sang the German national anthem and Horst Wessel (Nazi) songs in a church service – and claimed others joined him.[53] He also goose-stepped through narrow Warsaw streets singing Nazi songs.[54] Not a word about the disappearance of Warsaw's onetime huge Jewish population.

In my discussions with Viktor Braun in Bonn, he seemed to abhor Nazi atrocities but knew they happened. He was never with the *Einsatzkommando* murderers, but in the closing months of the war, in occupied Poland, was conscripted as a *Volkssturm* trooper, a ragtag military unit made up mostly of the very young and very old, this time in German uniform. *Volkssturm* men and boys were given bicycles and hand grenades in the dying days of the war. In a study of Soviet Germans, historian Ingeborg Fleischauer found that the majority of Soviet Germans did not embrace National Socialism as an ideology and actually were *victims* of the Nazi colonization plan for territorial expansion.[55]

One reason why survivors of German occupation living in Canada were reluctant to talk about their experience was evident in a case publicized in the *Globe and Mail* in 1999. A young man from Kotlyarevka, Johann Dueck, a herder like Viktor Braun, had returned from herding to find his village empty, all exiled. He became an interpreter for the occupying German army, immigrated to Canada after the end of the Second World War, and lived in St Catharines, Ontario. Some fifty years later, he was charged as a war criminal, a collaborator. The Canadian judge in the case eventually went to Selidovka, Ukraine, to hear testimony. There, Ukrainian witnesses explained the plight of the Soviet Germans: 'If you don't want to serve the Germans, it means you will join the partisans, but the partisans should be dead … and you were threatened with hanging.'[56]

It took almost five years for the case to come to trial. The federal war crimes unit tried to establish that Dueck had been a member of the Selidovka police unit that executed numerous POWs and civilians, including Jews. Defamed and hounded, the man's family mortgaged their homes and spent almost a million dollars in his defence. In Judge Marc Noel's final report, the federal judge found that Soviet secret police–tainted witnesses were not credible and that the man had been nothing other than what he had claimed, an interpreter in civilian clothes. Written up in the *Globe and Mail* as 'Witch Hunt for Crimes Not Committed,' Dueck was paid $750,000 in settlement of his court costs.[57]

In our discussions in Bonn, Viktor returned several times to a bizarre incident (he did not say where) in which a civilian had turned in a purported Jew who was detained and asked to say the Russian word for corn, *kukuruz*. Supposedly, Jews didn't pronounce the letter *r* in the same way as Germans or Russians or Ukrainians. Alone with the detainee, Viktor said he was terrified and told the man just to scram. Later a story was spread that 'a Jew had escaped' and Viktor feared for the man and for himself, as both were in jeopardy. What could he do? Desert his job as interpreter to return to former tormentors behind Soviet lines? One needs no clairvoyance to know his ending. The Soviets employed a squadron of shooters behind their own ranks who shot soldiers attempting to retreat. Desert and be caught by the Germans? Instantly shot as a traitor.

On both sides vengeance was relentless. If Ukrainian resistance fighters ambushed a German soldier, in retaliation at least ten persons, and sometimes the whole Ukrainian village where the event took place, could be slaughtered. There were no 'nice guys.' At this time and place of war, Viktor wanted to stay alive. All during his later life in the Soviet Union he feared that a discovery that he had been an interpreter could send him to prison, or worse. He never told his children about his role until decades later. In a 2000 family chronicle written by his daughter, the caution continued, but I discovered some details reading their EWZ files (German immigration and naturalization files), captured by the Allies at the close of the Second World War.[58]

Ostarbeiter Girls and 'Volunteers'

The history gets more complicated. Now I discover relatives on the other side of the tracks, ones *not* benefiting from the German occupation. Isaak Braun's family may have felt liberated, but the family of my father's brother, Heinrich, became victims. 'Bread baker' Heinrich had been arrested in 1938, largely because he was a German, and one would have expected that his wife and children would be among the advantaged new *Volksdeutsche*. Alas, Motya, Heinrich's wife, was Russian, persona non grata because she was a Slav, what Nazis called the subhuman *Untermenschen*.[59] Her children were 'mixed blood.' When the German army first rolled in, Heinrich's family thought their name Konrad would make them *Volksdeutsche*. They had not heard of the Nazi horror of 'German blood' being diluted, the revulsion for those of 'mixed blood.' The 'Only for Germans,' 'Only for Aryans,' or 'Forbidden for Ukrainians' signs appearing on stores and parks, meant them. They saw the occupation government self-protection (*Selbstschutz*) police unit beating non-*Volksdeutsche* for infractions of Nazi rules.

With a manpower shortage, Germany had begun rounding up prisoners of war and civilians in occupied territories (Poles, Ukrainians) to send back home as slave labour in German homes as nannies, in factories, and on farms. They were called eastern workers or *Ostarbeiter*. In Ukraine, the *Ostarbeiter* program resulted in the forced deportation of 2.3 million citizens (mostly women from rural areas) as cheap labour.[60] Initially advertisements had lured Ukrainians to 'work in beautiful Germany,' but volunteers were soon disillusioned. By March of 1942, *Reichskommissar* Koch, Nazi commander in occupied Ukraine, said that 450,000 *Ostarbeiter* a year were needed from Ukraine – 15,000 alone in German households – and round-ups began.[61] Heinrich's daughter Elizaveta told the story:

'One day a man wearing a dirty white armband with the word *police* in Ukrainian appeared and ordered us to report to the German-run Labour Exchange. There, a German officer ordered Lucia and me to go to Germany. I was fifteen and Lucia sixteen. We Ukrainian youths were ordered to assemble in a square. If you did not come willingly, you were ferreted out. Followed by our crying mothers, we were taken to train stations. I'm sure there were quotas, so many people for so many factories. Yes, and the local police protected their own children. It was so hard to leave Mama, and no one was there to help us or protect us. Sixty people from our area were sent to Westphalia.'

In a letter to my sister, Elizaveta wrote that the first year was hard. Food was poor. 'We were marched to the factory every morning, but when they realized we could not run away, they stopped guarding us. It was easier then. I cannot remember the names of our foremen, but some were good and some were bad.'[62]

Ostarbeiter were issued a two-by-two-inch patch of cloth, a blue and white square centring the word *east*, in German *OST*, to be worn on all clothes, to prevent escape. Each worker was issued an employment identification workbook with a photo that was kept by the employer. In German newspapers *Ostarbeiter* were depicted mostly not wearing their patches, but standing in courtyards of factories smiling happily, seemingly grateful to have a good job. Supposedly the OST identification patch was an 'honorary' badge![63]

Elizaveta and her sister Lucia worked at the Fabrik Narad in Westphalia, a factory producing enamel kitchen pots. They lived in barracks and received a loaf of bread a week and a daily watery soup. They were dependent upon the surrounding area for handouts of vegetables or windfall fruit. On one occasion, Elizaveta recalled, a truckload of sugar beets arrived and before the foreman could give orders to process them, the beets had been devoured to the last top by the hungry women in the forced labour brigade. Another time, the women went on strike, refusing to eat asparagus slop, instead spilling it on the floor. A policeman threatened, but there were no reprisals. Someone cleaned up the mess, but the food did not improve.

When Elizaveta told some of her story in 1995, she remembered having a good boss, and that workers in the camp were at liberty to walk on the streets. The wages were enough to allow them a movie a week or an ice cream cone. At times it was fun. 'I was always hungry, but then I was only fifteen. I was the youngest, the smallest. An old man, beside whom I worked, had me down to his house to meet his wife and have a meal. I think Lucia and me having a German surname and claiming German relatives gave us slightly better treatment.'[64]

Looking back on this experience in 1999, Elizaveta thought it likely had been easier to be an *Ostarbeiter* than to live at home. While they worked in Germany, the two sisters tried to contact their aunt, my father's elder sister, Helene Liebe, in Wernigerode in the Harz mountain region. 'People' had helped them to search for their Tante Helene. The answer came back, 'She no longer lives in Germany. She has moved to Sweden.' Who fabricated the Sweden story? Was it cowardice or caution? I don't know. My father's elder sister (married to a German theologian in 1906) lived in Wernigerode in the Harz Mountains area throughout the war years. We know Hitler's spies worked everywhere and that there was a Nazi 'Germanic purity' policy meant to separate German civilians from *Ostarbeiter*.[65] Tante Helene's son in Bremen, working for A.I.G. Farben producing war materials, had an anti-Nazi father-in-law hiding in his house. By the end of 1942, Tante Helene had lost two of her three sons in the war and had only that one son left in Bremen.

American troops liberated Westphalia in 1945. *Ostarbeiter* sisters Elizaveta and Lucia, released with other factory workers, found themselves cheered as war heroes. The Americans showered the prisoners with food, and, as Elizaveta said, 'We soon were swimming in chocolate.' But then, the return home. *Ostarbeiter* more politically astute than Heinrich's daughters chose to remain in the West, but most, overjoyed that Father Stalin and the Red Army had liberated Berlin, anticipated being seen as Soviet heroes. How shocked they were to be called collaborators. Elizaveta said, 'A Soviet officer appeared and informed us that we had been forgiven for assisting the enemy.' What crime? They had been 'exposed to and contaminated by the evils of capitalism.'

Many Soviet soldiers, certain the women had volunteered for work in Germany, began raping liberated *Ostarbeiter* young girls. Girls like

Elizaveta were accused of 'selling themselves to Germany for a crust of bread,' of being 'German dolls.' A Bolshevik saying was, 'Who but a traitor could succeed in returning whole from the enemy?'[66] Liberated POW Soviet soldiers, reviled as traitors and criminals, often were shot.[67] Stalin said that, rather than surrender, they should have killed themselves.

In June 1945 Elizaveta's worker brigade from Ukraine returned to the USSR via Czechoslovakia. Going through Poland was dangerous, for it had a long history of being invaded and mistreated by Russia. If a Soviet vehicle got into mechanical trouble and was marooned in Polish woods, its passengers would be strung up. The young women took a train filled with lecherous returning Soviet soldiers, but, Elizaveta stated, had the good fortune to be protected by a soldier whose sister was also an *Ostarbeiter*.

And here is another twist in the family Diaspora. While Elizaveta and her sister Lucia from Soviet Ukraine were forced to go to Germany as slave labour, her cousins from Paraguay (Justina's two youngest children) willingly came to Germany. Jutti Epp, the girl on the back of the sleigh escaping across the frozen Amur River, had grown up. Life in Paraguay was difficult. Her mother, Justina, with her six children had given up trying to farm in the dry Chaco and moved to east Paraguay where life also was a constant struggle.

When Hitler launched an international propaganda campaign to 'return to the homeland,' struggling immigrant Mennonite pioneers in Paraguay and Brazil had ears wide open. Mennonites who left the USSR in 1929 and the refugees from Harbin remembered how Germany had welcomed them. Settlers in Paraguay had kept in close contact with Germany, especially with Professor B.H. Unruh, who counselled them on many subjects and assured them of Hitler's determination to overthrow 'godless Bolshevism.'[68] In 1936, he had dissuaded a group of fifty families that had actually volunteered to immigrate to Germany. They had been enticed to join a 'Friesen colony' by a zealot in Germany who thought the Russian Mennonites in Paraguay represented the purest German bloodline.[69] To many in Paraguay, Nazism was unwelcome, but to others Hitler's call *'Heim ins Reich'* sounded like a rescue.

Justina's Mennonite community, in a settlement named Friesland in East Paraguay, was excited by the call from Germany. A buzz went around that farmers from Germany's Friesland province (Friesland was also a province in Holland) were offering Paraguayan youths free education and free passage to Germany. 'Aren't we lucky to be named

Friesland! A big SS man Hajo Schröder from Friesland, Germany, had read about the Friesland in Paraguay and decided to sponsor us.'[70] Even though dissuaded by B.H. Unruh and the German embassy in Berlin, parents in Friesland urged their youths to take advantage of a unique opportunity in a desperate economy.[71]

In Justina Epp's home, eighteen-year-old Abram and twenty-one year-old Jutti (as she told me) pressed their mother to go. Jutti wanted to be a nurse and there was no place to study in Paraguay. Abram thought studying agriculture at an agricultural college would help his future. Justina let them go.

The twenty-eight young men and five women from Friesland arrived in Bremerhafen, Germany, on 31 June 1939. Many years later, in Canada and long after the world knew about Nazi atrocities, Jutti delivered the following report at a reunion of Frieslanders in Abbotsford, BC.[72]

Friesland's mayor, Heinrich Rempel, was in touch with Herr Hajo Schröder in Germany near Bremen. Hajo Schroeder, a 100 per cent Nazi, had the idea to get able young people to come to Germany with whom he planned to set up a Mennonite village as they had had in Ukraine. We knew nothing of this. Everything was planned very quickly and in May our first group left by train for Buenos Aires.... It was all well organized and in two days we were on a steamboat to Germany. The travel costs for this part were arranged by 'Reichsen Nährstand.' It was 200 marks, half price for Heimkehrer [returnees].

We knew nothing about it and were without a care, but later found we had to put in four months of farm labour to repay that ticket. When the 'guys' (Jungs) heard some Plattdeutsch being spoken in an adjoining cabin, that was a surprise. A family from Brazil with a sister and elderly grandmother were 'returning to the Reich.' As we entered the canal at Calais, we heard news of the danger of war and were disturbed, but having heard so much about 'Kraft durch Freude' [strength through joy – a Hitler slogan] in Paraguay, we were anxious to see and experience Germany.

We arrived in Bremerhafen on June 29, 1939, and suddenly were told, 'Get ready to disembark.' We had expected to go to Hamburg and then on from there. Within the hour we were on a bus, and after a few hours we arrived in a guesthouse in the little town of Jever bei Oldenburg. All kinds of men, farmers and three women were waiting for us. We still didn't know what was going on, were famished and waiting for a good meal. All we got was tea. Suddenly the 'guys' in our group were called up by name and each one presented to a farmer. This seemed very suspicious.... I was called up and had to stand in front of a farmer who smiled at me with blue eyes and greeted me. I followed him to his Volkswagen and there stood a woman with gold spectacles.

Frau Gerken allowed me to sleep in one day, but after that it was 4:30 a.m. in the milking parlour. That was the introduction for all of us. I was fortunate to be permitted to eat with the family and in the cold winter to be in their warm living room. The other workers and maids ate in the back kitchen where there was a stove in winter. Work was carried on in summer until ten at night and in winter milking was done three times a day until ten-thirty. We were free after the milking every other Sunday. To stay for the noon meal meant that we also would appear to do the evening milking.

We learned to ride bicycles, and on our free Sundays several of us met in the Evangelische Kirche and after that at the water tower in Hohenkirchen. Here we exchanged experiences, our homesickness, and sometimes we cried, but I always told myself, this isn't the end. The farmers were very satisfied with the work of the 'guys,' who were all reliable.

War broke out on 1 September 1939. We knew what war was and were afraid. The year came to an end. I had paid for my passage, but there was no opportunity to leave since during wartime all were obliged to remain at their place of work. However, I did not give up and applied at the labour office.... the town mayor was able to get me free so I could enter nurse's training in Bremen in October 1940. After three years and passing examinations as a surgical nurse, again with much effort, I was able to enter the midwifery school in Stuttgart.

During the last years of the war several of our guys voluntarily joined up, but hoped not to be sent to the eastern front. My brother was among these. I wrote to several of them since they had no contact with their families and I became like their sister. Packages were only allowed to weigh 100 grams. Those guys who had not volunteered were conscripted, even though all of us were not citizens. Some of my letters were returned stamped, 'Fallen for the Führer and Fatherland.'

Of the twenty-eight Friesland men who were conscripted or volunteered, eleven were killed, but not Jutti's brother – renamed 'Arno' because Abram was considered 'too Jewish.' At Christmas 1939 the man who had lured them to Germany handed out copies of Hitler's *Mein Kampf* as gifts and told the group from Paraguay, 'Forget the Christian story and celebrate the solstice.'[73]

This the group rejected. Jutti told me about visiting her Epp relatives in West Prussia near Danzig, a city still virtually untouched by bombing until late 1944. Here she felt 'at home,' the language and cuisine reminding her of her mother.[74] During most of the war Jutti was in nurse's training or working as a nurse in various hospitals. She wrote that when a military pastor said, 'Too bad it didn't succeed,' about the assassination attempt on Hitler, she was afraid to say anything for fear of being overheard.[75]

Wounded in battle in the last days of the war, Jutti's brother recuperated but broke an arm skating and avoided being returned to active battle. Returning to Paraguay in 1947, he later moved to Brazil, where he developed a modern dairy farm – frozen semen sent in from abroad and the latest technology. Jutti also returned to South America.

Escape from Red Paradise

It is 1943. Encircled, the German army is bogged down at Stalingrad. In Mikhailovka, in occupied Soviet Ukraine, Hermine Braun and her children, working on the farm, increasingly become aware of refugees – Chechens from the Caucuses and Don Cossacks – moving *west*. By August columns of the German army are retreating, and when German occupation administration offices begin to close, all *Volksdeutsche* are ordered to join the retreat. Greatly troubled by the German collapse, the *Volksdeutsche* welcome the chance to escape reprisals by Ukrainian partisans and the Red Army.

On 10 October, Hermine Braun and her friend Agatha Unrau, allotted horses and a wagon – perhaps taken from Ukrainians – load up Hermine's sewing machine, a few clothes, a bit of bedding, a sack of flour, yeast, salt, and sugar. The weather is damp and cool, but with young people walking and mothers in the wagon guiding the horses (a cow tied behind the wagon for milk), they set out. German soldiers on horseback accompany a long column of wagons just like theirs.

The story of the Trek, when 350,000 Soviet Germans travelled in some cases hundreds of kilometres to German-occupied Poland, is told in other books.[76] On our visit to Bonn in 1999, Greta Braun told the bare details, describing the 'Michaelsburger' caravan making its way towards the mouth of the Dnieper River at the Black Sea. Near Kherson, they were encircled by advancing Soviet troops, each day more uncertain than the last. The refugee group waited ten days, encamped without shelter or cooking facilities. Resourceful as always, Greta said, 'We women dug holes in the ground, filled them with straw that we burned, and then placed our bread dough in the covered tunnels. Were those soldiers astonished when we opened the holes. They had never seen bread baked like that. And it rose high too!'

As the trek group waited, a commanding German officer told Greta's brother Kornelius to inform the women they very well might not escape. He hesitated. Panic might ensue if each mother grabbed a child and ran, but which child and run where? He was debating with himself when an officer announced that the army would mount one final counter-attack that very night, to try to break out. 'What joy in our encampment the following morning with the news that the Reds were pushed back!'

Nine trains stood on the Kherson tracks waiting to take away the retreating German military personnel and refugees. Locomotives fired up, the women and children boarded. Although Greta seemed uninformed about events in the larger theatre of war or politics, concentrating instead on fleeing the Communists, the devastation on the battlefield shocked her. 'Everything was burned black. It is just too dreadful to describe.'

Some refugees were moved almost entirely by train, but thousands of others from the Dnieper area walked beside horse-drawn wagons in long caravans through mud, rain, and snow before they reached the area of occupied Poland renamed the Warthegau. Part of the pre-Versailles Prussian province of Posen, it had been given to Poland after the First World War. In areas taken over by the Soviets in consequence of the 1939 Hitler-Stalin non-aggression pact, they had deported 880,000 Poles.[77] Similarly, in areas Germany had taken, she removed thousands of Polish nationals. The Nazis wished to make room for uprooted ethnic Germans from ancient Baltic and Eastern communities, the ones told to come *'Heim ins Reich.'* Some 60,000 were resettled in the Warthegau.[78] Polish nationals remaining in the land were treated harshly, and thousands were sent to Germany as Polish *Ostarbeiter*, the *PArbeiter*.[79] The Mikhailovka group, en route four months, arrived in the Warthegau in February 1944 and was greeted by Hitler Youth who helped them to move into rooms commandeered or taken away from Polish nationals. Many refugees sympathized with the Poles and felt badly about taking space others had been forced to vacate.[80] They knew what it was like to be removed from homes and have to see their communities destroyed.

In our visits with the Brauns in Bonn, little was said about Viktor's brother Yasha, youngest of Isaak and Hermine's children, except that he was short, had been separated from the family at the end of the war, and foolishly left the safety of the American zone to cross into the Russian zone (swimming across the Elbe River in search of his girlfriend). Nobody mentioned what I found in EWZ files from the German ministry of the interior captured by the American Army near the end of the Second World War. EWZ (*Einwandererzentralstelle*) immigration forms were filled out when the Brauns arrived in the Warthegau and were processed for German citizenship. Questions Hermine was required to answer demanded vital statistics: 'How German are you?' Hermine wrote, '100 per cent.' Another question asked the applicant to swear (or affirm) that there was no tainting of a German heredity with 'Jewish blood,' a space Hermine did not fill in. On 30 June 1944 in Reisen, Warthegau, Hermine Braun and her children were declared German citizens.[81]

Also in the EWZ file I read that Yasha, sent away for Nazi indoctrination, had left the farm in May 1943 and in 1944 was stationed (when last known) in Minsk, Ostland. Ostland was the German term for a combination of the occupied Baltic countries and White Russia. Yasha was a Hitler Youth in the *Kriegseinsatzkommando Mitte*. Yasha could have welcomed moving from collective farm rags into Hitler Youth uniform. Hitler Youth, a paramilitary organization for boys aged thirteen to eighteen, were drilled in marching, bayonet use, grenade throwing, trench digging, map reading, gas defence, pistol shooting, and crawling under barbed wire. Unlucky Yasha had just finished his training when the proud German war machine met Stalingrad. Promptly, he was pulled into active duty.[82]

Describing his conscription as soon as he reached the Warthegau, a young Mennonite wrote that he and all militarily eligible men and boys older than fifteen were forced 'to *voluntarily* join the Waffen SS.'[83] All but their youngest sons taken away in previous Soviet round-ups or through German recruitment in occupied Ukraine, many mothers now lost their remaining teenage sons. In German uniforms, these youths died in large numbers in the Battle of the Bulge. This battle in the war's coldest, snowiest winter, between December 1944 and January 1945, in the forested Ardennes of Belgium was the last major (and failed) Nazi counter-offensive against the Allies.

The mothers Hermine Braun and Agatha Unrau and daughters Liesel and Greta found work, Hermine as a cleaning woman in a post office and Liesel in the office of the local commissioner. It must have impressed them to see the old towns, the thirteenth- to fifteenth-century cathedrals, well-maintained town houses – so unlike their long-neglected houses in Ukraine. In early 1944 Allied bombing had not yet touched the occupied territories. At some point the four women moved from the Warthegau to the village of Kristindorf, near Berlin, where they again worked on a farm. Nobody knew where their men were – those arrested in 1937–8, marched away by the Soviets in 1941, or working as interpreters or German soldiers.

When they saw Germans frantically packing jewellery and silver into trunks and burying them in gardens, or children burning Hitler Youth medals, flags, and black scarves with the leather knot, it became obvious to the refuges from Soviet Ukraine that Germany would lose the war. Viktor, now in German uniform, was in the area of Elbing (West Prussia) on the Baltic Sea coast when Allied bombing and a strong push by the Red Army sent Baltic civilians fleeing west. Helter-skelter, by water and land, as described by Günter Grass in *Peeling the Onion*, thousands tried to escape the Red Army.

Viktor Braun's officers said, 'Every man for himself, see if you can survive,' and he threw away his uniform. Soon woods and byways were filled with shadowy men creeping west, not only to escape Russian hands, but also to evade German 'bloodhounds' searching for deserters to execute at a roadside as warnings to civilians to 'believe in the Führer' to the end. After Viktor reached the vicinity of Berlin, by coincidence he heard that his mother, Widow Unrau, Liesel, and Greta were in Kristindorf and found them just in time to attend his sweetheart Greta's twenty-first birthday.

The Brauns hoped the Americans would reach Berlin first, yet, as bombs rained in April 1945 and ancient cities and towns turned into rubble, they sought underground shelters. Burning cities like Dresden could be seen sixty-five kilometres away, and fourteen-year-old German boys sent to fight were mowed down by Russian tanks.[84] Soon the fighting was house to house, in every street, every village. Then it was, 'Horror of horrors! It's the Red Army in Kristindorf!' and Viktor, his mother, and sister were overrun.[85] 'The war is over!' [*Voina kaput!*], shouted Red Army soldiers. 'Germany has lost the war!' [*Fritzi kaput, voina kaput!*]

Viktor and Greta Braun did not talk about the wrecked vehicles, abandoned suitcases, dead animals, or corpses left on streets, or about Nazis' desperate acts – the killing of sick prisoners, force-marching remaining concentration camp survivors. Or about the horror of Soviet soldiers raping millions of German and refugee young women and girls. How surprised we had been at stories told by my mother's cousin, Tante Kathe, in British Columbia. A refugee in Berlin (she had trekked out of the USSR) at the time of Germany's surrender, she had hidden in cellars of bombed-out buildings and tried to shield young girls, dressing them in rags, pulling kerchiefs over their soot-streaked faces, and coaching them to hide under dirty burlap sacks. Russian and Western historians writing about the assaults on millions of German women and young girls vary in response. Some express horror, but others excuse the acts as justified revenge, 'understandable pent-up sexual need.'[86] If my relatives were raped, they never spoke of it. In all my discussions with women who immigrated to Canada after the Second World War, nobody wanted to speak about rape, but in her research Canadian historian Marlene Epp, in confidence, heard from raped Mennonite women.[87]

The Brauns also omitted mention of the round-up of German civilians in Soviet-conquered areas who, in a reverse *Ostarbeiter* move, became German *Ostarbeiter* sent to Belorussia and Ukraine to do forced labour and 'repair war damage.' Antony Beevor gave the figure of 68,680 civilians, mostly German women and children assigned to clean up war rubble in Soviet Ukraine.[88] Beevor stated that these thousands 'suffered at least as much' as their Soviet counterparts rounded up previously by the Wehrmacht in German-occupied USSR. Many were forced to leave behind dependent children, and worse, were repeatedly raped.[89] Soviet superiors punished their soldiers for rapes only if they became infected with venereal diseases (which women had picked up from previous rapes).

Many refugee and German women committed suicide rather than face being gang-raped by the Red Army. As revenge for the brutality the German Army had shown to Soviet citizens in the USSR, Stalin saw nothing wrong with the Red Army 'having fun' with German women and girls. The Red Army also hunted for Soviet refugees who had worked with the German military, men like Viktor Braun. Captured in uniform, such people were shot on the spot, as were Ukrainians and Caucasians who had worked for the Germans, especially as camp guards. Thousands of captured German soldiers were sent to the USSR to do ten years of hard labour.

Repatriated to the Fatherland, 1945–1950

At Yalta in 1944, Allied leaders had decided to assist the USSR when Stalin demanded that refugees from the USSR be returned or repatriated. Churchill and Roosevelt were more concerned with the safe return

Gültig bis zum *13. Februar* 19*31*.

(Ausstellende Behörde) , den **1 4. Feb. 1930** 192_

Personalausweis Nr. *239*

Paßersatz *Bmd: Jacob – 10. 12. 1926*

Familienname: *Konrad*

Vorname: *Peter*

Staatsangehörigkeit: *staatlos* | frühere: *Rußland*
| bis wann: *2. 12. 1929*

Beruf: *Landwirt*

Ständiger Wohnsitz mit Anschrift: _____

Gegenwärtiger Aufenthaltsort mit Anschrift: *Flüchtlingslager Prenzlau*

Geboren am: *3. April 1890*   Alter: *39* Jahre

Geburtsort: *Schöntal, Perekop, Krim*

Gestalt: *mittel* Haar: *schwarz* Augen: *blau* Gesichtsform: *rund*

Besondere Kennzeichen: *keine*

Es wird hiermit bescheinigt, daß der Inhaber die durch nebenstehendes Lichtbild dargestellte Person ist und die darunter befindliche Unterschrift eigenhändig vollzogen hat.

Unterschrift:
Im auftrag
Hoffmann

Unterschrift des Inhabers
Peter Konrad

Nr. A 54 Berlin Reichsdruckerei (7. 24)

Stateless passport issued to Peter Konrad in the refugee camp in Prenzlau, Germany, on 14 February 1930. This passport guaranteed a return to Germany, not the USSR, should Canadian immigration not accept or deport the passport bearer.

Portrait of the Jakob and Helene Konrad Family taken in Simferopol, Crimea, 1903. The portrait was made shortly before daughter Helene left for missionary training. Children (back row, left to right): Peter, Jakob, Justina, Anna. Children (front row): Abram, Maria, Gerhard, Heinrich, Helene. Photo Konrad Archives.

Portrait of Isaak Braun, his second wife Helene, and the Braun children taken in Davlekanova, Bashkiria, in 1910. Back row (left to right): Isaak, Peter, Jakob, Johannes, Luise; front row: (second family) Henry, baby Nicholas, Bernhard, Anna. Photo Konrad Archives.

Justina Konrad and Jakob Epp's wedding portrait, Crimea, 1908.
Photo Konrad Archives.

Motya and Heinrich Konrad with daughters Lucia and Elizaveta,
Maslianovka, Siberia, 1928. Photo courtesy Elizaveta Dovbush.

Gerhard, Lieschen, and her Froese parents in Spat, Crimea, on 12 March 1930. Gerhard Konrad, wearing a hat, is on the bottom step along with Lieschen's young brother Willy. Lieschen (with tie) stands beside her mother. Next is her father, the miller Heinrich Froese. Other Froese family members are not identified. Soon after this photograph the Froese family was exiled to Arkhangelsk. Gerhard Konrad photo.

Brothers Gerhard and Abram Konrad in Taldy Kurgan, Kazakhstan, in September 1959 at Gerhard's house. (Left to right) Abram's grandson Evgeny, his son Jakob, Abram, Gerhard, Klara (standing), Motya, Nastya, Abram's daughter Lena, and young Nelly in front. Gerhard Konrad photo.

Peter and Luise Konrad and children in Maslianovka, Siberia, in 1929. Back: Mary, Peter, Helen. Front: mother Luise holding Heinrich, father Peter Jakob holding Jakob. Photo Konrad Archives.

Family photo in Alici's album taken in 1931. Johannes and Anna Braun's children: (back) Alici, Heinz/Andrei, Hans; (front) Maria, Anni (image lost).

Peter and Selma Braun and children in 'the 1930s.' (Left to right) Grisha, Selma, Lora, Peter, Petya. Photo courtesy Henry Brown.

Andrei Braun at his mother Anna's house in Konstantinovka, Siberia, in 1948. He fetched his bride home on the back of his bicycle in 1949. Photo courtesy Alici Braun.

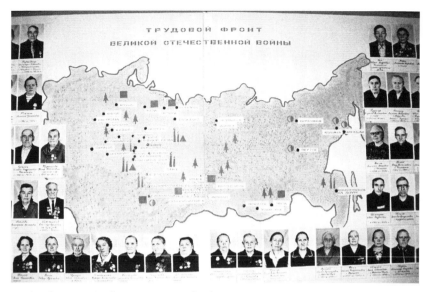

A display map in the museum in the former Mennonite village of Margenau, Siberia (within the former Mennonite high school), showing a map of Labour Army work sites and photographs of local 'volunteers' of the 'Work Front of the Great Fatherland War' – the *Trudarmiia*. Photo Anne Konrad.

Meeting Maria Braun, in the Intourist Hotel, Karaganda, Kazakhstan, 1989. Natasha and Volodya Braun/Milshin, Maria Braun, Andrei and daughter Vika Braun/Milshin. Photo Konrad Archives.

AnnaK's (Anna Konrad Wiebe Toews) house in Waldheim, Siberia, 1989, occupied by her grandson's family after daughter Agatha and Heinrich Klassen immigrated to Germany. Photo courtesy Heinrich Klassen.

Furnishings from some former local Mennonite village homes are displayed in Omsk Regional History Museum, 2001. Photo by author.

Harvey L. Dyck at the Tomsk prison cell door (with peephole) peers at the bunks and latrine bucket (right), June 2001. Photo by author.

Historians Boris Trenin (right) and Harvey L. Dyck (left) in the basement Museum of the History of Political Repression, a former OGPU-NKVD prison in Tomsk, 2001. Photo by author.

Reunion after forty-eight years. Gerhard (left) and brother Peter Konrad (right) in Canada, 1977. Photo Konrad Archives.

Discussing family history. (Left to right) Gerhard Konrad, Nelly Konrad, Lena Wiebe, Nina and Jakob Wiebe, Bremen, 1991. Photo by author.

Looking for family villages (Gorchakovo) in Bashkiria. Photo H.L. Dyck.

Author and Director Ramzil at the former Davlekanova Mennonite high school, 2001. Photo H.L. Dyck.

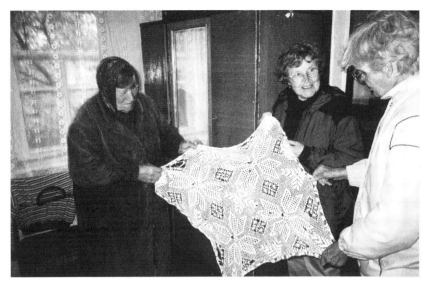

The last Plautdietsch-speaking Mennonite (at left) in Kotlyarevka, Ukraine, with author and (right) Maria Vasilevskaya, 2001. Photo H.L. Dyck.

The author with Elizaveta Dovbush in Snezhnoie, Ukraine, 1999. Photo H.L. Dyck.

Issyk, Central Asia, in early 1960s. Four exiled widows: (front, first left) Agatha Unrau and (far right) Hermine Hein Braun (wife of Isaak); (back, left to right) Shura and Yasha Braun, Liesel (Braun) Lammert, Viktor and Greta Braun, and another couple. Photo courtesy Johanna Schmidt.

Greta Unrau and friends at collective farm in Michailovka, Soviet Ukraine, take watermelons to river to sell, pre 1943. Photo courtesy Johanna Schmidt.

A monument to the 30,000 Mennonite victims of the Soviet inferno was unveiled in Zaporizhiia, Ukraine, on 10 October 2009. Inscribed on the base is 'Blessed are they who mourn.' Inscriptions in English, German, Russian, and Ukrainian read 'To Mennonite Victims of Tribulation, Stalinist Terror and Religious Oppression.' Photo T.A. Dyck.

ПРОКУРАТУРА СРСР

ПРОКУРАТУРА
ДОНЕЦЬКОЇ ОБЛАСТІ

340015, Донецьк-15,
вул. газети «Соціалістичний Донбас», № 2

ПРОКУРАТУРА СССР

ПРОКУРАТУРА
ДОНЕЦКОЙ ОБЛАСТИ

340015, Донецк 15
ул. газеты «Социалистический Донбасс», №

06 Х-89   № 13/2

На № _____ от _____

┌
Довбуш Елизавете Андреевне
Донецкая область,
г.Снежное, ул.Горького, 9, кв.3
┐

№ 3 4866

СПРАВКА

В соответствии со ст.I Указа Президиума Верховного Совета
СССР от 16 января 1989 года № 10036-XI "О дополнительных мерах
по восстановлению справедливости в отношении жертв репрессий,
имевших место в период 30-40-х и начала 50-х годов", постанов-
ление НКВД по Донецкой области от 9 октября 1938г. в отношении
Конрада Генриха Яковлевича, 1897г. рождения, уроженца с.Алексан-
дровки, Бердянского района, Днепропетровской области, до ареста
работавшего доставщиком материалов ЦММ треста "Снежнянскантрацит",
отменено, дело производством прекращено за отсутствием в его дей-
ствиях состава преступления.
      Конрад Генрих Яковлевич р е а б и л и т и р о в а н.

Прокурор Донецкой област:
государственный советник
юстиции 2 класса

В.Г.Синюков

Волновахская тип. З. 2111—30 т. 13-05-88

Elizaveta Dovbush received her father Heinrich Konrad's certificate of
rehabilitation in October 1989. He had been executed in October 1938. 'I have
cried very hard. After fifty-one years they declare him innocent …'

of their own POWs. Wrote Britain's Patrick Dean, assistant legal adviser to the Foreign Office, 'All those with whom Soviet authorities desire to deal, must subject to what is said below, be handed over to them, and we are not concerned with the fact that they may be shot or otherwise more harshly dealt with than they might under English law.'[90]

Soviet authorities often gave refugees whom they unearthed in Germany (people like Hermine or Greta Braun and Widow Unrau) sweet promises, like, 'You can return to your former homes. Your husbands and fathers will be there. There will be no reprisals, no punishment.' Greta told us that, tired of being on the run, some refugees sought out a Soviet repatriation camp, gullibly believing they would be returned to former homes. Others, overrun, had no choice.

In the Soviet zone of occupation, Viktor's younger brother Yasha and Greta's brother Kornelius were missing when the Braun and Unrau families were sent to Soviet detention barracks twenty-five kilometres from Kristindorf. After a month, the 'collaborators' were taken by bus to the German-Polish border and stuffed into cattle cars travelling east. By 1 December 1946, the Allies had returned 5.5 million people to the USSR.[91] Americans, known to have an army of many-coloured soldiers and to hand out chocolates, were thought less likely than other Allies to force repatriation. But Yasha Braun, aged twenty, in the American zone, focused only on his sweetheart in detention barracks in the Russian zone and waited for a night when boat traffic on the Elbe River was light, and then (who even knew he could swim?) dove into its cold waters and swam across into the Russian zone. Alas, he was told the bus taking his girlfriend and family members had left for the Polish border and an unknown destination, but revealed as a Soviet German, he was sent to cool his passion in a Ural prison work camp.

Meanwhile, the train carrying the 'repatriated' Brauns was headed for the Urals (15–30 per cent of similar repatriated died en route).[92] The train stopped at Solikamsk, once the salt cellar of the Russian Empire, but as of 1941 a centre of large pulp and paper mills. Newsprint relied on a steady supply of timber, and since indigenous Komi people sparsely inhabited the surrounding forested areas, the deportees from Germany were the increased labour force. The Brauns were now herded onto a waiting ship that took them 150 kilometres farther north up the broad Kama River into pine forests – and minus forty degrees in winter. It was the end of October when the 'prisoner' ship carrying the Brauns reached the port of Krasnovishersk, in the Perm region. Surrounded by armed guards, marched almost six kilometres, dragging along their belongings on wooden stone boats, they reached a prison lumbering camp complete with barbed wire and watchtowers. Women and men were in the same barracks, so mothers slept on the wooden planks of the lower berth of a continuous row of bed boards and Liesel and Greta on the top berths. Viktor slept in the narrow aisle. On wash lines overhead hung wet and dirty clothing or foot rags. The smell of sweat and cigarette smoke was mixed with coarse language and crying.

Liesel, Greta, and Viktor were assigned to cut trees – two workers at opposite ends of a saw. Once the trees were limbed, trunks were then cut into required lengths for the pulp and paper mill. Every worker was assessed a quota to cut each day and work carried on through all weather. But a siren sounding early in the morning – if it was colder than minus 40 degrees Celsius – meant 'stay indoors.' Against the bitter cold, 'repatriates' were given thin gloves and boots of woven birch bark to be worn over rags wound around the feet. Kerchiefs for women and caps with earflaps for men were each worker's own responsibility, as were coats. 'How happy we forced labourers were a few years later when felt boots became available in the local market and we purchased them with our skimpy salaries.' Food was rationed to 250 grams of bread a day for non-workers (about half a standard loaf of bread) and 600 grams for workers like Viktor, Liesel, and Greta. The bread was spongy, like dough, and included sawdust and chaff. Women often held it over an open fire at the tree-cutting site, toasting it enough to develop a flavour. Viktor told us that when he worked on the crosscut saw with another male, he could surpass his quota and earn slightly more bread. A worker like Viktor earned a salary of fifty roubles a month.

With such scanty rations, many starved. Mothers Hermine Braun and Widow Unrau, looking after kindergarten children in the camp and getting the scant portion of 250 grams of bread, took a handmade sled and a blanket to cover any food they might get, and bartered in widely separated villages for potatoes or turnips. They traded any item of 'foreign' clothing (from Germany), which was prized locally. One item Hermine did not barter was her son Viktor's leather vest with its rabbit-fur lining that saved him from freezing in the cold. After a year Liesel became the lumber camp accountant, and everyone in the camp benefited from honest accounts. Her predecessor often held back wages to line his pocket, an example of which Greta was quick to contribute.

WORKER. *'I want to ask for my monthly pay.'*
ACCOUNTANT. *'You've already received it.'*

WORKER. *'I've received nothing.'*
ACCOUNTANT. *'Here's your signature. See for yourself.'*
WORKER *(looking at the ledger, vehemently). 'That's not my signature.'*

But it was. Liesel quietly observing, being appreciced to the old accountant, told the worker later, 'He showed you your signature from the previous month. You should have looked at the date. That's how he cheats people.'

With his earnings, Viktor bought a one-room hut, and when Viktor Braun and Greta Unrau married, the two families moved in. A curtain strung across a corner of the room made the couple's bedroom. When Liesel married, another corner was curtained off. When babies arrived, the grandmothers looked after the children. In the early 1960s, after internal travel was permitted (except to their original homes in Soviet Ukraine), both families moved to the Alma Ata area and worked in a collective farm vineyard.

Also 'repatriated,' the *Ostarbeiter* Konrad sisters, Elizaveta and Lucia, had returned home during the corn harvest to find their village Snezhnoie in ruin. In retreat, the German army had set fire to villages, railways, and storage buildings, anything that might feed, aid, or assist pursuing Red Army troops. The girls joined their mother, Motya, now living in a dugout, and they found work. 'Had we told anyone that we were *Ostarbeiter* or that our father had been arrested, we never would have received a job. They sent such people into mines.' Elizaveta's first job was as an apprentice in a print shop and her sister's in the post office. A drought in Ukraine in 1946 resulted in a famine, but that was not their worst problem. Elizaveta wrote:

My sister Lucia gave some money to a fellow postal worker to buy flour for us, but she was swindled, got neither the flour nor her money back. Mama wanted to protest, but we feared for her to go alone, so both Lucia and I went with her. That made us five minutes late for work. For Lucia there was no problem, but my foreman confronted me and said I would have to be tried and sentenced because I had been late. They were sorry for me but could not risk losing their own ration cards by protecting me. I was advised to write a petition and voluntarily resign my job.

Having lost both a job and my ration card, I decided to write to Uncle Abram and Tante Nastya in Central Asia. I packed up and took the train to Moscow – that's as far as I had a ticket. Then I joined others who hid in wooden cattle cars, sleeping as best I could. It took us a month to get to Mama's sister in Frunze [Bishkek] in Kirghizia. Not having had anything to eat for twenty-

four hours when I arrived, I felt utterly lost, but thank God, Mama was pray-
ing for me. My aunt did not recognize me. She had not seen me since I was
three years old. I rested there. My aunt bought me a ticket to Alma Ata where
I wanted to meet Lena, the daughter of Uncle Abram and Tante Nastya who
was attending college in Alma Ata and was on her winter break. There was a
cousin, a daughter of an uncle on my mother's side, who lived in Alma Ata, a
paediatrician, and I was her guest. I met Uncle Abram's daughter, my cousin
Lena, who bought tickets so we could go to Molani by train and then by vehicle
the forty-three miles [seventy kilometres] to the border of China.

Tante Nastya lived near the border. I was supposed to carry an identity pass-
port, but didn't have one. Uncle Abram came to a village at the border where
the guards knew him well. They were friends. He brought me felt boots and
two fur coats. One coat we placed on the floor of the wagon and the other one
we used to cover me. Lena sat on me and that's how we got into the village of
Aksu [where Abram Konrad and hundreds of others had been deported]. Uncle
Abram had to go to the local police to register that his niece had come for a visit,
but since I had no passport the police said, 'She has to be gone within twenty-
four hours.' I was terrified. Uncle Abram and Tante Nastya went to the head
of police where Tante Nastya fell on her knees to plead for me. She said I would
die on the way. They allowed me to stay for 6 months.

So I could stay there until the fall. Here there was food, no starvation. Tante
Nastya had a goat, potatoes and bread. Uncle Gerhard had a cow, a calf and a
pig. I worked for both uncles and aunts and sent parcels home to my mother.
Tante Nastya treated me like her own child – what she did for her own children,
she did for me. At Tante Klara's [wife of Gerhard], she made me do all the work.
I was to be her maid, do the milking, take the cow to pasture, work the garden,
and carry water from a distance. Uncle Gerhard was away from home [a truck
driver] and Tante Klara wanted a record player, to flirt, to party, and to dance
with Russian officials. We did not enjoy each other's company.[93]

Returning to Snezhnoie, Soviet Ukraine, in the fall of 1947, again not
revealing her past, Elizaveta got a job with the railway, weighing trucks.
Her sister Lucia, a postal clerk, worked her way up in the system and
kept this job her entire working life. Their brother Evgeny (Eugene),
released from the Red Army, became a truck driver.

Evgeny, mother Motya, and the two sisters moved into a barracks
where they had one room and a kitchen. They repaired the space, all
contributing their wages. When Evgeny wanted to marry, his fiancée
said there was no room for another woman in that 'apartment.' Elizaveta related bitterly, 'I was pushed out. My brother got drunk when

his fiancée said this, whereupon Mother asked me to leave. I did not get one rouble and I had done much of the repair and given all of my money for it. They treated me like this. I've suffered all my life.'

Lucia had married a Russian communist miner and moved out. When we met her in 2001 she had a full-size house and fairly large garden. Her mother, Motya, stayed with son Evgeny, his wife Ludmilla, and looked after their child, Tanya.

Eventually Elizaveta married Emelian Dovbush, a Ukrainian Romanian. His family had been exiled from Romania in 1947 and by the 1950s had ended up in the same Snezhnoie barracks. Elizaveta's job with the railway gave her a pass that allowed her to travel on her once-a-year holiday. She told us that over the years she visited Lithuania, Latvia, and Estonia, and saw Moscow and Leningrad. Twice she visited her Konrad uncles in Taldy Kurgan, Kazakhstan. Sometimes she took along her niece Tanya. In 1990 she wrote a letter to try to contact her relatives in Canada.

7

Prisoners and Singers in Siberia, 1941–1954

Maria in the *Trudarmiia*

After we had corresponded with Maria Braun (we met in Karaganda) for some years, she wanted to give us gifts (being too proud to be only a recipient) and asked what we would like. I replied, 'Write your auto-biography.' Starting in 1992 and for two years, she mailed a chapter to me, another one to my sister Mary, alternating to ensure that at least some arrived in spite of censors in the postal system. She began with her father's arrest:

After Papa [Johannes] was gone, Mama sold everything so we could repay the debts. Mama was very ill with intestinal problems and could not eat, always had to vomit....

So I worked at the collective farm until June 1941. We already had bought ourselves many things, for example bedding, and the war came. I was eighteen … they took us away to Siberia where there was so much snow that the houses could not be seen for the depth of the snow.

In 1942 my sister Anni and I were forced into the Trudarmiia.

This was a new term for me, *Trudarmiia*, also called the Labour Army. With workers needed for Soviet industry and to produce military sup-plies, on 7 October 1942, Stalin had ordered that the *Nemtsy*, German-speaking men between fifteen and fifty-five and women between sixteen and forty-five, were to be rounded up – even from deporta-tion sites – for the *Trudarmiia*.[1] The implication was, 'Your countrymen attacked our Fatherland; Russian people suffered; you Soviet Germans have to pay for it.'[2] Sent west across the Urals, Maria and her sister Anni reached a forced labour work site and began digging deep trenches for pipes in the area of Ufa. Maria wrote:

The trenches were twenty-five metres deep [this seems impossible], and we were so young and had nothing to eat. Whenever we found some potato peelings we cooked them and ate them. Once we poisoned ourselves with the peelings. We used to go to the holes where they poured out the water and all the garbage from wherever there were kitchens.

Workers in the *Trudarmiia* were given hand tools: spades, saws, hoes, crowbars, pickaxes, and wheelbarrows. In winter, ground was frozen two feet down and Maria would chip away with a pickaxe until small chunks loosened. Working under such conditions in inadequate clothing, unable to meet prescribed quotas, her rations were reduced. Maria had been told to bring her own underwear, bedding, and a bowl and spoon for a soup that was typically 80 per cent water with a few sunflower shells, grass seeds, rye flour, or bran thickening, and an occasional fish bone. Only as the war progressed and workers caught onto the system (and guards were complicit) did she and her fellow workers begin to find ways to fudge the numbers for work completed and get their full food ration.

Forced workers like Maria wrapped rags around their feet since shoes – canvas-covered tops with wooden soles or woven of birch bark – were hardly waterproof or warm. I once saw a replica of a Labour Army Camp barracks in a Toronto exhibition. The uninsulated wooden building had tiers of bunks on either side and one small round stove in the middle. The splintery bare bunk was there, but without the fleas, lice, and stench of urine and wet rags.

Maria worked in various camps, in a brick factory where

the kilns were so hot that our faces were always as though they had been burned. That's where I got the fever [malaria] and was so ill that I spit up blood. I was as thin as a skeleton and sister Anni was swollen thick from hunger.

In 1944 she and her sister decided to desert:

Anni and I decided to break out. If we got home, good, and if we perished, what difference did it make where we died? It was March. We went by foot and we also stood on the steps of trains. I almost could not walk any more because I was so ill. Everywhere the snow was melting and we walked with wet feet.

Of course it was wartime, and if anyone was caught escaping, they were sentenced harshly. When we arrived in a village at sundown – we always arrived in the evenings so that nobody should see us – we looked for the bathhouse in a garden. There we undressed, and it was so warm that we could dry out our clothes and footwear. In the early morning when it was still dark we would leave. That's how we travelled.

One day I was so ill that I couldn't go any more and I said to Anni, 'You go alone. Let me die here.'

She cried and begged me, 'Maria, please come!'

'No, I can't do it any longer,' I said.

Then she went. As I raised my head to look after her, all I could see was a small dot. Then I wept too and I think I must have prayed. Suddenly Anni was standing in front of me again. She had returned. 'I couldn't continue without you. I couldn't leave you here,' she said, begging me to come. She helped me to my feet and we continued.

I found an empty can with which I dipped some water on the way and I drank. Anni didn't know this and I got sicker and sicker. The fever wouldn't leave me. In a village we helped to dig up the garden and we were given some food to eat.

The sisters were caught and taken to a local headquarters where they were assigned to carry beams at a construction site, but because of her malaria Maria would carry only two or three and then be unable to continue. Beside an old cast-iron heater in a small hut where workers warmed up, she lay down, thinking she was about to die.

The administrator came to oversee how the work was progressing and asked, 'What's lying there, Comrade Procurator?'

'A jacket,' she replied.

'No,' the man persisted, 'That's a person.' His foot nudged me.

'Yes,' we told him, 'that's what the woman had said to us; she wouldn't give us written permission to go to the infirmary. We'd try to escape.'

'Come,' said the procurator, 'I'll give you a note to the infirmary."

So then they took me to the infirmary and put me into the section for lung infections because I was spitting up so much blood. I lay there for a week and then they examined my lungs in X-rays and found that my lungs were healthy. After that I was taken to the convalescent wing and there I remained for a month while Anni was working. They had given her food now and she was allowed to be in the barracks. I had a good woman doctor who was very kind to me.

One day Anni said, 'They want to deport us back to the place from which we ran away.' So then I decided to ask the kind doctor to write a medical note ordering me home to recuperate. At first she did not want to do this because she thought I was being let out of hospital too soon, but finally she agreed to do it after I begged her.

So we set out on foot that same night and continued our way home. We also would take the train at times, but never sat in a passenger car. They caught us six times after that, but let us go each time. In May we got to a small station where the people already were digging up their gardens, and so we asked for some work to help dig the garden. We got work from a woman with a young child who lived with her mother. As we started to dig, my raging fever returned and the old woman said to me, 'Maria, go inside! You can't dig.' But Anni dug. We stayed there for a week, and exactly on 11 May was Anni's birthday, and the old woman asked her what she could cook for her for her birthday. 'Fried potatoes and rivel milk soup.'³ How happy we were that day! After a week the old woman talked it over with the stationmaster and they bought us tickets to get home. It was a long time to get home and when we got to our house I looked through the window and saw our mother sitting there sewing for other people and she did not recognize me. So I said to Anni, 'You look inside.' And when my mother looked up and saw Anni's face in the window she shrieked, 'My children!' That was a wonderful reunion.

Home for ten months, always on the verge of death, Maria lay in bed. The doctor had no hope for her, but an old man in the village recommended a herbal cure that worked.⁴ The threat of a six-year prison sentence for desertion facing them, she and her sister returned to the labour camp:

Now they sent us to the forest. Of course that was not women's work, but we had to do it. Felling trees and cutting off the branches to heap up and burn. The trees had to be cut into six-metre and four-metre lengths and the snow came up to our waists. We had almost no food and were expected to work hard. I was assigned to ride on a horse, with several girls to load up the logs. It was very heavy work.

Once we were loading a birch log, and one end already was on the wagon and the other end needed to be raised and, as it was being manoeuvred, the piece holding the top end on the wagon began to splinter and so I sprang forward to secure the piece. As I lunged to hold the weight, I felt this sharp tearing pain inside my body as though my insides were being torn apart, and then I was in the infirmary. For a long time I was unable to sit. That's how I tore out

my uterus, and now still my uterus keeps prolapsing into my vagina, a very
heavy cross for me to bear. When I had recuperated I had to return to the same
work, to drive the logs down the hill over all the stumps, a hard job.

Maria's autobiography also touched on personal relationships within the camp. She mentioned the problem of guards taking advantage of and often raping prisoners, once barely escaping this fate herself. Usually the guards were not punished.

Whoever was in charge of us Germans did whatever he wanted. He'd stand
there at the bottom of the hill when it already was pitch dark, and it was impos-
sible to work any longer, and he'd wait to see the first one to say, 'It's time to go
back.' I always was the first one and then he would get on his horse, race ahead
to the kitchen and tell the cook to reduce my food ration, 'Braun, 200 grams of
bread.' So I had to suffer a lot, but God was with me.
*   We had an evil overseer who did whatever he pleased. One day he wanted*
to drive into the deep forest with me. It was in the winter and he intended to
rape me. At work, I had to seat myself in the sleigh with him and we drove
off, his driver holding the reins. We came to a river that was frozen and as we
approached the bank of the river, I hurled myself out of the sleigh, and because
the horse was travelling on slippery ice, they had to continue for some distance
before they could turn around. Meanwhile I had escaped into the nearest house.
The driver came into the house and said to me, 'Maria, come at once. Mr Tut-
anon is waiting. Come immediately or you'll be sorry.'
*   'I don't care what the consequences are,' I said heatedly. 'I'm not going!' I*
remained with the woman of the house until the evening and then returned.
My horse had been standing and waiting for me since noon. Nothing hap-
pened. Later I found out that Tutanon had been reported for what he was doing
to us girls, and he was removed from the camp. Then we got a boss who was
good to us Germans. We were such hard workers. On Sundays the new boss
would come into our barracks with his two children and listen to us sing. We
Germans can sing really well. And then we would be happy and enjoy our-
selves.

Love affairs flourished in the labour camps, but Maria wrote nothing about births. We know from other sources that babies were born in these camps. Maria wrote:

A young man fell in love with me and jilted me and I thought I would die.
But life continued and he did this to quite a few other girls. That's how life in

the forest was. I sang a lot and played my guitar. A young Russian came to our camp on furlough and he heard me singing and playing guitar. Later he wanted to go out with me and I was afraid because I didn't know what kind of a person he was, good or bad, but I went out with him. When his holidays were over, his father was an official in our camp, he told his father, 'Look after that young woman. Make sure she doesn't go out with anyone else.' His father was good to us Germans.

My boyfriend was three years younger than I was. So off he went to do three more years of service. We wrote letters to each other. When he had completed his term of duty he came back and he brought me back my picture. 'My mother doesn't want me to marry a German,' he told me. How I wept! We really loved each other. So then he married a Russian girl, but he must not have been happy with her because one day he walked by me with his wife and he got hold of my elbow and demanded to talk to me. I pulled away from him and said, 'I've got nothing to talk to you about.' After that I always avoided him when I saw him coming. This continued until 1946.

When the war ended in 1945, Maria was not released, and two years later she again decided to escape. Such attempts often failed.

In 1947 a woman friend and I decided to break out. We walked through the forests for three days and three nights. Finally we came to a railway station and here we jumped onto the train as it was leaving, and did not sit in any seat, but managed to avoid being noticed. At the next station we tried to find a train carrying fish and we sat in that car. And then when we got to the next station we looked for another unlikely boxcar and we kept this up until we were halfway home. Then they caught us. But the stationmaster was understanding and asked us, 'Why are you sitting in a car when the train is in a station? You have to keep hidden when the train stops, until the train is moving.' And so he let us go. We continued on the train and got to the home of my friend. I stayed for two days and her parents bought me a ticket to ride home.

Back home I worked at cleaning and then I took a four-month course in dairy management at the state collective farm. Immediately the first month that I was working, a woman came to me and wanted me to give her some cream. She was the pred, the boss of the farm, and her name was Mrs Froese. 'I can't do that,' I protested. 'If I give you cream, I have to pay for it. It belongs to the state. I'm not allowed to give it away.'

'Good,' she retorted, 'You'll pay for this!' She banged the door. The next day I'm called to the police station and they say to me, 'You escaped from the Labour Army, right?' I acknowledged that I did. So then they threw me into

jail. And after I had been in a local jail for several days, they transferred me to another jail, and then they put me on a train and I got to another jail. And so I was transferred from jail to jail until I got back to where I had escaped, near Ufa. And so I was kept for various times in nine different jails altogether, a month here, two weeks there. In total it took four months for me to get back to Ufa. There I was taken to court and sentenced to four months in jail, which I had already served. I was sent back to the forest.

In one of the prisons I had been in, in Omsk, there had been an outbreak of typhus and so all my hair had been shaved off. It was in March and was still very cold, and all I was wearing when I left home was a thin dress and so I was very lightly clothed for the cold prisons. In prison they gave us soup made from thistles and thistle balls, instead of meatballs.

Once I was sick and had swollen patches on my arms, on my breasts, and in the morning I had a temperature and so I remained lying there. When everyone returned they called a policeman and he forced me to go with him to an icy cold room, where no human being ever belonged and he shoved me into this space and locked the door. There stood iron bedsteads and so I sat down on one of the beds and began to sing. It was bitterly cold in there. The policeman knocked on the door and said, 'Stop singing!' So I asked myself, who could stop me? So I continued to sing. In the evening a female policewoman unlocked the door and asked, 'What are you doing here?' I showed her my swollen parts and explained everything to her, so she was angry with the other policeman and said what a rogue he was. So she took me back and gave me my blanket and I could lie down and rest again.

Maria's last years of forced labour were spent in a logging camp. To get to her work site she had to walk fifteen kilometres, but her singing continued.

There was a blind man in the camp who played on his harmonica and I used to sing when he played, so we were a musical team. On holidays it was a little easier. Then we could practise. And those times I would sing and play my guitar. We performed musical numbers and did some small plays from books. When the holidays were finished I had to return to the forest.

Maria's mother applied for her release and in 1949 sent her a document, which her boss did not show her. When her mother wrote, 'Why aren't you coming home? I've sent you papers,' Maria discovered the deceit. With new papers in 1950, finally 'free,' she was accompanied by a guard until she was delivered to the local police back at home. Still an 'enemy of the state,' and under the *Spetskommandatura* law,[5] she had to report monthly to the police. The woman who had turned her in before now asked Maria to work for her. Maria's reply was tart: 'When I was home before, you made sure I got stuck in jail, and now you're asking me to work? Get out of here, shameless woman!'

In the hotel room in Karaganda, Maria had told us something of her married life. Released after eight years of forced labour, she had worked in house construction and as janitor in a school. She met twenty-seven-year-old Nikolai Milshin in a bar and knew 'he was trouble' but wanted a home of her own. Milshin, deserted by his wife, had two little girls and Maria wanted children. A doctor had said her herniated uterus would prevent her from having children. She moved in with Milshin in 1952. After four months the ex-wife came and took the girls and now he had to pay child support. At first Milshin was good to Maria, but they were poor and she was stuck. Contrary to medical opinion, two weeks after living with Milshin, she was pregnant.

Maria had three children: Jura, born in 1953, Andrusha in 1955, and Volodya in 1958. Maria complained that her husband drank, beat her and the children, could pick up an axe and chop up a table, and the boys were frightened of him. She gave us the impression the relationship did not last long, but I discovered that it lasted for nineteen years. They separated in 1971. During this time Maria worked as a nurse's aide in a hospital in Kulunda, bringing home bread the patients had not eaten and sometimes leftover soup. After she retired, her pension was fifty-seven roubles. She continued to have health problems because of her prolapsed uterus, but refused medical help. She had a garden and lived alone, a hardship in the deep snow or when coal had to be shovelled for the winter. At the age of fifty-two, in 1977, Baptists converted her.

In our conversations in Karaganda, Maria appeared fearless, but the Soviet system had affected her and her family. She worried about the future of her sons and grandchildren. Deaf son Andrusha had been jailed for two years for drunkenness, and his wife left her children alone to run about on the streets all day without food. Maria got them for the summer holidays and wanted to teach them her religion, but her daughter-in-law wanted none of this. In any disagreement she would yank them back home. 'But I wouldn't give her the satisfaction of letting her see me cry! Oh, no, then she'd have the victory.'

With the help of American dollars from my extended family, the following year Maria was able to buy a small house and move to

Slavgorod near to son Volodya and Natasha. In subsequent years she reported that she had a lung problem. 'It might be cancer,' she wrote, 'but I've worked in Soviet hospitals and I'm not going there.' In 1993 my sister Lill, bringing jeans and other gifts for her family, saw Maria for the last time. At that time Maria said a pair of shoes would have cost her 12,000 roubles and a pair of jeans 18,000 roubles. On pension, she was receiving 500 roubles a month. Commenting on her experience in the Labour Army, she told my sister, 'When I stand in a store and hear people complain, I think of how we had to scrounge in slop pails that people threw out.'[6]

In the next years of perestroika, with republics of the former Soviet Union breaking off, mail was disrupted, letters often failed to arrive, and our correspondence became unpredictable. I had planned a visit to Siberia for the next summer, when her sister Alici wrote that Maria had died – the news arriving long after the fact.

Alici and the Golden *A*

Another woman who sang in prison was Maria's sister Alici. During the term of the Hitler-Stalin non-aggression pact (1939–41), as hostility towards the *Nemtsy* eased, Alici left Kotlyarevka. Invited by her Tante Katya Neufeld, Alici moved to Omsk, where she acquired teacher qualifications.

Here she had a friendship circle of Mennonite young people that included her aunt's family members, all in the same house. All of them were active Christians. In their free time, Alici and the young people loved to sing together. Heinrich Hildebrand played the mandolin and guitar sweetly enough to melt Alici's heart. Hildebrand was drafted into the Red Army, but they corresponded in triangle-shaped love letters. In Riga I saw such letters in a museum dedicated to victims of oppression. Like pinned butterflies on a black surface, the small triangles, each a page folded into an origami 'hat,' had messages inside and addresses outside – an invention for unavailable envelopes.

Alici told us about this part of her life in 1999 when Harvey and I visited her home in Shakhty. Qualified as a teacher, teaching German, she was posted to a school seventy kilometres out of Omsk. It was 5 November 1940 and Alici, seated in the teachers' office, was entering her pupil's marks for the first quarter into a ledger when two young policemen barged into the school. 'Where is Alici Braun?'

'She's sitting there.'

'Up! Show us where you live!'

Alici shared rooms with two other teachers and took the men to their lodging. In her room, one policeman ordered her roommates to do a body search for weapons while the other one ordered, 'Don't touch anything!'

'What have you done?' blurted out her roommate.

Alici, sobbing, shook her head. She had no idea.

One of the secret police officers found Alici's letters, a small stack including her triangle-shaped love letters from Heinrich Hildebrand and, pocketing these, ordered, 'Dress. You're under arrest.'

Pushed out onto the street, twenty-one-year old Alici was made to kneel face down in the freezing mud while her colleagues stood by, horrified. She was then hustled into what she described as a 'caged vehicle' with other arrested persons and taken to a local jail where she was forced to disrobe and be shaved 'everywhere.' Seventy-nine-year-old Alici still burned in shame as she told of this humiliation. 'Imagine, me, young, pretty, twenty, and that … An old man offered me a basin to get washed afterwards and then I was thrown into solitary confinement. I was in such shock, all I could do was sing. I sang and sang. I sang folk songs, hymns, all the religious songs I knew, and nobody stopped me. I kept thinking they would soon let me out, that it was a great mistake.'

The next day she asked for a scrap of paper and wrote a note to Heinrich Hildebrand, folding it into a little triangle, saying, 'I'm arrested. *Aufwiedersehen!*' She handed it to a guard and asked that it be sent to Heinrich's army address near the Polish border in Lutsk, Ukraine. 'Imagine, he got the note! Immediately he wrote to his brother Kornelius, who was studying at a medical institute in Omsk. All his friends there contributed to give me some food in prison. They were going to give me some the next morning, when they all were arrested. I met Kornelius in prison, working as a doctor. He had been sentenced to five years. He's dead now. So is Heinrich. At the outbreak of war in 1941, he was wounded in battle on the front in Bessarabia (Moldavia) and died there in hospital.'

Since Alici had been arrested before Hitler's surprise attack, during the Hitler-Stalin non-aggression phase, I suspected it must not be because she was a German-speaker. She told me that by the time she was tried a year later, eleven of her friends and relatives had been arrested. Among the number was her uncle, seventy-year-old Franz Peters, the so-called kulak driven out of his home and onto whose wagon she had thrown a loaf of bread in 1931. Returned to Omsk from his five-year banishment, he was living in a dugout. Also arrested were Alici's land-lady, her Tante Katya Neufeld, and her cousin Heinrich Neufeld, who lived upstairs. Two more Neufelds living in Omsk were arrested, as were two Mennonite cheese-makers and the father of Alici's friend Leni Froese. Froese was an agronomist on an experimental farm.

What all had in common was that they were Mennonites qui-etly practising their religion. Was that the motive for the arrests? An attack on religion? Andrej Savin, Novosibirsk historian, found that an Omsk NKVD functionary, writing specifically about Mennonites, had advised the NKVD to be even more vigilant after the Hitler-Stalin non-agression pact. He said the pact gave greater opportunity for German spies to operate; Mennonites needed more surveillance.[7]

Two days after her arrest, Alici in her short sheepskin coat, escorted by two policemen wearing long fur coats, was hustled onto a train and under guard taken to Omsk. Here she was placed in a room near a main street, where, since this was the 7 November Bolshevik Revolution holiday celebration, she could hear a parade outside. When she tried to look out of the high window, she was threatened with a revolver. Sleeping on a cement floor, Alici waited eight months before her trial came up. 'To that day I kept thinking there was a mistake. Surely, they'd release me.'

Prisoners were not to talk, sit, or sleep during the day. Bright lights and interrogations came at night. At any time a guard could check on her through a peephole in the door. A small food window could be opened to offer a thin soup. At night a guard came to escort her to the interrogation room where she had to sign her name to the date and time of the 'interview.' Her clothing, including underwear, was removed and searched; any personal belongings like hairpins were taken. Confiscat-ed personal belongings were not returned. To ensure that the accused would never see them again, the clause 'with confiscation of property' was added in a court verdict. A prisoner was permitted to request pen and paper to make a complaint or petition, but such letters rarely went beyond the prosecutor's desk drawer.[8] Over and over the interrogator asked her questions, told her to sign an admission that she opposed the Soviet system, was hostile about her father's arrest, had 'praised capi-talism,' and received letters from abroad.

'I was innocent. I knew it was dangerous to venture any opinion and never talked about my father's arrest. I knew the danger.'

Soviet interrogators alternated between threats and seeming kind-ness, and during her interrogation Alici was threatened that her mother would be arrested if she did not sign. Another time she was threatened that three men would rape her, and at another session she was told she would be thrown into a room with starving rats. Always she declared her innocence. At her trial in a closed court she was found guilty and sentenced to six years' imprisonment. Another arbitrary year was added later. At the sentencing all the prisoners with her demanded a final word, and in her statement Alici said, 'I have always worked and I will continue to do so to the best of my ability.' She signed a document with the same words. Why? I asked. 'I wanted to prove that I was a good citizen – and maybe I hoped for a reduced sentence.' Siberian historian Andrej Savin found she was sentenced according to Article 58: 2, 10, and 11 of the criminal code, for anti-Soviet propaganda.[9]

In that prison, and later when she was moved to other prison camps, Alici always scrutinized new recruits being marched into camp – miserably clothed, hungry, wasted men who soon died and regularly were replaced by new trainloads. 'I kept looking. Was that one my father? That one? "Father?" I'd ask, but was always mistaken.'

I asked what happened to the others with whom she had been arrested. She said that a second trial of the eleven was held in 1941, after the German attack. In it, four of the men, including her cousin Heinrich Neufeld, were condemned to death.[10] Over and over Alici lamented his fate, this 'exceptional husband.' Upon hearing his death sentence, Heinrich had wept and asked Alici, 'Will you tell my little son that I must die?' Neufeld's son was a year old. His wife was not told of his execution and faithfully waited years for his release. Alici's Tante Katya Neufeld was given ten years. Her daughter and brother Franz Peters both died in prison.

Quietly, as an aside almost, as we sat on her green bench outside her house in Shakhty, Alici suggested that the father-in-law of her cousin (stepfather of Neufeld's wife) was the person who had denounced Heinrich, adding his name to a list of persons who were then arrested. After the arrests, her Aunt Neufeld's home was confiscated, and Heinrich's wife and her young son had to return to her mother's village outside Omsk. When the boy turned four, his mother was dragooned into the Labour Army.

Alici remained in prison from 1940 to 1948.

We sat around her small table in the brick house as Alici talked softly about her prison years. She spoke German, a language her sons did not understand, and they kept bringing in more and more mineral water and wine bottles. Placing them on the table, granddaughter Dasha said, 'The visitors can't drink our water.'

I asked what conditions were like for female prisoners and Alici was reticent, suggesting there were unwelcome memories, so we let it pass. But a day later, outside in the shade of the tin-roofed former garage, sitting on a bench that her son Vanya had built, she touched my arm and volunteered more.

When I first arrived at the prison camp an elderly prisoner watched me carrying heavy bricks and advised, "Don't work so hard.' Then he asked, 'How long is your sentence?'

I replied, 'But I'm used to working hard.'

'Think of the six years,' he advised. 'Better you pour water on the bricks. You'll never last the way you're going.' He studied me and then, as he headed for the office, he threw over his shoulder, 'Better I place you on a different duty.'

The next day I was given an 'invalid assignment,' working a sewing machine, stitching soldiers' underwear and other clothing. It was piecework: sew so many garments and get 400 grams of bread, or go above the quota and get 700 grams of bread. I got 700 grams. I lived in barracks, on the second floor. We were along the Irtysh River near [or did she say 'in'?] Omsk.

One prisoner, someone assigned as a repairman for the machines, got a crush on me. He began leaving little gifts on my machine. Once it was a meal voucher for food from the administrators' section, better than the watery inedible fish-head soup portioned out daily to us. Another time it was a golden A fashioned from thin twisted wire, and at Easter the man came right next to me as I sat stitching a heavy cotton uniform. 'Christ is risen' [Kristos voskres] he whispered and quickly pecked me on the cheek.

I was totally upset. Nobody used that greeting anymore. In bygone times when religion was tolerated, I would have replied, 'He is risen indeed' [Voistino voskres], but now? What trap was he setting for me? Soon thereafter I was removed to an even 'lighter work' assignment where I discovered that my admirer was a married man, the husband of the supervisor of the prison clinic. Sometime later, his wife, the supervisor, called me and four other women into the clinic for a 'complete' gynaecological examination. She stayed around until the medical examination was completed, and when the results confirmed that I was still a virgin, she left the room.

After this 'test' I was moved to another prison. Here the barracks were so terrible – full of regular criminals, orphans ['wild children'] allowed to grow up on the street in crime, thieves, women arrested for prostitution or vagrancy, wife murderers, rapists, the criminals we called the urki. It was impossible to sleep even a night.

I asked for a change and was moved to a barracks inhabited by political prisoners like myself, professional people, doctors, druggists, and so on. This

prison manufactured plane parts, but I was again placed on a construction bri-
gade, again assigned to carrying bricks. Soon I fell ill, had a rheumatic attack,
and landed in the prison infirmary. Many prisoners died in hospital, many of
plain starvation. Another Mennonite, near death himself, gave me some bread
and showed me photographs of his family. 'If I die,' he said, 'you take my food
package from my family and return these photos to them. Tell them what hap-
pened to me.' Mothers and wives sent parcels to prisoners, hoping against all
odds that they would discover the family member was still alive. The parcels
contained dried breads, cooked potatoes, onions, sugar, sometimes lard.[11] When
prisoners died, a name tag was tied around a toe, and the naked corpses were
piled up on a wagon, driven to a giant hole, and dumped into a mass grave.

When I finally did get out of prison, true to my promise, I found the collec-
tive farm where his wife and daughters worked. I discovered them singing oh
so beautifully, and told them how, in my arms, so to say, their father had died.
It was very sad, but at least they knew where and how he died. But where was
my father?

Sometimes, telling her story, Alici and I would just sit silently, waiting for our emotions to subside and her hands to stop trembling. Then
she would take my arm and resume. She had stayed in this second
camp of political prisoners until 1947 and another young prisoner had
fallen in love with her, a Mennonite. Sitting on her green bench among
the piles of bricks in her backyard on that hot June day in Shakhty, the
almost-eighty-year-old Alici sighed deeply, but then her eyes twinkled
and she smiled. 'You know, if I had only not disliked his thick glasses so
much, I might be living in Germany now with all the other *Aussiedler*!'

The new suitor worked in the infirmary. When she landed back there,
he offered to procure Aspirin for her rheumatism. 'But there were his
glasses.' She snickered, 'I couldn't help laughing whenever I saw him,
not openly, but I didn't encourage him.'

'And Obratsov, your husband?' I asked. Obratsov. A Russian,
wouldn't he be ridiculed for associating with a German, an enemy of
the people?

'Obratsov was not taken in by that propaganda. After I recovered
from my illness, I was assigned back on a construction work brigade to
carry bricks, but soon reassigned to work in the prison infirmary. Here
I had to carry messages to the clinic statistician [tallying the deaths], a
man called Ivan Obratsov.' Alici sighed, 'Oh yes. He fell in love with
me right away.'

'And you?' I wondered.

'No, not right away. He was a jovial man, told funny stories, and slowly I began to like him. Of course I could tell he was attracted to me. But you couldn't reveal anything in public. Immediately one of us would have been sent to another prison. I surprised myself actually. One day a hospital official asked me, "Alici, do you love Obratsov?" Without thinking I answered, "Yes." That was the turning point. "It will be tough later on," the official said. So, unofficially as it were, we became engaged.'

Obratsov, born in 1891, was in fact the same age as Alici's father and also had the same name (Johannes is Ivan in Russian). He had been a Communist official, a boss or *Nachalnik* working in Ulan Ude at a Soviet airdrome when Stalin embarked on his Great Purge. Married and the father of a son, Obratsov was arrested in 1937. He had been put into a tall narrow barrel into which water had been slowly added till it reached his neck. Signing for crimes he had not committed, he got a ten-year sentence. Before he completed his prison term in October 1947, his wife left him. Alici was due to be released in November of the same year, so they decided to go to a city in Uzbekistan to find a warmer climate. He let her know he was leaving by train but had no address.

Alici filled out Form A and was officially registered as a 'former prisoner' instead of 'convict.' It was a month after her fiancé Ivan had left. She travelled to see her mother, but after a few days, said, 'I'm going to join Ivan. I vowed to be true to him.' What could her mother say? That nice young Hildebrandt suitor of seven years ago was gone. So were all the young Mennonite men Alici might have married, scattered in Labour Army camps, perished, or deported if they had managed to survive the war. Alici was twenty-eight and single. What protection was there for a *German* woman? Married to a Russian, Alici would not be hounded as an enemy.

'What possessed me?' Alici exclaimed as she told me the story, 'I was foolhardy. Going to a strange place, no means, and no address. I knew only the name of the city where Ivan had gone, far east to St Andizhan in Uzbekistan.'

As he told her, when Ivan Obratsov had arrived, he had taken a room and found work. Often he talked to his landlady and her children, telling them about the 'beautiful lady' who was his bride.

One day one of the children said, 'She's coming today.'

'Who is coming?'

'Your beautiful lady. She's arriving today.'

Obratsov thought children had wondrous imaginations, but why not humour the child? He decided to go to the train station.

Alici had indeed arrived that day. When she got off the train she sat down on her suitcase and said to herself, I must be crazy. How will I ever find Ivan in a big city? Where shall I go? How can I begin?

Ivan looked, saw the thick braid circling her beloved blond head, her dear shoulders slumped as she sat on her suitcase. Quietly he tiptoed behind her and covered her eyes. 'Guess who!'

'Was that coincidence?' Alici asked me, 'or was it meant to be? Imagine, my Vanya found me!'

So they lived together in his room for two years and Alici found work in a hospital. One day in 1950 Alici came home from work to find her husband missing. An order had come to rearrest all men who had survived in 1937. For a whole summer she searched for him. When at last she found him, they embraced, and he told her he was being sent north to a prison in Krasnoyarsk, a major centre for political prisoners on the Yenisey River in a region of mountains and taiga.

'I begged and applied until they let me join him,' Alici continued. 'Then I lived there with him in the prison camp. Ivan worked again as a prison clinic statistician.'

It had been difficult, both sleeping on the prison floor. Because so many had been exiled to Krasnoyarsk, any living space had to be paid for. When her husband became ill, the prison authorities allowed them a room. In this room her two sons were born, Volodya in 1951 and Vanya in 1953. The camp had many professionals and Alici was able to train as a nurse. In 1962 Ivan's prison term expired and they moved out of the prison yard. Often when political prisoners like Alici or her husband completed their terms, they found work in the same area. Also, *Germans* were forbidden to return to their former homes in Soviet Ukraine or Crimea. Ivan found work in the preparation of furs and Alici as a nurse. They built a small log house and later bought a four-room house, which Alici thought was very large. 'It had a corridor.' They had a cow and raised two pigs at a time, to sell.

Alici suffered a heart attack and after being hospitalized for two months, classified as an invalid, was told to seek a warmer climate. They decided to move to Shakhty in the Rostov area because Obratsov's son from his first marriage had lived there. The son, a pilot, had been killed in an accident, but his widow, a gynaecologist, welcomed them. In Shakhty the Obratsovs eventually bought the brick house in which we found Alici in 1999. Their sons were seven and nine when they arrived in Shakhty, and the boys never were told about their parents' repression until both were rehabilitated, declared innocent of all original charges. There was no compensation for innocent imprisonment.

I wondered how Alici felt as her eldest son Volodya, a zealous Pioneer, Komsomol, and Communist party member, went on to attend a NKVD institute in Rostov and became a high-ranking member in the police and Party. 'He said he joined because he wanted to know how they operate, from within,' Alici told me. 'Do you understand such logic?' When the Communist Party fell and Party buildings were cleared out in 1991, Alici's Soviet policeman son Volodya was ignominiously escorted out of his privileged office, and when we met him he was a guard in a bank. Nevertheless, driving me around Shakhty on a morning sightseeing tour in his shiny black car, he took a detour through the police headquarters and the men on duty saluted him.

Alici's husband died in May 1987 and Harvey asked if we could visit his grave. Alici's son Vanya drove us a short distance up a small hill to a fenced off cemetery with many small wrought iron enclosures that included metal mini picnic tables and wooden benches where relatives come to leave food, a table for the dead. What none of us could have guessed was that this burial plot would include Alici and both of her sons before my book was concluded.

Although her two sons were married, Alici felt a great heartache about a divorce in the family. 'I have two sons but three daughters-in-law.' Volodya had left his wife of twenty-two years and had been living the last four years with a vivacious woman called Nadia. On the bright side, Alici noted, Nadia had cured Volodya of his drinking. Regularly he used to come home drunk and, locked out by his wife, knocked on his mother's window (just two houses away) where Alici would get up to let him in. Also, Volodya took more pride in his own garden and house now, which the first wife had neglected. Together with Nadia, Volodya had started growing tomatoes and potatoes, even helped picking the sweet cherries in their orchard. The day we arrived he was bare-chested, watering vegetables. They both helped Alici more frequently, Nadia washing dishes at the coldwater tap with bubbling good humour.

Alici's younger son, Vanya, was a director in a ceramics factory where he had been a long-time employee. A chain-smoker, Vanya had been critically ill and overworked the previous winter. The hospital where he became a patient had no resources, so every day his wife, Tanya, took the two-hour bus trip to bring clean sheets, food, and medicine, and to bathe him. Vanya and Tanya's daughter, Dasha, her grandmother's delight, stayed with Alici before and after school while her parents were at work. In 1999 she was twelve and an accomplished gymnast, practising every day for a ribbon dance in honour of Pushkin's two hundredth birthday, a celebration on the coming weekend.

The evening before we left, Vanya and Tanya (with help from Volodya and Nadia) arranged a great backyard feast for us visitors. Into a huge pot of boiling water sitting on a hot plate that they had moved outside went an armload of dill from Alici's garden. Piles of crayfish followed the dill and soon emerged lobster-red on a platter. Dasha, whispering to her Babushka Alici, 'So expensive,' was told, 'Don't talk.' Pickled tomatoes, thin green cucumbers, and fresh bread appeared. Wine bottles came out, along with cognac (they remembered Harvey wasn't a big vodka fan), and as she allowed her glass to be filled, Alici said her church forbade it, but she would join us for toasts, 'just this once, of course.' Nothing was too good for visitors from afar.

Her future was very uncertain, Alici said, since her rheumatoid arthritis was getting worse, her toes beginning to curl one over the other. She shook her head, 'Like my mother, my poor mother.' How she dreaded the winter, living alone and having to carry in scoops of coal for her stove. There was no telephone. The wires on the street were always stolen. 'When I'm resting I lie and think and all the horrors of long ago whirl around in my head ... I remember from when I was four years old ...' Her children brought her a loaf of bread regularly, but she asked, 'What if they forget?' Harvey and I saw how desperate things were when we took a walk, climbing a nearby hill to look at a massive Shakhty war monument erected to honour the victims of Nazism. The metal lettering from the memorial had been ripped off a stone wall, to be melted we supposed, and stone tablets listing names of the victims also had been removed. Memorial tablets used as stepping-stones or steps. I worried for Alici's safety.

'Of all of our family, Alici got away the best,' Maria had told us in Karaganda. 'Why would she say that?' Alici asked when we repeated this. 'I always lived in fear. I never told my neighbours that I had a criminal record. I was alone here as a *Nemka*. After many years I was summoned to appear at the local police headquarters and I almost died of fright, but it turned out they just wanted to give me my rehabilitation documents.'

'How did your mother discover your fate?' Four years after she was arrested, Alici said, someone from Omsk had appeared in her mother's village and told Anna Braun that her daughter was in prison. Her mother had roasted some Zwieback and taken the train to Omsk, but when she arrived at the prison she was told Alici was not there. She left a note and her package of roasted buns. When that package finally reached Alici in her new prison, she discovered the family she had left in Kotlyarevka, Ukraine, was in Siberia.

'Have you ever found out about your father?'

Alici said that in a document dated 28 May 1960, Anna Braun had been notified that Johannes Braun had died of liver cancer on 27 August 1942. Such letters during Khrushchev's day were common and were rarely believed. In 1999 Alici still did not know how long he had been kept in prison, if he was sent to the 'High North,' as his family thought, or if he had died of natural causes as the Khrushchev-era letter stated. Harvey's work in state and party archives had led him to believe the most likely scenario for persons arrested in 1937 or 1938 was execution a few months after arrest. Family members could now write to get the facts, and I resolved, upon returning home to Canada, to become that family member.

In Alici's sitting room were two portraits, one of her and her husband and the other of the two young sons. In her bedroom, on the wall opposite her bed, hung another portrait. This one beside her guitar, a portrait she saw every night before she closed her eyes, was of her father. She often wept for this dear lost man, her father Johannes.

We left Shakhty with Alici's son Vanya driving us two hours to the Rostov airport in early morning darkness. Two of only eight passengers flying to Kiev, and the only non-nationals, hassled about our exit permission forms, I felt a shadow of what it was like to be in the grip of a bureaucracy. When Vanya hugged and impulsively kissed my cheek on our farewell, I felt an overwhelming ache for what the whole Soviet system had extracted from families – not only my relatives, but hundreds of thousands of families.

Millions of families with similar stories suffered in that system. Not gassed, but confined in prisons and concentration camps, starved, overworked, tortured, or shot, they were killed slowly in what Columbia University historian Istvan Deak had called the Soviet 'freezing chambers.'[12] Families in the USSR like those of Johannes and Anna Braun, of Isaak and Peter Braun, of Anna, Heinrich, Gerhard, and Abram Konrad would forever bear the scars. People of my father's and mother's 'Russian homeland,' my parents' siblings' and their families cut by that red sickle, who knew or would ever remember them?

Returning home, I began to reconstruct details. Alici's accusation that a stepfather could have denounced his son-in-law to the authorities was disturbing. And who was the dastardly person who denounced Alici? I thought back to that first letter my parents had received from a woman in 1946, that first person who knew that Alici had been arrested ('went the way of her father'). She was a Sara Janzen and just happened also to be the wife of that stepfather who purportedly denounced Alici's cousin Heinrich Neufeld.

My parents corresponded with this Sara. In fact, they knew her well from their time in Siberia. Sara had been a young widow with a daughter when she married my father's eldest brother. My father's brother died of typhus before their child (another daughter, named Helene) was born. Sara then married the man who supposedly denounced Alici's cousin Heinrich Neufeld. Alici had lived in Omsk with her Aunt Neufeld and her family – including Heinrich Neufeld and his wife.

I recalled how Alici had pulled out a scribbler with hand-copied poems and pointed to one composed for the engagement party of her cousin Heinrich Neufeld and his bride, the married couple living upstairs. She had said, 'That was your relative too, the Maria who married my cousin.' When Alici had said this, I had no idea what she meant and forgot to ask. We were poring over the poem, reading it together, finding a German song we both knew and singing it. Now it was clear to me why Sara had known about the arrests of Johannes and Alici. She had heard it from her daughter who lived in the same house.

If this stepfather, Sara's husband, had denounced people, betrayed his family members, I wanted to know if he benefited or suffered for it. I wrote Alici, specifically asking what she had meant, suggesting a father-in-law had put his son-in-law's name on a list to be arrested. She wrote back, 'Yes, yes, he had him shot.'[13] It kept niggling, this accusation.

In 2002 I made the acquaintance of Sara's younger daughter, the one named Helene – and that was that child of my father's eldest brother who died of typhus. This Helene had recently immigrated to Germany. At first I did not know she had also lived in the same house in Omsk with Alici. As she told us about herself, I thought I might find out more about her stepfather and her brother-in-law Heinrich Neufeld. On a visit to Germany in 2005, Helene talked about her career. She had been studying agronomy at an institute in Omsk, living with her elder sister when her brother-in-law Heinrich Neufeld was arrested. 'What a fine person he was, such a devoted father.'

I asked about her stepfather (privately wondering if he had benefited from denouncing others) and she said he was the assistant to the *pred* of the collective farm, did not have to work on the fields, but sat in the office, ordered supplies, and supervised the workers, but was conscripted into the Labour Army. He was released after eighteen months. Whenever I mentioned Alici, she changed the topic. I thought, no wonder, imagine if Alici knew and told me that Helene's stepfather was responsible for Heinrich Neufeld's arrest. I fretted how to forgive someone like that. Did he do it to save himself, and under what circumstances? Did he think the more people he denounced, the better his own chances of good treatment? Condemning eleven people, six members of the same family, and a son-in-law too! And how did Alici find this out?

I reviewed Sara's dozens of letters to my parents (she was a regular correspondent from 1956 until her death in 1977), found she wrote warmly about her family and focused on her and her husband's continuing faith, the ins and outs of religious oppression. I noted that daughter Helene got advanced education (enemies of the people, that is *Germans*, were customarily denied higher education), had a good job as an agronomist, had paid holidays at spas, received good medical attention, and did not share her mother's faith. After Sara became crippled with arthritis, her husband wrote about prayer meetings, Bible studies, and worship services on Sundays.[14] Whatever he may have done in 1940 seemed long forgiven or accepted as coming from the dreadful Stalinist past. He seemed devout.

I reassessed the case. Who else would have known and had contact with Alici's friends and relatives in Omsk? Why was Helene so prickly when I mentioned Alici? Could it be that she, young Helene, not her stepfather, had reported the names? School children who spied on their parents or siblings were rewarded. Helene lived in the Neufeld house and knew members of the family *and* Alici's friends. She was never conscripted into the Labour Army (as were her sister and other German women and girls between sixteen and fourteen), but was able to continue her studies. Accused at the time of buying her way out of the Labour Army, she explained, 'It was all on the level. The school director told me, "As long as you maintain your high marks, I'll protect you. But you have to promise not to go home to your mother so often." So my little brother had to stop school and take in the butter. I stayed in school and became an agronomist.'[15]

When Alici died in 2003, in a letter I mentioned this to Helene. She wrote back that she had reported Alici's death to one of Alici's relatives in Germany and had asked the relative, 'Did Alici write you anything?' The relative assured her that Alici wrote only about her garden. Why would she ask this question? In a letter in 2006, among other topics, I asked, 'What was your problem with Alici?' She stopped writing to me. I wrote again several times, but the woman who always answered too soon, a regular correspondent, failed to reply. My letters were not returned by the old age home where she now lived. Was this a guilty conscience? Was it self-defence, to avoid remembering the event? Even a year later when I emailed the old age home asking about her (had she died?), I received no reply. Was it possible that this schoolgirl who knew everyone arrested, who was allowed to continue her education as her brother-in-law and her landlady's family and relatives were arrested, could have been cajoled into becoming an informer?

Missing Red Army Soldier Hans

There was still the mystery of Hans Braun, brother of Maria and Alici, Anna's son conscripted into the Red Army in 1939 and gone missing. In his mother Anna's first letter to my parents in 1961, she thought he might be in Canada:

24 June 1961 …
Yes, dear ones, my dear son must be with you there somewhere. He was registered at our previous address [Kotlyarevka]. Immediately I wrote to the director of the school in Ebental, as well as to the pred of the state farm [sovkhoz] in our little village. I received the answer from both that such a person was not there during the war, nor after the war…. If he is still alive somewhere, it would make me very happy if he wrote me a few lines. Tell him to write immediately or write something about him. Of course, if he is there, he'll read this….

My children are spread everywhere. Alici lives in Krasnoyarsk, a three-days' journey, Maria has moved with her three sons to Alma Ata, and Anni lives ten kilometres away in Kulunda with her four children. I have thirteen grandchildren and live with my youngest, Heinrich (Heinz), who has three girls and one boy. I receive a pension of eight roubles, fifty kopeks, a great help and joy to me? We live well? We lack for nothing? Thanks to my in-laws Jakob and Anni I have clothes. A thousand thanks to them. I'm still drinking the coffee they sent. The shops here are fully stocked?

Thank you for the photo you sent. Peter, you look like yourself, but Luise, I can hardly recognize you. You look so young and plump. I have to keep looking at you. From my heart, I wish that God might preserve your good fortune so you may walk through life together. Our sister-in-law Hermine is ill, probably has lung cancer. If it is God's will I'd like to visit her in August when I visit Mika [daughter Maria]. Then I'll write you about her. Greet all the relatives and give my son Hans a kiss from me if he should come to see you.

With kisses, A.B.

The obvious question marks in her letter suggested opposites, especially 'full shelves' in stores. Even in 1989 when we met Maria Braun, having stopped at many places in the former USSR, people were queuing for scarce goods, rushing to line up upon rumours of the arrival of a new shipment.

Imagine my parents' surprise and joy when, three months after receiving Anna's letter, they found her missing son. Using the International Red Cross, Hans Braun was located, not in Canada, but in Germany. My parents wrote to him and he replied,

Munich, 10 Oct. 1961
Dear Aunt, dear Uncle and Children,

We received your letter with great joy. I recalled that I had an uncle named Peter Konrad living in North America, but I thought he lived in New York. Immediately I returned from captivity in 1955, I wrote to the mayor there but received no reply. Now I understand why.

Yes, dear Aunt Louise [sic], I had no idea that my father had a sister, and my happiness is even greater knowing this now. I know very little about Papa. Either I was a very unobservant boy or Papa told very little about himself or his family as a precaution. In that witch's cauldron, one had to be on guard at all times. Now I hope to learn more about my dear aunt.

Many thanks for the photos. Such lanky fellows are a delight to see. My boys are still young, but healthy and happy, making much mischief for their dear mother, Traudl.

Warm greetings from Hans and family

Put in contact, Hans wrote to his mother, Anna, in the USSR, and by June 1962 she was waiting for a parcel from him. Her rheumatoid arthritis had advanced and she had moved in with her daughter Maria, now living in Kulunda. Maria's newly bought house was mouldy and crumbling, so her husband Milshin was removing rotted beams and renovating as Anna lived in a barn. By day, Milshin worked as a carpenter and Maria in the Kulunda clinic. Anna wrote, 'We have had *difficult* years' and 'I weep day and night. Often I think of my beloved, if he saw me now.'[16]

On 31 January 1963, Anna wrote that daughter Maria suffers from the damage to her health from her years in the Labour Army and her daughter Anni, also in the Labour Army, has died at age thirty-seven. Hans's wife, Traudl, had reported from Munich, 'Hans was overjoyed to meet Peter Braun from Canada. They felt happy. But Mama, how much happier we would be if you could come to us. Come to us.' On 3 March 1966 she wrote that her children could not imagine how my parents could host all their guests. 'Here we struggle just to stay alive.'

On 9 March 1967 Anna wrote that her son Hans had written asking to know more about his father. 'The children hardly knew their father. He was always having to read newspaper articles to keep abreast....' Totally crippled, Anna died 13 December 1968. She was spared knowing the following great sadness in her family.

Hans's last letter was written to Maria, who forwarded it to Alici, who passed it over for me to read when we visited her in Shakhty in 1999:

München/Neubiberg, 10 July 1976
Dear Sister Maria and all dear ones,
After a long delay, today I want to reply to the letter you found so difficult to write. We are very happy that your Tamara [Tanya] has had a little daughter. Jura, the happy father, must be your favourite son and he also is the hardest working, both on the job and at home, isn't he? Yes, dear sister, how do you feel, being an Oma? How quickly the time goes by, first a child and then a wife. Poor Mika [Maria], life has handed you many sore trials. But because you have conquered them so bravely, your children will have a much easier time.

Yes, each one of us has been tried and each, in his or her way, has passed the test because all of us have been able to establish our own families. Only, among us happiness has not been divided equally. Anni had to leave this world at a young age and, of us all, likely she suffered the most. Judging by her, we all are doing better. You know how difficult it was for Mama when all of us were torn asunder and each of us has had to take the path appointed for us. After the difficult years, Alici has found a firm anchor. I mean, considering the circumstances of us all, I think she has had the best luck through her husband. I imagine him to be a good and faithful father of her family and that she has earned peace and tranquillity.

Yes, dear sister, life tests every person most severely and the question is whether one can meet this hardness through strength, love, or humility. How are things with Heinie? Is he a strong man who can master all difficulties? He was the best of all of us as a child, whether in learning or in love for our Mama.

How do you get along? It must be nice when brother and sister can give each other advice or sympathy during difficult days.

Here we live our modest lives and each has a duty to fulfil. Traudel looks after the welfare [of the household] and I earn the necessary money. She is a good housewife. The children are learning everything they need for the future. The eldest one, Volker, is doing his third year of apprenticeship with Die Post to become an electrical technician. The next, Reiner, is taking his final examinations to complete secondary school (matriculation needed to enter university), and the little one, Silvia-Alici is entering a business school in fall. All leave the house to catch a bus between six and eight in the morning. Now dear sister, your brother and his family greet you most heartily. Also a thousand greetings to Alici, Heinz, and all their families.

Your Hans

Alici then handed over a letter that Hans's wife, Traudl, had sent Maria in April 1977. After this letter Maria had written again and again, but Traudl never replied.

Dear Maria with Children,

I have to write you sad news. My dear Hans died on 22 March. Because of his prisoner-of-war experience, he was subject to frequent depressions and he could no longer face life, so he shot himself. The children and I simply cannot believe that he has left us alone. I always expect him to come through the door. I have wept many tears and had many sleepless nights. But I must continue my life, even though it is most difficult.

Most likely I will have to sell our property. The children are well, but I am not in good shape. For five years I have been going to work three days a week. Dear Maria, I don't know if the address is correct, since I don't know Russian.

Heartfelt greetings for now,
from Traudl and children

As she spoke of her brother, Alici's eyes had filled with tears and she had begged me, 'Couldn't you find out more? Didn't some Canadian relatives visit him in Munich? Didn't Traudl mention a visit from a Peter Braun?' She gave me a small snapshot of Hans's young family posing with our Aunt Kay and Uncle Nick Braun from BC. 'Maybe he told them something. Could you ask?' I promised to try. Like in all suicides, survivors search for a cause, look into themselves for something they might have done to prevent the death, and subconsciously want someone to take responsibility. Why wouldn't Hans's wife write again?

Why, in his last letter to Maria, did Hans only say she was a 'good housewife'? Was it impulsive, a rash response after a marital dispute or work problem? Why did it happen so long after his captivity? Was it delayed trauma?

When we returned home I phoned my Aunt Kay (in Abbotsford) who had visited Hans and his family in Munich in the late 1960s or 1970s. Aunt Kay told me that she had noticed how fastidious Traudl was. Then she added, 'I don't remember everything. Ask Peter. He was there.' Aunt Kay and Uncle Nick's son Peter taught at McGill University and lived in Montreal. After his mother told him the nature of my request, we had a phone interview. Peter, a cousin I remembered as a boy with a violin, now a professor of biochemistry, told me he first met Hans in July 1962, shortly after Hans had been connected with his mother. Peter was on a backpacking tour of Europe, a twenty-three-year-old student whose parents told him to look up this newly located relative. They met in a small village on the outskirts of Munich.

'I walked up and as he saw me, he just stood there and wept. He clasped me, just held me and cried and cried. He had recognized me as a Braun right away and said I was the first family member he had seen since he left home in 1939. I will never forget that meeting. I was born in 1939.'

Peter said it happened forty years ago, but he had kept a diary. He described Hans as a handsome, 'dashing' forty-year-old, very 'Braun' with wavy, dark blond hair and fair complexion. 'But you could see he was a man who had suffered. There was sorrow in his face, the sadness of a man who has suffered deeply, silently.'

Peter contrasted handsome Hans with his 'exceedingly plain-looking wife, Traudl.' Hans and family lived in the village of Traudl's Swabian parents, a working-class farming area just outside Munich (now a suburb). Hans had achieved all the outward signs of a good life, a Bavarian-style house, a wife and family, but he hardly saw his children since he worked long hours, driving a taxi in Munich.

Peter stayed three days and said Hans could not stop talking about his past. In the Red Army, he was stationed at the Polish border when captured. Soviet propaganda trained him that all Nazis were evil, but when the German soldiers treated him well, he 'realized not all of them were monsters.' He agreed to be an interpreter, listening to Soviet radio transmissions to infantry divisions. At the end of the war, in Wehrmacht uniform when captured by the Red Army, he disguised his identity, passing himself off as a German national. Had the Soviets known his true origin, he would immediately have been shot as a traitor. As a German POW, he was sent to a Siberian prison camp where he suffered greatly. Just over half of German POWs survived in Soviet captivity. It was difficult to pretend he did not understand Russian, to be tortured, starved, and dehumanized in prison camps, never called by name but by numbers on his back and cap.[17] Constantly suspected of being a traitor, he was determined that his tormentors should not have the satisfaction of seeing him die.[18] Peter, brought up in a pious home, vividly recalled that Hans did not believe in a religious God but attributed his being alive to his willpower and hatred of the Soviets who had stolen his father and destroyed his family. 'The belief that I would survive became my God. I refused to give up that thought.' With a bitter smile, Hans had kept repeating, 'I survived.' He had to live to mourn the dead, to be a witness to the truth.

At the end of Hans's ten years as a German POW in the USSR, German chancellor Konrad Adenauer negotiated the return of POWs, and in 1955 Hans returned to Germany with a prisoner buddy from the Munich area. He married his friend's sister, received a veteran's assistance package to help begin civilian life, and used it to buy a good car that became his livelihood, his taxi.

Over and over, Alici had searched for answers. Why would a man take his own life? I asked myself the same thing. When Harvey and I had been in Bonn in 1996 visiting the Viktor Braun family, hadn't one of them let fall that a cousin in Central Asia got the idea Hans was rich and begged him to buy her a car, and hadn't the Bonn Brauns asked him at one time to sponsor their family to immigrate to Germany? From her letters I knew Hans had sent care packages to his mother. The weight of all those suffering siblings and relatives in the USSR appealing for help, his own family situation, the unresolved pain of his lost father, the loss of friends, the bitterness of war, cruel prison practices – all these nightmares could lead to despair. Who can plumb the depths of such experience? For me, the most telling clue was what Hans told Peter on their parting. Peter had asked what troubled Hans the most and Hans had said, 'What tormented me most is that I didn't know about my family in the USSR, where they were. If I only had somebody who loved me, I'd feel secure.'

When I wrote Alici, telling her what Peter Braun told me, she fell ill. Should I have saved her the pain, I asked myself? Was it better not to know – even if she asked to know? Was it right to withhold? Later Alici wrote she was grateful to know Hans had refused to break under

Soviet torture. She wrote, 'He did it for us.'[19] What did she mean by 'he did it for us'? Faced with huge losses and defeats at the fighting front after Hitler attacked the USSR, Stalin, stunned by the attack, blamed the military and to galvanize his soldiers never to retreat, approved a secret police order that families of deserters or captured soldiers were to be arrested and punished or destroyed.[20] 'He did it for us' meant that Hans's silence saved his mother and siblings. This was tested when the Germans captured Stalin's son Yakov. Furious that his son had not committed suicide rather than be captured, Stalin had Yakov's wife Julia arrested. The Germans offered to exchange Yakov for captured German Field Marshall General von Paulus in 1943, but Stalin refused the swap. When Yakov threw himself on the wire of the POW camp in Lübec, Germany, electrocuting himself, his father praised him as a hero.[21]

Hans was one more of Stalin's victims. In the end, tragically unable to escape his tortured past, ironically Hans did what Stalin wanted and killed himself.

8

Survivors

Deserted Wife and Defiant Daughter Lena

On my twice-annual visits to BC, where I sat with my father in the retirement home and where we looked through the box of 'Russian' photographs, AnnaK was a surprise to me. 'You had a sister called Anna?' It was like the time my father pointed to a woman in a group photograph and said she was his dead sister Susana. Susana died when my father was very young, but Anna? Yes, the one who had a 'no-good husband.' Usually cautious not to reveal family skeletons, my mother had let that slip out.

With so many Annas in the family, I am calling her AnnaK. AnnaK was the mother of little Lena, whom we originally met prancing at her grandparents' golden wedding anniversary and whom I first met in person in 1991. School out, I flew to Europe, rented a car, and drove to Bremen to see Uncle Gerhard and meet up with Harvey returning from his research in Odessa.

AnnaK's daughter Lena had lived with Uncle Gerhard and his daughter Nelly in their Bremen apartment for three years, but now she had her own place in Neuwied on the Rhine, two hours by train from Bremen. By 1991 she had lived 'in the West' for thirteen years. I had stopped to see Nelly first and, as we entered Gerhard's apartment, we found Lena and Uncle sitting elbow to elbow at a small table eating a hearty beef soup. Lena had dropped in at his apartment, found him badly bruised from a fall and, with nobody there to help, took him to the doctor. She had him bandaged up and had even washed his woollen pants that stank of urine. Gerhard, recovered from a recent heart attack, was ninety and Nelly, in her mid-thirties, lived in Göttingen in a bachelor pad with a spiral staircase. I was with her the Sunday evening she received a phone call that Gerhard had fallen, but she had told me, 'Lena is there. Everything's looked after.'

In her blue, short-sleeved sweater and navy skirt, square and muscular, Lena resembled 'happy workers' harvesting grain on Soviet posters. With her strong jaw and her greyish-brown hair pulled back severely into a generous bun, she impressed me as one tough-minded lady. Not one to wait long to speak her mind, she pointed to a greenish plastic 'hot food keeper' on a small table at the entrance. 'Look at this mush. That's what he has to eat. That swill!' She stood in the narrow hallway and conspiratorially asked me, 'What is that Meals on Wheels? One hot meal a day?' 'Lena's a great cook,' Nelly had said, 'The way she makes *Kotletten*! Numm.' Nelly and I had driven at a leisurely pace, visited the ancient Hanseatic League city Lübeck that I had studied decades ago. The salt trade was big then. Clearly we should have come sooner.

'He can't live alone any longer.' Lena looked hard at Nelly.

'I know, I know.' Nelly suddenly sounded tired. She had not expected the bruises and, pampered child of a much older father, was not used to this reversal of the child–parent relationship. 'I'll phone, tell my boss I'm staying home longer with Papa.'

Things settled down. Warmed by the unusual bounty of attention, Gerhard became talkative and Nelly began to phone around, to see if the Evangelical Church pastor had leads on retirement homes. Out came Gerhard's album of pictures and he and Lena began to tell stories as I asked questions. At times, when we looked at certain pictures, Gerhard seemed a little confused and his laughing and crying got stitched together, a piano-wire sound, thin and easily broken. Often Nelly insisted, 'Papa, we know, we know.' Not I.

They talked about Siberia, the grandparents, their houses, and much as I wished them to slow down, one of the three always rushed to turn the page. Lena told about the golden wedding anniversary, about Smolianovka where Justina Epp had lived, about our grandparents' house and 'Down the street lived my mother.' At last we were coming to AnnaK.

Quiet by nature, AnnaK had married young Mennonite farmer Peter Wiebe in 1913. From my father's story of Kolchak's White Army, I recalled that Wiebe, conscripted as an orderly on hospital trains filled with lice-infested soldiers carrying typhus, had contracted the disease and died in March 1920. His wife AnnaK had two young sons and was pregnant with Lena. AnnaK remarried and become Frau Dietrich

Toews, but as soon as we got to the 'Toews' part, Lena changed the subject. 'Look, this was the house plan,' she said, drawing a diagram.

With Nelly assuming responsibility for her father, Lena returned to her home in Neuwied on the Rhine and Harvey and I visited her there a few days later. Seated at her kitchen/dining table, she told us her story. During her first three years after immigrating to Bremen, she had attended language classes, cooked, and worked in a library, but, qualifying for a pension, she moved to a Bonn suburb, where she experienced a religious conversion and joined an evangelical church. When more *Deutsche* from Siberia immigrated to Germany, including a daughter of her sister Agatha, she decided she preferred living among Soviet German immigrants (*Aussiedler*). Did she say another sister, an Agatha? Agatha, I learned, was a child of AnnaK and her second husband. We would eventually find her living nearer to Frankfurt.

Assigned an unfinished apartment in a housing block, Lena hung her own drywall, wall papered, painted, and installed a bathroom. She had a bedroom, a spacious all-purpose living-dining room, and small kitchen, and she rented a plot of land a few streets over where she kept a large garden, complete with a garden house. Her sturdy rows of raspberries, raised beds of strawberries, flowers interspersed everywhere, a large cucumber bed, and neatly staked tomato plants were a pleasure. She collected rainwater in barrels to sprinkle over the plants. Since one of Agatha's children and her family lived nearby, Lena provided them with her pickled cucumbers and garden preserves.

In Gerhard's apartment we had not reached the Soviet period or found out what happened to AnnaK, but now Lena wanted to talk about her mother's 'no-good' second husband. When AnnaK married smooth-talking widower Dietrich Toews, Lena was one-and-a-half, and not till she was six did she know he was her stepfather. 'After that I never sat on his lap again.' Our Grandmother Konrad had warned AnnaK, 'Once a servant, always a servant,' and I asked Lena what that meant. She looked disgusted. Obviously Grandmother had known that Toews was servile, 'And he was just a barber!' At the table where we had eaten Lena's famous *Kotletten*, she sighed and added, 'But my mother was a widow with three young children, so what could she do? He was a young widower with a six-month-old daughter. So that's why.'

Lena explained that when Stalin introduced his first Five-Year Plan, workers like her stepfather Toews did not feel threatened. She paused, 'Weren't they all children of a kulak? Therefore kulaks too?' AnnaK and family had moved into the grandparent Konrad's empty home and lived there for four years. Although Toews felt safe from the Communists at first, even in a 'workers' paradise' there was no denying his family contained 'counter-revolutionary kulaks' who had fled. More and more fingers pointing at them, in 1934 Toews decided to take Justina Epp's route, to go to the Amur River. They got to Lake Baikal, this 'wonder of nature' that stretched 650 kilometres, at places 80 kilometres wide, and somewhere along this lake the family stopped at a town and her stepfather found a place to stay in unheated, deserted barracks – a roof over their heads, but not much more.[1] There were six children: Lena, her two elder brothers, Jakob and Peter, her two younger sisters, Agatha and Anni (children of AnnaK and Toews), and Toews's daughter Katya.

'We slept in rags on a dirty floor. Although Stepfather Toews got some work as a barber, we were starving. He had a reputation as a ladies' man and that's why our family had no food. He spent it on ladies.'

They were in the cold barracks and four-year-old sister Anni, hollow-eyed, kept crying for bread. One day she stopped crying, stopped begging. Her mother saw the child lying motionless on her heap of rags and rushed to her. Anni's eyes were open. 'Anni, Anni!' The mother screamed, but the body was limp. A Russian woman sharing the barracks came over to see what the commotion was about. She predicted, 'Open eyes on a dead person mean another family member will die within the year.'

Someone had to earn money, and seeing his anguished mother and dead little sister, AnnaK's eldest son, Jakob, offered to go back to Waldheim where his step-grandmother Toews lived. Aged twenty, he would look for work. 'He had just enough money to buy a suit of clothes, but instead of clothes, he bought another ticket and took one of my sisters along to Waldheim so there would be one less mouth to feed in the Baikal. He took his stepsister Katya so the Toews family would be less critical.'

When Jakob applied for work on the Waldheim collective farm, local officials asked, 'Why didn't you join the Komsomols to help build socialism?' Unable to get work in Waldheim, he finally got a job as a bookkeeper on a neighbouring collective farm, saved his small earnings, and sent help to his mother and sisters in the Baikal. One day he showed up at Oma Toews house in Waldheim, saying he was not feeling well. He went to bed and, diagnosed with typhus, was dead in four days.

Day after day in the Baikal, AnnaK, her two remaining daughters, son Peter and husband Toews, waited for a letter from Jakob. Day after day, Lena ran to the post office before school. One day there was a letter. 'Was I happy! At last, a letter.' Quickly Lena grabbed the letter, dashed home, handed it to her mother, and ran back to school, but still was late. 'As punishment for being late I had to stay after school, but I raced home and when I got there I found both my mother and brother Peter sobbing. The letter, it turned out, was not from my big brother, but from Oma Toews. In the envelope was a photo of our Jasha lying in his coffin.'

The destitute Wiebe-Toews family returned to Waldheim, Siberia, and were given one room in the home of Oma Toews. Urged by his mother and siblings, Dietrich Toews soon returned to the Baikal to look for work. 'He sent back one parcel to our family in the room at Waldheim, but no money. He took up with a Russian woman and only once did we hear from him again.' Lena thought Toews continued to barber, but like thousands of other men, was arrested during the 1937–8 Terror. And that was all Lena would say about Dietrich Toews. But, going through my parents' letters, I read that Toews had survived the Terror years. In 1956, a letter from Sara Janzen in Omsk stated that Toews found out AnnaK and the children had built themselves a small house and he wanted to return. His wife, soft-hearted, would have allowed it, but the children would not.[2]

Lena said that her mother never was the same after her son Jakob died. Quieter than before, she still had to support her children and earned small sums by digging potatoes, cleaning, knitting, sewing – anything for a few roubles or kopeks. Oma Toews did not give them any money or food, but the children worked. Lena helped her mother dig potatoes on a share basis – dig eight sacks for someone and the ninth sack is yours. She recalled working to help support the family at age nine – before moving to the Baikal.

In return for my room and board, I was sent to be a maid and nanny while my stepsister Katya and younger sister stayed with Ma. I hated being a 'slave,' especially as there was a lazy daughter in the house whose job it was to let out the family cows for the cowherd who herded the village cattle to the common meadow. Regularly the daughter slept in and I shooed the cows onto the street in time. One day I got tired of it. The daughter slept in and the cows missed the herder's call. The daughter woke up and screamed at me to chase the cows out fast and I yelled back, 'That's it. I'm leaving.'

'You can't,' shrilled the daughter, 'Your father authorized you to work here.'

'He's not my father. He can't tell me what to do! Ma can tell me what to do, not Pa. And my Ma says we're digging potatoes and that's where I'm going. So goodbye!'

Seated in her apartment in Neuwied, excited in her storytelling, the more she recalled, the more she lapsed into Plautdietsch.

Another time Agatchen was sick, and in the kitchen Oma Toews had been baking because there was a birthday in her family. As soon as I walked into the house, I smelled an aroma of cookies. It filled the house and seeped into our room where little Agatchen lay sick and hungry. So I said, 'Why doesn't Agatchen get anything? She's ill and hungry and they have food.' [Mama, woaromm tjrijcht Agatje nuscht? See ess krank, enn ahr hungat, enn see habe too aete.]

*   'Lena, Oma Toews won't give anything.' [Lena, Oma Toews jeft Die muscht.]*
*   'I'll go ask. Isn't Agatchen even her own flesh and blood, a Toews?' [Mama, da woa etj froage gohne; Agatje ess doch een Toews, gaunz dijchet frindschauft.]*
*   'No, no, I'll go.' [Nae, nae, etj woa gohne.]*
*   So Ma asked for a bit of food for sick little Agatchen and Oma Toews went to a cupboard and pulled out a dry, mouldy crust of bread. 'Here, take this.' [Hiea, nemm dit.]*
*   When Ma came back with Oma Toews's gift, I was so angry, I determined to give the old woman a piece of my mind. I wouldn't interrupt the celebration in the parlour, oh no, but I would catch Oma Toews in the kitchen. As Oma Toews entered, I stuck out my chest and told her, 'That crust of bread, that old dry, mouldy crust of bread you gave your hungry grandchild will haunt you. Just wait. You've got that on your conscience and don't you think I'll ever forget. God will judge you, so don't think he doesn't see you.'*

With these words, seventy-three-year old Lena shook her head, 'That's what happened.' Years later when old Oma Toews became ill, the daughter who received the birthday cookies couldn't be bothered to nurse her, even begrudged her mother food. At that time, Lena, living in her own house, heard through the village grapevine that old Oma Toews was sick and not being tended. She decided that sick people, regardless of who they are, must get food. She prepared borscht, made a mousse, and baked something, put the food into two pails, and walked to the Toews house.

A hated step-aunt, on her knees washing the kitchen floor, looked derisively at Lena, 'Humph, you're here? Want to see the old lady?'

Lena ignored her look and tramped right over the newly wet floor through the familiar house to the bedroom of Oma Toews.

'What? You Lena?' Oma Toews was astonished.

Lena set down her pails, got a bowl from the kitchen, and slowly spooned the old woman her savoury soup. 'I told her, "Just eat now."'

The old woman's tears rolled down her face. She closed her eyes and her voice choked. 'That crust of bread is so dry, so dry.'

'Let's forget about it.'

'I can't forget. How could I have been so cruel?'

Lena said nothing but continued to dip into the soup and urged another swallow.

'Now I know,' cried old Oma Toews. 'Now I know.'

Finishing the tale, Lena nodded, 'In a stroke, perhaps of divine justice, the wicked daughter soon after caught typhus and died.' She paused. 'Then a son, a "decent son," came home and nursed his mother.'

Telling her stories, Lena jumped from one time period to the next, each anecdote told with more fire, and I wondered, with such a strong personality, how did she manage under rigid Soviet regulations? In situations where most people became cowed, fearful, and panic-stricken, how did she keep her defiance? Perhaps her early start as a fighter put others on guard. Perhaps the village administrators in Waldheim were a trifle more lenient, being fellow Mennonites, some even Party members. Like her Uncle Gerhard, she had an uncanny ability to size up a situation and exploit any opening. As she told her story with bravado I saw how it was possible, by believing yourself above a situation, to live in the Soviet world and keep some dignity. This impression was confirmed in Lena's further stories.

Deserted, scrapping bits of food together, doing her odd jobs, and trying to raise her children, AnnaK had appealed to a new manager at the Waldheim Collective Farm, who gave the family work. They decided to build themselves a house, working at night. At one end of the village there was a pond bounded on one side by clay soil. After the day's work the family would go to the pond, take off their clothes, and, holding them over their heads, wade through the muddy water breast-deep, and make clay bricks out of the scooped up clay. Like children at a seaside, they filled wooden forms with clay mud and tipped out bricks, and the pile of bricks drying in the sun grew. Soon the bricks were mortared into walls and a house emerged, not large, and not beautiful, a space free of Oma Toews. Until her son Peter was drafted into the Red Army in 1939, AnnaK's life improved slightly.

By 1939 religion had not been taught for ten years and many Mennonite children were becoming atheists. AnnaK had continued to teach her children about God and to speak her Mennonite Plautdietsch, not Russian. Daughters Agatha and Katya Toews followed in her footsteps, but Lena Wiebe wanted to enjoy life. After the day's work, young people of the village gathered at the club in the former church, and here Lena liked to dance, whirling to romantic music played by a band.

They met at the dance club. He was a Russian Baptist and his name was Nikolai. Lena, black-haired, outgoing, saucy, was four years older. Even at seventy-three, Lena's eyes shone as she described Nikolai in his uniform: 'Oh, Nikolai was a handsome soldier!' They both knew time was short and weren't they in love? They became engaged. People shook their heads. A Russian and a *Nemka*? Romeo and Juliet, a doomed alliance.

On Sunday (she would never forget it), 22 June 1941, as usual, Lena went to the dance club, but today she did not come to dance. She had just heard on the village loudspeaker that Hitler had invaded the Soviet Union. Slowly she walked into the club and told the club manager. Instantly the dance music stopped. Waldheim was, after all, a mostly German-speaking village. 'Now we'll get it' (Nu woa wie daut tjriee), Lena predicted as the dancers slowly left the building. Now her village would be hated more than ever.

After Nikolai left for war, Lena discovered she was pregnant. She wrote him and he told his relatives to advise her to get an abortion. When they relayed this information, she exploded, 'How could he say that? A father wanting to do in his own child! He'll be down on his knees to this child. Very well, it will be my child and I will have it.' In the icy month of January 1942 Lena decided to give Nikolai one last chance to accept fatherhood. Bundled up in heavy winter clothing, she boarded the train, stopped off to deliver a packet of food and letters to her brother Peter at his Labour Army work camp, and, bringing a suitcase of goods from Nikolai's family, continued to his military post. She saw him briefly, but he said little, so when Lena's baby was born, she named him after her dead brother.

I had asked how Lena was able to avoid deportation and the *Trudarmiia*. The German Army never occupied Siberia, so Siberian Mennonite villagers, unlike those in Ukraine, were not exiled, and the Labour Army exemption was easy to explain. It was the 'doomed alliance' that saved her. *Trudarmiia* rules exempted pregnant women and mothers with children under the age of three.

During the four years Nikolai was away, Lena did not know if he was dead or alive, heard not a word from him. She worked and AnnaK minded her baby. And then one day at the end of the war, Nik's relatives shouted out to her as she went by, 'Nik is home!'

'When? How?'

'They arrived last night.'

'They?'

'He wants to see his son.'

'I won't let him near my son. You tell him he won't ever get near my son!'

Reflecting in 1991, Lena suggested that Nikolai might still have returned to her, had she not been so stubborn. She studied her son's photograph that lay on the table in front of us and sighed. 'Yes, although Nik's girlfriend Larissa was pregnant, he wasn't married yet, was he? And who knows?' But then she seemed to relive the moment and added defiantly, 'It was the idea of my son being cheated, of him being disappointed – that, I would not tolerate. Every day little Yasha came home telling me that the papa of so-and-so had come home from the war and when was his papa coming? To have Yasha's papa come back only to disappear again? No way! I wasn't disappointing my son this way. Better he never saw his father.'

By now Lena was tired of the hard work on the collective farm. Saved from the *Trudarmiia*, she looked for openings. Her child had an advantage because his father was Russian. Taking a chapter from *Gone with the Wind*, the Mennonite Scarlet O'Hara plotted how to save her Tara and buy herself a better life. If she married a Russian, she'd be able to get different work. *Nemtsy* had no rights, but Russians were not called fascists or enemies. Russians were not under surveillance, subjected to *Spetskommandatura* restrictions on travel and social contacts. She decided to marry a Russian. Her mother said little when Lena told her of this resolve, but Lena's sister Agatha told me that both she and AnnaK were shamed by Lena having an illegitimate child and that Mennonite villagers looked askance at Lena Wiebe flirting with Russians.

Swaggering into the collective farm office, Lena noticed a good-looking, blond truck driver called Igor Kuznetzov. Handsome, in her late twenties, she turned on her charms and Igor fell for her in no time. They married, and not long afterwards Lena got a good new job as manager of the local state store. Scarlet O'Hara, according to plan. The one hitch was that Igor had a great thirst for alcohol, and when Lena warned him she didn't like this, it made no impression. What could she do, gone on weekends? 'You know, a truck driver is on the road much of the time.'

Lena and Igor moved into their own house, but AnnaK continued to look after Lena's little Yasha. Early every morning Lena walked the five kilometres to the store, opened up at nine, stayed till sundown, locked up, and walked back to pick up Yasha. Immediately after she took the job, she dismissed the former manager's assistant. 'He was an incompetent, took bribes, and did backroom deals.' Not that this was uncommon under Communist rule. Often when goods came in, a storekeeper kept items off the shelves to sell privately at a higher price when stocks were depleted. The system might be corrupt, but not *her* store. What, risk being charged, when Lena and the other *Nemtsy* were already suspected as enemies? She'd rather do the assistant's job herself. So she swept floors, stocked shelves, took inventory, and sold liquor only for medicine. 'Those were my conditions.'

Shortly thereafter, into Lena's store came one of the Toews relatives who had eaten birthday cookies when little Agatha Toews lay ill and hungry. Smiling importantly, Toews walked up to her counter and bantered, 'Oh ho, our cousin has a high position now. Store manager!'

'Cousin?' Lena's voice was scathing. 'You weren't my relative before and you're not my relative now. So don't you cousin me! I was a Wiebe and you were a Toews. That's the way it is now too.'

It was 1948, another day in the Waldheim state store. In walked Ewald Goertzen, former head of the collective farm, the *pred.* In the days before Lena's marriage, he had sat in his warm office while she and other women and girls shovelled manure, carried buckets of water, or lifted heavy sacks of feed. Ewald got his position on the collective farm by becoming loyal to Marxist-Leninism. But having also become a drunkard, he had been dismissed from his job. 'Can't you give me a job?' he begged. 'I'll do anything – sweep floors – anything, just please give me work.'

How the worm had turned, Lena thought. Not his officious manner, not the careless bookkeeping, no, nothing other than the bottle had done him in, the colourless, odourless vodka. And she, Lena Wiebe, was dead set against hiring an alcoholic. But, listening to his whining, Lena remembered when her mother had begged for odd jobs and how gnarled her mother's hands had become. Now she sat at home and welcomed Lena every morning. It was Ewald who had given her mother that first job at the collective farm. 'Well, on one condition. Not a drop of alcohol, do you understand? I keep one case of liquor and that is sold for medicine. No drinking. Is that clear?'

'I promise. I promise!'

For a month everything ran smoothly. Lena checked in the back store-room where Ewald lifted and sorted, received and packed. They locked up together and went their separate ways. Then one evening Lena found Ewald sprawled across the back room table, with open bottles lying all round him. Goods were spilled from the warehouse shelves, money was lying scattered about, and the back door was wide open. She collected the money, tied it up in a bag and hid the pouch inside a row of containers, got a bucket of water, sloshed it over the drunken man, and proceeded to tidy up the mess. Who had come to the back and bribed Ewald to trade liquor for goods? The cold water took effect and Ewald began to blubber. A man who wet his trousers, what a sight.

Lena pushed him by the arms and they began a slow walk. Supporting the stumbling man, Lena hoped the dusk would hide their slow silhouettes from watching eyes. When they reached the outskirts of Waldheim village Lena steadied Ewald: 'Now you're on your own. No way am I going to be seen slip-sliding down main street with the likes of you!' Somehow he got home and the whole thing never got out, not in the scrutiny of the store inventory or in any other way. Years later, Lena's sister Agatha told me of more incidents where Lena helped others (giving out a piece of bread after dark), but 'never cheated the government. She would cover a debt herself rather than have it discovered by the authorities.'

But Lena worried about her mother.

AnnaK listless in bed, had little energy to listen to Lena's report of a day's events. Only sixty, she was an old babushka in cheap worn slippers, the type of poor peasant, back in her youth in Crimea, she would have seen sitting in the sun on a bench in front of a mud-bricked hut. She kept remembering a carriage pulled by matched horses, remembering her sister Helena going abroad to study (holding a parasol in that portrait from Germany), remembering blossoming acacia trees. More and more AnnaK brooded on her girlhood and talked about heaven's streets of gold where there would be no more tears, where she would see Jesus. She prayed for Lena to be converted, but Lena was not interested. The Waldheim village was filling with non-Mennonites who did not want any religion, but AnnaK clung to her faith. When a few of the men dragooned in 1941 returned, AnnaK remembered her first husband, Peter Wiebe. How weak and emaciated he had appeared returning from Kolchak's War. Then typhus killed him. 'I'll die soon,' she said, 'I can feel it.'

'It was June 1948,' Lena told me. 'Before I left for work as usual at seven o'clock, I came to my mother's bed to check, and that morning Ma wanly reached out and stroked my face. "I'll be gone when you come back tonight," she said and smiled such a loving look that it cut right into my heart. "No, no," I protested. "I'll try to leave early tonight and we'll try a hot plaster on your chest. Just rest. I'll be back early."'

Yet when Lena hurried in at seven that evening, her sister Agatha had washed their mother and closed her eyes. And that's how my father's sister Anna, the one he never talked about, died in Waldheim, Siberia.

Anna Konrad Wiebe Toews
(1887, Crimea – 1948, Siberia)

Lena mourned the loss of her mother, but she had her son, Yasha, and Russian truck-driver husband, Igor. It was spring again and one week-end, still during the time of *Spetskommandatura*, Pentecost coming up, Lena and Igor had agreed that Saturday would be a good day to plant potatoes. On Friday Lena sensed something was wrong, but she made Igor his breakfast and reminded him not to go out drinking, to come home in time so they could get an early start in the morning. They both left for work. As she put Yasha to bed that night, Igor still had not come home and Lena fumed about his miserable drinking habit. The next morning it was raining hard, not a good planting day. In mid-morning there was a knock on the door.

'Is Igor Kuznetzov home? No?'

The policeman handed her a summons. Lena thought the summons would be about Igor's drinking and she should at least warn him. Going to his place of work, a surprise awaited her. At the garage the other drivers told her Igor was on his days off. He always had five days on, five days off. Didn't she know? Lena did not know that, but she did not let on. Imagine, five days off! Just where had he been spending those days?

Surveying the amused men, Lena recognized one of Igor's friends leaning against the garage door. 'Hey, Misha,' she asked, 'you know where Igor is?' Misha shook his head. She knew immediately he was covering for Igor and decided on a new approach. 'Are you by any chance driving to Issil Kul?' She referred to a town some distance away. 'May I get a lift?' Lena had no permission to take such a trip, since under the *Spetskommandatura* laws she was forbidden to travel more than a few kilometres, but that was a detail she ignored.

They drove for twenty kilometres and then Lena admitted to Misha, 'I lied to you. I don't need to go to Issil Kul. I need to tell Igor that the police have come looking for him. Can you tell me where he is? I won't tell him how I got there or that you gave me a lift. It's the summons that is important.' So then Misha told her where Igor was and let her off on the main road leading into that village.

The rain had stopped. As she walked along the rutted dirt road filled with puddles, she noticed a young woman wobbling on a bicycle but decided not to ask her anything. Where best to get information? Aha, the village well was always a source, a meeting place where truck drivers often stopped for a drink of water. People got to know them. Standing at the well were two women, an old babushka gesticulating at a younger one balancing a heavy pail on her head.

'What's going on in the village?' Lena asked the babushka. She had noticed celebrations, with people outside their houses drinking and laughing.

'Oh,' said the crone, 'there's a wedding. It's already the second day of the wedding. A young girl, well a woman actually, since she already had a child from a soldier who deserted her – a village girl, she's marrying a truck driver, a chauffeur.'

'Really,' Lena's eyes lit up. 'How interesting. And who is the lucky groom, the chauffeur?'

'Well, I'm not sure, but I think Igor is his name.'

'You know, Babushka, I'm Igor's cousin and I've come to tell him he has a summons.' Lena whispered conspiratorially into the old woman's shawl, 'It's rather important. Could you point out the house of the bride – where I could tell him?'

'You're his cousin? I'll show you the house. I'm going that way too.'

As the old woman and Lena walked along the street, Lena began to think what could happen to the old crone when the truth came out. Fireworks enough without involving this old one, so why share the truth about Igor? Lena told the old woman to just keep on walking. No, no, she would tell nobody how she found the house, nothing.

As Lena walked towards the house where the carousing grew louder, she was puzzled. She knew Igor inside out, a weak man, but could not guess what would have drawn him into this deceit. He wanted something from this circus, but what?

In front of the house she stopped and stood with folded arms. Soon neighbours came out to watch. A sturdy woman with a flushed face opened the door and Lena called out, 'Who is getting married here?'

"My daughter.' The woman at the door sounded proud, important.

'It's dangerous to drink. It's dangerous to get married.'

'How so? Dangerous to get married?' the woman laughed and, looking around for support, peered inquiringly at Lena. 'You're joking.'

'No, I'm not joking. By the way, where is your daughter?'

'She's gone to get some herring. She left on her bike just a while ago.'

Lena thought, it's the one I noticed when I came from the main road. Good I didn't ask her for directions. Lena was beginning to enjoy this charade. She sweetened her voice and asked innocently, 'And – might I ask – who is the bridegroom?'

'Igor Kuznetzov. He's a chauffeur!'

'So may I meet the new husband?'

Around her the village onlookers, wedding guests in various degrees of intoxication, were beginning to smell trouble and looked at her suspiciously.

'Who are you? Yes, who are you?'

Lena braved them all. 'I'm Igor's wife.'

Quickly the little crowd disappeared and soon sheepish Igor emerged from the wedding house. Dishevelled, apprehensive, his usually tidy blond hair that had attracted Lena when she first saw him in the office at the collective farm now pointing in all directions, his voice slurred, he began to upbraid her. 'Lena how dare you …'

She cut him short. 'How nice that you can just take the weekend and get married! Isn't that something! Here the police come to my house looking for you and you're off in this village – getting married!'

'Shh, Lena, shh.'

'You really think you're something! Maybe you think you're Adolf Hitler! Haha, Berlin is burning and he is in his underground bunker getting married!'

'Go home, Lena! Go home. I'll come home. Just don't make a ruckus.'

'Ruckus? Who's the one making a ruckus? Oh, I'll go home. I'll leave right now. You just go on with your wedding, but let me tell you this. When you get home your belongings will all be in a nice bundle outside and you won't step a foot into my house. Not ever again!'

With that last barrage Lena turned around and stomped up the street, heading towards the main road where she would hitchhike a ride back home. As she neared the highway, she noticed a cyclist and as it came closer she saw it was indeed the same young woman she had seen before, only this time there was a parcel of salted herring in the carrier of the bicycle. The bride. As the bicycle bride was about to pedal past, Lena grabbed her tire so firmly that the cyclist almost fell off.

'Why did you do that? What's the matter with you?' the woman screamed.

'You're the bride, right?'

'What's that to you?'

'To me? Oh, that's just dandy! You see, I'm Igor's wife. Your Igor is married.'

'Already married?'

'Yes. To me.'

The new bride stared at Lena. 'What's your name?'

'Lena Wiebe.'

The bride recognized that it was not Russian, but a German name, one of the 'enemies of the state.'

'He would never marry you!' She spit out the words. 'A *Nemka*? Never!'

Lena didn't know what overcame her, but she smashed the sneering bride in the face with her fist. 'Take that from a *Nemka*!'

The bicycle tipped and herring spilled in the mud. The fallen bride, whimpering and cowering, put up her hands to defend herself, but Lena turned and walked determinedly to the highway.

Reaching home, Lena was so exhausted she lay down, and before she knew it, Igor was through the door and begging her, 'Please let me explain. Let me explain!' He was on his knees beside the bed. 'I can explain everything.'

Emboldened by her silence, Igor now showed a little spirit and asked almost respectfully, 'What did you do to the bride? You should have seen her face!'

Again Lena answered nothing and Igor shook his head. 'She's going to charge you.' He almost crowed, 'She'll charge you. She'll report you.'

'Hah. Whom will she charge? She had it coming.'

'What did you hit her with? Her whole face is a map.'

'Just my fist.'

'But her face, her eyes. She's all bloodshot.'

'Let her be. And what about you? Shall I show you how I did it?'

'No, no, no, but she'll charge you.'

Lena sat up on the bed facing Igor. 'Charged. You'll be the one who gets charged. Charged! Three wives! All living! Just how are you going to explain that to the judge?'

Igor 's mouth fell open.

'And just how is your bride going to explain to the judge about all the home brew bottles I saw standing in that house and on the tables. Since when has it become legal to make home brew? How many years in jail is it for making illegal booze? Do you know that? Five? Ten?'

Igor's boldness was crumbling. He shifted his position.

'Oh no,' Lena pointed her finger at him. 'It's you who will go to court. There'll be no court case from your bride against me. You're the one who has the summons, and do you know what for? I've opened the letter. Bigamy! What's the penalty for that?'

'Okay, enough, enough. I'll tell you what happened.'

And so he did. Igor's plan was to marry the daughter with the herring in order to persuade her parents to sell their two cows and give him the money. He had told them he could take the money from the sale of their two mediocre cows and buy one really superior cow for them. Of course he never intended to buy the good cow, but to abscond with the money and use it to pay the child support that he owed from his first marriage. Yes, he knew about the summons. It was not the first time he had received a summons to pay child support. Yes, a first wife. He was going to tell her.

'That's a piece of news,' Lena said, 'on one day to find out not only that you have a first wife and a son, but also a third wife. What a revelation.'

As Igor began to cry, Lena stormed on. 'Lucky thing I have had no child of yours or you'd have to marry another cow.'

By then Igor begged her to forgive him, saying he never had wanted the girl with the herring, but Lena, only Lena, and could she please take him back. Lena thought of her own son, Yasha, and how difficult it was for a child to grow up without a man around. She thought how the *Nemtsy* were still very restricted because of the regulations of the *Spetzkomandantura*, and she finally sighed and said, 'On one condition. That you never go to that village again.'

In the following years Lena left Igor because he drank too much and landed in jail. She moved to nearby Issil Kul where she ran a gift store. Here her business partner absconded with a large sum of money, and Lena, knowing the books would be audited, personally borrowed everywhere to restore the sum. She herself spent years repaying the debts. When Yasha was ten years old, Lena took his father, Nikolai, to court for child support payments so Yasha could go on in school. The judge wanted to force Nikolai to pay Lena half his salary, but she told him, 'No, that's too much. He's got two other children.' (Nikolai had married Larissa). 'Am I going to take bread out of their mouths?' When

Nikolai suggested she withdraw her court action entirely, she laughed, 'Well, I'm generous but not stupid.' They settled on a fair amount and the child support helped her to build herself a small house.

Sitting in her Neuwied apartment where her walls were decorated with framed puzzles of castles and mountains, Lena relished telling the details. Hadn't she done it before, built a house with handmade bricks? She had three loads of clay and a load of straw dumped on her allotted site and the neighbours thought this young woman was crazy. Lena calmly hired three brothers to come after their work and put up a frame. Since they lived some distance away, the work proceeded slowly until she decided that cooking them supper would save time. They'd come to eat. So she left them a snack of cold coffee ('chicory blend is the only decent coffee'), some bread and cheese, and when she came home from her work, she cooked them a good meal. The frame was up in no time. Now with little Yasha's help, she made the bricks. In bare feet, they mixed clay with chopped straw and stamped. They wedged branches between frame studs and stuffed clay mixture into the walls, layer by layer, to fill in the walls.

In 1955, when the hateful *Spetskommandatura* curfews finally ended, people felt freer to communicate and began to look up relatives. Lena moved into Omsk, worked in another store, and lived with her Uncle and Aunt Wiebe. She had a portrait taken of a handsome, buxom woman, firm and determined, posing with her son. Yasha was bright and bold, like his mother. Having completed his schooling, Yasha was called up for his two-year military service. From near Leningrad, he wrote his mother regularly. Lena joked with him that he'd soon be getting married, but he laughed, 'Oh, I'll never leave you, Ma. No wife could separate me from my mother!'

In Omsk Lena's Uncle Wiebe would tell Bible stories at his home, and relatives would meet after work for Christmas Eve, even though New Year's Day was the holiday. On nights when Lena's Uncle Wiebe, speaking in Plautdietsch, told the Bible story of Christmas to his grandchildren, Yasha often was present. In March 1966, Lena's son fell into the Irtysh River during an altercation and died. At that moment, she remembered the teaching of her mother, AnnaK. Her mother had said that to have eternal life, one must be saved. Would she see him again? Did he have time in the last minutes to get right with God? Surely in those last moments he would have called out to God. She remembered the last Christmas when, instead of dressing up like Father Frost in his red and white suit and handing out gifts to the children, he had chosen to go with her and listened to Uncle Wiebe. He must have called on God at the last moment, her son, dearer than all the world. Lena the unbeliever gave her son a Christian burial.

One of the people who comforted Lena in her enormous grief was a man we will call Grigorii. Some time after the tragedy she began to live with him, and though he was 'a decent sort,' she did not want to marry him. She had never been married legally, Lena explained to us in 1991 – and this was after she had become baptized in Germany and was a member of an evangelical church in Neuwied. Igor was still married when she married him, and she had just been engaged to Nikolai. Grigorii was her third partner, not third husband.[3]

Lena, much like my father, was a marvellous storyteller. Brazen, she saw through sham and couldn't abide hypocrisy. She had a good sense of humour, but not about religion. She was generous and spirited. Perhaps her self-confidence was her best asset. Lena outsmarted the system when she could, but openly. In matters of honesty and work ethic, she was true to her upbringing and traditional Mennonite teaching. She was fortunate to live in Siberia where the 'German' villages remained essentially intact, in spite of revolution, war, and discrimination. A majority of Waldheim villagers were Mennonites, so she had a community with a common past, a cocoon. She was not uprooted or relocated. She never lost her formidable spirit, her identity, or her sense of self-worth. She overcame the system, rather than the reverse. It was the passive mother, AnnaK, who bore the pain.

Lena's Sisters: 'Religious Fanatics'

Amalia

Lena's brother, Peter Wiebe, had survived the Red Army and the Labour Army and by 1960 lived with his wife, Amalia, and three sons in Taldy Kurgan, Kazakhstan. After Peter died, Amalia immigrated to Germany and I met her in Berlin. Her son Peter, a medical doctor who had arrived two years previously, had sponsored her. In the early 1990s it was relatively easy for Soviet Germans to get exit permits. Amalia was living with Peter and his family in a Berlin subsidized apartment. Peter had a hospital locum – a position that most immigrant medical doctors found almost impossible to get. Another son, Viktor, and his family recently arrived in Berlin were living at the Paul Gerhard Stift, a Protestant type of cloister and a temporary residence for new immigrants. After three years in France on a research exchange from the Academy of Sciences in Novosibirsk, Viktor, a geneticist, his wife, Marina, an architect, and two children had decided to immigrate to Germany because they feared the door for *Aussiedler* might close. Called *Spätaussiedler*, 'late arrivals,' they received smaller stipends and shorter language training than emigrants like Gerhard's daughter Nelly or their aunt Lena Wiebe.

Amalia was a thin woman with a stern, narrow face and grey hair pulled back severely in a knot. I had written that I was looking for life histories but made a big mistake by arriving at her son's apartment with a notepad. At first Amalia gave me only monosyllabic answers, affirmed a few known facts, and, when asked for an opinion, said she didn't know, she couldn't say. Suddenly she rose from her seat and said curtly, 'Come, I'll show you my pictures.' We went to her bedroom. On a narrow bed were several large square pillows covered in pure white starched pillowcases brought from Taldy Kurgan. She said she had brought almost nothing and had burned most of her letters and pictures, except those of her immediate family. 'What good were they? I thought I'd never see any of those people again. I remember your parents' golden wedding picture, all those people. I never thought I'd meet someone from Canada. I could have taken it, but I didn't know.'

We looked at Amalia's few remaining pictures now inserted into a book on the history of the Paul Gerhard Stift. She had carefully cut a three-quarter-inch slit into four corners of each page of historical text and inserted a photograph, covering portraits of elderly deaconesses. Examining pictures, she relaxed and began to talk.

She had met her husband in Tabashar, Tajikistan, both having been sent here after their release from the *Trudarmiia* in 1947. Both were destitute, without proper clothing or money, and separated from their families. They married in 1948. 'No formal wedding, just a registry in the municipal office.' Amalia sat on a chair with photographs in her lap, speaking in monotones. 'We had nothing, only a straw mattress. Peter got work in a uranium mine. We built three walls to make a one-room house. It was a long, garage-like building with thirteen adjoining one-room homes. We added number fourteen. Peter died of cancer. Others who worked in the mine, all, all died of cancer. Two sons were born in Tabashar: Jakob in 1949 and Peter in 1953. Our third son, Viktor, was born after we moved to Taldy Kurgan in 1956.'

Her parents, Jakob Frick and Margarita Schaaf, had worked in a spinning factory before being removed from the 'workers' list.' Ten days later they were given twenty-four hours' notice to be exiled. Their story hardly varied from that of the Braun family. Unloaded in eastern Siberia, near Barnaul, they were told to fend for themselves, and her family traded clothes for food, gathered wizened potatoes left over after harvesting, tried to get a little money by sewing for others, or worked on a collective farm. Amalia and her sisters, commandeered for the *Trudarmiia*, were sent into a labour camp to cut trees in winter and to cut hay with scythes in summer. They built makeshift huts of grass and camped out in the hayfields, where they were practically devoured by mosquitoes.

'In 1946 we were told, "Now you're out of the *Trudarmiia*. You're going to Tajikistan." Both men and women from different forced labour camps were sent to Tajikistan. When I got there I whitewashed and painted the insides of homes. That's how I met my husband, Peter. He was a bricklayer.'

The following day, Amalia and I sat on a bench in front of the Stift where we could watch who came and went in the courtyard. I no longer carried pencil and pad but listened attentively as Amalia spoke quietly. Whenever anyone went by, she placed her hand on my arm in a 'don't say anything now' warning, and we waited till the passerby was out of earshot. At no time did her face betray any sign of emotion.

We talked about Amalia's husband, how he was conscripted into the Red Army in Waldheim, and about his time in the Labour Army. We talked about living in Taldy Kurgan, Kazakhstan. 'Peter was a religious man. He was a Christian. He had to do things honestly.' Amalia paused to see if I understood her cryptic comment about the widespread habit of Soviet citizens helping themselves to government building supplies from worksites. 'That's why it took us longer to build our house.'

It was Gerhard Konrad, Peter's uncle, who had invited them to move to Taldy Kurgan, Kazakhstan (Gerhard had lived there since 1952). Gerhard had brought some tin for a roof and helped build a two-bedroom, mud-brick house, and Amalia made the air-dried bricks for the stove with her own hands. To grow vegetables or fruit in the sandy soil, narrow canals along the streets provided irrigation. Amalia planted oak and maple trees, as well as fruit trees and grapevines. 'Gerhard helped us a lot,' she said. 'He was smart, capable, and sly.' She dipped in and out of time periods, ever alert, always halting when someone passed. Her husband had almost died of starvation when he was in the *Trudarmiia*. He was taking what he thought would be his last bath when he accidentally scalded himself and ended up in the infirmary. 'His luck.' Just at that time he received a packet of food from his mother, enough for him to gain strength in the two weeks he was in recovery.

Since Peter Wiebe was a blacksmith, he was able to retire at the age of fifty, ten years earlier than the norm. He received seventy roubles in pension and Amalia, still working, sixty roubles. The eldest son found work as a truck driver, and the other two sons both completed ten years of school (Soviet high school ended in the tenth grade). Bearing in mind Soviet hostility towards ethnic Germans and Stalin's attempt to wipe out their culture, it was difficult for the Wiebe sons to be accepted into programs of advanced education, yet son Peter Wiebe took the medical exams and passed. He had two changes of clothes: his 'school' clothes and his 'sports' clothes. When he had to do the compulsory two months of harvest work demanded of all university students, he wore his sports clothes over his school clothes for warmth. He came home, got his clothes laundered, and returned to school, and somehow he got by.

The youngest son, Viktor, the geneticist, wanted desperately to go to university, but there was no money. He worked two years, did his compulsory two years of army service, and got into university only to find he had forgotten far too much. Then his father died and his mother took money he had been saving up for years to buy a car, sold their cow, and then divided the money four ways, giving each a quarter, and with their 2,000 roubles the sons managed to attend university.

On Sunday we attended church with Amalia in the Paul Gerhard Stift chapel where she was a parishioner. It was the fiftieth anniversary of the Hiroshima bombing. As we sat in a sparse congregation among blocks of deaconesses in grey dresses and white caps, the minister strode to the front in his black gown. Behind him, perhaps symbolic of the Wiebe family, fluttering up again and again against the modern stained glass window, summer butterflies attempted to break through the beams of light.

In all the times we met, Amalia never asked questions, never made a negative or critical observation, never blamed anyone, was always factual, almost robotic. Careful, watchful, she had survived the Soviet system by registering no emotion – so different from her husband's sister, Lena. But Lena never experienced labour camps and dislocation, and never hosted secret house church meetings in constant fear of the door being knocked down by the secret police, never kept a secret faith. Lena faced down her attackers, was always a step ahead of the authorities. But what of those who survived by keeping everything bottled up, by looking down, by learning *not* to see anything, hear anything, and especially not to say anything? Could I expect Amalia to be forthcoming, express opinions, having known only intimidation? When I asked her how people lived with daily injustice, she said, 'You have to accept things as they are. We can't change things.' Then she was silent.

Also living in Taldy Kurgan were my father and Gerhard's brother, Abram, his wife Nastya, and his family. I knew little about Abram and asked the Wiebe brothers about him. What did they know? Nelly had told me Abram was russified: 'He didn't want to speak German. He drank. Well, his wife was Russian, but her children were the despised *Nemtsy* who did not want to be *Nemtsy* – one especially. The son wanted to take his wife's name when he married.' Amalia Wiebe's sons in Berlin agreed with Nelly that our Uncle Abram had become russified: 'It was understandable. And yes, his children resented his German background. His only daughter, Lolya (Lena), was married to a big Soviet Pooh-Bah with medals across his chest and connected to the Soviet space program. So she was very pro-Soviet. Her father had to be careful. But Nelly is wrong, Abram was never a drunkard.'[4]

Nelly had no ties with Abram's children. 'I did not accompany my father when he visited the Wiebes, or Abram and Nastya. I had schoolwork and children's activities.' I asked why Nelly's mother, Klara, and Abram's wife, Nastya, did not get along, why Gerhard went to visit his relatives without his wife. Nelly had found her Tante Nastya grandmotherly, very kind, but her mother, Klara, kept a grudge against Nastya for blurting out to Gerhard's adopted son, Otto, that he was adopted. Likely Nastya thought his mother, Klara, would have told him long ago, or Klara used this as an excuse. Nelly said, 'My mother had to be very careful, especially with the Wiebes, who were religious. Religious fanatics. Mama hated that. You could lose your job.' *Religious fanatic* was used in Soviet propaganda to denigrate believers. The Wiebes met in houses for underground church services during 'thaw' intervals when the government relaxed its searches, but Gerhard and Abram never attended these meetings. Nelly had said, 'When someone at work didn't drink, right away you knew it must be one of those underground Baptists. And the Wiebes' father was very strict about that; why, he even had church services in his house. Religious fanatics!'

Observing the two sons in Berlin, it was clear to me that Amalia and her husband's religious training had uneven results. Although they were raised at home to be God-fearing, the boys' schooling triumphed. As doctor Peter stated, 'I grew up an atheist and I'll stay an atheist, but I respect people who are religious.' Against all odds, the sons had persevered to get an advanced education and professional degrees. Peter had worked in a forensic lab in Taldy Kurgan and Viktor was a researcher at the Academy of Sciences in Novosibirsk, yet both still experienced discrimination and were maligned as traitors and Nazis. Peter's first marriage collapsed after his Russian wife called him a fascist. Then the fall of Communism turned everything upside down. Suddenly it was important not to be a Communist and advantageous to be a German or – where they lived – to be a Kazakh. Communism had wiped out religion, but not nationalism. Everywhere Amalia's sons heard, 'Kaza-khstan for the Kazakhs,' and knew they didn't belong. The Wiebes taught their sons faith, but the sons wanted to fit into a Soviet world. Gerhard did not teach his children faith and they too grew up atheists. In villages like Lena Wiebe's Waldheim where people had been able to remain in their communities, traditions and religion continued, but in places of exile, how could one family sustain the pull to conform? Trained to adapt, it may be ironic, but when they reached Germany, Gerhard's family had their children christened and even Nelly was con-firmed. 'I didn't believe, but it was the thing to do.' By trying to remain invisible, conforming, one could survive. To lose one's faith could be the price of a Soviet upbringing.

Agatha

Lena's younger sister, Agatha, had immigrated to Germany before Lena Wiebe died suddenly of a heart attack. When I met her in 2005, she was a widow living with her eldest son Peter's family in the ancient town of Marienheide in North Rhine–Westphalia, an area of low hills, forests, small lakes, and meadows. German immigrants from Russia (*Russlandsdeutsche*) had been attracted here by its many metal and plas-tics factories. Driving up a hillside, we found a cluster of steep-roofed, white houses, nearly all built by Mennonites from Lena Wiebe's village of Waldheim, Siberia. As we knocked, a young girl in a long skirt called, 'Oma,' and an elderly woman in a dark tunic, wearing large round eye-glasses, and the familiar roses-on-black kerchief tied at the nape of her neck appeared in the doorway.

Agatha, now Widow Klassen, invited us into a living room, and soon a dark-haired teenaged granddaughter in long skirt offered, 'Some-thing to drink? Tea? Coffee?' From open doors, peeping out like mice, more of the twelve grandchildren in the home emerged. The first thing Agatha said was, 'You have to stay here. My sons have room.'

Agatha and her husband, following their children, had immigrated to Germany from Waldheim, Siberia. Her son Jakob and his wife, Irene, told us they had left good jobs in Omsk and that 'if you forget about religion and politics, it is possible to live well under communism.' Last to emigrate, the youngest son, Heinrich, living in the house his grandmother AnnaK and her children had built, waited to move because his father-in-law had permitted his daughter to marry Heinrich only on the promise they would not emigrate. He thought Christians should continue to witness to their faith in the USSR, now that 'religious fanatics' were no longer being arrested and it was wrong to leave for Germany.[5] The father-in-law died and the young couple immigrated.

The sons Jakob and Heinrich lived a five-minute walk downhill from Peter in adjacent houses. We lunched at one home, had dinner in another, went for walks or visited in one of the three living rooms. Everyone wanted to tell stories of life in the USSR. It was a change not to hear horror stories, but endless jokes, satiric *Krokodil* jokes, and happy memories. The Klassen men were machinists or engineers in local factories. One wife was a nurse and another laughingly explained, 'I'm a floor cosmetician' (cleaner). The son with the dozen children (Peter), whose wife had died a year ago, was urged to start 'looking around.' Even mother Agatha suggested another wife was due.

Secure in their transplanted 'Waldheim' village, the family had kept AnnaK's faith. Part of an evangelical Baptist church community, they now met three times on Sundays, with Bible study Tuesdays and prayer meeting Thursdays. Women wore head coverings and long-sleeved shirts and dresses, and a church youth group numbered 150.

Much of our time with the family was spent telling jokes. Agatha said gallows humour jokes had always circulated within her Mennonite community. There was the one, about the man who said, 'Just think, for a hundred roubles I can buy a horse. But why would I want to buy a horse when for the same money I can buy two chickens?'

And the one told during the Khrushchev 'thaw' (1960 to 1964) that was critical of the rampant deception that made the system work: Khrushchev visits an old friend in Soviet Ukraine and asks, 'How's it going?' The friend says, 'Not good, not good. I work and work and still am starving, but others have enough of everything.' Khrushchev says, 'You sleep too much.' 'But I work day and night. I'm so tired I almost fall over.' Khrushchev repeats, 'You sleep too much.' He goes back to Moscow.

Khrushchev's friend sits at his window late at night and sees his bosses and his fellow workers carrying pails and bulging pillowcases. His brain lights up. After this night he too stays awake at night, and in three years has everything he needs: furnishings, food, and clothing. He is so happy he decides to take a present to Khrushchev. He brings a pail of honey. He sets down the honey, knocks on Khrushchev's office door, goes inside, and says, 'Have I got a present for you.' Turning to retrieve the pail, it's gone. He says, 'I see nobody sleeps too much here either.'[6]

Agatha remembered her favourite schoolteacher in Waldheim, who cautioned the pupils (with a twinkle), not to refer to 'our guys up there' [*onse Jungess doa bowe*], referring to Stalin and his court. That teacher disappeared. In 1937 and 1938, twenty-two men from Waldheim were arrested, ten one year, twelve another, about half the village men. Of these, five survived to be released at the end of the war. One died mysteriously on the way home and another came back crippled. Agatha knew who in Waldheim had denounced those twenty-two names on the list – everyone in the village knew. To be accepted back into the village, one of the men repented, but not enough. He wrote on a piece of paper that he was sorry and sent it to the schoolteacher's widow, but she never forgave him. Said Agatha, 'He should have done it in person, and that would have been better.'[7]

Agatha described night-time 'church' meetings, moving furniture to prepare a small space for a service. Hunting for 'religious fanatics,' Soviet officials often barged into a home where the windows had been darkened with a blanket. Arrests were made, especially if children were present. Any 'brethren' who conducted services were arrested. Agatha's father-in-law was jailed for thirteen years.

Agatha was saved from the Labour Army in 1942 because she was the only remaining tractor and combine driver left in Waldheim after the men were forced into the *Trudarmiia*. 'As our yearly wage we got ten kilograms of grain to use for bread, but if the collective farm was short on its quota, they took it back. To survive, we had our small garden plots at home but had to make deliveries from these too.' She had married six months after her mother, AnnaK, died and raised a family of five children. Both wife and husband worked on the collective farm, managing their own garden plot after hours. If a nasty *pred* controlled the farm, collective members went hungry. Agatha said wistfully, 'Christians have to tell the truth, but there was a neighbouring village *pred* who secretly stashed grain away in a building that looked like a house and did not report the correct numbers. His workers had bread for the winter. He was a good man, a Ukrainian.'

Agatha's husband had been in the Red Army, then the Labour Army, and came back home with his clothing in tatters. He had left a suit of clothes with a friend, but the friend had sold it to buy food, so Lena the storekeeper found him a proper pair of pants to get married. The family lived largely from their garden, a cow, some chickens, and a pig they were allowed to own privately. To pay their taxes, they grew sugar beets, processing them into syrup, which they sold. Annually, from their small private holding they were obligated to deliver 100 eggs and forty pounds of meat to the state. In elections every adult villager was required to cast a ballot. Once far advanced in pregnancy, Agatha refused to go to the polling location. The officials would not allow her husband to vote for her until the last minute before poll closing time. Then the village got its required 100 per cent turnout.

Like her sister Lena, Agatha kept her head high through Soviet times, benefiting by living continuously in one village among her own people. She was able to retain her traditions and to keep her language and religion. But living always in a small village, she also kept its prejudices. She thought my uncles Abram and Heinrich Konrad had married 'Russian women' because they had difficulty finding suitable mates, 'what with the shame of their father having had a bankruptcy in Crimea.' She thought Gerhard had difficulty being accepted by his in-laws because they were 'rich people.' She thought her group of *Russlandsdeutsche* were the only 'pure Germans' ('These others are all mixed up; we kept within our group').

Subjected to similar Soviet restrictions on religion and civil rights, Agatha's children had not, within the village, been subjected to the kind of discrimination suffered by their cousins in other parts of the USSR. They did not bemoan their Soviet past. They had survived it together within their community and had no identity crises. They had learned trades rather than sought academic careers and thereby avoided being disappointed at exclusion from advanced education. They had not been exiled. They had kept their family traditions and an ethic of hard work and honesty. By complying on the outside, privately they had kept their Plautdietsch language, a sense of humour, and their faith. They did not see a difference between Baptist and Mennonite. As they said, the difference did not matter since God was above all that. Baptists had successfully absorbed Mennonites into their churches, so that the majority

of Mennonites emigrating from the USSR to Germany after 1980 identified themselves as Baptists.[8]

Encapsulated as they had been within their Mennonite/Baptist village while in the USSR, I wondered how the next generation would
fare, subjected to an open society and secular German culture.

Did Gerhard Stay Lucky?

Gerhard and Lieschen Konrad were in Alma Ata, Kazakhstan, at the
outbreak of war in 1941. Bedridden, Lieschen had permission to stay
behind when suspect ethnic minority groups were exiled, but she said,
'No, if I'm going to die, I'd rather be with you.' In November, with
hundreds of other deportees, Gerhard and Lieschen were sent 600 kilometres into a semi-desert. Then, loaded onto oxcarts, the deportees
were sent into the Taklamakan Desert. For 200 kilometres, the caravan
crossed a barren landscape of sand lizards and snakes until it reached
Aksu at the southern foot of the Tian Shan Mountains. In Aksu, a traditional Islamic Uygur/Han Chinese territory, the deported Germans,
Koreans, Tatars, Greeks, Ukrainians, and other undesirables made dugouts for shelter. Assigned work on collective farms, denied all basic lib-
erties, and kept under constant surveillance, Gerhard's beloved wife
Lieschen lasted six months, till June 1942.

I wondered how able-bodied Gerhard had escaped conscription
into the *Trudarmiia* when German males, including soldiers in the Red
Army, were deployed in 1942. Gerhard had died before I could ask,
but on a further trip to Germany, his daughter Nelly solved the puzzle.
Her father, a good mechanic, could repair engines, create parts, and
drive any vehicle. When the exiled ethnic minorities reached Aksu,
they found themselves in a border area of the Japanese puppet state
Manchukuo. It had teemed with military personnel, but with the German army advancing rapidly in Soviet Ukraine, suddenly all service-
able military vehicles had been rushed to the European warfront. Left
for the remaining Party officials and skeleton military staff were piles
of broken down vehicles, decrepit trucks, and a few tractors – nothing
the brass could use for their own transportation.

Local Party bosses and police who inspected the Labour Army camps
and collective farms, or attended meetings, did not relish travel on oxcart
or camel. They wanted to be driven in a car, preferably by a chauffeur.
As Nelly told me, 'One of a very few able men not yet arrested by 1941
and rarer yet, a skilled mechanic, my father was told to put together

a vehicle from all the ancient parts. He built a car, but because it was a jerry-built contraption, only he knew how to drive and maintain it.' So the mechanical wizard Gerhard became a chauffeur and mechanic who repaired a car that broke down on remote trails. 'One day my father was called into headquarters and given a letter to be delivered to a distant location. Just one thin letter – imagine. He was also ordered to wait for a reply. He was dumbfounded. Why waste scarce petrol, when a stamp would do? But knowing better than to question orders, he arrived at his destination and waited two whole days before given a return letter. When he finally got back to the Aksu detention camp, everyone said to him, "Weren't you lucky! While you were gone, the military police came and took away so-and-so for the Labour Army."'

This scenario repeated itself several times. Woebegone it was, but when officers needed a passenger vehicle, one with a mechanically skilled driver had been found.

So Gerhard became an anomaly, a male among hundreds of women in the detention camp, a prize for women seeking a mate. The *Trudarmiia* dragnet had removed all young single women, but not mothers of children under the age of three. Twenty-five-year-old Klara Scheller Kelm had a little son, Otto. Klara, raised in a family of Swabian German colonists from the North Caucuses, deserted by her husband, was a teacher of German. Gerhard was reluctantly dragged to a social gathering one evening, where Klara attended with her son. Little Otto stood looking around the room, spied Gerhard, and running up to him shouted, 'You're my papa!' So, little Otto on his lap, Gerhard met Klara.

Having children had been Gerhard and Lieschen's unfulfilled wish. Nelly thought that Gerhard had taken Lieschen to many 'cures' in a futile effort to become pregnant. Another relative told me she thought a horse had kicked Gerhard in the testicles when he was a boy and that rendered him infertile. The children Gerhard and Lieschen had reared for Lieschen's sisters had always been returned to their surviving parents, but here was an instant family available, a child that wanted Gerhard as his father. After Klara received her divorce papers, they married and Gerhard adopted her child.

This little family continued on at Aksu for another eight years, Gerhard chauffeuring and truck driving and Klara graduating to work in a clinic. By 1947, when Elizaveta arrived in Aksu for her six-month visit, as described earlier, she noted that both Gerhard and Abram Konrad (also exiled to Aksu after 1941) had accumulated livestock and improved their living conditions. Both drove government vehicles but never used them personally. Although the war was over, they still were *Nemtsy* and 'enemies of the state' under wartime regulations of the *Spetskommandatura*. Constantly reporting to authorities, they never travelled more than a kilometre without permission. Rules of the *Spetskommadatura* did not permit 'enemies' to move, but if Gerhard's boss wanted to take his chauffeur with him, that was different. In 1952 Gerhard and Klara were moved 200 kilometres to Taldy Kurgan, a border town between China and Soviet Kazakhstan.

Located in an area inhabited by Kazakhs, a mix of Turkic and Mongol nomadic tribes, Taldy Kurgan had been founded by Cossacks loyal to the tsar who had settled here and built a fortress. When Kazakhstan became a Soviet republic in 1936, plans were swiftly made to access its resources and introduce Soviet policies (ergo, Gerhard's job at the collective swine farm in Semipalatinsk). As early as 1936, the forced resettlement of Soviet citizens had begun to change the population mix. A secret document had ordered fifteen thousand German and Polish households from Ukraine 'to resettle' parts of Kazakhstan.[9] From the area of Alma Ata, three thousand households were 'resettled': two thousand to grow tobacco and one thousand to grow sugar beets on collective farms.

When Gerhard and Klara arrived, nomads still lived in yurts in rural areas around the town, but a primitive irrigation system watered large sugar beet farms that fed sugar factories. In the town itself a ditch or canal dug along streets released water at set times to homeowners to irrigate small gardens and orchards. Taldy Kurgan church properties had been confiscated, and one parcel of 'land,' a large Orthodox Church cemetery, had been levelled and subdivided. Here Gerhard was given a building lot with an ancient apple tree. Faintly recalling the biblical injunction that all flesh is as grass blown by the wind, he set about constructing his house. He framed his house and then stamped mud, straw, and sawdust between the studs to make a wall half a metre thick – cool in the thirty-degree summers and warm in the minus-thirty-degree winters. Later he added a summer kitchen and orchard.

In March 1953 Joseph Stalin died suddenly. This was the time of the 'doctors' plot.' Stalin claimed Kremlin doctors belonging to a Zionist group were conspiring to murder Soviet leaders. The run-up to the plot had begun after the end of the Second World War, particularly after 1948 when Israel was created. Anti-Semitism in the USSR had escalated and Stalin had begun an 'anti-cosmopolitan' campaign against

Jews, attacking them as 'alien bourgeois elements,' enemies, and 'allies of Israel and the USA.' Thousands of Soviet Jews had been arrested, expelled from jobs, and exiled, and it was feared that Stalin was planning a new purge before his death.[10]

For the intimidated peoples of the USSR, the death of their dictator 'Father' was shattering. At his state funeral in Moscow, overcome with grief and loss, hysterical people in the street were trampled to death. Schoolchildren cried, and in Taldy Kurgan, Gerhard's stepson Otto, thirteen, wearing his red Pioneer scarf, about to join the Komsomol Communist youth organization, wept openly. Not one anti-Soviet word had been risked in Gerhard's home. Not once did he dare talk about his own past. Otto was growing up ignorant of his parents' experience.

Who knew what would happen now?

But after Stalin's death, the tight surveillance of ethnic minorities maintained through the *Spetskommandatura* eased. The end of the draconian law meant the 'unreliables' with their identity cards no longer had to report to the police, could travel without permission, write letters internally, and meet together. Soon Gerhard's wife, Klara, was allowed to teach German in a local elementary school and Gerhard, released as official chauffeur, became the driver of an ambulance – a tuberculosis-prevention clinic on wheels. He kept this job until 1967, then drove a mobile blood clinic for six more years, as he told us with pride, a 'new bus from Czechoslovakia.' With these freedoms, in 1957 Gerhard risked writing my parents his first letter since 1930.

As already noted, Gerhard had invited his nephew Peter Wiebe and his wife, Amalia, to move to Taldy Kurgan and helped them to settle. Freedom of movement allowed other relatives to move to Taldy Kurgan. My father's brother Abram, his wife, Nastya, and their three children soon lived five kilometres from Gerhard. Abram worked as a chauffeur, as would his two sons. One might expect these relatives to meet often, but brothers Gerhard and Abram saw one another separately. As we noted, Gerhard's wife did not care for Abram's wife and also avoided the Wiebes.

On 10 October 1955, when Gerhard was fifty-six, Klara gave birth to the baby Nelly. When people asked why a child appeared so many years after they married, Gerhard said, 'The wonderful thing about this baby is that she will live "free."' Until that time children born of exiled parents had to be registered as 'exiled,' but after Khrushchev's famous attack on Stalin, the category of 'exiled' was removed.

By 1960 Gerhard had slowly contacted his siblings – those scattered within the Soviet Union and also in Canada, Germany, Paraguay, and Brazil. He cautioned everyone, 'Don't write to Abram. His children don't want it.' A letter Gerhard wrote to his sister Marichen* in Brazil in 1963 was published in the Canadian *Mennonitische Rundshau*. (He would have disapproved.) In the letter he reported driving an ambulance on mostly asphalt roads, that his wife was teaching, and that daughter Nelly was in kindergarten. He had become a grandfather when son Otto and his wife, Ira, both students, had a baby girl. Ira's mother looked after the baby while her parents completed their studies. Gerhard's orchard produced apples, apricots, plums, cherries, and grapes, and the garden yielded vegetables, strawberries, and raspberries. By plane, Gerhard, Klara, and Nelly had visited Klara's brothers in Karaganda – brothers his wife had not seen in twenty-three years. Motya and Elizaveta had visited Taldy Kurgan and Abram had paid them a return visit for three weeks. He ended with 'We are in need of nothing.'[11] From the letter I noted a relaxation of travel regulations and also that the brothers were paying attention to Heinrich's family.

The last line of Gerhard's letter, meaning 'send me no parcels,' was misunderstood by my parents. When relatives in the USSR wrote they had 'everything,' people abroad construed this was written for the censor, and continued to send parcels. A parcel in 1968 contained a customary display rug to mount on the wall above a sofa for Abram and Nastya, two sheets for the Wiebes, the Johanna Spyri's *Heidi* and a nightgown for Nelly, and a doll for Gerhard and Klara's granddaughter. In his thank-you letter Gerhard mentioned that Nelly was practising the piano as he wrote (I noted they owned a piano), but cautioned my parents *not* to send parcels and *not* to write to his son Otto. They had invited Otto to visit Canada. It was possible for him to visit East Bloc communist countries, but not the West.[12] Correspondence between the USSR and Canada was restored, but there were things not permissible to say and wise not to ask. Gerhard remembered the danger of gifts from abroad. Now it was not because the Soviets feared Hitler, but that they did not want to show their bare cupboards to the West.

On one of my visits with Nelly in Göttingen after Gerhard had died, as she told her father's stories and we were looking through her father's photograph album, we got to a photograph of a group under a grape

---

* Maria, called Marichen by her family, reached Germany in 1929 but was denied entry to Canada for health reasons. In 1932 she joined her sister Justina (coming from Harbin) aboard ship in Le Havre and then immigrated to South America with her.

arbour at the back of a house in Taldy Kurgan. There was little Nelly, about four, and Abram's two sons, one wearing a Ukrainian embroidered shirt, sitting on low stools in the foreground, while a relaxed Gerhard held a mandolin and Abram had a guitar on his knee. I was struck by how much this unknown Uncle Abram resembled my father – strong features, dark wavy hair, the confident pose, broad shoulders, smiling eyes. Gerhard's wife, Klara, grinning, was behind her husband, and Abram's meek-looking wife, Nastya, sat calmly facing the men. In the background was Heinrich's wife, Motya, no husband – hunchbacked, with head covered in a white kerchief. The next photograph was of a funeral cortege, a flatbed truck carrying a coffin followed by schoolchildren mourners walking along the street in parade formation. Large wreaths with bannered messages decorated the coffin of Gerhard's wife, Klara. Recently retired from teaching, she had died after six months of cancer treatments.

In January 1975, Abram died. The cancer that killed Klara and Abram may relate to Soviet Kazakhstan's red sky created by surface and underground nuclear tests – 500 tests in forty years. People saw the mushroom clouds but did not dare to ask and were left exposed to high levels of radiation. Even now, East Kazakhstan still has one of the highest cancer rates in the world.[13] Abram's two sons died of cancer, as did Klara and Peter Wiebe – five of fourteen relatives in Taldy Kurgan.

From Gerhard's letters after Klara's death, I had learned that Nelly applied for university admission and was initially told, 'You're a *Nemka*. Grab a shovel and start digging,' so she got a small job playing piano for the House of Pioneers. Finally accepted into a language program at the university in Alma Ata, Nelly had come home during a semester break to again accompany Pioneer ballet classes on piano when Gerhard told her the news: he had a German visa with papers ready to leave the USSR. The West German Republic had an agreement with the Soviets to accept Soviet Germans for family reunification and he had a German nephew in Bremen, son of his sister Helene Liebe (married to German theologian Carl Liebe in 1906).

Initially the official in Taldy Kurgan had refused to forward Gerhard's application: 'A nephew is not a close enough relative.' Gerhard then had written to ask my father, a brother, to request that the Soviets comply with their stated policy to permit family reunification. Six months later, when my father's letter was presented – reapplication was permitted every six months – the same official sat back in his chair and smirked, 'You know, Comrade, reunification works both ways.

Your brother could move to the USSR instead of you moving to the West.' After six months again (March 1976) Gerhard had to get a second German visa to replace the one expired. My parents' letters to him at that time numbered fifty.[14]

Was it Gerhard's proverbial luck or was it coincidence that exactly in 1976 he acquired that most desired of all Soviet possessions – a car? Ten years earlier Gerhard had put his name on a list of people applying to purchase a car and had saved up for it, but years had rolled by and, no car forthcoming, the money somehow got used up. In 1976, a shipment of ten cars specified to be sold only to pensioners arrived in Taldy Kurgan. All the names yellowing on the list for years were put into a lottery and in the first run-off draw, Gerhard's name was pulled. What irony, he thought, all these years I've wanted a car, and now that my children are away at schools and my wife is dead, my name pops up. Well, it's beginner's luck. Anyway, I haven't the money.

But, sure enough, in the second draw, Gerhard's name was among the ten prospective buyers. What to do? There had been a change of personnel at the local government office, so now, with the car lottery ticket in his pocket, he went again to police headquarters to apply for an exit visa. Speaking politely to the new officer in charge, he asked, 'Comrade, are you aware of the recent world conference our Soviet head of state attended? The officer looked perplexed.

'Do you know about the Soviet signature on the Helsinki Accord?

'Helsinki Accord?'

'Freedom of travel and family reunification is in the signed agreement.'

The official, surveying the application, looked up at grey-haired Gerhard. He turned to his subordinate: 'What about this old pensioner? What good is he to the state anyway?' He took Gerhard's application. 'I'll send it in. Let the higher brass deal with Helsinki. Imagine, Helsinki?'

Gerhard knew but did not explain that on 1 August 1975, in Helsinki, Finland, thirty-five European countries, Canada, the United States, and the USSR had signed a document, the so-called KSZE Final Agreement, guaranteeing basic human rights and freedoms, including freedom of travel. So now came the high stakes. Gerhard still carried the lottery ticket for the car. Should he buy the car? What if he finally received permission to emigrate? No longer having the funds, Gerhard gambled to do both – to buy the car and to emigrate. To pay for the car he decided to sell his house to his neighbour who had a son about to be married. The sale was conditional on Gerhard's being able to rent the house until the following summer. House sold, money in hand, he took his lottery ticket to the authorities and drove home with his new Lada.

All his neighbours thought he was crazy, selling his house to buy a car. Where would he live? Gerhard hid his real intent but dropped hints that he was driving to see his son Otto, who had moved recently to Tashkent, Uzbekistan. Even in the 1970s, any intention to emigrate to the West was interpreted as anti-socialist, so Gerhard maintained total secrecy in his arrangements. He had learned to trust nobody with politically sensitive information, not even his brother's family. Abram's children would be very upset, and anything they said or did could jeopardize his plans. As well, it could lead to retaliation, demotion, and cancellation of their jobs – a worry for Abram's daughter married to a Party man in the Soviet space program at the Baikonor Cosmodrome.

When Gerhard told Nelly (studying at a language institute in Alma Ata), they decided she should write her final exams before they left. When I talked to her about it years later, Nelly told me how odd it had felt, coming home for her school break and asking the neighbour if she could pick an apple from the tree in their yard. 'Yes,' her father insisted, 'it's not ours anymore.' Son Otto was decidedly upset. What effect would his father's move have on his career and on his wife's aspirations? Both he and his wife had good government positions: his wife as a medical doctor in senior management in the Ministry of Health and Otto in the top-secret aeronautics field. And how would it affect their two daughters, their plans, with one studying to become a medical doctor and the other a dentist?

While Otto kept silent at home and remained unhappy, Gerhard's gamble paid off. On 28 June 1976 he received the visas, granting permission for him and Nelly to leave the USSR. Somewhat pacified with the promise that he would now have Gerhard's new car, Otto made an arrangement to receive letters at a business address. In Taldy Kurgan, Otto and Gerhard signed papers handing over the car, and, with the Lada now his, Otto helped to drive it to Tashkent. When Gerhard shipped his belongings to Tashkent by train, the neighbours thought Konrad was moving to be with his children. That made sense.

One other person privy to his plans was Lena Wiebe, manager of a store in Omsk. Lena flew to Taldy Kurgan, arriving at midnight, and was welcomed at the airport by Gerhard in the Lada. Appearing on the doorstep at the home of her brother Peter, her sister-in-law Amalia was flabbergasted. 'Have you fallen from the sky?'

'Well, I had to say goodbye to Uncle Gerhard.'

'He's leaving?' Amalia was speechless. Then she said, 'But we live here. Why didn't he tell us?'

Lena reminded her how dangerous it was to say anything good about the West.

When I met Amalia in Berlin in 1995 she mentioned that episode, and, still chagrined, she asked, 'Why couldn't he tell us? We wouldn't have told.' Then she repeated, 'Gerhard always knew things before they happened. How could he always know?'

Gerhard's last letter from the USSR was written on 28 June 1976. Briefly he stated he had permission to leave and expected to arrive in Friedland, Germany, at the end of July. He and Nelly packed two suitcases each, which was all they were allowed. Soviet regulations forbade any photographs, but Gerhard took his most important ones nonetheless. From Tashkent they flew to Moscow where the custom's officer saw the photos and exclaimed loudly, 'Send these to your relatives,' but whispered, 'So take them, quickly.'

On 28 July 1976 Gerhard and Nelly landed in Frankfurt, passed through the refugee reception centre at Friedland, and within two days were in Bremen, the home of nephew Hannes Liebe. At that time the German government fully and generously supported all ethnic Soviet German immigrants as part of their *Umsiedler* program. Ethnic Germans were granted immediate citizenship with full civil rights, pensions, welfare, language training, education, and compensation for lost properties in the USSR. These attitudes and policies have changed since 1975, and Germany has reduced its handsome support of immigrants from the USSR, but for Gerhard they were wonderful.

After a short stay in temporary housing, by September 1976, granted a pension, Gerhard had settled in a subsidized one-bedroom apartment in a Bremen suburb. Nelly had arrived wearing the long braid much beloved in the USSR, and immediately her cousin whisked her off to a beauty parlour to get a short haircut, 'to fit in.' Then came a visit to a dress shop. '"You have to look more sophisticated," she told me. I let it all happen, but it did not make me feel welcome.'

Coming from Central Asia where demands were simple, Gerhard furnished his flat mostly with items Germans had put out on 'furniture discard' days. Nelly, frequently away at school, slept on the couch. With free language study and student welfare assistance, she would emerge ten years later with a master's degree in Slavic languages at the University of Göttingen. The German government paid compensation for the family's losses and once again Gerhard attended church and added religious expressions in his letters to my parents. He sponsored Lena Wiebe's emigration.

In the following ten years Gerhard visited Canada, the South American relatives in Brazil, and his niece Maria Liebe Reich in Switzerland. He went on European tours as well as to health spas. Once, describing a wonderful holiday at the hot springs in Bad Pyrmont, he wrote a cryptic comment that made me think there were secrets of his survival that he had never told. Describing how, snow falling, in the hot outdoor pool, he had started a snowball fight, he wrote, 'For the first time in my life, we threw snowballs like boys and girls – though I have swum in icy water several times in my life in an emergency.'[15]

In 1991 Communism collapsed. To people like Gerhard, it was almost unbelievable. We saw him that summer for the last time. Sitting hunched on a straight-backed chair in his apartment, fingering a pastry, he looked up as we chattered excitedly about developments in Moscow. With his blue eyes fierce, he asked the question none of us could answer. 'All the hardships, the millions of deaths, in the end, what did they do to – and for – my country?'

After Gerhard's heart attack in 1986, he had rather lonely last years, suffering indignities and neglect. A grandson of his long-suffering sister AnnaK and his wife, recent immigrants from the USSR, gave him loving attention, but his Bremen nephew and his niece found it uncomfortable to identify with increasingly unpopular *Russländer* relatives. His children preoccupied with their own situations, he found an unexpected friendship in a dear woman called Friedchen, another lonely person whose children lived in the DDR, a place difficult to visit until the Berlin Wall came down. My Uncle Gerhard died in a Bremen old age home on 10 September 1993 at the age of ninety-two. He was buried in the lovely old Osterholzer Friedhof, a cemetery where his sister Helene Liebe also was buried.

Gerhard had survived where others perished – partly through luck, but also bravado and a quiet intelligence and ability to judge situations. There was some dissimulation and much survivor's guilt. The incident in the cement factory, which he had described to Harvey and me, was troubling. When I read letters he had written to my parents from the USSR, I had an overwhelming feeling of loss. How affectionately he

asked about his siblings, how he tried to keep alive the family connections, to honour the past without naming it, to be a humane person
in a non-religious state, to be pleasant even when he knew evil intent
lurked beneath many a surface. He had survived a systematic tyranny,
but it took its toll. As long as he lived in the totalitarian state, he fought
it in his mind, but once he came to the 'free West,' he lost something,
became a stranger. He was endlessly polite, ever trying to please the
aloof North Germans. He graciously accepted class-consciousness and
snobbery. He tried to blend in, but he was never at home. The man of
his Russia stories, the Soviet citizen with all his ghosts, how could he fit
into a world living for the present moment?

9

Destinations and Endings

Elizaveta in Donbas

As I was discovering the missing members of my extended family, I wanted to see the places where they lived or had lived, to see what remained, to get a feeling for their surroundings. Avoiding a seven-hour bus trip, in 1999 we had taken a taxi from Zaporozhye to see where my father's brother Heinrich had lived with his family and where he was arrested. His daughters still lived in Snezhnoie. Harvey had been here previously and we had been in contact with Elizaveta for almost ten years. We came with financial assistance collected by the family in Canada, clothing, and a year's supply of vitamins, painkillers, and other items – the extended family continuing our parent's 'parcels.'

Elizaveta's house was one quarter of a green-roofed bungalow that had a narrow garden in front and an outhouse in the backyard. She ushered us to sit down at the table set up beside a single bed in the middle of her one-and-a-half-room house. I looked for some family resemblances in this gaunt woman with grey hair cut short and parted on the side, thick glasses, and orange polyester dress. Her husband, Emelian, shorter, less angular, smiling throughout the visit, hardly spoke. Staring down at us from above the customary rug on the wall were two blue tinted portraits of Elizaveta's and Emelian's parents, taken before 1930. In his portrait, Heinrich Konrad wore a soft cloth cap, dark shirt, and a white tie. Motya wore a small gold brooch on her dress. Another photograph, on the single commode, captured Motya as an old babushka, haggard in a white kerchief. The two single beds in the room – one piled high with heavier comforters, and the one we sat on – doubled as couches. The half room was a kitchen. From it our hostess brought a metal pot and began to ladle out a mustard-coloured chicken soup, including chicken feet. In a mark of largess she spooned a dollop of butter into each already rich plate. 'Eat! Eat!'

Harvey asked Elizaveta if she wanted to accompany us to Shakhty to visit my cousin Alici Braun. At first she said no, but five minutes before we were to leave she had changed her dress, grabbed a handbag, and was ready. Elizaveta and my cousin Alici in Shakhty were friends from previous meetings. Both had joined Baptist churches within the last decade; both had lost their fathers; both had married non-Germans, and both were related to me – Elizaveta on my father's side and Alici on my mother's.

Neither Elizaveta nor her sister had children of her own and I wondered if their childlessness had anything to do with time as *Ostarbeiter* – remembering girls were considered fair game for gang raping by victorious Soviet troops. I also wondered what would happen to Elizaveta when she became old or lost her husband. My cousin Alici had told me that old people without children to look after them last no longer than three days in the state homes for the aged. 'They tear out each other's hair.'

Emelian got out a cardboard box filled with jars of home-canned plums and pickles –'For you to take home to Canada' – and the driver opened his trunk for the box. When we insisted that we also had to see her sister Lucia, Elizaveta complained, 'I was deathly ill in winter. I called up her husband – he has a car – I asked him to drive me to the hospital, but he refused. He said he was nobody's taxi.'

'Yes,' Emelian added, 'She phoned them you were coming. Did they bother?'

'Lucia's husband was a big Communist,' Elizaveta reminded us. 'Down on his luck since the fall of the Party, but that's who he was. Never wrote to thank you, did she? I'm always the one writing, sending cards. It's a lot of work. She's never done it.'

I sensed the tension and thought Elizaveta was right. There is always one child more faithful, more devoted, but, like the brother of the prodigal son, least acknowledged. Quietly I decided to reduce Lucia's share of the money we were giving. We drove the short stretch to Lucia's, Elizaveta and her husband with us.

Another solidly built woman with grey hair cut short, her legs laced heavily with varicose veins, came running out through her garden as we opened the gate. Her thickset husband, a grin on his face, ambled behind. Sobbing, Lucia hugged Harvey, then me, and between gulps, wiping tears with her apron, said, 'Come in! Come in! Eat, eat!' We faced another table fully set with vodka bottles, boxed chocolates, stewed tomatoes, and bread. Again Lucia sobbed, 'We haven't received our pensions for three months. No money for gas. The drought last year meant no fruit. Fortunately we had canned plums the year before. I don't have the goats anymore. Goat milk was my medicine. It kept me going, but now there's no milk and my health is gone. My husband has no work ...'

'Calm yourself, Lucia,' urged Elizaveta.

Harvey complimented Lucia on her home-canned pickled tomatoes, and, following her example, picked one up with his fingers and sucked it. 'Very tasty.'

When Lucia's husband brought out three giant jars of tomatoes, pickled cucumbers, and paprika peppers, as well as a bag of potatoes, I quickly pressed the restored original sum of American dollars into Lucia's hand. As we left, Lucia hugged us while Elizaveta looked on stoically. The gallon jars joined Elizaveta's smaller ones in the back of the taxi and we continued our trip. The food came in handy in Shakhty.

Throughout the days and nights of our visit in Shakhty, Elizaveta wore her polyester purple dress (bought to celebrate an anniversary thirteen years ago) and patiently sat as Alici and I conversed in our common childhood language – German. Elizaveta said she had learned little German during her years as an *Ostarbeiter*, having been with Ukrainians. Alici would interpret perhaps a quarter of what was said, so it seemed there was competition to have 'guests' to themselves.

I learned a few details from Elizaveta in Shakhty, but most of my questions had to wait until May 2001 when we met again, this time in Zaporozhye. Our visit began with a memorial event at the site of a village massacre. Harvey had negotiated agreements with local officials and villagers for the placement of a marker, and members from Mennonite families whose grandfathers, fathers, uncles, or other close relatives were the murder victims had come for the unveiling. It was rare for Ukrainians to see Soviet atrocities of the past acknowledged (monuments often celebrate heroes, not victims), but many villagers who attended the ceremonies said the massacre had been wrong.[1]

At this time we invited Elizaveta to accompany us in the Intourist bus to see the sites of former Mennonite villages. Knowing nothing of her father's Mennonite past, she now saw where our ancestors had once lived and what remained of their brick houses, schools, churches, mills, and planted forests. Seated beside a friend who interpreted for me, she peered out of the bus window saying, 'It's the first time I've seen that.' Like many elderly women, she wore an oversized, grey, shaggy mohair sweater ('Alici gave it to me twelve years ago'), headscarf patterned with orange and brown flowers, and sturdy brown shoes. I asked about her marriage. 'After living together thirteen years, his family asked, "Haven't we been good to you?" So then we married and I took his name.'

Driving by the huge statue of Lenin at the banks of the Dnieper River, I asked what she thought of these reminders of Soviet times, and she said for her the Brezhnev years were better than now. In spite of her family's traumatic experiences, Elizaveta was nostalgic for the communist era. Under Communism hadn't there been full employment, free rent, subsidized bread, even a small vacation, but now who but the rich could live? 'Democracy has not helped us. Conditions are terrible now with all the robberies and stealing. Even the dead are not left in peace. Stop your experiments with us, I wrote to Kuchma (president of Ukraine in 2001). You Banderists from the west have spoiled everything!' (Stepan Bandera was the leader of the Organization of Ukrainian Nationalists from 1940 to 1943 and 1945 to 1959. He was murdered by a KBG agent in Munich and became a hero, particularly to western Ukrainian nationalists.)

I asked about compensation Elizaveta was to get from Germany as an *Ostarbeiter*. Germany had paid, she said, but the local Ukrainian officials had absconded with the funds and it now was a court case. She hoped the rumour that the German government was to send money out individually was true. There were notices telling where to address applications and she had written. Our interpreter said that compensation depended on length and place of work, and so on, but would not exceed three thousand marks per person. She had helped many Ukrainians fill out applications. Elizaveta asked if I could write a letter to Germany about her compensation. (She did get her three thousand German marks.)

Elizaveta told what happened to her mother after she and Lucia were sent to Germany. During the Nazi occupation, *Volksdeutsche* had been moved into homogeneous German villages, and 'Slavs' like Motya were evicted and installed in homes emptied of Jews – or any *Volksdeutsche* living among Ukrainians. Motya and her young son, Evgeny, had been sent to the large Ukrainian village of Guliai-Polie, which was the infamous home of Nestor Makhno, the anarchist bandit leader who had terrorized the region with his black flag and army, following the

Bolshevik Revolution. How did Elizaveta experience the mass murders of Jews? 'I was sent to Germany as an *Ostarbeiter* soon after the occupation. What did I know?'

When the war ended, her mother was able to return to Snezhnoie, still not knowing what had happened to husband or daughters. Over the following years with the hardships and her struggle to survive, Motya slowly began to lose her mind. Elizaveta, sobbing, told about her mother's last years. Sometime in the mid-1970s her mother had started to wander about the town at all hours of the day or night. Once, Elizaveta passing an old woman lying in the ditch, thought, 'That looks like my mother's shawl. Can two old babushkas have identical shawls?' At this time Motya was living with her son Evgeny and his wife. Alarmed, Elizaveta went to her brother's house, and his wife said, 'No, Mother-in-law isn't here, hasn't been back since yesterday.'

Elizaveta found someone to accompany her back to the ditch where she had seen the old woman and together they carried Motya home.

How old was she? 'About seventy.'

During later years, Motya seldom recognized her children and, after anguished discussions, her children decided Motya would have to be taken to a mental hospital fifty kilometres away. Four days after Motya's committal, Elizaveta visited her mother only to find her cowering in a corner, unable to walk, unfed, calling for her husband to rescue her. 'This isn't a hospital. This is a prison!' her mother wept. 'I've raised three children and look where they have taken me!'

Elizaveta packed her mother up, got on a bus, and, with Motya still calling out to her long-gone husband to help, brought her mother home to be with her and Emelian. Before her long illness, Motya had requested a religious funeral, and when she died in 1983 at the age of eighty-seven, her daughter tried to follow her mother's wishes. When churches reappeared, Motya had attended the Baptist church regularly, but Elizaveta refused to go. Now Elizaveta informed the church of Motya's death, and members of the congregation came over immediately and sang hymns in the house. While the funeral procession made its way along the street, Communist neighbours jeered and shouted, but the Baptist group kept on singing. Elizaveta said, 'Those scoffing people were the Orthodox who served the high and mighty, but not the poor.' After experiencing the caring and love of the Baptist group, Elizaveta began to attend her mother's church and eventually became a member. She was baptized in a small lake in 1989.

Her brother Evgeny never approved of his sister's religion. Elizaveta, childless herself, was very fond of Evgeny's daughter Tanya, but blamed his wife for not looking after her husband. She knew he had tuberculosis but didn't want him to stop working and she never bothered even to visit him in hospital. After Evgeny died, his widow and Elizaveta had words that resulted in the loss of Elizaveta's access to young Tanya.

Estranged from her sister, feeling she had no family, left with just bitter memories, Elizaveta decided to get the truth about her father. Heinrich was forty years old when he disappeared and, had he survived, would be ninety-one. She wrote to the Soviet authorities and was informed that her father had been charged with 'sabotaging work in the bread factory and participating in the creation of a national, fascistic, diversionary, insurgent organization.' In prison for six months, he was found guilty by a secret troika, sentenced, and shot on 16 October 1938. No mention was made of his place of trial, execution, or burial, but he was 'rehabilitated.'

'After fifty-two years, now they declare him innocent!' she had written to my sister Mary. 'How much hardship we have had to go through. I have cried very hard. I wanted to put flowers on his grave. This pain will remain with me to the end. I walk to the market past the police station where my father was imprisoned and my heart bleeds. Why did this happen?'[2]

The official document, typed on cheap, yellowed paper, is full of blots and spelling errors and stamped with a purple seal:

5 October 1989
Elizaveta Andreevna Divbush
Donetzkoy Oblast
Snezhnoie, Gorki St. 9, #3
Certificate
In accordance with Article 1 of the Ukaz of the Presidium of the Supreme Soviet of the USSR of 16 January 1989, numbered 10036-X1, 'About the additional measures for the restoration of justice for the victims of repression during the period of 1930s–40s and beginning of 1950s' the decision of NKVD of Donetsk District of 9 October 1938 in relation to Heinrich Jakobovitch Konrad, born in 1897 in the village of Alekandrovka, municipality of Berdiansk, District of Dnepropetrovsk, who, prior to his arrest, worked as a shipping clerk at the CMM Trust, has been reversed and his file has been closed because of nonexisting grounds.

Heinrich Jakovlevich Konrad is rehabilitated.

SEAL
V.G. Seniukov
Procurator
sub. Crown Attorney for Donetsk District Court Council, 2nd class[3]

The Road to Memrik

In 2001, my husband and I went to find Kotlyarevka. By taxi we drove three hours in the rain to find the village where the family of Johannes and Anna Braun had lived in the former Memrik settlement. The back windows of the taxi were tinted, hard to see through, but we could make out flat fields of black soil, and tree-lined village streets where sixty-five years ago Johannes would have been issuing tractors and seeding drills to plough and plant fields. Today we drove by iron-red slag heaps, leftovers from dying mines. Cows and calves chained on stakes grazed freely on new grass along the way.

Our taxi driver spoke little and remained in the car whenever we stopped. We ordered a bowl of borscht at a rundown restaurant and passed a square of apartment blocks where Anna Braun had stood outside the Selidovka prison gates. In the light drizzle we saw a blond woman in a black pantsuit waiting for a bus and asked, 'Where is Kotlyarevka?' 'It's here,' she answered. 'This is it.' Of course, the villages had been amalgamated into one collective farm. We slowed down to look for recognizable Mennonite-built houses – brick with the gable facing the street. 'There's one!'

The brick had been whitewashed and the door and window frames been painted a deep blue, but keeping tradition, an enclosed garden in front of the house had poppies and peonies beside rows of sprouting vegetables and a straight row of marigolds. On the dirt sidewalk an elderly woman in a brown dress and kerchief was eyeing us as she guarded a goose and several goslings. When our interpreter asked if this was a *Nemtsy* house, the woman burst out laughing, 'I'm *Nemka*!' Instantly she began to speak in Plautdietsch: 'I'm the only one left in all the three German villages, the only one left. Come in! Come in.' She opened a garden gate and our interpreter was stumped, but Harvey and I understood her and happily followed.

Anna Petrovna Isaak was a Mennonite, and sure enough, her husband was one too. She showed us the smaller of two houses, the one that formerly had a *banya* or bathhouse and was the summerhouse, and the main house, her husband's parental home, his village. Deported in 1941 (like Anna Braun and her children), dropped off on the barren steppes of Slavgorod, after the war ended he had ignored regulations (forbidden to return to Ukraine), returned here, and after some years reclaimed his parental house.

'Look at the floor boards,' said our hostess. 'They used to be the ceiling.' We admired the house, saw the *Himmelsbett,* a double bed with lace-edged bed coverings and embroidered pillows, a showpiece in every Mennonite parlour in bygone days, and quickly agreed when she suggested we walk just down the street to her son's house. 'It's bigger, original Mennonite, and he has the furniture from long ago. The museum in Donetsk took the sofa bed, the *Schlopbank.* They came and got it but never paid us.'

In the son's house a young daughter-in-law was rolling out dough and making small dumplings. 'Here's Oksana. She's making *pelmeni.* Do you know them? I see you are wondering why there's so much furniture. Well, after we Germans all were exiled, you know, in 1941, the *pred* took all the best furniture from the empty houses and took the best house too. You know they had to leave everything behind. My son bought the house with the furniture after "the Fall." But we've all handed in our applications. If we get our papers, we're moving to Germany. We're taking only the clock.'

Harvey's eyes brightened as he recognized the authentic Mennonite furniture from pre-Revolutionary days. Hutches, a very fine armoire, a chest of drawers similar to one a Mennonite cabinetmaker-farmer handmade for our family when we lived in Alberta, bedsteads, chairs, and the pendulum clock, rare and much sought after today if crafted by the Kroeger workshop in Khortitsa. The house still had the barn attached in the original building style where a firewall, stairs, and pantry separated house from barn, all under one roof. We climbed up to see a large attic. Here, in days before the Bolshevik Revolution a family had stored sacks of grain and smoked sausages in the wide brick chimney. My parents told us watermelons used to be stored in grain sacks and kept till Christmas. The present owners used the attic to dry clothes and onions. Another set of steps led to a cellar, but we forewent it because Harvey wanted to negotiate for the furniture.

The son owner arrived home from his job as a chauffeur taking miners to the shafts and, yes, he was interested in selling for American dollars, but where would the furniture go? Again Harvey thanked his good fortune. He was organizing the next international conference on Mennonite topics for the bicentennial of a Mennonite presence in Ukraine in 2004. He wanted a museum display and here was the opportunity. 'If you do get your immigration papers and sell the furniture, please contact us first.'

Harvey hoped to donate the furniture to the Melitopol museum, but in the interim it could go to the Mennonite Centre in Molochansk, the former Mennonite town of Halbstadt. Here North Americans had bought one of their own former school buildings, and restored and converted it into a community and social service centre. Staffed by volunteer directors from North America and local employees, the centre had tried to follow the Christian principle of returning good for evil. North American Mennonites sought to give assistance rather than seek retribution.[4] None had asked for compensation or demanded a return of properties – not that the Soviet, Ukrainian, or Russian governments had ever suggested they would make amends this way.

As we left, I asked about the lake my cousin Alici mentioned, the one to which her mother's boarders came for the good country air. 'Oh yes, just drive around the corner. And the mill is still there too.' The son came along as a guide, and we found the lake, now a large pond filled with weeds and algae. We were serenaded by a chorus of frogs and birds. 'This was a good place to fish, but no more,' the son told us. 'The village manager sold the waterfront and now you dare not step near because you will be trespassing. That's your perestroika,' he said acidly. 'What used to be village property is now trespassing.'

'You did not want perestroika?'

'Oh no, it happened overnight. Everyone began stealing and selling things. They stole all the metal, even railway tracks and especially anything copper or aluminium. They'll steal anything with metal. They sell to foreign countries. They get more money. There used to be a canning factory over there. Come perestroika, the people stole the bricks, the contents, everything.' He pointed to a building on the far side of the pond. 'The mill is still working and with its original German machinery. An original oil-pressing plant also is still in operation, also with its original machinery.'

I asked about the tractor station and collective farm office (former Mennonite church) and he said, 'You can still see the foundations where it was, facing the street. Under that tall grass.' Did he know about a large school in the district? 'Oh, it's gone too, all gone.' The 'large school' had been Alici's Ebental Internat.

In the fields around us stood decrepit and vandalized collective farm buildings. Somewhere among the houses, one had belonged to Johannes and Anna Braun. In this village Johannes Braun the agronomist had received his awards for farm management. Here that fateful December day in 1937 he had rushed home at noon telling his wife to pack his things before his arrest. He would have been taken to the local police station, that concrete building we passed near the little café where we got the bowl of borscht in Selidovka.

On our return we stopped a distance out of Kotlyarevka at the Zhelanaia train station where Alici had left for Siberia, where her brother Hans left for the Red Army, and where Anna Braun and her three children had waited to be deported. A high, brick water tower remained at the station, as did four sets of tracks. To get to the station from the road, we had to cross the tracks, so where were they kept, the hundreds waiting to be exiled? Weeds don't speak. One train, its locomotive painted bright green, with locked doors and out of service, was at the station. Who remembered that September day in 1941 when Anna and children were pushed into a coal car? In a garden behind the station we could imagine shadows, whispers, and cries of the long ago deported.

As we drove through the one-time Memrik settlement, the guide kept talking about thieves, closed mines, closed factories, and high unemployment, and I kept trying to picture my Uncle Johannes and his family living here in the 1930s. Had the same trees lined the street? Here a woman shepherded a red cow and there a man pulled a handcart filled with cans of milk to sell in the village. Was it that way then? Or, like my uncle, had all memory of the past just *disappeared*?

Footsteps in Ufa

That same summer, 2001, we took the Trans-Siberian Railway, and with frequent stops along the way got to areas of the Gulag, places of exile for many of my relatives. With us was my forty-five year old cousin Nelly who, born in Taldy Kurgan, had lived in Germany since 1976.

Nelly (Uncle Gerhard's daughter) joined Harvey and me in Moscow, and soon we were in a sleeper compartment of the streamlined train – four passengers to a car with two padded red leatherette bench seats and a small table covered in a white linen cloth. Above each seat, a top bunk contained four folded sets of sheets, pillows, and blankets.

31 May. *The clacking sound speeds up and multiple train tracks and buildings disappear. At the outskirts of Moscow, I stare out of the window trying to locate dachas among the tall pine trees. Will we see the cottages where my*

parents hid? I try to imagine thirteen thousand people hiding here, but see no buildings....

1 June. We wake up on our narrow bunks to see the Volga River. The train halts at Samara, a city where my mother's uncle, Baptist Elder Jakob Wiens, lived – grandfather of Soviet dissident Georgi Vins, the Russian Baptist prisoner of conscience who was traded for a high-level Soviet spy caught in the West. The station is new, but the blocks of Soviet high-rise apartments are old stark grey. It's a brief stop to purchase drinks and food from vendors. Through rain-streaked windows we see flooded black fields, miles of bush, and small wooden houses [izbas] in Russian villages seemingly unchanged in a hundred years.

Wet fields and sandy red hills give way to Ural foothills with slopes in ochre and green. Beside the tracks, foxtail fronds wave in the wind. We reach a prairie and see why this area has seen so many wars – soldiers can just march across these plains! Spring yellow buttercups and white vetch compete with rubbish heaps and rusted metal beside the rails taking us east. Train after train. Nine tracks. Here, a flock of sheep and there, garden patches. Backs bent, people are planting vegetables in straight rows, onions already high. These 'dachas' are not for holidays, unless you count weekly trips out to weed and water survival gardens. They begin as far as sixty miles outside a city....

3 June. Twenty-eight hours after leaving Moscow, concrete grain elevators and massive apartment blocks loom up at the confluence of the Ufa and wide Belaya Rivers. We are in my mother's territory, the place of her childhood and home of her missing brothers Johannes, Peter, and Isaak Braun. High above the river, on an escarpment, a huge statue of a horse and rider, a Bashkir hero, defines the city of Ufa. We cross a long bridge into the once-ancient fur trade centre (its emblem is the marten) that now has a fine museum, opera house, a university, and giant flour mills.

A small group of Mennonites from southern Ukraine had built nineteen villages and isolated estates on this frontier of the Tsarist Russian Empire.[5] My Braun grandparents had pioneered on this virgin steppe near foothills of the western Ural Mountains, an area inhabited largely by Russians, Tartars, and Bashkirs. My grandfather's farm in Gorchakovo village was thirty kilometres from the Trans-Siberian Railway town of Davlekanova.

We are ten time zones from Toronto. We take a taxi into the old city centre. Our vintage hotel is across the street from the city square that includes a modern mall and a huge monument. Is it Lenin? No, it's a giant world globe....

4 June. *Sunday morning in Ufa and a breakfast of eggs with dark orange yolks. Why is every main street named Ulitsa Lenina and why are there so many Lenin statues? When Grandfather Braun, who frequented this city for business, walked these same streets, were they named Ulitsa Romanovka? We walk past log houses with fretwork-trimmed windows looking for the address Alici gave us for her granddaughter Katya, the geologist looking for gold. She with her young husband, Pavel, and son live in student housing. When we find the dark, one-room basement apartment where residents share a kitchen, it reminds me of an unfinished basement laundry room and we wonder where they sleep the child. Katya is away on fieldwork so we spend a Sunday with husband Pavel exploring the city.*

5 June. *Monday. Leaving our suitcases at the hotel, we scramble to the train station to take the electric commuter train to Davlekanova, miss it (time change again) and hire a taxi. After driving eighty miles, we arrive at the same railway station pictured in my guidebook, a red-cover book of memoirs compiled in Canada by former Mennonite residents of the Davlekanova settlement, the 'Ufa Reunion,' which becomes my Mao's red book. From this Davlekanova train station my mother left home to begin her teaching career and from here she left for Moscow in 1929. Her brother Isaak lived here after his unsuccessful attempt to reach Moscow in 1929, and perhaps her brother Peter, the 'collective farm secretary,' has footprints here too.*

We walked into town and found the town's one hotel looking deserted, but with a 'bank teller' opening, behind which a tiny receptionist asked, 'Have you registered with the AVIR?' Oh dear, the AVIR. In Soviet days, to get permission to stay, all travellers were required to report to a registry office within forty-eight hours of arrival. We found the AVIR office and presented our visas and passports, only to have a middle-aged official begin a typical Soviet-style hostile interrogation: 'Do you have a visa for Russia? What is your business?' Harvey and I had obtained a one-month visa for all parts of Russia in Moscow, but Nelly still had to do that in Ufa. Exasperated, Harvey finally asked, 'Is this a closed city?' From experience in Soviet days, he knew a meek approach was ineffective. 'Wait ten minutes.' The henna-coiffed official disappeared into another room and, as others went in and out in no time, we waited. Without comment, she finally returned our stamped passports and we thanked her. 'Bol'shoe spasibo.'

Back at the hotel the now-friendly receptionist collected our twelve roubles a night and apologized, 'Very expensive. Our luxury room.' Down a hallway thick in faux French baroque plaster, the 'luxe' suite used only by the Party brass was a cold-water, two-room suite generous in dust, with a bathroom where a newspaper was the toilet tissue. The bedroom had thin, lumpy mattresses but was graced by Greek statue mouldings. The sitting room had a couch for Nelly as well as a glass-front cupboard with six wine glasses for bygone visiting government inspectors.

It was raining, but, cameras and my red Ufa book ready, we set out to find my mother's past. We filmed log houses and shops, trying to match the pictures in my book. 'That bazaar must be the same market square.' Unable to find any Mennonite-style houses or large buildings like my mother's school, we focused on the train station that looked exactly like the one in my Ufa book. As we took pictures, out of the train station popped two men in brown jackets, black pants, and oversized, round-topped police hats, the *militsia*. The older one in a leather jacket demanded, 'Who gave you permission to take any photographs? What do you think you're doing filming the railway station? Show us your papers! We've had complaints you are taking pictures in the town. Hand over your film.'

Ready to say *mea culpa*, Nelly's Soviet upbringing showed immediately, but I opened my red Ufa book and pointed to a photo of the same station as Harvey asked, 'Who says we are not allowed to take photographs? Do you know we are foreign visitors to your city – Canadians?' Nelly was quaking. What Soviet citizen questions police? For a short time we faced each other and then the police retreated into the station and minutes later came back out to apologize. Nelly was upset: 'Me they treat like a nobody, and you, you foreigners get respect.'

Umbrellas up, we continued to search for Mennonite houses and my mother's high school until a woman on the street told us to inquire at the Palace of Culture in the town square. We found it deserted except for an oversized white statue of Lenin and, speaking German, were wondering if the centre would be open, when a friendly voice behind us said he would check it out for us. Jamil, a tall young man in a brown suit and tie, as we discovered subsequently, was the director of sports at the centre. 'Emil in German,' he smiled, 'Jamil in Bashkir. My German? I was stationed in East Germany two years for my military service.' He introduced us to museum director Massar Mukhametzyanov and we arranged a return visit for the afternoon. When we told Jamil about our quest, looking for my mother's school and traces of my Braun relatives, he offered to drive us to the school. 'It's on the other side of the railway tracks.' We had searched the wrong side of the tracks.

Jamil stopped at gates of a low, green building behind a larger building, and – another coincidence, or was it something more? – precisely
at that moment, walking through the gate, came another Bashkir, again
in a suit and tie. Director Ramzil, head of the College of Civil Engineering in the green building was delighted to meet us and said his college was planning to move into the larger building in front of us. Yes,
it was what we were looking for, the former Mennonite Davlekanova
High School, my mother's school! At that moment I recalled the voice
of my mother, how she had longed to attend here, how she had pleaded
against the rage of her stepmother ('Girls don't need higher education;
I didn't go'). Here were her happiest girlhood memories. She and her
'cloverleaf' of friends.

Pleased to talk to someone who knew about the school's origins, the
director said the building had been a military headquarters from 1955
to 1997 and was being renovated. He allowed us inside the former high
school and we were soon impressed by lofty ceilings, large rooms, and
wide halls. We saw a large gymnasium and many rooms in use now
by primary classes. We knew that the downstairs rooms had once been
teacher accommodations and that the auditorium in one wing of the
school had once served as the Mennonite Brethren church. I pictured
my mother and her younger brothers, eager students sitting in the
audience for worship services or performing on this stage (my mother
recited poetry). As we walked through the grounds it felt like a miracle
that the school still existed, still breathed a spirit of friendship in spite
of its fate.

Taking the day off to show us around, Director Ramzil invited us into
his white Lada. We stopped at the city hall, a former Mennonite doctor's
house, where we were introduced to the mayor (who proudly posed for
a photograph). Making a phone call, the director invited us to a noon
meal in a special restaurant in a flour mill. In a private room, as we were
served borscht, meat and vegetables, blini, desert, vodka toasts, and
tea, he proudly stated this was the largest milling operation in Bashkiria, 'And your people started it.' We were amazed that someone in the
former USSR knew and valued the fact that Mennonites had introduced
machine agriculture into the region before the Bolshevik Revolution.
Soviet citizens were not usually told that 'Germans' built the first flour
mills and introduced grain-growing on this Bashkir plain. Had there
been no Revolution, how different our history would have been.

Back at the museum, Director Massar, impressed by a visit from a
fellow historian from abroad, had called in a television crew to film an

interview. He (a Tatar) and Marina, his Russian assistant, were the only two historians in this part of Bashkiria. We saw her tracing a map by holding up the original on a window. Marina had studied at the Bashkir University in Ufa, the one we saw on our Sunday tour. Among many artefacts telling the story of Bashkir peoples, the Davlekanova museum also had a small Mennonite section including photographs, a 'special recipe,' an earthenware 'unbreakable' pot, a few dishes, spoons, and other objects. This again surprised us. In southern Ukraine where Mennonites first settled, their history was not visible in museums until the 1999 international conference and museum exhibition in Zaporizhzhia. The Ukrainian TV and print media had provided broad coverage and people then looked at schools, factories, and other public buildings and realized many were Mennonite-built. Director Massar wanted a copy of my Ufa book (which was out of print, but I sent one to him later). He knew about Mennonite milling and educational contributions. He mentioned the deportations, saying, 'We're sorry they moved away. Come back.' As we both knew, it was not 'moved away.' He said a local KGB building had been used 'to deal only with Germans.' Opposite the former KGB site, a onetime synagogue also was out of use.

I inquired after my uncle Peter Braun. In 1929 when my parents had stopped off in Davlekanova en route to Moscow, my mother's brothers Peter and Isaak Braun and their families still lived here. I knew that Isaak and family left, but what happened to brother Peter or other Mennonites here? Were they all deported? Were there records? The director said he would investigate. I also wanted to find the villages where my mother, grandparents, and great-grandparents once lived.

Side by side in a buggy, my mother aged eight and her little brother Isaak, two, were driven to Karanbash, a village some fifteen kilometres from their home, to stay with their maternal Wiens grandparents till their mother returned. She died on the train en route to a hospital. A stepmother soon arrived to take charge of a household with four boys and my mother. Where was Karanbash? With no taxis in Davlekanova, Director Ramzil volunteered to drive us in his Lada over muddy roads to look for the home of my great-grandparents Jakob and Elizabeth Wiens who had died before the Bolshevik Revolution.[6]

On the way to Karanbash, we saw distant ridges of the Urta Tau Mountains, foothills of the Urals. We passed green and wooded rolling hills surrounded by fields of black soil and the college director said that within the bare fields there used to be estates of Mennonites named Neufeld and Hottmann. As we approached Karanbash, we found we had come too late. Most of the village was gone. We saw a few broken down barns and newer Soviet houses and looked for a cemetery. Perhaps my great-grandparents or other Wiens relatives would have left markers, gravestones. Seeing us search, a man and woman appeared from behind a dilapidated barn and Director Ramzil asked the woman, 'Do you remember anyone living here named Vins (Wiens)? Any German houses? A cemetery?'

'Get your ass over here,' she called over her shoulder to the old man behind her.

An elderly man, a bit drunk, in rubber boots, hit his head trying to remember, 'Vins, Vins, no? Some Germans?'

'Those are terrorists,' cried the woman. 'My pile of hay has been stolen.'

Ignoring the outburst, the director tried another Mennonite name: 'Thiessen?'

'Do you have permission to come snooping over here?' shouted the woman.

'Thiessen? Thiessen?' the old man hit his head again and nodded. 'There were Thiessens. I'll show you.' He tramped through tall wet grass to one of the barns, whose brick sides had fallen in, surrounded with piles of manure. 'This was a German building.' He looked us over. 'If you give me something, I'll find you the cemetery.'

We followed him to a higher part of a small pasture, past a garbage pit. 'This is it.' Several metres farther he pointed to a clump of lilac and elderberry bushes. 'They planted those. We didn't have trees like that.' Elderberry is a common native bush.

'Do you know the name of the Davlekanova chief of police?' the college director asked our guide. 'He was my student.'

Instantly the elderly man and woman scuttled behind the decrepit barn.

Hidden in the underbrush in the lilac grove, I saw a blue forget-me-not, a memento of my unknown great-grandparents. Better than a gravestone, this gentle, enduring flower would be my marker.

As we returned to Davlekanova, the director stopped the car at 'a Mennonite house' on the 'German' side of the railway tracks. 'These are Germans, Driedigers. You should meet them. Maybe they know if your uncle was deported in 1941.'

The homeowner said her grandmother was deported, but her husband, who came back, had died. She knew no Brauns. Would her husband have known? She replied, 'If you don't ask right away, it's lost.'

'There's one more German family in the town,' suggested our guide director. He dropped us off near the railway overpass where an elderly woman at the door turned out to be a daughter of a medical doctor pictured in my Ufa book. Her family home was seized in 1931 during dekulakization, and today was the mayor's office, the city hall we saw earlier. The Neufeld daughter was deported in 1941 but was allowed to return after Stalin's death. 'Not many came back. No, no Brauns. Come inside. My three sons married Russian wives so I never get an opportunity to speak German. I miss it.'

Asked if she associated with the other 'German' family, she threw up her hands. 'You can't talk to them. They're far too religious. Nobody laughs any more. We used to laugh so much. Have you had supper? Yes, well, you'll eat again.'

She ladled out fried eggs, fresh radishes ('water three times a day, rain or shine, and you'll get ones as big as mine'), and thick slabs of bread. Her eyes lit up when I pulled out the red Ufa book. Seeing the pictures, she exclaimed, 'That's my nephew! My parents!' She turned to Nelly: 'You're Nelly? That's my name too. And your father's name? That's my name too! Nelly Grigorovna! Think of it, we're alike!'

Nelly at last was happy, giggling, getting over being seen as only an interpreter for us foreigners. She claimed she purposely spoke broken Russian at times, but people still guessed she was Soviet-born and not the German on her passport. We were running into a few problems with her resentment about being asked to translate my questions and not to add her own opinions to answers. Yet I sensed she felt far more relaxed here than in Germany, where by now she had spent half her life.

As for information about my mother's brother Peter Braun, we got none.

6 June. *Today we look for the village of Gorchakovo, the Braun grandparents' home. Our directors have found a driver with an American car, an elderly Lincoln large enough for six – driver, Harvey, Nelly, museum director, a TV cameraman, and me.*

Mennonite villages in the Davlekanova settlement were widely scattered – unlike in southeastern Ukraine – and pioneers here were an entrepreneurial adventurous type, mixing freely with non-Mennonites. In his notes, my grandfather Braun mentioned friends among the Russian Orthodox clergy as well as local Bashkirs and Tatars. Nobody knew where the village was located, but we checked my red book and set out in good humour. My grandfather had driven to Davlekanova with horse and buggy, back and forth every week, sometimes several times. How far was it? At first we drove on a new roadway, freshly gravelled, but the side roads were rutted deep in mud. At the bottom of an incline we stopped to allow a cowboy on horseback to take a herd of red cows across the road.

The museum director asked him where we could find Gorchakovo, but he did not know. He said this cow crossing was what was left of a one-time 'German' estate, the Thiessen estate. I listened. Before the Civil War, for a semester, my mother had taught at a Thiessen estate, had seen the large Christmas tree in the big house. Could this be the one? Thiessen had built houses for his workers and it seemed the short row of brick dormitory-style houses on one side of the road at this crossing were remnants. In the Civil War, activists had arrested Thiessen as a capitalist enemy, killed him, and burned his grand house. A woman emerged from one of the houses and leaned across her gate as Nelly translated my questions.

The woman said that the village teacher had documents about the estate, that the large horse barn was here till ten years ago, but was now demolished, replaced by a store. She said Thiessen had planted the tall pines in front of the row of houses. 'We don't have trees like that. Yes, when the Germans were here it was clean and beautiful, but look how everything has deteriorated.' The director thought she could be right about the trees.

But we were looking for Gorchakovo. After we had driven almost thirty kilometres, we watched a yellow truck slowly grind up a hill and asked the driver for directions to Gorchakovo. He pointed the way he came: 'Down there.' Soon we had left the Lincoln in mud up to its axles and were tramping through mud ourselves. All we found were a few houses between puddles where geese and goslings nibbled grass beside a dirt roadway. Nothing even faintly resembled a Mennonite village layout.

Always find the oldest person was our motto. After knocking at windows of a few houses we found the oldest inhabitant, with a Mennonite name, Mr Enns. Was it our luck again? Alas, Enns had come here as a child in 1932 after the rest of his family had starved in Ukraine, and he knew little about the earlier inhabitants. He shared the local tale that a rich 'German' had lived in Gorchakovo, someone with many horses and cows, and when the Revolution came, the rich 'German' escaped by plane, leaving the local people overjoyed to butcher his cattle and hold a feast. Plane?

Since Gorchakovo had a large church in my mother's day, we asked about any large buildings, but his answer was, 'No.' There might have been a cemetery, but houses were built there now. In southern Ukraine, where warring armies had passed back and forth, many Mennonite-built houses still exist, so without a warfront here, why had log houses disappeared? Davlekanova still had many old log houses and brick buildings. But not Mr Enns, or his Tatar wife, or anyone else in Gorchakovo knew about my mother's village or her brothers.

Still, seeing the landscape where my mother grew up, the rolling hills, the blue ridges of the distant Ural Mountains, the black fields, and many wood lots where her brothers roamed reminded me they once were young, not missing, not merely men who had *disappeared.* Grateful for our reception and assistance by the Davlekanova directors, we returned to the white catkin-strewn streets of Davlekanova. Catching the evening electric train back to Ufa, I knew my mother's village existed only in my Ufa book, but in the Davlekanova School her memory was alive.

7 June. *We are about to take a taxi to the railway station when I realize I have left my money belt under my pillow. It contains my Visa card and American dollars for the needy relatives we plan to meet in Slavgorod. Dashing back to the hotel, we see a woman in a blue smock (the cleaner) at the concierge's office putting down a phone. 'We were phoning the train station to tell you we found your papers.' 'See,' says Harvey, 'I told you Russians are honest people.' The concierge waves away our thank you money, 'Don't miss your train.'*

Our suitcases are too heavy and the train station is overcrowded. All travellers seem to carry huge plaid-patterned, plastic, zippered bags, and pushy old men with medals across their chests wave their canes at you in waiting rooms. War veterans get the seats. Our four-person train compartment has a new companion on a top bunk.

Trans-Siberian Rail to Slavgorod

The Trans-Siberian was taking us to meet Maria Braun's children, her brother Heinz, as well as Peter Braun's daughter Lora who lived just across the border in Kazakhstan. We stopped in Chelyabinsk, a major deportation destination, walked streets where Russian log houses alternated with monumental Soviet-style buildings, theatres, concert halls, and a KGB building. A cathedral – closed by the Soviets and used as a horse barn – was now a concert hall where tonight's concert was to be played on an organ donated by 'the Germans.' Were the slave labourers who worked here forgotten? My travel book stated sixty thousand died at one industrial plant nearby. We met a local journalist named Nachtigal, a Mennonite name, who worked from a Catholic centre and was digging up the history of local repression. Originally from Kotlyarevka (like my Uncle Johannes), his father arrived here in 1941 and became a forced labour conscript. His mother had trekked out of the USSR in 1943 and got to Germany but was 'repatriated' to a labour camp here in 1945.

8 June. *Omsk greets us with hordes of mosquitoes. Everywhere white poplar pollen is sifting onto streets and rain-wet sidewalks. We are eleven time zones from home and daylight lasts till eleven at night. These are the 'white nights.' Our hotel room overlooks the River Om, a quiet river compared to the mighty Irtysh River on the opposite side of the city. Harvey has arranged to meet a fellow historian, Pyotr Vibe, director of the Omsk State Museum of History and Regional Studies, and we tour his dimly lit museum. Vibe, who has a Mennonite father (Wiebe) and German Colonist mother, researches Soviet Germans. Later we find a restaurant and eat the national dish, pelmeni.*

9 June. *Today we will look for Maslianovka, home of the Konrads. With Museum Director Vibe, his driver and white Volga, we set out for the 'German villages.'*

We found the Lubinskaya train station on the Tiumen-Omsk line where my parents and elder siblings boarded the train in 1929. At the former Mennonite village of Chukraievka, now a dacha suburb of Omsk, we looked for 'Mennonite houses.' Pyotr Vibe called them 'German' and was reminded, 'Mennonite houses.' The Soviets may have lumped us together, robbed us of our name, but we'd reclaim it. Though both Mennonites and German Colonists suffered and spoke German, our culture, response to politics, and religion differed widely.

Nelly knocked on the window and the housekeeper, Mrs Flaming, came outside. (Flaming was an infrequent Mennonite name.) She said the owners had left the house as it was and moved to Germany, but they might come back. She allowed us to see the interior and since Mennonite homes all had the same house plan and furnishings, in my mind it was similar to my Konrad grandparents' home – as it once was.

The house had the Dutch-style stove (*pech*) bricked into the kitchen to heat the adjoining rooms. It had a *Schlopbank*, the wooden 'sleeping bench,' a sofa by day with a drawer that pulled out at night to sleep two. The parlour boasted a treadle sewing machine and the obligatory *Himmelsbett* piled high with pillows and the best (lace-edged) linens. Mottoes (cardboard-backed with floral designs and Bible verses) hung on the parlour walls. The attic, once used to store grain, now housed a sausage-maker, a wooden butter churn exactly like the one we had in Alberta, a porcelain coffee mill that mounts on a wall (Mennonites, immigrating before the Revolution, brought them to Canada), a butcher knife, cookie cutters, and other kitchen objects – 'things we brought to Siberia from the Molochna [Ukraine].' The museum director recorded the artefacts, planning perhaps to bargain for them.

The walls of the house appeared to be a metre thick and, made of mud and wattle, were plastered over and whitewashed inside and out. The windowsills were wide enough for a dozen geranium plants in cans. A chute in the kitchen ceiling allowed grain sacks from the attic to be dropped through. In the cellar we found piles of potatoes and carrots bedded in sand, while gallon jars of crab apples in syrup and pickled tomatoes were lined up on a shelf. It seemed frozen in time, the way it was when the original family left.

Mrs Flaming told us a Soviet official wanted the house in 1941 so he shot the owner, a grandfather. Not long afterward the parents were sent to the Labour Army, leaving eight children on the street. Mrs Flaming also pointed out the foundation remains of a onetime church, a steam mill, and 'over there at that house, #29 was a school.' As we were leaving, she held up a copper kettle: 'It's original too, from them.'

Maslianovka, the last Siberian home village of my grandparents and parents, was about twelve kilometres from Omsk. It appeared as a mean and deserted village where small nondescript houses with unkempt yards filled one side of a dirt road. There were no public buildings. Pyotr Vibe had been in Maslianovka ten years ago to collect 'German' artefacts and I wondered if any were from the homes of the Konrad families. They had lived on two side of the street: my grandparents, my parents, uncles Abram and Heinrich, as well as an aunt, AnnaK. We knocked on a window and found a woman who spoke German. As she curbed a chained dog guarding her house, she told us she arrived here in 1933, at the age of two. She knew nothing about the Konrads. Her husband was 'German' and she, a Volga German, was exiled here in 1941. 'You should have come ten years ago,' she said. 'They have all left for Germany.'

Yes, there used to be houses on both sides of a much longer street. The school was gone. Church? Maybe that old foundation. Standing beside his mud-spattered car, Pyotr Vibe mentioned that the last time he was here there had been a store. In Chukraievka the houses survived. Why had these houses disappeared? We asked if Maslianovka still had a cemetery, and she pointed to a grove of trees behind an open field. My grandfather Jakob J. Konrad was buried in Maslianovka. So was Lena Wiebe's father. 'You can cross my field to get to the cemetery or drive around to a narrow lane from the road.'

Vibe and the driver took the car, but we walked towards the forest. Following a path past birch trees to a clearing covered in wild strawberries, we heard birds singing. A sagging picket fence enclosed the cemetery, and inside were numerous new concrete slab grave markers surrounded by metal fences, some with red stars and a few with crosses. Two newer-looking gravestones from the 1980s had Mennonite names on them, 'Enns' and 'Wieler.' Weren't they the sisters who wrote to my parents, those in my box of 'Russian letters'? The older section of the cemetery was covered in birch trees and underbrush. 'Lucky to be dead,' Uncle Gerhard had said, and I recalled how my father never believed in visiting cemeteries. Would he be happy that trees covered his father's grave? Nobody had turned it into a pasture or built a house on it. Nature had given him a birch tree.

A swarm of mosquitoes attacked us as we returned to Director Vibe's white Volga (Soviet brass used black Volgas). On a road thick with mud gumbo, we passed black fields dotted with more glades of white poplar or birch. The car got stuck and the driver flagged down a van to pull us out with the kind of rope that seems to be kept in every trunk. In the traffic tie-up, as we passed a large exhibition grounds this weekend displaying new military equipment, Vibe quipped, 'Do you know that Omsk manufactures tanks and missiles? It's secret. Tell people we make refrigerators that shoot and sausages that fly.'

Back at home I checked the letter box and reread those from the Wieler/Enns sisters. In one letter, Agatha Wieler wrote,

Early in January I went outdoors one evening and looked up at the moon. Strange, I thought, one quarter of the moon is red. I took a closer look. From under a cloud, dark as night, a fiery stake long as a hand emerged and seemed to hold back the moon. As the moon tried to move ahead, fearsome to behold, half a hand pushed itself forward and appeared to threaten the moon, forcing it to stop. The whole drama was over in a moment, but as I continued to look, I saw a star and it also disappeared. What can all of this mean?[7]

When I had first read her letter I thought of Soviet nuclear tests, but then of the red moon that occurs in a total lunar eclipse. She quoted the Book of Revelation, the 'last trumpet,' so a larger metaphor was meant. A red quarter moon, a vanishing star, a stake ... ?[8]

From Wieler's letter, it appeared that a disproportionately large number of men and women of this small village were arrested or disappeared ('were taken').

In many ways Omsk touched me more than Ukraine. It was my father's city. For my cousin Alici it was prison. When we walked the streets and passed a military yard with a high yellow brick fence topped by barbed wire, I asked, 'Was this Alici's prison?' When we passed the NKVD headquarters fortress and saw a plaque on the wall dedicated to the memory of Soviet police guards who 'died as soldiers,' I wondered, did they guard Alici?

10 June. *We are on another exploration and this time Museum Director Vibe accompanies us to find Waldheim, the village of Lena Wiebe and AnnaK.*

The road to Waldheim was impossible to navigate because of the deep mud, so we changed plans and headed for Margenau, another prominent Siberian Mennonite village before collectivization, and the place where my father's brother Heinrich briefly attended high school. Margenau's main street still had the double row of houses, but Kazakhs had moved into former Mennonite homes. All the poplar trees that once lined Margenau's streets in old photographs were gone, replaced by telephone poles and strings of light bulbs suspended high across the road. We asked for directions from friendly people living in green-painted houses. Vibe knew the director of the local museum housed in a school built by Mennonites. Grigorii Zaretsky and his blond wife, in shorts, were outside the house hoeing their straight rows of vegetables, but, upon Vibe's explanation of our interest, he dashed indoors and emerged in a white shirt and grey pants. His wife came back in a dress. Zaretsky had the key to the school (which was locked for summer holidays) where he had taught for twenty-seven years and started the museum. His mother was a Volga German deported in 1941 to Margenau to live with the resident Mennonites. 'They intermarried, got along well,' he said. Born in Margenau, he thought his father, an orphan, had been adopted by Mennonites and that Volga Germans (mostly Catholics) and Mennonites had met for underground church services in homes.

In the school museum we saw a large map labelled 'The Labour Front of the Great Fatherland War,' featuring photos of village *Trudarmiia* survivors. The faces had labels reading 'volunteer' and 'war hero,' but all were German and Mennonite names. It upset me to see them described as volunteers, but it got worse. Prominent in the next space was a large coloured portrait of Pavel Morozov, the boy who denounced his father and thereby became a Soviet child hero. I asked why this boy was still being so prominently featured in 2001 and Zaretsky said, 'It's part of history,' but added, 'I didn't consider him a hero.' The picture was offensive, but I kept quiet. This was Zaretsky's home, his history – sadly so incomplete.

On the return to Omsk we stopped at the railway station Piketnoie where my Konrad grandparents lived the first years in Siberia. It was where they experienced a pogrom – a story my father loved to tell and retell. It happened eighty years ago. The family had been robbed, bound, and put into the cellar, but they survived, and the stationmaster had investigated the theft after the raid.

The station was neat, painted green, and inside a woman seated at a panel of blinking lights was monitoring incoming and outgoing trains. Where was my grandparents' farmstead? My father had said, 'There was the railway station, a bush, and then a lake.' 'Oh, that's across the tracks,' said the traffic controller. An old woman in boots and kerchief stopped chasing her chickens long enough to tell us the barracks we saw across the tracks had been built in Soviet days and a space was allotted to her. Gone too was my father's bush, and a small lake was a couple of kilometres away. We returned to the station, sat on the benches inside, and took a few pictures.

11 June. Today was an Omsk City walkabout. In a park we found a memorial to the victims of Communism, the first we had seen. Tall, shaped like a Russian Orthodox church cupola, the memorial rested on four pillars engraved with names of places of deportation and slave labour camps. Soil from those prisons and slave labour camps was under the floor of the memorial, and in the centre, in an open pit was an eternal flame. The Memorial Society was recognizing Stalin's victims.

It was a bank holiday, Independence Day. We walked along the Irtysh River and sent off telegrams at an Internet café. The telegrams were to relatives we wanted to meet on our next stop in Slavgorod – Maria Braun's children and her brother Heinz. Also Lora Braun, daughter of my mother's brother Peter. The only place open was an art gallery where a painting captioned *Independence Day 1991* posed a dilemma for citizens trained to take orders rather than use personal initiative. A sea of people waiting for orders surrounded a pulpit filled only with crumpled paper. The painting suggested that one day even the present state might acknowledge its past.

Slavgorod. 13 June. We arrived at the station in Slavgorod at 11:30 in the morning. Maria Braun's entire family was waiting at the station. There was Jura, Maria's eldest son, with wife, Tanya, and twelve-year old son, Zhenia; Volodya, Maria's youngest son, was with his wife, Natasha, and their twelve-year-old daughter, Nastya; Andrei (called Andrusha), Maria's deaf son, was with his wife, Natasha, and their children, Igor and Vika. Vika, the little girl with the big bow in Karaganda, was now twenty-one, a slim blond woman in a long dress. Volodya and Andrei lived in Slavgorod, but Jura and family had driven twelve hours from Kemerovo to meet us. Jura was a bus driver, his wife, Tanya, a construction engineer. All the men were dark-haired, lean, and tall, had sunken eyes, and smoked cigarettes endlessly.

Rolling our suitcases, commenting in Russian on our pull-up handles, they accompanied us along a dirt street to our hotel. The walls in the large foyer of the 'five star' hotel were covered in murals, but our cold-water room was dusty. Nearby, in a gated military compound, Volodya and Natasha's apartment was spacious, had a shiny wooden wall unit in the living/dining room, plush chairs, two bedrooms, and a balcony. We were invited to a feast: *pelmeni* soup, cold cuts, breads, cheese, pickles, tomatoes and cucumbers, chocolates, nuts, cherries, and pastries. We were aware of the huge expense and generous traditional Russian hospitality.

Maria's sons – Volodya and deaf Andrusha – seemed much alike, yet their wives, both named Natasha, were opposites. Volodya's dark-haired wife, Natasha, was an outgoing, gutsy lady, a storekeeper. When Communism collapsed and most factories in Slavgorod closed, Dark Natasha had rented space in an empty aircraft factory turned into a mall. She travelled to China on a bus with armed guards and brought back toys she sold in her brightly decorated stall. Her husband, Volodya, in the army when we first met in 1989, now was a customs officer at the Kazakhstan-Russian border just out of town.

Blond Natasha, Andrusha's wife, felt uncomfortable, and it was obvious that she and her deaf husband were the odd ones out. Petite, curly haired, and slim in brown skirt and blouse, she used sign language with her husband. When she told us her daughter Vika had lived with Maria Braun and become a Baptist, the others smiled smugly. Andru-

sha worked as a locksmith but was paid mostly in kind (coal, vegetables). He had a small disability pension of twenty roubles a month,
and the others thought his wife should get a job, not just 'sit at home.'
The twelve-year-old cousins, Jura and Volodya's children, observing
us Westerners using a knife and fork, nudged each other and slipped
forks into their left hands. In Soviet days, knives were often prohibited,
a custom still in evidence in second-class hotels we frequented.

In the banter that followed, we observed the next generation, children of the repressed who had little knowledge of and little interest
in their parents' past or heritage. They focused on day-to-day problems. Andrusha and his family had financial problems. Their daughter
Vika, prodded by her grandmother, had begun a sewing program but
dropped out when the factory closed. Her Uncle Jura asked her why
she did not look for other work and she replied, 'Why should I?' We
detected this air of hopelessness among other young people we met.
Her brother Igor, eighteen, was shortly to leave for his compulsory
military duty and his parents hoped he would learn a skill in the army.
Jura and Tanya said that if he were their son, they would buy him out,
to prevent him from being sent to fight in Chechnya. It cost 10,000 roubles, but it was possible to get out of military service. The engineer
Tanya was dismayed that the Soviet system had trained people to follow orders rather than to take initiative.

Maria Braun's sons spoke fondly of their mother, but also of their
Uncle Andrei (Heinz), the one Maria called greedy and mean. They
were proud of their grandfather Johannes Braun: 'Such a singer. He
even sang for the tsar.' Dark Natasha was proud of *her* grandfather.
He was a 'big Communist' who had his children stand up and sing the
'International' before all meals. 'My parents were Communists, but I
visited the cathedral in Novgorod, liked the candles, incense, and singing, and decided to have my children baptized Orthodox.' Then Blond
Natasha said she liked the singing in Vika's Baptist church, where she
went a few times. They sang hymns before meals. Quickly she added, 'But I don't believe. In times like these, how can you believe?' She
told us the Baptists were very kind and prepared everything at Maria
Braun's funeral. Also German Baptists sent busloads of good clothes,
Christmas gifts, and supplies to the Slavgorod church. 'It helps out.'
To this Dark Natasha said, 'I might change religions too, if I benefited!'

In the afternoon we visited Maria Braun's grave in a cemetery on the
open steppe. A few rows over, a funeral was in progress. With a small
school bus as hearse, about twenty people were watching a silent bur-

ial. Bolsheviks long ago had forbidden any religious services or songs at funerals and good Communists still followed the rules. The body had been laid out at his home the night before. To me it was a bleak sight, death without comfort. Maria's grave was surrounded by a metal fence and had a stone with her name and dates. Andrusha had given us flowers to place on it, since there was no room for him (with all of us) in Jura's car. Jura also showed us the small cinderblock house where Maria had lived the last years. Maria had saved money sent by relatives in Canada to pay for her own funeral and had given each child several hundred dollars.

The next morning, Harvey, Nelly, and I were the only visitors at the Slavgorod museum. We listened to a stock Soviet lecture that 'Russian durum wheat is better than Canada's' and looked at photographs of Red heroes of the Civil War 1918–21 (but none of Whites), and Red Army uniforms and medals from the Second World War. There was no mention of oppressed people or the Labour Army. We then visited the Slavgorod 'German Centre.' In an attempt to stop the flow of immigrants from the former USSR, the German government was supporting a cultural centre. Here we met a Catholic teacher who described their programs: camps, women's and *Trudarmist* clubs, and language classes. Ruefully she admitted her program was so successful that *more* rather than fewer people wanted to immigrate to Germany.

On a drive through the town with Jura and Tanya, we stopped at a former prison, a three-storey, crumbling, yellow brick building, the front of which was being reconstructed. Harvey thought it was a former flour mill. A battered brick wall surrounded the site and strings of barbed wire dangled from the top. The windows were bricked in, leaving small openings covered with iron bars. A rubbish heap at the entrance was filled with broken glass, plastic bottles, old clothes, a chamber pot, rusted bits of iron, and weeds.

As we stood looking at this former prison, a man carrying firewood stopped and told us his wife's family were arrested in 1937 and 1938. 'Shot right in this yard.' Another woman on the street, seeing that we were visitors, stopped and told us, 'We were eleven children and our father was shot here.' She started to cry. 'He was an engineer.' They were coming out of nowhere, the ghosts of all the tormented and lost. Strangers wanted us to know a tragedy took place here, a travesty. Yellow mills meant to grind flour had crushed lives. Who was responsible? Had paranoia run wild, and no one person, but a thousand subordinate Stalins had been at work? A week later on a branch line to Kulunda, a

train attendant heard us speaking German and asked, 'Are you Plautdietsch?' She was from a village near Kulunda where deported Mennonites from Soviet Ukraine were dropped in November 1941. Her
grandmother had told her, 'That mill in Slavgorod, the yellow mill, was
the Friesen mill, a Mennonite mill. That's where they took all the men
to prison.'[9]

On our next day in Slavgorod we drove to Andrusha and Natasha's
house for lunch. They lived in a grey, cement-brick, three-room house
and had a potato patch in the front yard. The garden had rows of tomatoes, onions, garlic, and cucumbers all carefully hilled. Paths were laid
out in a small orchard, and a cherry tree and rhubarb were planted
behind the house. We all removed our shoes as we stepped inside the
common sitting/eating room. Here Natasha slept on the couch. The
children Vika and Igor each had a small bedroom curtained off, with
narrow beds. In the larger bedroom used by Andrusha was a substan-
tial chest of drawers built, they proudly told us, by their father, Nikolai
Milshin, Maria's husband. Hadn't she told us he destroyed furniture?
Dark Natasha said the boys took after their father, and Tanya agreed.
Her husband, Jura, could do anything: sew, cook, and do carpentry. 'He
even cleans.'

In the chatter Jura told us his mother and father had never been legally married. 'When I was born, they told the registry clerk they were
getting married soon, so the clerk said, "Fine," and registered me as
a Milshin. Then two years later when Andrusha came along and they
still weren't married, he said, "You're not married. The baby's name is
Braun." Same for Volodya: Braun too.' We also discovered that Andrusha was deaf as the result of childhood meningitis. His mother persuaded officials to pay for his schooling at a residential school that
taught him sign language. Then at a trade school he learned plumbing,
but jobs had dried up since all the factories were closed following the
collapse of the Communist government. To change the topic to happier
subjects we moved into the garden, where Harvey plucked a long blade
of grass and used it as a whistle. Soon all were trying the same trick,
even whistling through onion blades.

In Vika I was reminded of Laura in *The Glass Menagerie*. Slight, her
fair hair parted in the middle and held back with a ribbon, blue eyes,
long skirt, she sat unnoticed until I asked to see her bedroom filled with
pink and puffy plush animals. She confided she had begun a sewing
course but had dropped out. She pulled out her photograph album
and happily showed me photos of her church youth group. She had

no camera, but they shared pictures of their outings, visits to the sick and elderly, and a trip to Gorno Altaisk in a bus given to her church by German Baptists. She passed her hand longingly over wedding photos of friends in her group. When Vika nursed her grandmother during the last two years, Maria Braun had cajoled and urged her to study, to get an occupation. She sang in the church choir, attended weekly Bible study, and was baptized at sixteen. I sensed her family hoped she would get that 'gentleman caller.'

The following day we visited the 'German rayon,' a pre-Revolution settlement consisting primarily of Mennonite and German Colonist villages. Wherever we went, we always sought out the oldest inhabitants, and on a street in Grishkovka, one of fifty-three former Mennonite/German villages, we found a woman named Friesen, who spoke to us in Plautdietsch. She recalled the arrival of deported 'fifth columnists' from Soviet Ukraine. Her stepmother had taken bread, potatoes, and tea for them and had gone to the village authorities demanding that shelter be found for these people dumped out onto the street. 'They were put up in a closed kindergarten, but soon were sent off again to work in Labour Army camps.' Another old woman came up to us on the street and asked, 'Do you speak Plautdietsch?' She was rescued from starvation because an aunt came to get her from the place she was exiled. Touch anyone here and out poured a similar story. I hoped someone collected them.

The administrative headquarters of the *Deutsche rayon* was in Halbstadt, a large village where the German government had invested in building a street of German-style 'show' houses. Local people told us it might look good, but only the bosses lived here, so what change was that? Halbstadt's tree-lined streets had well-maintained front gardens and traditional Mennonite fences. The local archivist wanted to have a memorial built here to remember the repression, but Moscow had turned down a request for funds to create a new museum in a former Mennonite house. We talked to the cultural representative in the Cultural Centre, who lamented that all the people who moved into town after local Mennonites immigrated to Germany did not want to work on collective farms. They were people who sold their houses in Novosibirsk where real estate prices were higher, moved into cheaper houses in Halbstadt, drank up their assets, sold again, and moved into yet cheaper houses in Slavgorod. He complained that Germans were being discriminated against with higher taxes because 'we are *Nemtsy* and we work hard.' Hadn't Solzhenitsyn written that Germans, set down in any wilderness, could turn it into a land of plenty by dint of their powerful work ethic?[10]

In the village of Kusak, on another tree-lined street with painted picket fences, we met a man in a sweatshirt and training shorts who directed us. 'There's an old *Mennist* up the street. Go talk to Wiebe.' Another Wiebe. At the *Mennist* house, we removed our shoes and found the traditional Mennonite house with rooms in their pre-revolutionary places, the house joined to the barn. Mr Wiebe had lived here all his life, as had his parents. Mrs Wiebe, baking what appeared to be my mother's Zwieback buns (a Saturday ritual), invited us to sit in their parlour [*groote Stow*], and the interview began. Their village was still a collective farm named Kolkhoz Engels. Five villages had been amalgamated in 1975, and farming the ten thousand hectares had been successful until people began to leave for Germany.

Mrs Wiebe was baking for her grandchildren because her visiting son was flying back home to Germany. She had altogether thirty grandchildren, most in Germany, but she and her husband had no wish to emigrate. 'What do they do there?' she asked. 'Look at someone else's tree? That Germany has spoiled everything for us, taken away our children, our neighbours. And our collective is going downhill. You should have been here ten years ago. Then it was something.'

Now seventy-one, Mrs Wiebe, buxom, her round face framed in glasses, handed out large mugs of hot water and passed us a jar of instant coffee. 'Add as much as you like.' She recalled her deportation from the Zaporozhye area in 1941. Given six hours to pack, her stepmother (her father was already arrested) had butchered their small pig and salted the meat for the journey. There were blackout regulations, so her stepmother covered the barn door and windows, but someone opened the door and a patrol noticed and arrested her. At headquarters, the police supervisor shouted, 'Shoot her!' Her stepmother went on her knees, 'I'm being deported tonight. Who will look after my children?' They let her go. It took a month to reach Siberia. At train stations, gawkers who had listened to Soviet propaganda stood waiting to see the 'monsters' being deported. 'They were surprised we Fritzies and Fascists did not have horns and tails.' Unloaded in Semi Palatinsk, Kazakhstan, they were fortunate to be put into an empty kindergarten. Her brothers aged one and two had starved to death and her stepmother was sent to the Labour Army. Alone, she became a beggar, but everyone was starving. 'It's forty years ago, but I never forget it.' In 1944 an elder married sister from this area came to get her from the detention camp and she had lived here ever since.

As Mrs Wiebe was telling her story in German and Nelly was translating into Russian for Tanya, abruptly they left the room. Later I asked Nelly what was wrong. 'It got too much for Tanya. She said her communist grandparents suffered too. She was not taught these stories.' At night I kept seeing Mrs Wiebe and thinking my mother could have had a similar fate. A woman who jumped when unannounced guests appeared, scurried to get out her preserves, offered a meal – so like my mother. And then there were Tanya's grandparents who suffered in the war and whose story I was not hearing.

I was upset not to be able to speak directly with Tanya or Maria Braun's children, was becoming irritated with Nelly's constant giggling and table manners. Expected to eat all our meals with the relatives and knowing the outlay of food was expensive for them, I took small helpings. I asked myself what I was actually objecting to. Was it her unconcern for Party membership, the 'piece of paper' that I saw as acquiescence? What was wrong with me? Right and wrong were blurring. But Nelly was a casualty too. Trying desperately to blend in wherever she was, at heart this was where she could relax. Raised in a Soviet culture she knew as normal, she too was uprooted. What an upside-down world.

Andrei: On the Kulunda Steppe

Volodya and Jura, their wives, we, and two children in two cars were driving sixty-five kilometres from Slavgorod over the Kulunda steppe to meet Heinz Braun. For Volodya and Jura and families it was a visit with their 'Uncle Andrei.' And for me it meant that at last I would see the place where the deportees, Anna Braun and three children, were dumped off the train in December 1941. As we drove, Jura, reminiscing, told us he practically grew up with Uncle Andrei, that he and his brothers regularly walked back and forth the ten kilometres from their home in Kulunda to the farm, that he loved the farm. Jura had started work on the railway at fourteen, but often visited there after his work. Sensing her son's obvious affection, I wondered why his mother, Maria, was so antagonistic towards her brother. Heinz Braun lived in Konstantinovka, a Russian-Ukrainian village, a *sovkhoz* or state farm. Maria had never mentioned Konstantinovka.

Along the way we noticed cattle being herded by lonely shepherds, but there were no fences. We reached a one-street village with a wide road allowance and tall power poles between unpainted and crooked picket fences. Behind the fences, log houses were topped with TV antennas. A few wooden sheds, barns, and garden patches filled each yard. Mid-village, in front of the farm director's office, a faded blue slab resembling an upended aeroplane wing was a Second World War memorial.

His sister Alici had told me Heinz had only four years of schooling and after losing his father, he had helped earn his own living. 'Mama got silkworms, teeny tiny ones, and all of us children walked a great distance and carried home bundles of mulberry branches on our backs, tied with a rope. The payoff came when the first cocoons were delivered and we could go to the state store and buy bread. If there was enough left for a few metres of silk, Mama sewed dresses for us three girls, and the two boys got silk shirts. Oh, joy!'

When our two cars drew up at 'Uncle Andrei's,' a cluster of people rushed towards us. As we hugged one another, I looked to see if Heinz resembled my mother's idolized brother Johannes. At seventy-four, Heinz was short, had a trim build and a full head of white hair. His wife, Maria Rogodza, lines of hard work written on her face and arms, wore a kerchief tied back over grey hair, a checked apron, and short-sleeved print dress. A daughter, Katya, a young woman in a miniskirt, purple sweater, and henna hair that was cut pageboy style, had come from Kazan, bringing her twelve-year-old son who regularly spent summers with his grandparents at the farm. A tall, close-shaven man with a moustache and slightly Tartar eyes was introduced as Heinz's son Kolya. The woman in a denim vest and a smile of metal teeth was Kolya's third wife, Nina. The two young boys standing awkwardly in the background were Katya's son and another grandson.

Jura's wife, Tanya, smiled, relaxed, and soon, chattering happily in Russian, the women, including Nelly, moved into a summer kitchen beside the house. Here an electric stove and a table were covered in enamel pots, pans, and food preparations. As Heinz and I turned to each other, the astonished Slavgorod nephews called out, 'What? You speak German?' Heinz laughed, 'I used to practise it as I drove my tractor. Prrr prr, nobody knew. They would have called me a fascist. I never thought I would use it again, and now ...' Tears welled up as he looked at Harvey and me. 'Alici sent us your pictures.' I wanted to continue without my interpreter, but after a while I called Nelly in so

Heinz could speak more freely. We sat on a wooden bench and Heinz told his story.

He did not like being called Heinrich or Heinz, only Andrei. He remembered school in Kotlyarevka, seeing pictures of Stalin, Lenin, Karl Marx, and Friedrich Engels at the front of the classroom, and he so much wanted to be a Pioneer, to wear the red scarf and march into the radiant future. 'But they would not let me. We were enemies of the people.' By 1937, before he was arrested, his father had been awarded prizes as a top agronomist, once being awarded with a bicycle and once a gramophone (later reclaimed). 'He was a fine mechanic too, kept all the machinery at the tractor station in working order.'

Andrei was nine when his father was arrested on 23 December 1937. 'After that my mother burned all our pictures except ones of my parents and the dead grandparents.' The nine-year-old boy became a herder. For twenty kopeks per cow, he took out five or six of the village cows to the common pasture, herded them throughout the day, and returned them at night.

He remembered being deported from Kotlyarevka in 1941, the train being hit by a bomb. 'One mother went berserk and, leaving her children, ran across the tracks. She went crazy.' The train took five weeks to reach Siberia and by then 'everyone was so covered in lice, you could scrape them off.' When they arrived in Siberia, snow came up to the roofs of houses. People had been dropped off along the track, in Slavgorod, in Tabun, and his family in Kulunda. 'Village bosses were waiting to examine us, to assess which of us deportees to choose as workers.' Heinz – I had started calling him Andrei – did not know what happened to those unfit to be 'workers,' the very old or very young.

'The collective boss saw me, a boy of thirteen, my sisters aged fifteen and seventeen, and my fifty-year-old mother and decided we were to be his farm workers in Konstantinovka. Asking where we could live, he said, "Go, find something." We got a chicken coop and later moved into a dugout.' His sisters and mother working on the collective farm, Andrei immediately became a cowherd. Over the sixty years in Konstantinovka, not much had changed in that job. Seated on the 'babushka bench' traditionally found beside the picket fence facing the street, we saw the present cowherd, stick in hand, wobbling on a bicycle behind a few cattle. Andrei opened his barn door to let his cow and heifer onto the street and, as the herder swung her stick, Andrei's animals joined those trotting to a common pasture.

Alone with his mother, how did they manage? 'In 1944, the grain harvest was fantastic and we together earned enough to be able to buy a house.' He indicated the building behind us. 'Twice we made additions.' In a few years he had changed from cowherd to tractorist, a highly valued job, better paid too. He even got put on the 'hero wall' reserved for workers who had overproduced their quotas. Andrei was proud of his work, his contribution to the farm, his assimilation.

Andrei's eyes sparkled as he continued, 'I could still enjoy myself. I noticed girls.' In the next village lived a good-looking milkmaid, much desired not only for her dark eyes but also as one of the heroines of the collective farm who won awards of excellence – in other words, a *Stakhanovite*, a model Soviet citizen, a person meant to inspire others to double or triple their work output. Maria Rogodza, champion milkmaid, looked smart in her clinical white smock and cap standing beside a hand-operated cream separator, and Andrei, champion tractorist, knew he had to win her. But Andrei Braun had set his aim high. He, an enemy of the people, desired Soviet hero Maria Rogodza? Not so fast, said her village boss, the *pred*.

'A few men were after her, but I fought them off,' Andrei admitted. 'And I won. I went to her house and drank a few glasses of vodka with her parents. I helped her onto the back of my bicycle and peddled home. That was 1951. Well, we had a somewhat better wedding nine days later. We're married fifty years now and you could not find a better wife than my Maria. So my mother said, "Give her a day or two off work to get used to things here. She's just married and new in this village." Well, the *pred* from her village came over and gave her such a tongue-lashing, told her she was a terrible person, and so berated her that she felt like lying down across the railway tracks. He had wanted her for himself, you see, and he was mad. He wanted to beat me up too. I didn't care how he took it out on me because it was all for love. People do violent things for love.'

Andrei paid for his victory. After capturing his bride, he was given a much higher work quota and when he had more awards due him, the *pred* denied them, saying, 'You're a German, an enemy of the people. You have to do three times the regular hours to make up for all our men killed in the war.' New bride Maria was devastated no longer to be the star *Stakhanovite*, but a lowly wife of an enemy of the people. 'But children began to come and we were happy.'

In typical Russian custom, the baba or grandmother – Andrei and Maria were living with his mother, Anna Braun – looked after the babies as the parents worked. Of their six children, only three were alive in 2001. Two young daughters had died of cancer at ages two and three. Andrei was sure his little girls died because of radiation from the atomic tests at nearby Semipalatinsk. 'We never knew. Nobody told us.'

As champion tractorist, Andrei won awards – money (we presumed the jealous *pred* was gone) and even a trip to Moscow. He carefully saved, had set aside a thousand roubles for each child and even enough for his and his wife's funerals, when along came perestroika. 'It ruined me, ruined everything. Wiped out my savings. Then the factories closed and everything closed and look at it now. Perestroika!'

To change the subject I asked if he ever heard what happened to his father. Andrei repeated the familiar tale of the 1960s Khrushchev letters, the ones saying their men died of natural causes. 'They sent my mother, retroactively, two months of my father's wages. She bought a coat and boots.' These letters were not trusted.

I asked about our Uncle Peter Braun, whose family I had been unable to contact. I mentioned that Peter's wife, my mother's friend from her teaching days at the estate, had written to my parents about a daughter Lora living nearby, only some sixty-five kilometres across the border in Kazakhstan. We had no visas for Kazakhstan, but Lora did not require a visa to come to Russia. We had telegraphed her to meet us here. Had she written or phoned?

Andrei suggested we try to phone Lora from the farm office, and while Harvey and Andrei surveyed the ruins of the barely functioning collective farm, Nelly accompanied me to the farm office. We tried to place a phone call to Lora Braun, but after an hour we gave up. Later we found that Lora had no phone. Transferring money to her was impossible unless she had a bank account, which she did not, so I ended up writing her a letter filled with questions – translated into Russian by Nelly – when we were back in Moscow. I hoped the Russian envelope and stamp would speed a delivery.

Andrei's wife and family had outdone themselves in preparations for our visit. As in Alici's place, the house was freshly whitewashed and there was new wallpaper indoors. The adults were invited to a sitting room where extra tables were covered with new vinyl tablecloths and where bottles and bottles of vodka, wine, beer, mineral water, and champagne filled any open spot. Katya and her mother must have worked for days for this Barbette's Feast. Dishes included pickled herring, cold soup called *Okroshka*, sausages, mashed potatoes, fried meat, meatballs, pickled red peppers, pickled tomatoes, canned tomatoes, ikra, cucumbers, salads, mountains of bread, and a dessert of dark red fruit compote. 'Drink! Drink!' said our hosts. We made toasts, but dis-appointed them by not being vodka drinkers. 'So let's toast in wine – or brandy.' Katya told us Baba Anna would take only a sip of vodka and afterwards eat bread. 'She spoke German to us children and was very religious.' Maria Braun's sons nodded. 'Baba Anna died in Kulunda when she was living with us.'

A large framed portrait of Anna and Johannes Braun looked down on us from a place of honour in the centre of the living room wall. For-mally dressed, how innocent they were, how young. I wondered how many celebrations this portrait had seen, singing sessions, drinking orgies, funerals. 'Let's sing!' Andrei called out.

Kolya's wife, Nina, leading with a Ukrainian song, Kolya playing a guitar, they began to sing lustily. Maria Braun's sons, the nephews, and their wives joined in. All kept looking at Andrei, the man of the hour, and he sang powerfully. Acknowledging our attention, he claimed, 'I can sing any range, tenor, baritone, or bass.' As songs poured out, someone called, 'Your turn. Give us a Canadian song.' We sang, 'You Are My Sunshine.' More Ukrainian and Russian songs followed, and then Andrei suggested, 'A German one?' His family beamed as Andrei joined Nelly, Harvey, and me:

Hab oft im Kreise der Lieben
Im duftigen Grasse geruht
Und mir ein Liedlein gesungen
Und mir ein Liedlein gesungen
Und alles, alles war wieder gut.

Oft in a circle of loved ones
Resting on newly mown grass
We sang us a little song
We sang us a little song
And always, everything again was fine.

A short time after this gargantuan meal we were called back for the Russian national soup, *pelmeni*, salads, sausage, cheese, and *blinchiki* (crêpes). A third meal towards sundown offered dried smoked fish and thick slabs of home-baked bread and tea.

We noticed Andrei enjoyed alcohol ('less now,' his children said), and that he was emotional and devoted to his family. He had tried sincerely to become a Soviet person, to discard his parents' traditions and religion. He complained that his jolly sister Maria, who loved to play her guitar and sing at evening drinking parties, had, alas, become a 'religious fanatic.' (Was this the reason for the poor relations between Maria and her brother?) Yet, outwardly Soviet, Andrei had not been able to erase a fond memory of his German first language and his parents. With all his efforts to acculturate, his awards as a superior *Stakhanovite* tractorist, he still knew something had been stolen from him – and that he would always be a *Nemets*.

Throughout the visit, Andrei's son Kolya was flirting with Nelly, hoping to inveigle an invitation to visit Germany. We asked about their economy. There was no market for extra milk or meat from their red cow, and no vehicle to drive produce to market. Andrei had been forced to sell his car to pay for a heart operation. Without cash, how did they manage? 'We eat potatoes and can vegetables.' Both families had a long garden strip behind their houses filled with rows of hilled potato plantings and tomatoes.

Katya took out the family photograph album and, contrary to what Andrei had said, his mother had not burned every photograph. When Andrei boasted that his Grandfather Peters was 'a rich man with running water indoors and twenty-six pairs of oxen,' his daughter Katya sighed. She was unemployed and her father kept telling her to take any job, but she reminded him she had a university degree, suggesting she could not possibly work like her parents, do manual labour. He blamed perestroika for this attitude, but Katya said her generation disagreed with her father and saw its benefits too.

At a snapshot of Andrei's elder brother Hans, the one in the Red Army who ended up in Munich, I asked who found out about his being in the German Army. Andrei said a Red Army soldier from Omsk saw what happened. Urged to drop his buddy, Hans had refused to abandon his wounded friend and was captured by the Germans. So now I knew how Alici found out about Hans, from her brother Andrei. 'Why,' Andrei demanded, 'why did it happen?' The 'it' he referred to was the suicide. Yes, why did any of it happen?

So much more could be asked and answered, but the Slavgorod men had to return to work, and sadly we piled back into the cars, to drive into the night on the endless steppe. Was it Stolypin who ordered trees and bushes planted along roads for signposts when winter blizzards made this steppe a white desert? That's the way I felt after this visit, lost in a snowstorm, the story of Johannes and his family swirling around me. Once we meet people face to face, we see so many things differently. Maria's sons loved their father. Andrei was not mean or greedy with Maria's family, as she said. Wherever we turned there was brokenness. Would there be no redemption?

We made several more stops along the Trans-Siberian, finding footprints of the disappeared everywhere, but especially gripping was Tomsk, three thousand kilometres from Moscow, a closed city until the fall of the USSR. Here, in a former KGB building, its basement being restored by Memorial – a human rights society – we met historian Boris P. Trenin, director of the museum and editor-in-chief of a newly released book, *Pages from the History of the Tomsk Area 1940–1956: Unwilling Siberians.* Trenin told us that six hundred thousand kulaks were exiled to a swampy area north of Tomsk in the 1930s, and 20 per cent of them died in the first year. More deported 'unwilling Siberians' arrived in 1941 and yet thousands more in 1942. He was sure they were buried in a mass grave in a nearby ravine. He said, 'We did not have serfdom in Siberia before the Revolution. It came after 1917.' In front of the building, Memorial Society had erected a small marker in memory of the 'Victims of Bolshevism.' Trenin insisted it was not Stalinism, but Bolshevism, and that others worked with Stalin to do the murderous deeds.

With Trenin we visited the former KGB prison cells, tiny rooms off a dark narrow corridor where guards once patrolled. Passersby knew this was a prison because they saw steam rising from a barred small window below street level. A tunnel connected cells to another building with more cells, where more guards watched more prisoners. Prisoners to be executed were taken a ten-minute ride away.[11] A Tomsk museum guide in a building across the street told us she did not believe what Trenin had told us and that state officials denied it too.

In a later *New York Times* report, Clifford Levy wrote that Trenin met some retired KGB officers who admitted that in the 1930s, twice a week, prisoners were executed and thrown into the ravine.[12] Levy also wrote that Trenin was being denied access to KGB archive files – a measure that seemed to be the result of an attempt by Russian President Vladimir Putin (an ex KGB agent) to control how the Soviet past is being presented.[13]

Was Peter a Communist?

On our visit to Konstantinovka on the Kulunda steppe, we had been unable to meet the daughter of my mother's brother Peter Braun. I had a few scraps of information on this uncle. My cousin Viktor Braun in Bonn had said our uncle was a Communist. That was why he did not try to immigrate to Canada with other members of his own or his wife Selma's family. His sister-in-law Anna Reimer in Ontario had told me that exit documents for Peter's family were ready in 1924, but they had not come for them.[14] She also said my grandfather Braun had 'enticed' the couple to come to Gorchakovo, promising them half the farm.[15] I had that anecdote in Grandfather Braun's sermon note about Selma, saying she was 'on the run,' that she and the children were starving and received money from Canadian relatives in the mid-1930s. The historian in Davlekanova had promised to find whatever he could about the Peter Braun family in local archives.

I was rereading my mother's diaries, and, leafing through 1963, came to 10 August: 'Attended a wedding and a letter from Russia, from Anna.' A letter from Anna? Which Anna? Anna Braun? On 13 October, it was 'Thanksgiving in church. Missionary report,' and then '9 Nov. Peter and Selma are alive.'

So my mother knew. Both were alive. After more than thirty years, of her three brothers in the USSR presumed dead, one had survived. Already in 1963, when I was living in New York, she had known. Combing through the 'letter box,' I found letters from Selma's two sisters, Lily Wiens in Manitoba and Anna Wiens Reimer (my mother's pupil) in Ontario. I learned how difficult it had been for exiles within the Soviet Union to find each other. It could take years, come by accident, or never happen.

A relative of Lily Wiens in Manitoba had received a letter from Russia mentioning that someone named Maria Neufeld was looking for siblings who had immigrated to Canada and gave her address. In the wild hope that this was her sister, Lily wrote to the Russian address, and – it was her sister. The story repeated itself with Selma and Peter Braun. In 1961, a sister-in-law of Anna Reimer in Ontario telephoned, saying she had received a letter from someone in Siberia who knew a person named Selma who had relatives in Canada and was asking if anyone knew their whereabouts. Anna got the address, wrote a letter, and it was her sister Selma. After thirty-five years the sisters began to write to each other. When the sisters – Anna in Ontario and Lily in Manitoba – sent sisters Selma and Maria in USSR each other's addresses, those sisters discovered they had been living within eight hours' by train from one another. Each had thought the other dead.

The first letter from Selma was written to Lily in Manitoba:

Dear Sister Lily,
First, a loving greeting with Psalm 103. Quite unexpectedly and in a wonder-
ful way, the Lord has brought us together again after thirty years. We cried so
hard when we received that letter from Anni [Anna Wiens Reimer] as well as
when we looked at the photograph of you. I always have to cry when I look at
the picture. How you've changed! If Anni had not written who was who and
where each one is standing, I wouldn't have known you. And that's the way
it would be if you saw us. We don't have a picture of ourselves, but now we
want to have one taken.... Dear sister, it seems unbelievable that I am writing
to you. I lie awake the whole night and can't sleep. I always have to think of
you. Now we also have Mika's [sister Maria] address and I have written to her
already. She lives not too far from us and I will visit her soon.

Dear, dear brothers and sisters, if we could now talk face to face, how much
we would tell each other, how much has happened during these forty years that
we have not seen each other! We are doing all right now. We have our own
small house, and Peter gets his pension so that we have enough to live, but we
have had to experience such things that are impossible to describe. We have two
children left, out of five. You'll remember Lora, and Heinie was born in 1935.
Both are married and live not too far from us. The very youngest, Eduard, died
at home. The two grown-up ones, Grisha and Petya, are no longer alive. With
Job I have to say, 'The Lord has given. The Lord has taken. Blessed be the name
of the Lord.'

I must close for this time. Greet all our brothers and sisters affectionately.
P. and S. Braun
Lora sends her greetings to everyone.[16]

When my mother began corresponding with Peter and Selma, mail
to the USSR took months to arrive and each side wrote carefully, aware
of censorship. In the dozens of letters that Selma wrote to my parents
after 1963, she disclosed little of what had happened to them. After
three decades without information, she asked if perhaps *my* mother had
heard from Peter's brothers Johannes or Isaak. Selma's letters contained
nothing remotely critical or political. We know about the *Stasi* (Ministry for State Security or secret police) and its thousands of employees
engaged in opening and reading letters in East Germany (DDR), a long-
established practice also in the USSR. Selma wrote about garden and
weather, garden, weather. They owned nine hens, one rooster, had piglets to butcher in fall, but no cow for a long time. 'Last year we could

still get tinned milk for our coffee, but this year there is none.' They grew vegetables as well as gooseberries, raspberries, black currants, and a few strawberries.

Selma mentioned her family:

You remember Lora. She is married and has five children. The eldest is fourteen years old and the youngest will be two in May. However, she is not having a good life. Heinrich has only one son, Petya, who just turned seven this January. This spring they are having another little one. Our daughter-in-law is called Susa and she works in the hospital. Petya is always with us ...

You write us about Hermine [wife of Isaak], but please tell us where she and the children live.[17]

My mother sent the address of Hermine, Isaak's wife, who was then living in Alma Ata. In 1964 Selma and Peter managed to visit her:

First, an affectionate greeting of peace with Psalm 12.... Yes, how happy you look surrounded by your children. And for us, there were ten, if they had all grown up.... Now I want to tell you that in July we visited Isaak Braun's children Viktor and Liesel. We heard a lot about Hermine, about her difficult illness and her death. We also heard much sad news about Isaak, which cannot be described. I always weep when I think of how he had to suffer!

Liesel also told us a lot about her unhappy life with her husband, who mistreated her so badly that she twice landed in a mental institution. And now she is unable to hold down a full-time position, has to do light work because of her mental health. She is having a difficult time with her three children. Dear ones, you are so many there and are doing well, could you help Liesel a little, like my brothers and sister in Canada do for us? ...

The watermelons are beginning to ripen, but here so much is stolen from the gardens. Peter and I take turns keeping guard until 12 and 1 o'clock at night. It is too much of a shame if they should tear up everything after we have had so much work with the garden ... There aren't many potatoes this year. There was very little rain this summer, but maybe they will still grow a little after the rain. Here the winter is very long and the summer is too short....[18]

In a following letter Selma wrote she still wept for her grown sons Grisha and Petya 'in their hunger and misery.' Ten children, and half did not grow up? But ten children meant that the parents were together at least until 1935 when the youngest, Eduard (who died at home), was born. From Selma's letters, I slowly put together that they now lived in the foothills of a mountain chain in a small village beside the Ida River. At that high altitude the weather was extremely raw, with snow covering the tops of houses. There were snow tunnels between the house, barn, and outhouse. Often in the spring the river jammed up, with ice chunks cracking against the side of the house, forcing the elderly couple to scramble to carry their few belongings into the attic before the house flooded. Until a comforter was sent from Canada. they had no proper bed coverings, just rags. With chronic health problems, they comforted themselves with 'Whom the Lord loves, he punishes.'[19] Selma loved flowers and poetry and often quoted scripture or lines from a hymn; she remembered birthdays and wrote about their granddaughter. She discussed Liesel's unhappy marriage:

Liesel writes that she received the package you sent and was so happy to get it ... you ask if her husband will return. He has deserted his family three times and took up with another woman. Also, he told her once, 'I'm going to get you into the insane asylum, your mother Hermine underground, and the children into an orphanage.' ... All three children said they didn't want him anymore.... Liesel also says that it is a lot his fault that Hermine died. But we don't want to judge, because he is the judge who will judge correctly.[20]

In their village most men drank to excess, and daughter Lora's husband, a Volga German, was no exception. Selma and Peter missed a community of believers, felt cut off and lonely. Once a month, by bus they drove seventy kilometres into Ust Kamenogorsk to attend a communion service and stay overnight with friends. Unless they hauled bucket after bucket to water their vegetables during the brief, hot summer, they would starve. When Selma wrote, 'There are only two German families left,' I assumed there used to be more and that this was a deportation site for Soviet Germans. In 1967 when Selma's sister Maria moved to their village with her daughter and son-in-law, Selma was less lonely.

Selma and Peter enjoyed books from Canada, and Anna Reimer seemed to be able to get more sent through than my parents – she also sent narcissus bulbs. Letters with a religious tract or booklet seldom arrived. Selma requested the book *Ben Hur*, which my parents sent, but it never arrived. One could gauge the intensity of the Cold War by the mail – poor in 1968 when the Soviets invaded Czechoslovakia. When books did arrive, Peter read them to Selma, after her eyesight became weaker. Wool from Canadian sisters kept Selma knitting, but her handwriting was getting shaky. Blind in one eye, in 1970 Selma wrote, 'Andrusha and Sonya [their names had been Heinrich and Susa] work hard. I can't write details about them. You understand, don't you?'

To help celebrate Selma and Peter's golden wedding anniversary in 1971, Viktor and Liesel Braun came from Alma Ata, and a photograph was taken.[21] In 1972 Peter fell while shovelling snow and broke his left hand – a sorry thing for a seventy-seven-year-old man. There was more thieving, with even flowers being stolen at night unless the old folk watched vigilantly. After Liesel Braun wrote that the plum harvest was overflowing and invited them to come and dry as many as they wished, they again visited Isaak Braun's children in Alma Ata and enjoyed singing with musical accompaniment in a church service. That summer saw a drought in northern Kazakhstan and there was little feed for their few animals. In 1975 no books were getting through, not even from Anna Reimer. By 1976, aged eighty and eighty-one, they found the garden work difficult and Peter's hand hurt when he chopped wood, yet the irises were budding and the peonies blooming. In 1977 Selma wrote a final letter:

I am losing my balance and keep falling. My left leg and hand are shaking all the time and I am almost blind as well. Peter has to do everything himself now and he's not well either. From now on Peter will write to you, if you can read Russian. Wishing you the goodness of the Lord. Live well. May we meet again at God's throne.[22]

Peter wrote seven more letters in Russian, and at the time of his last letter in 1982, the couple were living with their daughter Lora in a cold, state-owned building. Both had debilitating medical problems and Selma was bedridden. Nothing in Selma's letters suggested (what Viktor had insisted) that Peter Braun had joined the Party. It seems what sustained this isolated couple was their Christian faith and their recovered links with family members. From their correspondence I knew nothing more about why they were 'on the run' in mid-1930 or ended up in Kazakhstan – or what happened to their sons.

On our Trans-Siberian trip, I had failed to meet their daughter Lora, but back in Toronto I heard from the historian in Davlekanova that Peter Braun had been a member of the local Davlekanova chapter of the All-Russian Mennonite Agricultural Association (AMLV).[23] Most of the leaders of this organization, formed in 1923 and disbanded under government pressure in 1928, were arrested in the early 1930s. The aim of the AMLV was to promote the restoration, development, and improvement of Mennonite agriculture as a whole.[24] Mennonites reasoned, why join a Communist organization when your own people were succeeding in improving agricultural production through AMLV. Though legal, the AMLV was viewed by the Soviets as unpatriotic and in competition with Soviet state plans for co-op agriculture.[25] Recent research in the Zaporozhye archives, supported by the interrogation records seen in 2007, shows that the Soviets viewed the AMLV as a German spy organization. Mennonites spoke German and resisted Bolshevism. Conclusion? They must be anti-Soviet. Judging by the arrest of most AMLV leaders, it is reasonable to assume that AMLV member Peter Braun was on a target list, but escaped. How?

I finally got some answers from Peter's daughter Lora:

5 December 2001
… Anne, I could not come to Kulunda because I did not have money and I could not send you a return telegram because I did not have money for that either. We live from one pension payment to the next and it is too small.… I have a husband and five children. Two of them live in Ust Kamenogorsk and two live with us. The youngest one lives in Germany. My mother had ten children but many were born premature or did not live long and we grew up as five siblings. The last one died when he was five and then we were three brothers and myself.

We were deported to Kazakhstan. We lived there one year, October 1941–2, and then they started to round us up into the Trudarmiia. *First they took my two brothers and then my father and then me. My mother and Andrei stayed back. My two brothers Grisha and Petya died in the* Trudarmiia. *Father was released from the* Trudarmiia *because his health was so terrible that he was expected to die anyway. He had only rags for clothing and was all swollen from starvation, but he walked home. Mama nursed him back to health. She sold everything she had to get him on his feet. I returned from the Labour Army in 1948 and since then I have been living in Verkh Uba.*

Lora had solved some riddles about my mother's early years. She wrote about life in Gorchakovo, about living with the Isaak Braun family in the same house, about her and her brothers Griesha and Petya playing with their young cousins Viktor and Liesel. She remembered driving to church, reciting poems for her parents, and then receiving presents on Christmas Eve. She wrote that her Uncle Isaak was a good preacher who often drove out to the Russian villages and who sang well. Her father had told her painful memories of his childhood:

There were five children from the first wife, and the stepmother had four children. I was four years old and Isaak was two years old. Luise [my mother], age eight, stood up for us. She took pity on us, was kind and loving. At the breakfast table stepmother, father, and their children sat on one side of the table and we children of our mother on the other side. They drank coffee with full milk, but we got skim milk. The children of our stepmother had white bread with butter, but we had black bread, and I don't know if anything was on it. Stepmother loved her own children but found fault with everything Isaak and I did. She never had one good word for us, or ever showed us any affection. One time our stepmother threw me into the pigpen. The pigs were so huge that I thought I would go insane, but our sister helped me out. My brother Isaak and I lived without love and tenderness and nobody needed us. How fortunate that we had our sister to share all our troubles and sorrows. My father never said anything to our stepmother about how she treated us.[26]

Lora also explained how and why her father, Peter, survived.

They started to hunt for my father, to jail him, but he had a good friend in the NKVD, and when they wanted to arrest my father one night, his friend always told him and we always escaped at night. We were all over Russia, running, and could not find a safe place. We were on the run and we had nothing to eat or to wear. We had a very difficult life, but thanks to my mother's relatives who twice sent us five dollars that we could take to the Torgsin where you could buy anything with dollars. They saved our lives.

In another letter she explained what had happened in 1924, when Selma's family had procured visas for them to emigrate, but Peter's family did not show up in Moscow:

My father and Uncle Isaak, their passports were ready in 1924, but they did not have money so Papa asked Uncle Jakob Braun to lend him money, but he would not give any. Papa said, 'I will work it off,' but still he did not give the money, and he was rich because his wife was from a rich family. He always laughed at Papa and Isaak and said, 'You cannot live because you are so poor.' Papa never spoke about him. When collectivization was enforced in 1929, of course there was no more individual farming. Because of that we are so poor.

We have always lived in the village of Verkh Uba. We have lived poorly all our lives and we are poor now, but I do not complain. Everything is in the hand of God.[27]

I now knew I had a grandfather who, in 1924, sold machinery (left behind after the pogrom at his farm) and used the money *only* for himself, his second wife, and their children. In my interview with him, as noted, Uncle Henry in Abbotsford had boasted that money was left over. With his stepmother, father, and younger siblings gone, Peter had next asked his brother Jakob (who left in 1929) for a loan, but Jakob had refused to help him. No wonder my mother said she had a difficult childhood in such a family! It was unusual that trustworthy friends within the secret police alerted or hid Peter when he was in danger of arrest. To have such friends, Peter Braun might have been pro-communist (my cousin Viktor's view). Lora wrote that her parents had given up their religion in the 1930s, but found it again in the 1950s. But why then was he 'on the run'? It could have been the AMLV connection.

The family's exile to Kazakhstan seems to have been part of the massive deportations of 'unreliable' ethnic minorities following Hitler's invasion of the USSR in 1941. In one letter Lora wrote their 'drop off' was a mining area at Sekisovka, a village forty kilometres north of Ust Kamenogorsk, in East Kazakhstan, where her father was a bookkeeper. In several subsequent letters she wrote about the *Trudarmiia*. Her father, and brother Petya had been in Prokopyevsk in the Kuznetsk Basin, the second-largest coal-producing area in the USSR after Donbas:

My father and brother Petya worked together. As the result of hunger and hard work, Petya caught tuberculosis. Later my father became sick.... As long as Petya was with Father, things went well, but after Father left, all his belongings were stolen and he was unable to go to work. He received no food and soon his tuberculosis became virulent. He was put into the infirmary and wrote my mother begging for money. She sent money, but as it went from one infirmary to the next, he got weaker and weaker, so that by the time it arrived he was dead.... My brother Griesha was sent to Kazan and from there south where he died of overwork and starvation. An acquaintance of our father told us this.[28]

Along with two thousand other German and other deported women, Lora was sent to the city of Sesran on the Volga River and remained there for five years and three months. I won't repeat all the horrors of being in the *Trudarmaiia* but will touch on a few excerpts.

All the things that we experienced there are too awful to write about. It has to be told. Due to hunger we grew white hair on our faces and people feared us.... marched to work and ... Watchtowers and guards were at every corner.... But where could you escape to.... We were assigned heavy manual work, digging a trench for an oil pipeline ... assigned a quota to complete each day ... always hungry ... our rations reduced ... 500 grams a day. Today not even swine would eat that bread ... I can't describe them all.[29]

The highest death rates were in the second half of 1942 when 25.9 per cent of all Germans in forced labour camps perished.[30] As forced labour workers, Lora's family had a 50 per cent casualty rate. (We can now view paintings of that Soviet program on websites.)[31] In our correspondence, Lora stated that many Germans originally exiled to Verkh Uba had died or had immigrated to Germany after 1980.

We were able to send Lora funds through her son in Germany and planned a visit in the summer of 2004, but she died in April. Lora's son Alexander sent us the news along with photos of her funeral – her children and grandchildren, dressed in cheap jackets, standing dejected behind her open coffin.

With Lora's sad letters my search for my missing relatives had ended. I had told their stories, and others could now share their sorrows. I hoped, as Andrei Makine wrote, they would be released into the world liberated from evil.[32] But then came an opportunity to read the interrogation files.

10

The NKVD Records

In Donets'k

We are in the Ukrainian Security Service (SBU) building in Donets'k. Two files given to us are thick, and one is slim. Reading quickly, Harvey skims through the files for an overview. The file for Johannes Braun includes twenty-five cases of men arrested at the same time; all except one are Mennonite names. We have only three hours to make notes, so he and Ludmilla translate as I write. At one point, overwhelmed by a migraine, I put my head down, and immediately the watchful guard telephones. What now? Will they tell us to leave? The next thing I know a tall white-smocked female doctor is taking my blood pressure. 'Just write, write,' urges Harvey, conscious of time.

'Have you eaten?'

When Ludmilla says I've not eaten all day, the doctor commands, 'You must eat.' She makes a phone call and the next moment someone brings in a cup of black tea with two cookies and packets of sugar. 'We'll check the blood pressure again in half an hour. Eat!' Ludmilla reads and I write. In half an hour two white-smocked women appear, one to watch as the other untangles the blood pressure cuff and retakes my blood pressure. 'A little better.' Write, write.

The handwriting on the yellowed pages is in purple ink, difficult to decipher (aren't confessions typed?). The name of the interrogator is Gnutov. (Would he have been seated behind a desk?) The interrogator has written that Ivan I. Braun, an enemy of the people, was arrested on 23 December 1937, is of 'middle class,' owned four horses, two cows, six small cattle, agricultural machinery, and sixty desiatinas of land, did not serve in the Red or White Army, and was not a Party member. Those points are probably correct. Another entry states I.I. Braun is a 'noble-man from the Omsk area' and again a 'former minister of the Baptist Brethren community.' Those false descriptions suit a Soviet purpose, making him out to be a *bourgeois* and religious *hostile* person. With false data and no real evidence, the aim is to turn an accusation into a proven fact. Lacking is any record of a prisoner being worn down by threats, sleep and food deprivation, or physical torture. The indictment reads,

Ivan I. Braun was a member of a counter-revolutionary, Trotskyite, Fascist, rebellious organization that existed in the Stalino district. The organization operated in the interests of fascist Germany. He is an enemy of the people who harmed collective farms and conducted counter revolutionary conversations. He is accused under Articles 54:2, 54:9, and 54:11.[1]

The following record of interrogation is two days after his arrest:

25 December 1937

GNUTOV. Are you a member of a counter-revolutionary organization and did you harm collective farms?

BRAUN. No I am not a member of a counter-revolutionary organization. I did some harmful work on farms.

GNUTOV. Explain how you are not a member of a counter-revolutionary organization, but harmed farms.

BRAUN. I had hostile feelings. I did agricultural work incorrectly and the director of the MTS tractor station, Vuvok, who was arrested as an enemy of the people, did not stop my destructive activity and gave me harmful directions.

GNUTOV. What contact did you have with Vuvok?

BRAUN. I worked under his guidance. Under his orders I ploughed the land, seeded, and harvested. I reported my work to him but had no direct contact with counter-revolutionary work.

GNUTOV. Did you know that Vuvok was a member of a counter-revolutionary organization?

BRAUN. I did not know that Vuvok was a member of a counter-revolutionary organization.

'Counter-revolutionary activity' (article 54 in the Soviet Ukrainian criminal code corresponds with article 58 in the Soviet Russian code) covers traitors, spies, subversives, saboteurs, anti-state propagandists, bourgeois nationalists, émigré agents, and hostile persons. In the ensuing interrogation, Gnutov accuses I.I. Braun (Johannes) of 'deliberately ordering shallow ploughing of land, decreasing the productivity of farm fields' – in other words, sabotage. As the interrogation continues, on paper – but who knows if in fact – Johannes Braun slowly begins to admit to more and more 'harmful work on farms.' A scenario of misdeeds develops.

Gnutov asks if Vuvok's 'harmful directions' resulted in Braun's not caring how the combines worked when harvesting wheat, and if his order for shallow cultivation of the land resulted in a reduction in the grain crop. Braun admits that following Vuvok's directions resulted in a loss of grain, a reduction in farm worker salaries, less fodder for the winter, and an anti-combine mood among the farmers in 1936 and 1937.

The line of questioning may have had something to do with a constant hunt for saboteurs.

Having secured an admission of wrongdoing in agriculture, Interrogator Gnutov turned to the second charge of organizing and being a member of a counter-revolutionary, Trotskyite, Fascist, diversionist, and rebellious organization existing in the Stalino district, Donetsk region.

GNUTOV. *Did you engage in counter-revolutionary work?*

BRAUN. *I confess that in 1936 in my home I spoke with Dietrich Dahl, saying that it is good to live where his father lives in America and that in Germany life is good. In Ukraine it is difficult or hard. We said that Germany will soon attack the Soviet Union and capture Ukraine and then Germans will live here as before.*

Braun's signature (Ivan I. Braun) appears on the bottom of each page. The next interrogation is dated twenty-four days later. Obviously this is a heavily redacted file with many interrogations missing. By this date the interrogator has pressed a confession out of one of the twenty-four men arrested with Johannes Braun. This person becomes the government 'witness' and now (who knows after how many nightly intimidation methods) Gnutov introduces his 'witness' H.P. Thiessen.

19 January 1938

GNUTOV. *H.P. Thiessen witnessed against you and said you were a member of an organization involved in counter-revolutionary activity. Do you admit this?*

BRAUN. *I admit that I am a member.*

GNUTOV. By whom, when, and under what circumstances were you recruited?

BRAUN. Heinrich Thiessen recruited me in 1935 under the following circumstances. I had known Thiessen since 1932 but we were not close. In 1935 Thiessen was elected chairman of the Petrovsky collective farm in Nikolaievka. At that time I worked as an agronomist in Selidovka. Because of my work I had relations with him as chair of a collective farm.

Since then we met often. He praised fascist Germany and said that the Soviet Union would win in a war. In 1935 Thiessen told me of a counter-revolutionary, Trotskyite organization and told me that this organization does rebellious work and has relations with other counter-revolutionary organizations in Donbas and that all the fascist work is supervised by the German consulate.

GNUTOV. What did Thiessen tell you about the counter-revolutionary organization?

BRAUN. Thiessen told me that the counter-revolutionary organization is under the direction of the German consulate. In a war with Germany against the USSR the organization will harm industry, railways, and agriculture. The counter-revolutionary organization must conduct an armed rebellion in the rear of the Red Army and thereby help Germany capture Soviet Ukraine.

Thiessen welcomed me to join the organization and I gave my consent. Thiessen gave me tasks to fulfil on the collective farm, such as sabotage. I received these tasks from Thiessen and I carried them out.

GNUTOV. What tasks did you carry out?

BRAUN. I personally recruited the following people.

Braun names the twenty-three other arrested Mennonite men: an elementary school teacher, a laboratory technician, a farmer, a former minister, a person who received a food package from North America, a person with relatives in North America, a former expediter, an accountant, a brigade leader on the collective farm, a cashier in Selidovka, two relatives, and so on. Among the persons named, the youngest is nineteen. Gnutov then asks his 'witness' Thiessen what he knows about Braun's counter-revolutionary activity. Thiessen says he knows that Braun recruited the twenty-three persons.[2] Gnutov then finds Ivan I. Braun guilty of enmity and of having carried out sabotage on the collective farm.

All of the men named in the file, including H.P. Thiessen, are found guilty and I.I. Braun is sentenced to death by shooting.

Nothing in the file tells if, where, or when this occurred, or how long I.I. Braun lived after he was condemned to death. An execution (a shot in the cervical vertebrae at the base of the skull or back of the head at the neck was standard) usually followed within six weeks. This happened at night in the basement of the prison where few would hear the shots.

Historian Kuromiya found that a burial site was excavated in 1989 at Rutchenkove outside Donetsk and that most of the bodies from the NKVD prison were dumped there.[3] He quotes an estimate of twenty-seven thousand to thirty thousand persons executed in Stalino oblast, with fifteen thousand executed in Donetsk between July 1937 and the end of 1938, over-fulfilling the Soviet 'control plan' by 15 per cent.[4]

As I wrote out the fraudulent questions and answers inscribed on yellowed paper seventy years earlier, I tried to imagine the brother my mother so greatly admired in the basement of this building. I remembered how his daughter Alici ached from the loss of her father, how she kept his portrait beside her guitar on her bedroom wall, the first face she saw when she woke up and the last face she saw as she fell asleep.

I had assumed that the answers were false but had not expected so much of the interrogation to be missing or fraudulent. In our visits with his children, Andrei and Alici had told us how Johannes received awards for good yields on the collective farm. They told me they saw the bicycle and gramophone.[5] Torture could have been used. On 25 December, two days after he was arrested, Braun denied belonging to a counter-revolutionary organization, and twenty-four days later he had led one! I compare this file with one in Zaporozhye where twenty-two interrogations took place (the survivor's statement) but only three were in an interrogation file given to a relative.[6]

What could be interpolated from this record?

Because of his higher level of education, position, and age (forty-eight), Ivan I. Braun was fingered as the 'ringleader' of a counter-revolutionary organization that never existed. Frantic about Hitler's anti-Bolshevism, the Soviets targeted ethnic Germans (including Mennonites) as traitors and fabricated evidence. To justify the closing of German consulates in the USSR, evidence was needed. As the Belkowez historians revealed, no ordinary Soviet citizen dared to approach a German consulate after the mid-1930s or wanted to work for the consulate in Kiev for fear of being arrested.[7] Even relatives of consular staff were arrested, so the story of a lowly agronomist from the Donetsk basin plotting with the German consulate is preposterous. German consulates in Kharkov and Odessa in Soviet Ukraine were closed on 15 November 1937.[8]

The twenty-four men, belonging to the same ethno-religious group, were seen as disloyal citizens, German spies. During the famine of the 1930s many of them with relatives living in Canada or abroad had received parcels or small sums of money, often via Germany. As previously mentioned, such activity, which was legal until 1936 – promoted by the Soviet government to meet its need for foreign currency from 1930 to 1935 – these 'Hitler's crumbs' were 'disloyalty.' Mennonites in the USSR had resisted communism fairly consistently. They had embarrassed the Soviets in 1929 by fleeing to Moscow. They had stubbornly held with their religion. They had relatives abroad who were anti-Bolshevik. This NKVD record shows how the Soviets aimed to get rid of them.

Heinrich's File

The SBU building was closing at six, and the female guard dressed in black was pacing. Quickly we turned to Case #24548 P.F., the file of Heinrich Jakovlevich Konrad, my father's brother.[9]

[Dates illegible]

QUESTION. *Give your background.*

ANSWER. *I was declared a kulak in July 1929.*

My brother Abram was in Frunze and invited me to come to Frunze. I wanted to leave for Mongolia in 1930, but was not allowed to go. In 1933, I left Mongolia. I corresponded with my brother Abram and with my wife's Mamentov family in the Caucasus.

QUESTION. *What did you do in Snezhnoie?*

ANSWER. *In 1937 I met with someone named Lupe and started to struggle against Soviet power. I did sabotage in the bakery.*

QUESTION. *Who is Lupe?*

ANSWER. *Lupe, dekulakized, lives in Snezhnoie. At the bakery he is a bookkeeper assistant.*

QUESTION. *What did you do at the bakery?*

ANSWER. *I added mouldy flour to the bread to adulterate it. I did this to make workers dissatisfied. I delayed the baking and the delivery of bread. I added mice to the bread.*

QUESTION. *Did you engage in any other activity?*

ANSWER. *No, no other activity.*

QUESTION. *Did you recruit anybody?*

ANSWER. *I did not recruit anybody. I know three people were recruited. I don't know them.*

On 15 February 1938, a neighbour of Heinrich Konrad had witnessed against him (he was arrested on 28 February 1938), and on 4 March 1938, another witness slandered him. On 17 March 1938, Heinrich admitted that he sabotaged the bread and was recruited by I.I. Schmidt to join an armed rebellion against the Soviet Union. Also that in 1933 he was involved in a counter-revolutionary organization, that he set fire to an electric motor, and added crushed glass to the bread.

He was found guilty by a troika.

On 9 October 1938, eight months after he was torn from his family, not able to take leave of his wife and child running behind the sleigh, in a dank prison, Heinrich Konrad was executed. Fifty some years later his daughter received a letter (case #12-530) – enclosed in the file – that he was innocent and was rehabilitated.[10]

We were still frantically scribbling when the time was up. 6:00 p.m. Friday closing. The guard kissed each of us on the cheek, leaving red lipstick. We thanked her and she asked Ludmilla if we were pleased with our reception. She suggested that next time we came we should give two days' notice.

Nothing in the file had said, 'We're sorry.' Nobody admitted it was a grave injustice.

Interrogation Records in Kherson

Having completed our responsibilities at a conference in Dnepro-petrovsk, Harvey and I began our seven-hour bus trip to Kherson. On good roads, we passed blackened fields of stunted sunflowers on a dry steppe. Situated near the mouth of the Dnieper River that empties into the Black Sea, Kherson was to be Catherine the Great's new city to rival St Petersburg. Prince Grigorii Alexandrovich Potemkin, Catherine's lover (some say husband), brilliant diplomat and general, chose the site, built the city, and laid out grand tree-lined avenues, parks, and squares, but died on the steppes. His tomb is midtown in the modest St Catherine's Cathedral.[11] The broad river had a harbour too shallow for a second St Petersburg.

In 1943 Hermine Braun and children, on their trek out of Soviet Ukraine, had waited anxiously in Kherson to be evacuated, and now we were here to examine the secret police file of her husband, father of Viktor, Liesel, and Yasha – my mother's little brother Isaak. On these streets, our quest seemed unreal. Early morning sidewalks were filled with elegant women (bleached blond or henna) in the shortest skirts, stiletto heels, and high boots, and men carrying leather purses that reminded me of metal lunch buckets carried by men of my childhood.

A clerk at the state archive directed us to an open staircase leading to a large reading room where several researchers pored over texts. After handing her a letter I had received from the Kherson archivist, Assistant Director Elena Stukalovo brought us Isaak Braun's file and said, 'Yes, you may use your computer. Yes, you may photocopy.' The reading room was bright with light. A large window overlooked a pink-painted school where teenagers loitered outdoors. Nobody monitored the four desks where researchers examined documents. The door to an adjoining office was open. At lunchtime an archivist walked us down the stairs, took us across a large square filled with orange and blue election posters and white booths sporting red hearts for Yulya (Ukraine's election was taking place in two days), and directed us to an outdoor café. Passing a colossal Lenin statue towering above beds of yellow marigolds, the archivist joked that Lenin 'guarded the White House.'

Seventy years after his arrest, in this city with fluttering election colours – not Soviet red, but orange and blue – it was hard to picture Black Raven trucks grinding to a stop at the nearby SBU headquarters and disgorging ragged farm workers smelling of sweat, hands tied behind their backs.

Isaak I. Braun's file, in a thick cardboard binder, contained forty-seven double-sided pages hand-sewn together. The pages, typed in purple ink, had a black ink stamp and a signature at the bottom, a USSR on the top. Some handwritten pages were difficult to read and some lines were underlined in red.[12] The helpful archivist, whose relatives had suffered similarly, offered to have the file photocopied before we left. She knew she would have to cut and redo the hand sewing. The only pages not to be photocopied were witness statements, but these we copied manually.

The document covered two arrests, the initial one in Kichkas in 1936 where Isaak Braun was released when his fellow 'criminals' were given prison sentences, and his rearrest in 1938 at the collective in Mikailovka. The 1936 documents supported what his son Viktor had told us in Bonn, that he was accused of holding religious services. Isaak had an advocate (Viktor's 'goodman') and a witness had mistaken him for 'Wall.'

But the file revealed more. We saw the names, social background, and occupations of the ten Mennonites tried with him in 1936. Two were registered preachers and four were from so-called kulak families dispossessed (dekulakized) in Mennonite settlements in Crimea and Molochna who had moved to the industrial area. One had a supervisory position in a local children's sanatorium, two more were from the Volga area, and one was a German Colonist accused of being resentful of Soviet policies and 'praising the regime of one capitalist country.'[13] The eldest man in the group, Ivan Vasilievich Leven (Johann Loewen), 'from a kulak family,' a Mennonite, sixty-two, was accused of being the most active leader. Isaak Braun did not seem to know the two men from the Volga region, recent arrivals in Kichkas. Like Isaak, all eleven men had moved to the Zaporozhye area to become 'invisible.' None of the eleven had previous convictions and all were described as 'active church figures,' ethnic Germans, non-partisan, literate, married, non-manual workers – not proletarians. The 1936 arrests suggest a crackdown on a targeted socio-economic class of religious German-speakers.

The men in the 1936 Kichkas group were tried together but were arrested on different days over a period of several months from March to May. All were accused of pretending to meet for religious services, but actually being a counter-revolutionary group working to overthrow the government, spreading false rumours about a 'saviour,' and attempting to influence children and adults to oppose the regime.

The process of obtaining false confessions became obvious. To extract a confession to use in confrontation against the others, it was the rule never to have them together in one cell. Church worker Loewen (Leven), a church organizer from a Mennonite settlement some 110 kilometres out of Zaporozhye, was arrested on 3 March. Isaak Braun – a lay missionary to the Russian population living around Gorchakovo, but never appointed as a preacher – was arrested on 8 March. On 4 April Gerhard Dyck was arrested. The next day two Klassen preachers were arrested, and on 7 April Josef Kreiter from the Kuban was arrested. The following day Franz Wall (Frantz Vaal) from Crimea became a prisoner, and two weeks later another two men were arrested. Finally, number eleven was arrested in a children's sanatorium on 12 May.

Nightly interrogations followed. When a closed court finally took place on 26–7 August, Isaak Braun had been incarcerated for almost six months. He was recorded as making this statement:

26 August 1936. I attended religious meetings. I heard nothing of counter-rev-

olutionary things there. There was nothing done with children. Jakob Klassen, David Klassen, Neufeld, and Vaal [Wall] visited my house, but there was nothing said that could be deemed as anti-Soviet. I completely do not know Martens or Toews. I did not listen to radio addresses. But Kreiter told me personally that he had heard broadcasts of speeches of Hitler and Goebbels. My father has lived in Canada since 1924. I received money that my father sent me.[14]

Sentencing was held off until 8 October 1936 when the Supreme Court of Soviet Ukraine upheld the verdicts. On the basis of articles 296, 297, and 302 of the UK USSR, the special panel sentenced preachers David and Jakob Klassen, Ivan Leven, and Ivan Neufeld, Vaal (Wall), Rempel, and Dyck to labour camps in remote parts of the Soviet Union for periods from three to seven years, but freed Isaak Braun.[15] Ironically, those sentenced may have benefited because they were gone from home when the massive purges took place in 1937 and 1938. Not known is how many survived their sentences and returned.[16]

At Isaak Braun's second arrest on 8 March 1938, he was first taken to a jail where a local investigator produced four witnesses to testify against him. Their statements were amazingly similar. In 1961 this farce of using government-appointed witnesses was acknowledged in a document containing a resolution of the Presidium of the Kherson Regional Court reviewing the case – three witnesses 'served in nearly all cases of those arrested in 1937–8 in Mikhailovka village.'[17]

As each 'witness' – one a fellow Mennonite – began to speak, Isaak knew he was doomed.[18] The witnesses were Abram Jakobovich Pankratz (a Mennonite), Andrush (Andrei) Abrams, David Abrams, and Robert A. Bikhe from Mikhailovka (Michaelsburg). All had identical backgrounds: they had 'low education' (*nizhne*), were ethnic German (could be Volynian Germans), and were proletarian. Two men claimed to have known Isaak Braun since 1936, disagreed on where he had lived, but agreed on his crimes. The accusations were inventions about the census, loans, elections, and, significantly, concerned Hitler.

QUESTION. Do you know of anti-Soviet utterances by the accused?

WITNESS PANKRATZ. Well, in his house he organized a group of Baptists and led them in religious services. In some of the services anti-Soviet things were said. He said positive things about Germany.

QUESTION. How do you characterize the political outlook of Braun?

WITNESS PANKRATZ. Braun was a middle peasant and a Baptist. He personally conducted services in his own house and he agitated among middle peasants in the village not to sign for some loans. The government had a campaign to get people to sign for some loans and Braun urged the middle peasants not to participate in the elections of the Supreme Soviet. He agitated for democracy. He said there is no democracy in the Soviet Union. He said Yezhov [head of secret police] and Stalin are not good. He said Hitler is good. He said soon Soviet power will end and Hitler will succeed. Russia will become part of Germany.

QUESTION. Do you know I.I. Braun?

WITNESS ROBERT BIKHE. He came from Donbas into Michaelsburg. He gathered in his house a circle of believers for prayer and religious services. And in 1938 when Trotsky was being tried, he said Trotsky was [something favourable]. Braun began to agitate among the population during the census. He said they should not report accurately. He said Soviet power will end and a different than communist power will come.

After being accused at the Michailovka village council office, Isaak Braun was taken to the town of Lepetikha (Velikaya Lepeticha) where the next day the NKVD officer Karmanov drew up a statement that accompanied Braun, and the men arrested with him, to NKVD (KGB) headquarters in the capital of the oblast at Kherson.[19]

Michailovka Village Council
B.-Lepetikhskiy district
9 March 1938
Given by the Mikhailovka village council and stating that citizen Isaak Isaakovich Braun, a former preacher, who arrived in Mikhailovka in 1936, has actively undertaken to organize a group of believers in Mikhailovka. He had a kulak farm, worked as a guard in the collective farm, did not show up at the duty post, but slept at home. On check-up he stated that 'I am not interested in being a guard at the farm.' He sought to undermine the work in the artel by categorically refusing to work in the busiest work periods, thus doing damage to the collective farm. In general, he is morally unreliable.

Resolution

In the town of B.-Lepetikha. The 8th day of March 1938. I, Karmanov, commissioner of B.-Lepetikhskiy NKVD of the USSR, having considered the materials incriminating citizen Isaak Isaakovich Braun, born in Gorchakovskiy uezd of Davlekanovskiy district in Nikolaev region, of average means, non-partisan, ethnic German, a volunteer in Kolchak's army, married, and convicted under article 54-10, of the crimes stipulated in article 54-10 of the UK USSR.

I have found that the undertaken investigation has established that Braun, possessing distinctly anti-Soviet attitudes and embittered against the Soviet authorities, systematically has carried out counter-revolutionary, fascist agitation with defeatist sentiments among people by holding disputes and debasing the activities of the party and the government.

The next pages in this file included a transcript of one interrogation in the NKVD headquarters in Kherson. Only one. We had to imagine four nights of interrogations, the questions, threats, and answers that preceded his 'confession.' In the interrogation Isaak Braun was asked about his religious activities, those leading to his 1936 arrest and those in Mikhailovka village. He now stated that he was set free in 1936, thanks only to the court having been in Zaporozhye.

ANSWER. They did not have full evidential materials since all of my anti-Soviet activities were done at the place of my birth; so the court accepted my testimony and my words, and thus acquitted me.

QUESTION. The investigators have the information that being distinctly disposed and embittered against the Soviet authorities, you systematically carried out anti-Soviet, nationalist agitation among the population. Do you confirm this?

ANSWER. Yes, I confirm and plead guilty in that having religious beliefs, I systematically undertook anti-Soviet, nationalist agitation. I said that life is much better in Germany. I referred in offending terms to the government of the Soviet Union and said that I would not defend the Soviet Union in the case of war, but would on the contrary go against the Soviet authorities and kill their representatives inside the country.

[Signature of the accused]

[End of page]

QUESTION. Under whose counter-revolutionary influence did you conduct the counter-revolutionary, nationalist, and fascist agitation?

ANSWER. No one influenced me in this. Being discontented with the Soviet authorities, I myself carried out the counter-revolutionary, nationalist agitation amongst the population. I plead completely guilty, that while holding religious beliefs, I systematically carried out counter-revolutionary activities to undermine the efforts in the village by the party and the government.

The transcript was read to me in understandable language and my words were recorded correctly. To confirm, I sign here.

[Signature of the accused]

Secretary of the Troika

[seal and signature]

Sheinberg

The wording of his signed confession may have been changed completely from what he said. He may have signed earlier on an empty page. Then too, men like Isaak Braun, trying to protect their families, could sign a confession after a threat to evict wife and children from their home. Isaak Braun was traumatized from his prison experience in 1936 (his son Viktor's testimony) and was in a vulnerable mental state following his release. Were the charges not so deadly, one could laugh at these inventions. I noted that Isaak Braun did not implicate others as 'fellow conspirators,' as normally required. In the end I saw a devout man brought to his knees, tears scalding his face as he was driven to sign his death warrant.

Six weeks after his conviction, a prison court condemned him to death. He then waited one more month for his name to be called shortly before midnight. Taken out, he was shot through the back of the neck.

The resolution of the Troika of UNKVD for Nikolaev region of 22 April 1938 on death by shooting of Isaak Isaakovich Braun, born in 1899, was carried into effect on 21 June 1938 at 24:00 [midnight] Acting comm.

Kherson city unit of UNKVD
[Signature] Pavlenko[20]

For twenty-three years, Isaak's family had lived in hope that he had been sent to the 'high North,' and in fear that he was dead. Finally, during Khrushchev's era, his daughter Liesel wrote to the KGB in Moscow. Her letter was in the file.

Head of Directorate of Labour Camps and Labour Settlements
Ministry of Internal Affairs of the USSR
10 March 1961
From: citizen Elizaveta Is. Braun
I, citizen Elizaveta Isaakovna Braun, am writing to you with an important request relating to my father. My father – Isaak Isaakovich Braun – was born on 30 March 1899 in Gorchakovo village, Davlekanovka district, Bashkirskaya ASSR, Ufa region, where he lived and worked. Later on, we moved to Mikhailovka village, B.-Lepetikha district, Zaporozhye region. He did basic jobs at the Engels Collective Farm. He was arrested on 8 March 1938, and there has been no news of him since. As a daughter, I am interested to know for what he was convicted. I ask you to consider my request and answer my questions.
[to this I affix] my signature
[Signature] Braun[21]

In 1961 the USSR Prosecutor's Office, Kherson region, conducted a thorough investigation and wrote that it had attempted to contact and interrogate the witnesses against her father to assess the veracity of their statements, but none could be located. It had attempted to find people who attended prayer meetings that Braun allegedly had organized, to question them if he used anti-Soviet agitation, and none were found. Finally, the prosecutor made a complete overview of the arrest in 1936, which was the basis for convicting him in Zaporozhye under article 54-10 (anti-Soviet agitation and propaganda), where he was set free. The 1961 commission concluded that holding services in his home was not illegal, and that Braun's communication with his father abroad was also not illegal. He dismissed the charges and declared Braun rehabilitated.[22]

With the prosecutor's letter, Isaak's family no longer waited for a letter; they knew he was dead. His wife Hermine died a year after reading that Isaak had been executed.

Perhaps – had Liesel seen the interrogation records – she would have known who the witnesses were. She needed the truth, but knowing the names of false witnesses and prosecutors would not bring back her father or erase his family's life of suffering. People like Liesel wanted acknowledgment, to know the truth, but turned for comfort, not to retribution, but to religious acceptance.

This was similar in other families. In 2004 an international conference in Zaporozhye celebrated the two hundredth anniversary of the arrival of Mennonites in today's Ukraine. Historians, dignitaries, and local Ukrainians as well as Mennonites from around the world gathered for lectures and public dedications.

At a ceremony in the former Mennonite town of Halbstadt, now Molochansk, an elderly woman approached a visitor from Paraguay, a son of a refugee who had trekked out in 1943 with the retreating German Army. She poked him and asked, 'Do you speak Plautdietsch?' and when he said he did, she said, 'We tried to leave in 1929, but were sent back. I came back here, but strangers were living in all the Mennonite houses. I thought all of you would return too, but nobody came. Why has nobody come?'

The man from Paraguay wanted to answer but could not speak for the lump in his throat. The woman saw his struggle and said, 'Now it's too late. But Mama always said, "In heaven we will all see each other again."' The visitor later wrote he had wanted to quote her the hymn 'Wehrlos und verlassen sehnt sich.'[23]

Wehrlos und verlassen, sehnt mein Herz / Nach stiller Ruh:
Doch Du deckest mit dem Fittich / Deiner Liebe sanft mich zu.

Defenceless and forsaken, my heart longs for rest and peace,
Then you spread your wings of caring, with your love you cover me.[24]

On the same occasion, in a faint voice an elderly man in a wheelchair confessed he had changed to a Russian name after his family disappeared. He really was Heinrich Neufeld, 'and my father was Aaron Neufeld. They're all gone. I'm all alone.'[25]

Thousands like him, how did they deal with the pain and loss? Were they made mute like Amalia, angry like Maria Braun? Like Andrei, did they turn to alcohol? As aged widows, did they struggle to survive? Like Alici and Elizaveta, did they mourn for a place where a daughter could lay a flower?

The interrogation files showed only how the Soviet system worked. Torture can get most people to confess to false charges. And the complicit interrogators? So often these agents later experienced the same fate as their victims. What a waste. Wasted lives. These yellowed pages did not bring to life the people they condemned. My uncles, the men, women, and children who suffered and perished have a different legacy.

They left a few photographs and letters. Their children and relatives recalled events, sad bits of memory coloured with an endless longing. They also left an invisible mantle of trauma on their descendents. My cousin Alici's sons both died, one murdered by an employee, the other under mysterious circumstances. Andrei (Heinz), having lost faith in God and in communism, died of advanced diabetes. Elizaveta's sister died for lack of medication. In their new country, two of Viktor's children suffered mental breakdowns and Gerhard's daughter and grandchildren who got baptized 'to fit in' were seen as foreigners. The list could go on.

Notes

Epigraph on title page from Agatha Wieler, Maslianovka, USSR, to Mr and Mrs P.J. Konrad, BC, 7 Feb. 1979, Konrad Papers, Toronto.
Epigraph on page 2 from Louis de Bernières, *Captain Corelli's Mandolin* (London: Vintage Books, 1995), 40. Used by permission.

Chapter 1

1 The secret police, founded by Lenin, was first called the All Russian Extraordinary Commission for Combating Counter-Revolution, Speculation, and Sabotage (Cheka). Names for the Soviet secret police were changed over time from Cheka to GPU to NKVD to MGB to KGB.
2 Translation by Harvey L. Dyck.
3 Alici Braun, Shakhty, Russia, to the author. Translation by the author. Unless stated otherwise, all further translations are by the author.

Chapter 2

1 Audrey Poetker, 'Five Poems,' *Mennonite Mirror* 20, no. 6 (Feb. 1991), 18, republished as Audrey Poetker-Thiessen in *Standing All the Night Through* (Winnipeg: Turnstone, 1992), 67. Used by permission of the author and Turnstone Press.
2 Anne Konrad, *And in Their Silent Beauty Speak: A Mennonite Family in Russia and Canada, 1790–1990* (Toronto: published by author, 2004).

Chapter 3

1 Maria Liebe Reich with the author, 1 July 1996, Zurich.

2 Lena Wiebe with the author, 16–17 Aug. 1991, Neuwied am Rhein.

3 Mennonite Zwieback are buns, not crisp, dry bread. The soft, doubledecker buns are customarily baked fresh every Saturday. Roasted, they keep well when travelling.

4 Sheila Fitzpatrick, *The Russian Revolution*, 2nd ed. (New York: Oxford University Press, 1994), 95–7.

5 A.I. Savin, *Ethno-Confession in the Soviet State: Mennonites in Siberia, 1920–1989; Annotated List of Archival Documents*, ed. Paul Toews, trans. Olga Shmakina and Ludymilla Kariaka, Russian Academy of Sciences Institute of History, Siberian Branch, Center for Mennonite Brethren Studies Fresno (Hillsboro: Print Source Direct, 2008). For information on co-ops and increasing hostility towards Mennonites, see 66–7nn327, 328; 71n350.

6 Herman Konrad with Peter and Luise Konrad, Clearbrook, BC, 25 Dec. 1980.

7 Lena Wiebe with the author, 16–17 Aug. 1991, Bremen.

8 Hiroaki Kuromiya, *Freedom and Terror in Donbas: A Ukrainian-Russian Borderland, 1870s–1990s* (Cambridge: Cambridge University Press, 1998), 165–6. During 1930, Stalin exported 4.8 million tons of grain and flour. In 1932 he exported 5.2 million from the Donbas. At the height of the famine of 1932–3, 1.8 million tons were sold (167).

9 Orlando Figes, *The Whisperers: Private Life in Stalin's Russia* (New York: Holt, 2007), 82.

10 Simon Sebag Montefiore, *Stalin: The Court of the Red Tsar* (London: Weidenfeld & Nicolson, 2003), 31.

11 Detlef Brandes and Andrej Savin, *Die Sibirien-deutschen im Sowjetstaat 1919–1938* (Essen: Klartext, 2001), 273–4. According to the OGPU Slavgorod, in individual rayons, 96–100 per cent of individual farms were dekulakized. Some landholders abandoned or voluntarily released their property ('self-liquidated'), while others were forcefully dekulakized for failure to meet quotas or fines (274).

12 Ibid., 274.

13 Ibid., 275.

14 Montefiore, *Stalin*, 40–1, reports that 26.6 million head of cattle and 15.3 million horses were slaughtered.

15 Terry Martin, *The Affirmative Action Empire: Nations and Nationalism in the Soviet Union, 1923–1939* (Ithaca, NY: Cornell University Press, 2001), 294. In 1930, 1,197 Soviet officials were murdered. Violence was greater in non-Russian and Cossack areas.

16 H.J. Willms, ed., *Vor den Toren Moskaus: Gottes Gnaedige Durchhilfe in Einer*

Schweren Zeit, Komitee der Flüchtlinge (Yarrow, BC: Columbia, 1950), 37.

17 Ibid.; Genesis 19:17.

18 Lynne Viola, 'The Best Sons of the Fatherland: Workers in the Vanguard of Soviet Collectivization,' *Slavic Review* 48, no. 4 (1989): 637–40.

19 Harvey L. Dyck, 'Collectivization, Depression, and Immigration, 1929–1930: A Chance Interplay,' in *Empire and Nations: Essays in Honour of Frederic H. Soward* (hereafter cited as *Empire*), ed. Harvey L. Dyck and H. Peter Krosby (Toronto: University of Toronto Press, 1969), 144–59. Dyck gives a figure of between 13,000 and 18,000 refugees (145); Brandes and Savin give 13,102, with 73 per cent Mennonites, 20 per cent Lutherans, and 6 per cent Catholics (*Die Sibirien-deutschen*, 285). Also see Larisa Belkowez and Sergej Belkowez, *Gescheiterte Hoffnungen: Das deutsche Generalkonsultat in Sibirien 1923–1938* (Essen: Klartext, 2004), 62–7.

20 Dyck, 'Collectivization,' 147.

21 Ibid., 149. On 2 November 1929, Boris Shtein, head of the mid-European division of the foreign Commissariat, warned the German foreign ministry that trains would be routed east, not west.

22 Jakob Rahn, 'Zwei Naechte in der Butyrka,' *Mennoblatt*, 16 Nov. 1989, 5–6.

23 Willms, *Vor den Toren Moskaus*, 98.

24 Peter Rahn, 'Autobiography' (unpublished, 1959), Fernheim Archives, Filadelfia, Chaco, Paraguay, 45; Jakob Rahn, 'Zwei Naechte,' *Mennoblatt*, 16 Nov. 1989, 5–6.

25 Brandes and Savin, *Die Sibirien-deutschen*, 287. Mennonites (3,885), Lutherans (1,260), Catholics (468), Baptists (51), and Adventists (7).

26 Dyck, 'Collectivization,' 156. Dyck stresses Germany's intense anti-communist sentiment combined with its strong sense of 'duty.' Belkowez and Belkowez discuss efforts to assist Siberians holding German citizenship (*Gescheiterte Hoffnugen*, 55–70).

27 Rahn, 'Autobiography,' 45.

28 Willms, *Vor den Toren Moskaus*, 62.

29 Brandes and Savin, *Die Sibirien-deutschen*, 292. Of 340 families, 121 were returned to Siberia (1,360 persons) in the Isil kul and Novo-Omsk rayons; 121 families (484 persons) registered as 'emigrated or left' returned to Siberia, leaving a loss of 219 families, with at least 186 families who had 'disappeared' to other regions or were deported. Forty-nine families succeeded in emigrating. Colonist Germans were less interested in emigrating than were Mennonites (291).

30 Brandes and Savin, *Die Sibirien-deutschen*, 298.

31 *Die Mennonitische Rundschau* (hereafter cited as *MR*), published 1880 to

2007, was a Mennonite periodical established initially for Mennonites newly arrived in North America from Russia. It became a Mennonite Brethren–controlled newspaper after 1945. *Der Bote*, a General Conference Mennonite periodical, began in 1924 in Saskatchewan. Both periodicals, in German, regularly reported on Mennonites and events within the USSR.

32 'Wanderungen,' *MR*, 29 Jan. 1930, 6. Refugees remaining in Möln include my grandmother, 'Helene Konrad, nee Klassen, age 74, Omsk, municipality of Ljubinsk, village of Maslianovka,' as well as 'Maria Wiebe, nee Konrad, age 34, son Jakob, age 7.'

33 'Familienliste der Flüchtlinge im Lager Prenzlau, Kaserne 3,' *MR*, 19 Mar. 1930, 7, lists the Peter Rahn family and my mother's brother Jakob Braun and family. 'Familienliste der Flüchtlinge,' *MR*, 26 Mar. 1930, 7, lists my parents, 26 Mar. 1930.

34 Luise Konrad, handwritten autobiography, n.d., Konrad Papers.

Chapter 4

1 Poetker, *Standing All the Night Through*, 87.

2 Gerhard Konrad, Kazakhstan, to P.J. Konrad, BC, 6 Jan. 1957, Konrad Papers.

3 Quoted by White Army General Anton Denikin, *The White Army*, trans. Catherine Zvegintzov (London: Jonathan Cape, 1930), 129. Latisis was a member of the Central Executive Committee. Legally entitled to extra rations of vodka, Latisis argued that his Cheka killers should also be entitled to their victims' gold teeth in compensation for their hard jobs.

4 Anonymous, 'Aus Minlertchik, Krim,' *MR*, 30 Jan. 1930, 9; *MR*, 9 Apr. 1930, 9. Letters written to relatives in Canada were submitted to be published as 'Anonymous,' to protect the writer in the USSR.

5 Anonymous, 'Aus der Krim,' *MR*, 5 Feb. 1930, 9; *MR*, 9 Apr. 1930, 9.

6 Author's recorded notes, 23 Aug. 1980.

7 Paul R. Magocsi, *A History of Ukraine* (Toronto: University of Toronto Press, 1996), 557; also in Colin P. Neufeld, 'Through the Fires of Hell: The Dekulakization and Collectivization of the Soviet Mennonite Community, 1928–1933,' *Journal of Mennonite Studies* 16 (1998): 16–22; and in Lynne Viola, 'The Second Coming: Class Enemies in the Soviet Countryside, 1927–1935,' in J. Arch Getty and Roberta T. Manning, *Stalinist Terror: New Perspectives* (Cambridge: Cambridge University Press, 1994), 65–99.

8 V. Peters, participant at 'Mennonite Inferno' conference, Winnipeg, 26 Sept. 1997.

9 Neufeld, 'Fires of Hell,' 13.

10 Hiroaki Kuromiya, 'Stalinist Terror in the Donbas: A Note,' in Getty and Manning, *Stalinist Terror*, 216.

11 Kuromiya, *Freedom and Terror in Donbas*, 2, 123, 157.

12 Anonymous, 'Spat, Crimea,' *MR*, 7 May 1930, 7.

13 'Letter from Borissovo, No. 2, to N. Klassen, Butte, Sask.,' *MR*, 7 May 1930, 11.

14 Anonymous, 'Ein Brief aus der Krim,' *MR*, 15 Apr. 1931, 6–7.

15 Anonymous, 'Ein Brief aus Sibirien,' *MR*, 16 Apr. 1930, 9.

16 Ibid.

17 Martin, *Affirmative Action Empire*, 249–51; Viola, 'Second Coming,' 76.

18 Kuromiya, 'Stalinist Terror in Donbas,' 217.

19 Anatoli Rybakov, *Children of the Arbat* (New York: Dell, 1988), 441.

20 Kaisha Atakhanova, 'The Monster of Semipalatinsk,' Resources for Environmental Activists, http://www.isar.org/pubs/ST/Semipalatinsk.html, finds 488 nuclear tests, including 26 above ground, 124 atmospheric, and 344 underground.

Rosemary Righter, 'Life under a Nuclear Cloud,' 1 Aug. 2002, Embassy of Kazakhstan, http://prosites-kazakhembus.homestead.com/Life_under.html, describes the poisonous effect on human health of the Semipalatinsk nuclear program.

'Semipalatinsk: 60 Years Later,' n.d., Bulletin of the Atomic Scientists, http://www.thebulletin.org/web-edition/special-topics/semipalatinsk-60-years-later, cites 467 nuclear detonations.

Togzhan Kassenova, 'The Lasting Toll of Semipalatinsk's Nuclear Testing,' Bulletin of the Atomic Scientists, 28 Sept. 2009, http://www.thebulletin.org/web-edition/features/the-lasting-toll-of-semipalatinsks-nuclear-testing, cites 456 nuclear tests, beginning in 1949.

21 Montefiore, *Stalin*, 125.

22 Jutti Epp Goering, *Eine Familiengeschichte und Eigene Erlebnisse* (Nanaimo, BC: printed by author, 2001), 4.

23 Pax (peace), is a term for American Mennonite men in alternative service. It was attributed also to Canadian volunteers in MCC service in Europe and South America after the Second World War. 'PAX boys' helped construct the Tran-Chaco Highway, simultaneously training Paraguayans to take over.

24 Herman Konrad to P.J. Konrad, Abbotsford, BC, 18 Jan. 1957, Konrad Papers.

25 The latter survived the Soviet terror and eventually immigrated to Germany after the fall of communism. Johannes died in 1917 and Wilhelm during the Russian Civil War.

26 Detlef Brandes, 'Ein Kulakenaufstand im sibirischen Halbstadt,' *Forschung zur Geschichte und Kultur der Russlandsdeutschen* 4 (1994): 107; Brandes and Savin, *Die Sibirien-deutschen*, 321–4.

27 John D. Block, 'Escape: Siberia to California,' 2010, chap. 9, Siberia Heritage, http://www.siberiaheritage.com/index.cfm?category=12&pagid=21. The United States admitted 16 Mennonites per month from Sept. 1929 to June 1930. More accounts of escapes across the Amur River are found in Ernst Eitzen, 'Paraguay-Sibirien; Reisebericht von Ernst und Elfriede Eitzen,' *Mennoblatt*, 16 Sept. 1997; and in H.P. Isaak, *Our Life Story and Escape: From Russia to China to Japan and to America* (Dinuba, CA: printed by author, 1977). Also see Wilmer A. Harms, *The Odyssey of Escapes from Russia: The Saga of Anna K* (Hillsboro, KS: Hearth Publishing, 1998); and Gerhard Ratzlaff, *Vater Abram: Von der Ukraine über Sibirien und China nach Paraguay und Kanada* (Asunción: printed by author, Asunción, Paraguay, 2004).

28 Russia and Japan fought for control of Manchuria during the Russo-Japanese War (1904–5); Japan occupied all of Manchuria in 1931 and created the puppet state Manchukuo in 1932. The Soviets captured Manchuria in 1945.

29 Detlef Brandes, 'Ein Kulakenaufstandt im sibirischen Halbstadt,' 103–4.

30 Belkowez and Belkowez, *Gescheiterte Hoffnungen*, 67.

31 Jutti Epp Goering with the author, 22 Nov. 1998, Vancouver, BC; and Epp Goering, *Eine Familiengeschichte und eigene Erlebnisse*. Also see Wilfred Martens, *River of Glass* (Scottdale, PA: Herald, 1980).

32 Ratzlaff includes a first-person account of the Shumanovka village escape but mentions no angelic intervention (*Vater Abram*, 58–60).

33 'Bericht über die Flüchtlinge in Harbin,' *MR*, 30 Dec. 1931, 7.

34 Epp Goering, *Eine Familiengeschichte*, 28–9.

35 Harms, *Odyssey*, 145. A report in Harbin in 1932 reports a Volynian German family forced to hand over two sisters as Chinese wives (73). A Russian woman is taken (92).

36 Ibid., 148.

37 N.P. Janzen, 'Bericht über die Flüchtlinge in Harbin,' *MR*, 30 Dec. 1931, 7.

38 Ibid. Also, Harms, *Odyssey*, 101–3; Isaak, *Life Story*, 118–23.

39 Janzen, 'Bericht,' 7.

40 The Nansen Mission statement read, 'In response to God's love in Christ / We welcome the stranger / Bringing new hope and new life / Through ministries of service and justice.'

41 Levi Mumaw, 'Hilfswerk Notizen: Ankunft Harbiner Gruppe Casado 4 Mai,' *MR*, 16 May 1932, 7; and Mumaw, 'Hilfswerk Notizen,' *MR*, 25 May

1932, 12. Levi Mumaw, MCC executive secretary at Scottdale, PA, stated that 370 Harbin Mennonite refugees, including seventy-eight families, had arrived in Paraguay on 2 May 1932. Two hundred Mennonites still remained in Harbin.

42 'Eindrücke der Harbinier Flüchtlinge auf ihrem Bestimmungsort in Paraguay: Kol. Fernheim, Paraguay, Schönau, No. 17,' *MR*, 31 Aug. 1932, 4–5.

43 Mara Moustafine, *Secrets and Spies: The Harbin Files* (Sydney: Random House Australia, 2002), 215.

44 Moustafine, *Secrets and Spies*, 275–6.

Chapter 5

1 Mennonites had been guaranteed freedom from military service by Catherine the Great, but in 1874 a law was passed eliminating this exemption. As a consequence thousands of Mennonites in imperial Russia immigrated to the United States and Canada. By 1880 those not emigrating had negotiated an alternative non-combatant service called the *Forstei*. Young men (eligibility determined by casting lots) lived in military-like settings (barracks, uniforms, and so on) and worked in forestry, hospitals, or other community services. During the First World War, many volunteered to work on hospital trains or were medical workers on the front lines. My father, in the *Forsei* from 1912 to 1914, served as a volunteer non-combatant at the Turkish front from 1914 to 1918.

2 Anne Konrad, 'Translucence,' in *Family Games* (Windsor, ON: Netherlandic, 1992), 7–16.

3 Agatha Klassen with the author, 29 Oct. 2005, Marienheide, Germany.

4 Ibid.

5 Brandes and Savin, *Die Sibirien-deutschen*, 320.

6 'Ein Massenmord von 40,000 Menschen im Soviet Paradies,' reprinted in *MR*, 3 Sept. 1930, 13; 'Kleefeld: Halbstädter Rayon,' *MR*, 30 Apr. 1930, 8; 'Sibirien,' *MR*, 11 June 1930, 6; 'Sibirien,' *MR*, 18 June 1930, 7–8.

7 Grandmother Konrad got to a German refugee camp in 1929. Unable to pass Canadian health regulations, she was first in Wenigerode, Germany, where her daughter Helene Liebe lived, then in Huebuden, Prussia, and joined Justina's family in Le Havre in 1932, to sail to South America. She died in Fernheim, Paraguay, in 1936.

8 A pud is the equivalent of about sixteen kilograms.

9 A verst is the equivalent of a kilometre.

10 Letter sent to Peter J. Konrad, La Glace, AB, postmarked 24 Dec. 1930, Konrad Papers. Translation by H.L. Dyck

11　Kuromiya, *Freedom and Terror in Donbas*, 157.
12　Ibid., 186.
13　Elizaveta Dovbush with H.L. Dyck, 31 Sept. 1995, Zaporozhye, Ukraine, Konrad Papers.
14　E. Dovbush to M. Epp, 22 Apr. 2002.
15　Nider, secretary of Molochansk District Communist Party Committee (Raikom KPU), 'Resolution of the Molochansk District Communist Party on the Results of Countering Fascist Influence and the Immediate Objectives of the Party Organization,' 25 Dec. 1934, file 29, inventory list 1, Communist Party collection R-286, Zaporozhye Regional State Archive (hereafter ZRSA); and 'Decision of the Bureau of the Dnepropetrovsk Regional Committee (Obkom), 14 Nov. 1934,' file 29, inventory list 1, R-286, ZRSA. This file is a report on progress in implementing the Communist Party (Bolshevik) of Ukraine's Central Committee Resolution in the Molochansk German district and other districts with German collective farms.].
16　Martin, *Affirmative Action Empire*, 326, 328–9.
17　Hiroaki Kuromiya, *The Voices of the Dead: Stalin's Great Terror in the 1930s* (New Haven, CT: Yale University Press, 2007), 16. Half a million Poles lived in the USSR (219).
18　Nider, 'On Implementation of the Central Committee of the Communist Party (Bolshevik) of Ukraine Resolution on Molochansk District,' 25 Dec. 1934, file 29, inventory list 1, R-286, ZRSA. The document includes 'Some Results of Countering Fascist Influence and on the Immediate Objectives of the Party Organization,' 'The Struggle against the Kulaks,' and 'The Revival of Party and Mass Work in Collective Farms.'
19　Nider, 'Resolution of the Molochansk District Communist Party': 'Along with the demand that collective farmers flatly stop receiving fascist crumbs, we oblige chairmen of village councils and collective farms, all communists and Komsomol members to demand a complete suspension of letters abroad and here. Charge Comrade Kuchmistiy to impose a rigid universal control over this matter at all post offices of Molochansk and adjacent districts.' Translation O. Shmakina.
20　Nider, to Comrade Popov, secretary of the Central Committee Bolshevik of Ukraine, Comrade Gavrilenko, head of steering party bodies of Central Committee Bolshevik of Ukraine, and Comrade Khataevich, secretary of Dnepropetrovsk Communist Party, 'On Implementation of the Central Committee of the Communist Party (Bolshevik) of Ukraine Resolution on Molochansk District,' 14 Nov. 1934, file 29, inventory list 1, R-286, ZRSA. In a report on 'The Struggle against Fascist Influence,' notice is taken of who

does and who does not accept foreign money transfers. In the Molochansk district, 937 transfers of German marks and 'fascist dollars' were received between 20 Nov. and 20 Dec. 1934. In Orlovo village (birthplace of my Konrad grandmother) 58 transfers arrived, forty-three persons refused to accept the money, but thirteen accepted. Of these thirteen, reportedly, four were wives and sisters of disenfranchised preachers, five were dispossessed kulaks, one was a pauper and two were persons previously expelled from the collective farm as 'Hitler's agents.'

21 Wm. Th., 'Etwas aus der Kolonie Alexandertal und dem Schicksal einer Familie,' *Bote,* 27 Feb. 1985, 2. A photo accompanying the article identifies the writer's mother as Auguste Thiessen.

22 Deputy Director Belov, Directorate of Foreign Transactions, VUK Torgsin (All-Soviet Association of Trade with Foreigners), Moscow, to Ekaterina Andreevna Braun, Molochansk, 4 Sept. 1934. The file contains a similar reply by a senior inspector of Torgsin [signature illegible], Kharkov, to Korneliy Bergman, Orlovo, file 29, inventory list 1, R-286, N93/1649, ZRSA.

23 Bureau of Molochansk Raipartkom (RPK), 25 Dec. 1934, file 29, inventory list 1, R-286, ZRSA.

24 Elizaveta Dovbush with Harvey L. Dyck, 31 Sept. 1995, Zaporozhye, Ukraine. There is some repetition of details in letters from E. Dovbush to Mary Epp: 12 Nov. 1999; 27 June 2001; 28 Feb. 2002; 22 Apr. 2002; 6 June 2002; 14 Nov. 2004, Konrad Papers.

25 E. Dovbush to Mary Epp, 5 June 2002, Konrad Papers.

26 Gerhard Konrad with the author, 1 Aug. 1984, Bremen, Germany. See also *Russian History Encyclopedia*, s.v. 'Alexander Chayanov,' http://www.encyclopedia.com/doc/1G2-3404100231.html. Soviet agricultural theoretician Alexander Vasilievich Chayanov taught statistics in the Kazakh Agricultural Institute in Alma Ata from 1933 to 1935. His emphasis on peasant contributions to the economy challenged Marxist interpretations. Arrested on 3 Oct. 1937, he was shot.

27 Kay Braun with the author, 15 July 1990, Clearbrook, BC.

28 Andrei (Heinz) Braun with the author, 16 June 2001, Konstantinovka, Russia.

29 Harvey L. Dyck's handwritten notes from 1 Sept. 1992, Shakhty, Russia, Konrad Papers.

30 Peter Rahn, *Mennoniten in der Umgebung von Omsk* (Winnipeg: Christian Press, 1975), 180–1.

31 Heinrich Goerz, *Memrik*, Echo Historical Series, trans. Eric Enns (Winnipeg: CMBC Publications, Manitoba Mennonite Historical Society, 1997), 74.

32 Ingeborg Fleischhauer and Benjamin Pinkus, *The Soviet Germans Past and*

Present, ed. and intro. Edith Rogovin Frankel (New York: St Martin's, 1986), 53–5. Communist-approved German-language schools functioned between 1919 and 1938.

33 Numbers vary. Orlando Figes estimates 4.6 to 8.5 million people died as a result of the famine between 1930 and 1933 (*Whisperers*, 98).

34 Robert Conquest, *Harvest of Sorrow: Soviet Collectivization and Terror-Famine* (Edmonton: University of Alberta Press and Canadian Institute of Ukrainian Studies, 1986), 53, estimates 5 million deaths; Alec Nove, 'Victims of Stalinism: How Many?,' in Getty and Manning, *Stalinist Terror*, 266, estimates 4.5 to 5 million.

35 A.A. Toews, ed., 'Erlebnisse der Witwe Susanna Hildebrandt, Neuhorst Alt Kolonie,' *Mennonitische Märtyrer: Der grosse Leidensweg* (Winnipeg: Christian Press, 1954), 2:75–7; Erica Jantzen, *Six Sugar Beets: Five Bitter Years* (Kitchener, ON: Pandora, 2003).

36 Peter Letkemann, 'Mennonites in the Soviet Inferno 1917–1956,' *Preservings: Newsletter/Magazine of the Hanover Steinbach Historical Society Inc.* [hereafter *Preservings*], 13 Dec. 1998, 10–11. Government directions were to dekulakize only 3 to 5 per cent of all peasant households. Also, 'Mennonite Victims of "The Great Terror," 1936–1938,' *Journal of Mennonite Studies* (Dec. 1998): 33–58. Letkemann finds that the ratio of Mennonites arrested during the 'Great Terror' (*Yezhovshchina*) was approximately 8 to 9 per cent, affecting one out of every five or six adults. Since most of the arrested were men, possibly as many as half of all Mennonite adult males were taken away (37). Also in Letkemann's 'Mennonites in the Soviet Inferno, 1929–1941,' 'Crimes of Communists against Ukraine and Her People,' ArtUkraine.com. http://www.artukraine.com/commcrimes/inferno.htm.

37 John Neufeld, 'Errinnerungen und Erlebnisse aus den schweren Jahren 1936–1943 in Sowjetrussland,' *Bote*, 9 May 1990, 8.

38 Anonymous, 'Aus der alten Heimat, Memrik, 1. Mai, 1935,' *Bote*, 12 June 1935, 5.

39 Goerz, *Memrik*, 89.

40 Ibid., 89–90.

41 Leo Thiessen with the author, 8 Aug. 1999, Toronto.

42 Wolfgang Leonhard, *Die Revolution entlässt ihre Kinder* (Leipzig: Reclam, 1954).

43 Roberta T. Manning, 'The Great Purges in a Rural District,' in Getty and Manning, *Stalinist Terror*, 189–91.

44 Goerz, *Memrik*, 92.

45 Helena Ens to Hans Heese, 1946, in Toews, *Mennonitische Märtyrer*, 2:276–8.

46 Anna Wiens Reimer with the author, 10 Aug. 1993, Oakville, ON; also

Anna Wiens Reimer, 'My Memories' (handwritten memoir, n.d.), courtesy Hank Reimer.

47 To avoid compulsory military service, thousands of Mennonites immigrated to North America in the 1870s. Others stayed to negotiate terms to fund and run their own alternative service camps. Essentially a forestry service, hence called *Forstei*, the recruits planted trees, established nurseries and model orchards, built roads, and more.

48 Estimates suggest at least two million citizens of German extraction held positions in banks, businesses, government, and the military, had married into Russian nobility, or lived in their own settlements in villages.

49 White Army leaders were General Anton Denikin (Ukraine), Mikhail Alekseye (Don area), General Wrangel (Crimea), and Admiral Kolchak (Siberia).

50 Wiens Reimer, 'My Memories,' 21.

51 Diane Reimer and Anna Reimer, *David and Anna: My Labour of Love* (Calgary: FDM Printers, 1995).

52 Reimer and Reimer, *David and Anna*, 109.

53 Ibid., 96–7. A.A. Toews, 'Ereignisse in der Alt-Kolonie – 1919 u. 20: Gerhard Wieler,' in *Mennonitische Märtyrer*, 2:269–70, identifies the driver. Peter Letkemann, email to author 5 Oct. 2000, identified Katya's fiancé Abram Siemens in 'Rossoschka,' *Friedenstimme*, 1 Oct. 1918.

54 Bertrand Patenaude, *The Big Show in Bololand: The American Relief Expedition to Soviet Russia in the Famine of 1921* (Palo Alto, CA: Stanford University Press, 2002), reviewed in *New York Review of Books*, 13 Mar. 2003.

55 N.N. Fransen, 'Amerikanische Fordson Trakors M.C.C. und Hershey Schkolade,' *Bote*, 23 Aug. 1989, 4–5.

56 Selma Braun to L. and P.J. Konrad, 18 July 1971, Konrad Papers.

57 Henry Brown with the author, 12 July 1997, Abbotsford, BC.

58 Reimer and Reimer, *David and Anna*, 123.

59 'Gortschokovw' [Gorchakovo], *MR*, 27 Apr. 1932, 7; 'Davlekanova,' *MR*, 26 Oct. 1932, 7.

60 Isaak Peter Braun, unpaginated sermon notes, handwritten, Konrad Papers.

61 Henry Brown with the author, 12 July 1997.

62 Helmut Huebert, 'The Majak Bible School of Davlekanovo,' *Mennonite Historian* 34, no. 1 (Mar. 2008): 9–10.

63 Gerhard Hein, *Vertrauen, Freuen, Danken* (Weienheim am Berg, Germany: Agape, 1992), 120. Born in Russia, brother of Hermine, Gerhard G. Hein was a German cleric with the Occupation forces.

64 Gerhard Hein, ed., *The Ufa Settlement in the Framework of the Older and*

Larger Mennonite Settlements in the Russia of Old; Ufa: The Mennonite Settlements (Colonies), 1894–1938, trans. Mary Enns (Steinbach, MB: Derksen, 1977), 155.

65 Jakob J. Niebuhr, 'Jakob G. Niebuhr Fabriken,' *Mennonite Life* 10 (Jan. 1955): 25–30, reprinted in *The Mennonite Encyclopedia* (Scottdale, PA: Mennonite Publishing House, 1957), 3:873–4. Niebuhr factories in Olgafeld and in New York (established in 1898) manufactured agricultural machinery, steam engines, and so on. In 1914 they employed 350 men and had an annual production of 450,000 roubles. In 1929 Gerhard Niebuhr fled via China and reached Paraguay. His son Jakob J. fled the USSR in 1943 and immigrated to Canada in 1947.

66 Gertrude Penner, 'Errinnerungen an New York, Ukraine,' *Bote*, 8 Apr. 1998, 9.

67 Frieda Pätkau Fast, 'Ausflug zum Dnjepr Staudamm in den 1930er Jahren,' *Bote*, 18 Oct. 2006, 6.

68 Anonymous letter dated Oct. 25, signed *Eure Eltern und Grosseltern* [Your parents and grandparents], *'Ausländisches'* [Foreign News], *MR*, 27 Nov. 1932, 6; Frieda Pätkau Fast, 'Ausflug,' *Bote*, 18 Oct. 2006, 6.

69 Toews, *Mennonitische Märtyrer*, 1:320. New-Einlage (Kichkas) is described as a 'sanctuary' for 'refugee' believers until 1935. Preacher Jakob Klassen had come from Crimea and Karl Friedrichsen from Ufa. Biography of Friedrichsen in Toews, *Mennonitische Märtyrer*, 164–5. More on Friedrichsen in Harold S. Bender, 'Mayak Bible School (Ufa, Russia),' *Global Anabaptist Mennonite Encyclopedia Online.* 1957. Web. 24 November 2010. http://www.gameo.org/encyclopedia/contents/M38286.html.

70 Kuromiya, *Voices of the Dead*, 245. Acronym·used as gallows humour for Torgsin: *Tovarishchi Rossiia Gibnet Stalin Istrebliaet Narod* [Comrades, Russia is perishing, Stalin exterminates the people].

71 Kuromiya, *Voices*, 218. Jews in Ukraine in 1937–8 comprised 5.2 per cent of the population and 2.6 per cent of the arrested. Poles made up only 1.5 per cent of the population, but 18.9 per cent of the arrested. Germans were only 1.4 per cent of the population, but 10.2 per cent of the arrested (284).

72 Toews, *Märtyrer*, 2:166, 168–9. Preacher Jakob Letkemann describes events during 1934–5. He escaped to Austria from the USSR.

73 Fleischhauer and Pinkus, *Soviet Germans*, 64.

74 Hans Rempel, 'Prediger Johann Rempel,' *Bote*, 9 Apr. 1986, 8–9. Johann Rempel, in prison seven months, was tried in Dnepropetrovsk. Witnesses were summoned from Kichkas to appear at the trial and report they had seen him preach, but they were forbidden to disclose proceedings to family members. Rempel was sentenced to eight years. Rempel's son, permitted a

brief visit, was shocked to find a man with totally white hair and a broken body. Himself in prison in 1938, this son heard from a witness that during the period of Advent, the four weeks before Christmas, his father had preached from Mathew 3:2, 'Repent, for the kingdom of heaven is at hand.' The Soviets said he was agitating for a different kingdom and therefore a traitor.

75 Toews, *Märtyrer*, 1:319–21. Wall reappears in Isaak Braun's interrogation files. Wall's wife survived to report that her husband, sentenced to five years as a political prisoner, was sent to the Altai Mountains to build a railroad. He corresponded with his family until 1939. His last letter stated he was swollen from starvation and ended with the words of a hymn encouraging steadfastness in faith in times of trial.

76 Helene Dueck, *Durch Trübsal und Not* (Winnipeg: Centre for Mennonite Brethren Studies, 1995), 29.

77 Reinhold Keil, 'Der Taiga ist das Gesetz und Staatsanwalt ist der Bär,' in *Heimat in der Fremde: Deutsche Aus Russland Erinnern Sich*, ed. Rudolf Pörtner (Düssseldorf: Econ, 1992), 222–4.

78 A.A. Toews, 'Pred. Jakob Letkemann und Leidensgenossen: Fürstenland, Süd Russland,' *Märtyrer*, 2:166.

79 Jakob Neufeld, 'Mein Dornenweg' [My path of thorns], unpublished memoir, trans. Harvey L. Dyck, Neufeld Papers, Toronto.

80 Gerhard Hildebrandt, 'Als Zieselmäse ein Sonntagessen waren: Kindheit in einem Mennonitischen Dorf in der Molochna-Kolonie,' in Rudolf Pörtner, *Heimat in der Fremde: Deutsche aus Russland erinnern sich* (Düsseldorf: Econ, 1992), 305.

81 Nina Markova, *Nina's Journey: A Memoir of Stalin's Russia and the Second World War* (Washington, DC: Regnery Gateway, 1989), 86.

82 H. Koop, 'Osterwicker Schulkinder ca 1932–33,' *Bote*, 21 Mar. 1990, 4.

83 Tina Baerg, 'Osterwicker (Saporoshje) Kindergarten 1937,' *Bote*, 30 Aug. 1989, 7.

84 Helen Rempel Wiens, 'Es war einmal! Wer erinnert sich?' *Bote*, 18 May, 1988, 5.

85 Ibid.

86 Lucy Braun, 'Sechste Klasse der Mittleschule Liebenau, Ukraine, am 12. Mai, 1939,' *Bote*, 14 Mar. 2007, cover page photo.

87 Helen R. Wiens, 'Ein Schülerausflug: Osterwick 1941,' *Bote*, 18 Oct. 1989, 12. The author identifies eighteen pupils with common Mennonite names. She states that the Russian (Ukrainian?) pupils were not in school following the German occupation of her village in August 1941.

88 Franz Thiessen, '1937 war ein besonderes Jahr: Mein Weg durch die

Gefängnisse und Straflager in der UdSSR,' *Bote*, 8 Mar., 5–9; 22 Mar., 5; 29 Mar., 9; 5 Apr., 9; 19 Apr., 9, 1995.
89 Rempel, 'Prediger Johann Rempel,' 9.

Chapter 6

1 A.A. Toews, 'Rote Weihnachten: Errinnerungen eines Schülers an Weihnachten in Sowjetrussland,' *Märtyrer*, 2:447.
2 Jakob Martens, 'Im Strudel des 2. Weltkrieges: Deutsche Invasion der Ukraine,' *Mennoblatt*, 1 Feb. 1997, 3–6.
3 Jakob A. Neufeld, *Tiefenwege: Erfahrungen und Erlebnisse von Russland-Mennoniten in zwei Jahrzehnten bis 1949* (Virgil, ON: Niagara, 1957), 57.
4 Martens, 'Im Strudel,' 4.
5 Herta Vogel, 'Minderjährige in der Hölle von Iwdel,' *Bote*, 2 Aug. 2006, 26.
6 Alexander Prusin with the author, Khortitsa '99 conference, Zaporozhye, 30 May 1999.
7 Erika Thiessen with the author, 7 Feb. 1998, Toronto.
8 Neufeld, *Tiefenwege*, 85.
9 Istvan Deak, 'Memories of Hell,' *New York Review of Books* 44, no. 11, 26 June 1997, 40.
10 Paul Robert Magocsi, *A History of Ukraine* (Toronto: University of Toronto Press, 1996), 631–2. The Soviets killed between 15,000 and 40,000 prisoners. Historian Kuromiya states that the Red Army massacred 10,000 in L'viv (Lvov) alone and Nazis killed 33,371 Jews at Babi Yar (Babyn Iar) (*Freedom and Terror*, 260).
11 Dieter Pohl, *'Brutale Praxis,'* in 'Hitler's Krieg,' special edition, *Der Spiegel* 2 (2005): 78.
12 Leo Thiessen with the author, 3 Dec. 1997, Toronto. The German field hospital refused to admit soldiers in Red Army uniform. Captured by the Germans, Leo went to a Soviet POW field hospital with a *Volksdeutsche* section. Here men lay on straw in an open field. German jeeps occasionally circled the area. Said Leo, 'They took the dead out, rows at a time. POWs were not given much help because there were too many of them. They couldn't keep up with all the new wounded.' He survived with the assistance of a caring nurse.
13 Ältester Jakob Tiessen, 'Meine Lebensgeschichte' [My life story], *Bote*, 10 Sept. 1997, 5. Tiessen told his story in three instalments (*Bote* 3, 10, and 17 Sept. 1997). He survived the Labour Army and was released at war's end to live in Siberia. He immigrated to Canada in 1980. Another survivor, then living in Iakovlievo, near Zaporozhye, Rempel recalled being marched

east with 1,259 German men under armed guard for one month until they reached Stalingrad. Put on barges and taken to northern work camps, after nine months, 360 of the 1,250 were alive. Jakob Rempel, 'Erinnerungen,' *Bote*, 3 Jan. 1991, 8.

14 Fleischhauer and Pinkus, *Soviet Germans*, 103–5. It was contrary to Soviet law to have a collective accusation of treason. There was no sentencing, as required by Soviet law, and by law, deportation of children under the age of sixteen was prohibited (105).

15 Ibid., 88–91.

16 Letkeman, 'Den Opfern zum Gedächnis,' *Bote*, 25 Apr. 2001, 16. Fleischhauer and Pinkus estimate 650,000 to 700,000 Soviet Germans from all areas were deported to the Asian USSR (*Soviet Germans*, 90–1).

17 Letkemann, 'Mennonites in the Soviet Inferno, 1917–1956,' 10.

18 Goerz, *Memrik*, 100; court file T-938-95, Federal Court of Canada Trial Division between the Minister of Citizenship and Immigration, Applicant, and Johann Dueck, Respondent, in the Town Hall, Selidovo, Ukraine before His Honour Judge Noël, held in the Town Hall, Selidovo, Ukraine on Tuesday, 2 June 1998. See other accounts in Dueck, *Durch Trübsal und Not*; Sarah Dyck, ed., *The Silence Echoes: Memoirs of Trauma and Tears* (Kitchener, ON: Pandora, 1997); J.B. Toews, *Journeys: Mennonite Stories of Faith and Survival in Stalin's Russia* (Winnipeg: Kindred Publications, 1998).

19 E. Hecht with the author, 9 June 1999, Cappeln, Germany.

20 Letkemann, 'Mennonites in the Soviet Inferno, 1941–1956,' *Mennonite Historian* 25, no. 2 (June 1999): 2.

21 Meir Buchsweiler, *Volksdeutsche in der Ukraine am Vorabend und Beginn des Zweiten Weltkrieges: ein Fall doppelter Loyalität* (Gerlingen: Bleicher, 1984), 345.

22 Ibid., 391.

23 Ibid., 337.

24 Erika Thiessen with the author, 21 Oct. 1998, Toronto.

25 S.W. with the author, 1 June 2004, Toronto. Person requests anonymity.

26 Anonymous, 'Zwischen Odessa und Perekop in den ersten Monaten des deutsch-russischen Krieges,' *Mennonitisches Jahrbuch 1949* (Newton, KS: Mennonite Publication Office, 1949), 12.

27 Hans Rempel, 'Die Heimat in Trümern,' in Toews, *Märtyrer*, 2:420.

28 Jacob D. Epp, *A Mennonite in Russia: The Diaries of Jacob D. Epp, 1851–1880*, ed. and trans. Harvey L. Dyck (Toronto: University of Toronto Press, 1991), 32–41.

29 David G. Rempel, with Cornelia Rempel Carlson, *A Mennonite Family in Tsarist Russia and the Soviet Union, 1789–1923* (Toronto: University of

Toronto Press, 2002), 91. Prior to 1917 Jewish traders controlled much of Alexandrovsk (Zaporozhye) local and export trade, 102.

30 Martens, 'Im Strudel,' *Mennoblatt*, 16 Feb. 1997, 3–4.

31 Horst Gerlach, 'Der Gebietskommissar und der Rajonchef,' *Die Russlandsmennoniten: Ein Volk unterwegs* (Kirchheimbolanden: GTS-Druck, 1992), 85.

32 Horst Gerlach, 'Griff in die Geschichte: Erinnerungen an die deutsche Besatzung in Russland, Hans Bohn und seine Zeit in Chortitza,' *Bote*, 13 Mar. 1996, 11.

33 Gerlach, 'Griff in die Geschichte,' *Bote*, 20 Mar. 1996, 11.

34 Karel C. Berkhoff, 'Was There a Religious Revival in Soviet Ukraine under the Nazi Regime?' *Slavonic and East European Review* 3 (July 2000): 536–67. The Nazis considered Baptists and Evangelical Christians 'harmless,' allowing them to preach, travel, and distribute literature, but Greek Catholic and Roman Catholic priests were persecuted (547). The Orthodox Church could function again but was watched. In 1942 Orthodox priests were forced to pray for Hitler on his birthday, 20 Apr. 1942 (563). In general, youth raised under communism were uninterested and there was not a large religious revival (564–5).

35 Dueck, *Durch Trübsal und Not*, 45.

36 Buchsweiler, *Volksdeutsche*, 351.

37 John Neufeld, 'Erinnerungen und Erlebnisse aus den schweren Jahren 1936–1943 in Sowjetrussland,' *Bote*, 6 June 1990, 9.

38 Karl Stumpp, 'Die Deutschen Siedlungen des Kronau-Orloffer Gebietes,' in *Heimatbuch der Deutschen aus Russland*, ed. Karl Stumpp (Stuttgart: Landsmannschaft der Deutschen aus Russland, 1958), 22–32. *Heimatbuch der Deutschen aus Russland* is a yearly periodical running from 1954 to 2008. The Stump article includes a comparison chart of Mennonite with Evangelical and Catholic (Colonist) villages in the Molochna settlement area: 229 Mennonites, most in 1932–3, starved to death (Kronau-Orloff region – now southeast Ukraine). Between 1929 and 1942, in the Kronau (Colonist) area, 380 men were exiled [*verbannt*] and in the (Mennonite) Orloff area, 409 men (perhaps because Mennonites had many lay clergy), 24. In 1921–2 and 1932–3, in the Kronau region 426 persons starved and in the Orloff region 229 people starved (lower numbers could be due to MCC soup kitchens in 1921–3 and Mennonites receiving money to purchase food at Torgsin from relatives abroad in 1932–3), 24. Stumpp (1896–1982) was assigned to undertake the survey by Georg Liebbrandt, then a prominent Nazi and also an émigré. For a discussion of the effect of the Stumpp survey on Soviet Jews, see Ingo Haar and Michael Fahlbusch, *German Scholars and Ethnic Cleansing* (New York: Berghan Books, 2005).

39 Peter Lohrenz and Therese Lohrenz, 'Errinnerungen,' *Bote*, 5 Mar. 1997, 5.

40 Horst Gerlach, 'The German Occupation of the Ukraine Mennonite Settlements 1941: Process and Consequence,' in *Die Lebensgeschichte der Familie Dürksen*, ed. Walter Dürksen (Paderborn: Verlagsbuchhandlung, 1998), 153.

41 Jacob Sawatsky, 'Zigeuner-Massengrab in Felsenbach,' *Bote*, 30 June 1999, 11; 7 July 1999, 11–12.

42 Buchsweiler, *Volksdeutsche*, 372.

43 Jake Neufeld with Harvey L. Dyck, Toronto, 22 Mar. 2007.

44 Johanna Schmidt, 'Familie Verzeichnis' (Bonn: unpublished family chronology, 2001).

45 Neufeld, *Tiefenwege*, 97.

46 Heinrich Winter, 'Die Neubelebung der Gemeinden in der alten Kolonie, 1941–1943,' *Bote*, 19 Nov. 1986, 12; and (front cover), 'Täuflinge in Osterwick 1943,' *Bote*, 20 June 1990, 1. Thirty-nine baptisms were performed in a school serving as a church.

47 Nic. Enns, 'Tauf Fest,' *Zionsbote*, 20 July 1947, 13. Preacher Nic. Enns reports 1,500 baptism candidates, walking three abreast and wearing white robes, were baptized in the Dnieper River, watched by a large crowd.

48 Berkhoff, 'Was There a Religious Revival?' 552.

49 Neufeld, *Tiefenwege*, 96–7.

50 Peter Wiebe, 'Aus dem Leben von Familie Peter und Tina Wiebe,' *Bote*, 28 Feb. 1996, 12. Wiebe was captured by the Americans in 1945, turned over to the Soviets as a German POW, and then given a ten-year penal sentence. He survived and immigrated to Germany.

51 Harry Loewen, 'Mennoniten unter deutscher Besatzung in der Ukraine,' *Bote*, 27 Apr. 2005, 28. Loewen's book review of Karel Berkhoff's *Harvest of Despair: Life and Death in Ukraine under Nazi Rule* includes a photograph of the march past.

52 Eduard Reimer, unpublished, untitled memoir written in 1980s in Germany, 60, no. 63, vol. 3333, Gerhard Lohrenz fond, Mennonite Heritage Centre Archive, Winnipeg. Conrad Stoesz, archivist, Mennonite Heritage Centre, Winnipeg, found this source for me. The author's name, Abram, was changed to Eduard during the occupation (75). The youths, eighteen and nineteen years old, were from the Mennonite villages of Klippenfeld, Hamberg, Wernersdorf, Liebenau, and Schönsee. There were four troops or divisions of *Schwadrons*: number one in Prishib, number two in Halbstadt, number three in Waldheim, and number four in Gnadenfeld. Numbers one and three were primarily Lutheran and Catholic 'Volksdeutsche' and two and four Mennonite.

53 Ibid., 68.

54 Ibid., 98. An episode in early 1942 describes Reimer catching a thief stealing a sack of oats, horsewhipping him, then turning him over to the German command, who investigated to see if the man was circumcised (58).

55 Fleischhauer and Pinkus, *Soviet Germans*, 93.

56 Testimony of Daniel Mateevich Podaliak, 2 June 1998, court file T-938-95,
in the Federal Court Trial Division between the Minister of Citizenship
and Immigration Applicant and Johann Dueck, Selidovo, Ukraine, 644–5,
671.

57 Kirk Makin, 'Witch Hunt for Crimes Not Committed,' *Globe and Mail*, 20
Feb. 1999.

58 'The EWZ files created between 1939 and 1945 by the Immigration Centre
(*Einwandererzentralstelle*) of the German government contain information
on approximately 2.9 million ethnic Germans processed by the centre for
immigration and naturalization during the war. These files presumably
include data on all Mennonites who came to Germany in the fall of 1943,
as well as information on their immediate ancestors.' Richard Thiessen,
'Mennonite Extractions from the EWZ Files,' Mennonite Genealogical
Resources, http://www.mennonitegenealogy.com/russia/ewz/ewz.htm.

59 P.R. Magocsi estimates that three million non-Jews in Ukraine were
victims of Nazi discrimination and extermination policies. Magocsi,
Ukraine, 633.

60 Ibid., 634.

61 Alexander Dallin, *German Rule in Russia, 1941–1945: A Study in Occupation
Politics* (New York: Macmillan, 1957), 452. There were 2,196,166 Ukrainian
Ostarbeiter. Andrew Gregorovich, 'World War II in Ukraine: Ostarbeiter
Slave Labor,' *FORUM Ukrainian Review* 92 (Spring 1995): 12–13. Ukrain-
ian Canadian Research and Documentation Centre (UCRDC) estimates
2,244,000 Ukrainian *Ostarbeiter* during the Second World War (13).

62 E. Dovbush to M. Epp, 28 Feb. 2000, trans. K. Peters, Konrad Papers.

63 Gregorovich, 'World War II in Ukraine,' 12.

64 E. Dovbush with Harvey L. Dyck, Zaporozhye, Ukraine, 31 Sept. 1995.

65 Dallin, *German Rule in Russia*, 439. Bormann's instructions were to 'maintain a requisite distance' between German citizens and *Ostarbeiter*.

66 Antony Beevor, *The Fall of Berlin 1945* (New York: Penguin Books, 2003),
109–10.

67 Ibid., 113; Erich Kern, *Dance of Death*, trans. Paul Findlay (London: Collins,
1951), 53–4.

68 Peter P. Klassen, *Die Mennoniten in Paraguay* (Bolanden-Weierhof: Mennonitischer Geschichtsverein e.V., 1988), 122; Peter P. Klassen, *Die Deutsch-Völkische Zeit in der Kolonie Fernheim 1933–1945* (Bolanden-Weierhof:
Mennonitischer Geschichtsverein e.V., 1990), 38, 45–6, 48, 50. When

Mennonites in Paraguay asked his advice about the 'Heil Hitler' greeting, Unruh replied, '*Heil Hitler* means that you sincerely wish the new leader of Germany well, just as believing Christians wish "heil" or blessing from God in whom the Führer honestly believes. Don't people sing Glory to you, Kaiser? So the Hitler greeting stands in third place [after God and Kaiser]. Have you not read 1 Peter 12:13–17?' (50).

69 Klassen, *Die Deutsch-Völkische Zeit,* 38. Teachers in a Mennonite school in Fernheim, Paraguay, who advocated heightened loyalty to Germany and Nazism were forced to leave the school.

70 Dietrich Rempel, 'Studienfahrt nach Deutschland,' in *Auf den Spuren der Vaeter: Eine Jubilaeumsschrift der Kolonie Friesland in Ostparaguay, 1937–1987,* ed. Gerhard Ratzlaff (Asunción: Cromos, 1987), 167–9, includes a list of war casualties (170) and photo of group (171).

71 Klassen, *Die Mennoniten*, 107; and 'Ein Junge Namens Willy,' *Mennoblatt*, 1 Jan., 1989, 6–7 (includes photo of the group); Ratzlaff, *Auf den Spuren der Vaeter*, 176–7, 188–9.

72 Justina Epp Goering, hand-copied speech, 31 May 1998, at Friesland Reunion in Clearbrook, BC, trans., Konrad Papers. A slightly altered version appears in her book *Eine Familiengeschichte und Eigene Erlebnisse* (Nanaimo: printed by the author, 2001), 45–7.

73 Epp Goering, *Eine Familiengeschichte*, 50.

74 Ibid., 57.

75 Ibid., 61.

76 Dueck, *Durch Trübsal und Not*; Marlene Epp, *Women without Men: Mennonite Refugees of the Second World War* (Toronto: University of Toronto Press, 2000); Neufeld, *Tiefenwege*.

77 Nicholas Stargardt, *Witnesses of War: Children's Lives under the Nazis* (Pimlico: Random House, 2006), 118.

78 Ibid.

79 Polish nationals were prohibited from teaching Polish. Polish children were to be 'Germanized,' taught 'obedience, order and cleanliness,' removed from their homes, kept in children's homes or camps, or adopted by German families and taught to become Hitler Youth. Ibid., 165–8. Three hundred and sixty thousand *PArbeiter* (a Polish *Arbeiter* was similar to an *Ostarbeiter* from Ukraine) were sent to Germany. Of these, 60,000 remained in post-war Germany and many emigrated. The German government made small 'help' payments in lieu of outright compensation for the years of labour. Jeanne Dingell, 'The Question of the Polish Forced Labourer during and in the Aftermath of World War II: The Example of the Warthegau Labourers,' 1998, http://www.remember.org/educate/dingell.html.

80 Neufeld, *Tiefenwege*, 179.

81 EWZ file 931,326, BC Mennonite Historical Society Archive, Abbotsford.

82 Hein, *Vertrauen, Freuen, Danken*, 107.

83 Martens, 'Im Strudel,' *Mennoblatt*, 1 Apr. 1997, 3–5.

84 W.G. Sebald, *On the Natural History of Destruction* (Toronto: Alfred A. Knopf, 2003), 23.

85 Two hundred thousand from Warthegau trying to reach Berlin were overtaken by the Red Army. Fleischhauer and Pinkus, *Soviet Germans*, 101.

86 Beevor, *Berlin*, 107–9; Catherine Merridale, *Ivan's War: The Red Army 1939–45* (London: Faber & Faber, 2005), 267–8, 275–7. 'They came upon another building and found the bodies of women who had been raped and then mutilated one by one, each with an empty wine bottle in their vaginas.... The problem was that sympathy for enemy females was actively discouraged; group pressure worked to bind the men together in their crime.'

87 Epp, *Women without Men*, 58–66.

88 Beevor, *Berlin*, 106.

89 Ibid.

90 Nikolai Tolstoy, *Victims of Yalta* (London: Hodder & Stoughton, 1977), 51–2.

91 Beevor, *Berlin*, 423. Allies returned 1,833,567 POWs (1.5 million were Red Army), repatriating 5.5 million persons to the USSR.

92 Fleischauer and Pinkus, *Soviet Germans*, 101.

93 E. Dovbush to M. Epp, 28 Feb. 2000, Konrad papers.

Chapter 7

1 Alfred Eisfeld and Victor Herdt, *Deportation, Sondersiedlung, Arbeitsarmee: Deutsche in der Sowjetunion 1941 bis 1956* (Cologne: Wissenschaft und Politik, 1996), 182–4.

2 Ella Becker, 'Mobilisierung 1942,' *Bote*, 15 Aug. 2007, 25.

3 This Mennonite soup is called *Seeti Malkschi Moos* in Plautdietsch. Fresh milk (or buttermilk) is heated, and 'rivels' or crumbs made of a mixture of flour and eggs are added to the boiling milk and cooked till the 'rivels' are done.

4 An old man from the village recommended certain herbs be heated and put under the bedclothes 'to smoke the fever out. The fever left and has not returned to the present day.'

5 Deportee Germans were under surveillance. Denied freedom to travel, they had to report to the NKVD twice a month, later once a month, and after 1954 once a year. They were denied secondary and higher education and were permanently denied the right to return to the places from which

they had been deported. In 1955 some civil rights were restored, but not the right of return. See Robert Friesen, *Auf den Spuren der Ahnen, 1882–1992* (Minden, Germany: Kurt Eilbracht, 2000), 367–71.

6 Maria Braun with Lillian Toews, Karaganda, 25 July 1993. Video recorded by Lillian Toews, Abbotsford, BC.

7 Andrej Savin, Novosibirsk, email message to author, 17 Nov. 2007, about 1940 FSB Omsk, federal secret police documents relating to the cases of Alici Braun and others.

8 Helene Celmina, *Women in Soviet Prisons* (printed by author, 1985), 22. Celmina, a Latvian émigré in the United States, was a translator of foreign articles when she was arrested in Riga in 1962. Given a four-year sentence, she was released in 1966.

9 Savin, email message to author. His information on Alici Braun was referenced to the secret police archive P-495, FSB Omsk, Federal Security Service Russia.

10 Savin to author. Heinrich Neufeld (arrested 31 Oct. 1940) and Ivan Neufeld (son of Franz Neufeld) were shot on 3 Aug. 1942. Helena (Elena) Ivanovna Neufeld and Elena Jakovlevna Neufeld were sentenced to ten years in prison (P-495, FSB Omsk). Franz Peters was sentenced to ten years in prison on 22 Apr. 1941. Katya Neufeld, arrested 29 June 1941, was sentenced to ten years prison on 6 Aug. 1941 (P-2779, FSB Omsk). Kornelius Hildebrand, medical student, arrested 17 June 1941, was sentenced to seven years prison on 5 Aug. 1941 (P-3157, FSB Omsk). In his email, Savin wrote that FSB documents 'of a prominent NKVD Omsk functionary' stated that the Hitler/Stalin friendship pact of 1939 opened the doors for *more* German spies. Mennonites should be monitored *more* closely as potential traitors.

11 Georgi Vins, *Testament from Prison*, trans. Jane Ellis (Weston, ON: David Cook Publishing, 1975), 47.

12 Deak, 'Memories of Hell,' 40.

13 Alici Braun to the author, 5 June 2002.

14 Heinrich Janzen, Omsk, to P.J. Konrad, 18 Feb. 1977, Konrad Papers.

15 Helena Blumenschein with the author, 25 Oct. 2005, Rheine.

16 Anna Braun to Luise Konrad, 8 Oct. 1962. Also 31 Jan. 1963, 3 Mar. 1966, and 9 Mar. 1967, Konrad Papers.

17 Johann Klippenstein, 'Leben und Leidenschaft von Ältesten Johann Penner,' *Bote*, 9 Mar. 1983, 3.

18 Donald Rayfield, *Stalin and His Hangmen: The Tyrant and Those Who Killed Him* (New York: Random House, 2004), 409. Death rates of German POWs in Soviet hands were twice as high as Soviet prisoners in German hands.

19 Alici Braun to the author, 22 Jan. 2000.

20 Montefiore, *Stalin*, 334, 335. In three weeks the Soviets lost two million men and thousands of tanks, planes, and guns. To terrorize the soldiers, Stalin issued Order 270 that families of captured men (which he termed deserters) be arrested, imprisoned, and denied all assistance.

21 Montefiore, *Stalin*, 394–5.

Chapter 8

1 In 2005 Lena's sister Agatha said their stop was in Ulan Ude (Lena had died before I could confirm this).

2 Sara and Heinrich Janzen, Omsk, USSR, to Mr and Mrs Peter J. Konrad, BC, 4 Apr. 1956, Konrad Papers. Enclosed letter (Heinrich Toews to Sara and Heinrich Janzen, Omsk) from Dietrich's brother stated that Dietrich survived the war and died of pulmonary tuberculosis in Waldheim, Siberia. Sara wrote that Dietrich's daughter Katya took in her father and his Russian wife (who then looked after Katya's children). Konrad Papers.

3 Sara Janzen to P.J. Konrad, 10 Sept. 1970, Konrad Papers.

4 Peter Wiebe and Viktor Wiebe with the author, 20 Aug. 1995, Berlin.

5 Sara Janzen, Omsk, to P.J. Konrad, 1 Feb. 1968, Konrad Papers. Janzen reported religious harassment on 4 May 1968, but that they would risk holding church services again and hope to escape notice.

6 Grete and Karl Fast, 'In Unna-Massen gehört: Ereinnisse, von Umsiedlern aus der Sowjetunion erlebt und erzählt,' *Bote*, 28 Mar. 1989, 9.

7 Agatha Klassen with the author, 29 Oct. 2005, Marienheide. See also Peter (Isaak) Derksen, *Es wurde wieder ruhig* (Winnipeg: Mennonite Heritage Centre, 1989), 186. A Mennonite preacher knew the (young) Mennonite woman who was his accuser. Sentenced to ten years, he survived. Upon his return, she begged his forgiveness.

8 Grete and Karl Fast, 'In Una Massen gehört,' *Bote*, 4 Jan. 1989, 9.

9 Eisfeld and Herdt, *Deportation*, 26–7. Fifteen thousand households meant 45,000 people.

10 Figes, *Whisperers*. See the case of A. Simonov (519–21).

11 Gerhard Konrad, Talde Kurgan, USSR, to Maria Goerzen, Witmarsum, Brazil, 'Letters from Russia' [Aus Russlandbriefen], *MR*, 7 Aug. 1963, 6.

12 Gerhard Konrad to P.J. Konrad, 7 Apr. 1968, Konrad Papers.

13 Mark MacKinnon, 'Forgotten Casualties of Cold War Remembered When the Sky Turned Red,' *Globe and Mail*, 9 Aug. 2004.

14 Gerhard Konrad to P.J. Konrad, 22 Mar. 1976, Konrad Papers.

15 Gerhard Konrad to P.J. Konrad, 4 Dec. 1976, Konrad Papers.

Chapter 9

1 Anne Konrad, 'Massacre Memorial Dedicated in Ukraine,' *Canadian Mennonite*, 10 Sept. 2001, 10. Also in Harvey L. Dyck, John R. Staples, and John B. Toews, *Nestor Makhno and the Eichenfeld Massacre: Civil War Tragedy in a Ukrainian Mennonite Village* (Kitchener, ON: Pandora, 2004).

2 E. Dovbush to M. Epp, 18 Feb. 1999, trans. K. Peters, Konrad Papers.

3 Translated by H.L. Dyck, Konrad Papers.

4 See Friends of the Mennonite Centre in Ukraine (FOMCU) or the Mennonite Centre Ukraine at http://www.mennonitecentre.ca/.

5 Gerhard Hein, 'The Ufa Settlement in the Framework of the Older and Larger Mennonite Settlements in the Russia of Old,' in *Ufa: The Mennonite Settlements (Colonies), 1894–1938*, ed. Gerhard Hein (Steinbach, MB: Derksen, 1975), 8. In 1926 the settlement's 2,529 Mennonites owned 10,222 desiatinas of land. (One desiatina equals about one hectare or two-and-a-half acres.)

6 'Karanbash, gouv. Ufa,' *Friedenstimme*, Halbstadt, Russia, 18 Apr. 1909 (obituary).

7 Agatha Wieler, Maslianovka, Siberia, to Mr and Mrs Peter J. Konrad, Clearbrook, BC, 7 Feb. 1979.

8 Agatha Wieler, Maslianovka, to P.J. Konrad, Clearbrook, BC., 23 Feb. 1979, Konrad Papers. Wieler, a neighbour of my parents when they lived in Maslianovka, mentioned this phenomenon in her report on what had happened to persons in her village: Franz Dück 'was taken.' Peter Loewen 'was taken' (his wife died and also three of his children). Dietrich Fast 'was taken.' 'They wanted to arrest my father, but when they looked through the door they saw he had died.' Abram Kröker 'was taken' in 1937. 'Papa's son' Jakob 'was taken' and his wife died right afterwards. 'Papa's son' Dietrich's wife, a 'kulak,' was sentenced to eighteen months in prison, leaving five children on their own. Wieler also wrote that twenty persons recently were baptized.

9 Peter Penner, 'Was Ich im Altai Sibirien gewonnen habe,' *Bote*, 27 Feb. 2002, 29–32. Photo of the Friesen mill, 30. Penner was born in Orlovo, German Rayon, Siberia.

10 Aleksandr I. Solzhenitsyn, *The Gulag Archipelago: 1918–1956* (New York: Harper Perennial, 1992), 400–1.

11 Boris P. Trenin with the author and Harvey L. Dyck, Tomsk, 21 June, 2001.

12 Clifford Levy, 'Purging History of Stalin's Terror,' *New York Times*, 26 Oct. 2008.

13 Clifford Levy, 'Nationalism of Putin's Era Veils Sins of Stalin's,' *New York Times*, 27 Nov. 2008.

14 Anna Wiens Reimer with the author, 10 Aug. 1993, Oakville, ON.
15 Reimer and Reimer, *David and Anna*, 123.
16 Selma Braun, Kazakhstan, to Lily Wiens, Gruenthal, MB, 22 Nov. 1963, Konrad Papers.
17 Selma Braun to L. and P. Konrad, Abbotsford, BC, 9 Feb. 1965, Konrad Papers.
18 Selma Braun to L. and P. Konrad, Abbotsford, BC, 23 Aug. 1964, Konrad Papers.
19 Revised Standard Version, Hebrews 12:6.
20 Selma Braun to P.J. Konrad, 19 Apr. 1965, Konrad Papers.
21 Selma Braun to P.J. Konrad, 18 July 1971, Konrad Papers.
22 Selma Braun to P.J. Konrad, 28 Nov. 1978, Konrad Papers.
23 Dimitrii Grigoriev, *Nemtsy Bashkortostana v kontse XIX–XX vv* (Ufa: Bashkir University Press, 2002).
24 Peter Letkemann, 'The Files of the Alrussischer Mennonitischer Landwirtschaftlicher Verein (AMLV),' *Mennonite Historian* 32, no. 3 (Sept. 2006): 4–5.
25 Brandes and Savin, *Die Sibirien-deutschen*, 102–3.
26 Lora Braun Ebert to the author, 18 Dec. 2002, Konrad Papers.
27 Lora Braun Ebert to the author, 1 Mar. 2003, Konrad Papers.
28 Ibid.
29 Lora Braun Ebert to the author, 1 Mar. 2003.
30 Katharina Neufeld, 'Mennonitisches Jahrbuch, "Die Aussellung" Russlandsdeutsche Zwangsarbeiter in der Sowjetunion 1941 bis 1946 im Museum für Russlandsdeutsche kulturgeschichte in Detmold,' *Bote*, 21 Jan. 2004, 12–14, 18–19. Included are statistics from Herman Arkadii of Saratov: there were 20,800 Germans in *Trudarmiia* on 1 Jan. 1942; 123,522 persons mobilized in October 1942 include 52,742 women who left behind 6,436 dependent children. In 1946, 203,766 refugee Germans repatriated to the USSR became new recruits for the forced labour camps, 23.
31 See paintings of the Soviet penal system by former prisoner Nikolai Getman, ArtUkraine.com, http://www.artukraine.com/paintings/getman.htm.
32 Andrei Makin, *Dreams of My Russian Summer* (New York: Simon and Schuster, 1997), 146.

Chapter 10

 1 Minutes of the Interrogation of Ivan I. Braun, 25 Dec. 1937, file 1a, inventory list 52(2a), collection R-117, Security Service Ukraine (hereafter SBU) in Donetsk Region; and Minutes of the Interrogation for Ivan I. Braun, 19

Jan. 1938, file 1a, inventory list 52-2a/1a, collection R-117, SBU, Donets'k. Recorded notes by the author from translations by Ludmilla Kariaka and Harvey L. Dyck, 23 Sept. 2007. Article 54 of the Ukrainian Soviet Social- ist Republic (SSR) Criminal Code corresponds to Article 58 in the Rus- sian Soviet Socialist Republic (RSFSR) Criminal Code. Article 58:2 targets bourgeois nationalists and separatists. Article 58:7 targets subversives. Article 58:9 targets 'wreckers' or saboteurs. Article 58:10 targets anti-Soviet agitation and propaganda. Article 58:11 targets 'hostile' groups.

2 The twenty-four persons named in 1937 were born in the following years: 1891, 1892, 1892, 1893, 1895, 1896, 1897, 1898, 1899, 1900, 1900, 1901, 1902, 1904, 1905, 1905, 1906, 1907, 1908, 1908, 1909, 1910, 1911, 1918.

3 Hiroaki Kuromiya, email to the author, 18 July 2009. Kuromiya thinks the execution record must still be with the SBU. The prisoner could also have died in custody from torture or a heart attack.

4 Kuromiya, *Freedom and Terror*, 239. Stalin sanctioned the use of torture (230) and he and Molotov signed the execution orders. A total of 4,265 ethnic Germans were arrested in Donets'k oblast from Sept. 1937 to Feb. 1938, and of these 84 per cent were executed (233).

5 Alici Braun, Shakhty, Russia, to Mary Epp, Abbotsford, BC, 4 Feb. 1992. Also, handwritten autobiography of Alici Braun sent to Mary Epp, 2 Nov. 1992, Konrad Papers.

6 Jakob Neufeld's file with three interrogations was seen by his son Jake Neufeld and historian Harvey L. Dyck in the state archive in Zaporozhye, 12 Apr. 2007. Jakob Neufeld's unpublished memoir, 'Mein Leidensweg' (9) states there were twenty-two interrogations. Jakob Neufeld Papers, Toronto.

7 Belkowez and Belkowez, *Gescheiterte Hoffnungen*, 106–7.

8 Robert M. Slusser and Jan F. Triska, *A Calendar of Soviet Treaties 1917–1957* (Palo Alto, CA: Stanford University Press, 1959), 119.

9 Case 24548 P.F., Minutes of the Interrogation for Heinrich Jakobovich Kon- rad, [number illegible] Mar. 1938, SBU Archive, Donetsk. From author's recorded notes, 23 Sept. 2007.

10 Procurator V.G. Senyukov, SUB Archive, Donetsk, to Elizaveta Andreiovna Dovbush, Snezhnoye, Ukraine, Certificate, 5 Oct. 1989, Konrad Papers.

11 Simon Sebag Montefiore, *Potemkin: Catherine the Great's Imperial Partner* (New York: Vintage Books, 2005).

12 Vol. 95, inventory list 4, R4033, State Archive of the Kherson Region (here- after SAKR), Kherson. Translation by Harvey L. Dyck, E. Davidova, and S. Markarov, Toronto.

13 Doc. 11, file 283, vol. 95, inventory list 4, R4033, SAKR. Accusations were

made against the following men: Preachers David Ivanovich Klassen (disenfranchised, literate, non-partisan, resident of Kichkas) and Jakob Petrovich Klassen (from the Mennonite village of Rosenthal – renamed Kantserovka – in a suburb of Zaporozhye, also literate, disenfranchised, and non-partisan). Ivan Genrikovich (Johann Heinrich) Neufeld from Münsterberg, Molochna settlement ('from a family of kulaks', disenfranchised, with no previous conviction). Gergard (Gerhard) Petrovich Rempel, age thirty-three, from Nieder Khortitsa, a largely Mennonite village near the Dnieper River and the new Dneprostroi dam (arrested at a children's sanatorium of the Zaporozhye Health authority). Gergard Ivanovich (Gerhard Johann) Dyck from Crimea (kulak). Frants Frantsevich Vaal (Franz Wall), also from Crimea (k̓ulak). Ivan Vasilievich Leven (Johann Loewen), age sixty-two, from the Mennonite village of Alexanderkron in the Molochna settlement (kulak). Gerhard Ivanovich Toews and Peter Gustanovich Toews are from the Volga region. The non-Mennonite Josef Karlovich Kreiter is a Soviet German from the Cossack village of Suvorovskaya in Kuban.

14 Doc. 14, vol. 95, inventory list 4, R4033, SAKR, outlines information on criminal case 612, 5 July 1961.

15 File 612, vol. 95, inventory list 4, R4033, SAKR. Translation E. Davidova. This file contains the findings of a preliminary judicial investigation by the Ukrainian KGB for Zaporozhye region. A special panel established that during 1933–6 a group in Kichkas, Zaporozhye, largely consisted of 'active church Mennonite figures' – preachers David Ivanovich Klassen, Jakob Petrovich Klassen – and kulaks – Leven, Vaal, Neufeld, and others. These men were said to be members of Mennonite religious communities that systematically gathered for prayer meetings that were often followed by 'counter-revolutionary talks of a nationalist nature, aimed at spiteful critique of the events run by the party and Government in the region, events aimed to rebuild the socialist structure of the village.' The group was accused of spreading provocative rumours about the imaginary persecution by the Soviet government of ethnic German people in their midst, as well as among collective farmers of German background. They were accused of 'singing high praises for an existing regime in one of the most reactionary states and admiring the ways of individual leaders of the above-mentioned regime.'

The following people were the active figures of this counter-revolutionary group: at Kichkas village, the preacher David Klassen and the kulaks Leven, Neufeld, and Vaal. Also Jakob Klassen from Kantserovka village [the Mennonite village of Rosenthal, in a suburb of Zaporozhye].

Pretending to hold religious rituals and prayer meetings, they ran counter-revolutionary, corrupting activity for both adult populations. In their believers they instilled a hope for the early end of Soviet power and in the forthcoming arrival of the 'Saviour.' They cited the inevitability of a war and the occupation of Ukraine by an imperialist state. The said persons, in a religious and nationalist spirit, subjected their youth to brainwashing. They tried to use all means to separate their children from communist influences, such as pioneer groups, the Komsomol, the club, etc. For this purpose, they organized parties with treats for children, meanwhile conducting talks with the children on religious topics. They urged the pioneers among them to abandon their pioneer groups and stop attending clubs and a number of other Soviet organizations. The said work was conducted personally by Jacob Klasssen, David Klassen, Leven, and Vaal. These people did their work through their own children and religious parents.

The specified group of people did not confine their counter-revolutionary activity to the walls of the prayer house, but a member of the group, Leven, carried out his counter-revolutionary, nationalist work among co-villagers without a sign of shame. He did not shun queues where he – Leven – would spread slanderous rumours of various kinds about Soviet authorities. He expressed his opinion of the upcoming separation of Ukraine from the Soviet Union by a capitalist country, thus indoctrinating the population in the counter-revolutionary spirit. His view was to get people to think about a need to provide support for the future invaders.

The accused Leven, being one of the active members of the said grouping, has repeatedly outlined his anti-Soviet views by complaining about the existing regime to the accused Rempel, Dyck, Petr Toews, and Gustav Toews. Apart from Gustav Toews, they fully shared his counter-revolutionary views. They opposed Soviet power by spreading all sorts of provocative rumours about the sham famine among ethnic Germans and the impending change of the existing regime. They tied this to the inevitability of war and counted upon the occupation of Ukraine by foreign troops.

As regards the accused Gustav Toews, despite being the object of intense counter-revolutionary indoctrination by Leven, he did not share his counter-revolutionary views. However, he did not oppose Leven either.

A no less important person, a member of this group, is the accused Neufeld, who was enlisted in the counter-revolutionary organization by his relative while still at his village of Minesberg, Molochansk district. The emissary Mishevskiy (a foreign citizen) and Ediger arrived in the village of Kichkas where, according to Ediger's instructions, they launched the counter-revolutionary activity, working on individual people with anti-Soviet sentiments. Their view was to prepare insurgent units to offer practical help to the invaders – which he briefly explained to his relative, the accused Rempel. The said Mishevskiyi and Ediger have already been convicted by the Special panel.

The accused Kreiter, while not being a member of the given counter-revolution-ary group, but being resentful toward some activities carried out by the Soviet authorities, repeatedly expressed his anti-Soviet views among his friends and relatives and praised the regime of one capitalist country. Further, Kreiter had one of the conversations on this matter with a member of the counter-revolutionary group, the accused Petr Toews.

The above is proved by confessions of the accused P. Toews, G. Toews, Kreiter and, during preliminary investigation, by Neufeld, and partial confessions of Leven, Rempel, and Vaal, as well as testimonies of witnesses Ivan Kozlovskiy, Maria Kozlovskaya, Braun, Funk, Dyck, and others.

On the basis of the above statements, the Special panel believes that the incrimi-nating accusations against all the accused are quite proven. However, the actions of Gustav Toews should be qualified as per article 54-12 of the Penal Code of the USSR since he was not involved in anti-Soviet activities himself. Instead he was indoctrinated by Leven, yet did not agree to join counter-revolutionary Activity, though he did fail to inform the appropriate authorities of Leven's counter-revolu-tionary activity.

As regards Kreiter's accusations, they should be qualified per article 54-10 p. 1 of the UK [the penal code] USSR, only as he was not involved in the organized counter-revolutionary group. With regards to the presented accusations against the accused BRAUN per article 54-10 p. 1 of the UK USSR, the Special panel deems those accusations unproved since the latter were not evidenced in the course of investigation.

David Ivanovich Klassen, age thirty-seven, Ivan Vasilievich Leven, age sixty-two, Ivan Henrikhovich Neufeld, age forty-seven, Jacob Petrovich Klassen, age forty-six, Frantz Frantzevich Vaal, fifty-four, Petr Gustavovich Toews, forty-nine, Hergard Ivanovich Dyck, forty, and Gergard Petrovich Rempel, thirty-three, are guilty according to article 54-11 and 54-10 p. 2 of the UK USSR.

Josef Karlovich Kreiter, fifty, per article 54-10 p. 2 of the UK USSR, and Gustav Petrovich Toews, twenty-four, per article 54-12 of the UK USSR are sentenced to restraint of liberty in correctional labour camps in remote parts of the Soviet Union for the term of:

David Klassen, Leven, Neufeld, and Jacob Klassen – seven years each; Vaal, Rempel, and Dyck – five years.

Kreiter and Petr Toews are sentenced to three years each, and Gustav Petrovich Toews is sentenced to imprisonment in general institutions of confinement for two years with loss of rights per paragraphs 'a,' 'b' and 'v' of article 29 of the UK USSR. Klassen, Jacob Klassen, Leven, and Neufeld are sentenced to five years each. Vaal, Rempel, and Dyck to three years each. P. Toews and Kreiter to a year and a half each. Gustav Toews to one year without confiscation of property due to lack of it.

The accused Isaak Isaakovich Braun, thirty-seven, is to be acquitted due to fail-ure to prove the submitted accusations per the Court and should be released from custody immediately.

Before the sentence takes effect, the preventive punishment toward all the accused is to remain the same, i.e., continued custody, crediting the time of preliminary custody for: Leven – from 3 March 1936, Dyck – from 4 Apr. 1936, David Klassen and Jacob Klassen – from 5 Apr. 1936, Kreiter – from 7 Apr. 1936, Vaal – from 8 Apr. 1936, P. Toews and G. Toews – from 22 Apr. 1936, Neufeld – from 7 May 1936, and Rempel – from 12 May 1936, all up to the day of the present conviction.

The accused owe the Dnepropetrovsk college of advocates the following amounts for legal support provided to them: D. Klassen, J. Klassen, Leven, Neufeld, and Vaal – 150 roubles each; Rempel and Dyck – 100 roubles each; Toews and Kreiter – 50 roubles each. The court-related costs are to be covered by the state.

This sentence can be appealed at the Special panel of the Supreme Court of the USSR within a five-day period from the date of presentation to the convicted of copies of the present sentence.

Investigator of Ukrainian KGB at the Cabinet of Ministers of the USSR for Kherson region – captain (signature) (Kolot)

16 Doc. 11, file 283, vol. 95, inventory list 4, R2033, SAKR.
17 Captain Kolot, 'Conclusion of the Criminal Case #11748 regarding the Accusation against Isaak Isaakovich Braun,' 10 June 1961, doc. 13, vol. 95, inventory list 4, R2033, SAKR. Captain Kolot, investigator of the UKGB at the CM of the USSR for Kherson region, concludes, 'An examination of a number of cases of arrested citizens in 1937–1938 in Mikhailovka vil-lage has also established that the said witnesses – and particularly Bikhe, Abrams A., and Abrams, D. – were regular (staff) witnesses and were questioned in all cases.'
18 L. Podvysotskiy, chair of the Presidium of Kherson regional court, 'Resolu-tion of the Kherson Regional Court, 20 July 1961,' doc. 16, file 95, vol. 95, inventory list 4-1/38, R2033, SAKR.
19 Zabolotnyi, commissioner of Lepatikhskiy NKVD of the USSR, 'Resolution to Bring Charges against the Accused, 8 March, 1938,' doc. 12/a, file 95, vol. 95, inventory list 4-1/38, R2033, SAKR. Also Captain Dmitrichenko, investigator of the UKGB at the CM of the USSR for Kherson region, 'Investigation File on Charges against Isaak Isaakovich Braun,' 6 June, 1961, doc. 12/a, file 3669 F/SN/1, vol. 95, inventory list 12/a, R4033/4, SAKR.
20 Sheinberg, secretary of the Troika meeting at UNKVD for Nikolaev region,

22 Apr. 1938, 'Extract from the Minutes, No. 42,' citing file 97058, vol. 95, inventory list 4, R2033, SAKR. This file finds Isaak Isaakovich Braun guilty of being 'sharply counter-revolutionary minded,' of trying to emigrate, of 'spreading libellous rumours about the allegedly hard life in the USSR,' and of 'praising the fascist regime of Germany and Hitler.' Also guilty of 'agitation to oppose the election to the Supreme Soviet of the USSR,' of 'insurgent tendencies, terrorist intentions,' and being 'against the sign-up for "Defence of the USSR loan."' Translation E. Davidova and S. Markarov.

21 A. Khuraskin, assistant regional prosecutor, USSR Prosecutor's Office, Kherson region, to Captain A.E. Dmitrichenko, citing file 11748, USSR Prosecutor's Office, Kherson region, Secretariat of UKGB.

22 Captain Kolot, 'Conclusion, 10 June, 1961,' doc. 13, vol. 95, inventory list 4, R2033, SAKR.

23 Heinrich Ratzlaff, 'Wehrlos und Verlassen,' *Mennoblatt*, 16 July 2004, 4–5.

24 Carl Rohl, 'Wehrlos und verlassen sehnt sich,' in *Sing the Journey Hymnal: A Worship Book* (Scottdale, PA: Faith and Life Resources, 2005), 93–4. Translation by Jean Wiebe Janzen.

25 Edwin Neufeld, 'Ein einsamer Mann in Molochansk,' *Mennoblatt*, 1 Aug. 2004, 4.

Selected Bibliography

Allen, William Sheridan. *The Nazi Seizure of Power: The Experience of a Single German Town, 1930–1935*. Chicago: Quadrangle Books, 1965.

Applebaum, Anne. *Gulag: A History.* New York: Doubleday, 2003.

– 'Inside the Gulag.' *New York Review*, 15 June 2000.

Bacon, Edwin. *The Gulag at War: Stalin's Forced Labor System in the Light of the Archives*. New York: New York University Press, 1994.

Baitalsky, Mikhail. *Notebooks for the Grandchildren: Recollections of a Trotskyist Who Survived the Stalin Terror*. Translated by Marilyn Vogt-Downey. New Jersey: Humanities, 1995.

Beevor, Antony. *The Fall of Berlin 1945*. London: Penguin Books, 2003.

Belkowez, Larisa, and Sergey Belkowez. *Gescheiterte Hoffnungen: Das deutsche Generalkonsultat in Sibirien 1923–1938*. Essen: Klartext, 2004.

Bohdan, Vladimir A. *Avoiding Extinction: Children of the Kulak*. New York: Vantage, 1992.

Bonner, Elena. 'The Remains of Totalitarianism.' Translated by Antonina W. Bouis. *New York Review*, 8 March 2001.

Brandes, Detlef, and Andrej Savin. *Die Sibirien-deutschen im Sowjetstaat 1919–1938*. Essen: Klartext, 2001.

Buchsweiler, Meir. *Volksdeutsche in der Ukraine am Vorabend und Beginn des Zweiten Weltkrieges – ein Fall doppelter Loyalität?* Gerlingen: Bleicher, 1984.

Bullock, Alan. *Hitler: A Study in Tyranny*. New York: Harper & Brothers, 1952.

Celmina, Helene. *Women in Soviet Prisons*. Celmina, 1985.

Conquest, Robert. *Harvest of Sorrow: Soviet Collectivization and Terror-Famine*. Edmonton: University of Alberta Press and Canadian Institute of Ukrainian Studies, 1986.

Cottrell, Robert. 'L'Homme Nikita.' *New York Review of Books*. 1 May 2003.

Dallin, Alexander. *German Rule in Russia, 1941–1945: A Study of Occupation Policies*. New York: Macmillan, 1957.

Daniels, Robert V. *The Stalin Revolution: Foundations of the Totalitarian Era*. 3rd ed. Toronto: Heath, 1990.

Deak, Istvan. 'The Crime of the Century.' *New York Review of Books*, 22 September 2002.

– 'Heroes and Victims.' *New York Review of Books*, 31 May 2001.

– 'Memories of Hell.' *New York Review of Books*, 26 June 1997.

Der Bote, Ein Mennonitisches Familienblatt. Letters, memoirs and articles in biweekly issues 1929–2007.

Derksen, Peter I. *Es wurde wieder ruhig: Die Lebensgeschichte eines mennonitischen Predigers aus der Sowjetunion*. Winnipeg: Mennonite Heritage Centre, 1989.

Die Mennonitische Rundschau. Letters, memoirs, and articles in selected issues 1924–2000.

Dueck, Helene. *Durch Trübsal und Not*. Winnipeg: Centre for Mennonite Brethren Studies, 1995.

Durrell, Gerald. *The Drunken Forest*. New York: Penguin Books, 1983.

Dyck, Harvey L. 'Collectivization, Depression, and Immigration, 1929–1930: A Chance Interplay.' In *Empire and Nations: Essays in Honour of Frederic H. Soward*, 144–59. Toronto: University of Toronto Press, 1969.

– 'Reform without Class War: Mennonite-Bolshevik Dialogue and Conflict in the 1920s.' *Preservings* 13 (December 1998): 2–5.

– *Weimar Germany and Soviet Russia, 1926–1933: A Study in Diplomatic Instability*. London: Chatto and Windus, 1966.

Dyck, Sarah, ed. *The Silence Echoes: Memoirs of Trauma and Tears*. Kitchener, ON: Pandora, 1997.

Eisfeld, Alfred, and Victor Herdt. *Deportation, Sondersiedlung, Arbeitsarmee: Deutsche in der Sowjetunion 1941 bis 1956*. Köln: Verlag Wissenschaft und Politik, 1996.

Epp, Frank H. *Mennonite Exodus: The Rescue and Resettlement of the Russian Mennonites since the Communist Revolution*. Altona, MB: Canadian Mennonite Relief and Immigration Council, 1962.

Epp, George K. 'Mennonite Ukrainian Relations (1789–1945).' *Journal of Mennonite Studies*, 7 (1989): 131–44.

Epp, Jacob D. *A Mennonite in Russia: The Diaries of Jacob D. Epp, 1851–1880*. Edited by Harvey Dyck. Toronto: University of Toronto Press, 1991.

Epp, Marlene. *Women without Men: Mennonite Refugees in the Second World War*. Toronto: University of Toronto Press, 2000.

Epp, Peter. *Ob Tausend Fallen: Mein Leben im Archipel Gulag*. Gummersbach: Memra-Verlag, 1988.

Epstein, Jason. 'Always Time to Kill.' *New York Review of Books*, 4 November 1999.

Evans, Richard J. *The Third Reich in Power, 1933–1839*. New York: Penguin, 2005.

Fast, Karl. *Gebt der Wahrheit die Ehre*. Winnipeg: Canzona, 1989.

Figes, Orlando, *The Whisperers: Private Life in Stalin's Russia*. London: Penguin, 2008.

Fitzpatrick, Sheila. *The Russian Revolution*. 2nd ed. New York: Oxford University Press, 1994.

Fleischhauer, Ingeborg, and Benjamin Pinkus. *The Soviet Germans Past and Present*. New York: St Martin's, 1986.

Friesen, Leonard G. 'Mennonites & the Soviet Inferno: Reflections on the Symposium.' *Journal of Mennonite Studies* 16 (1998): 91–4.

Friesen, P.M. *The Mennonite Brotherhood in Russia (1789–1910)*. Translated by Abraham Friesen, Peter J. Klassen, Harry Loewen, and J.B. Toews. Fresno, CA: Board of Christian Literature, General Conference of Mennonite Brethren Churches, 1978.

Friesen, Robert. *Auf den Spuren der Ahnen*. Oerlinghausen: Eilbracht, 2000.

Friesen, Rudy, with Sergey Shmakin. *Into the Past: Buildings of the Mennonite Commonwealth*. Winnipeg: Raduga Publications, 1996.

Garros, Veronique, Natalia Korenevskaya, and Thomas Lahusen, eds. *Intimacy and Terror: Soviet Diaries of the 1930s*. New York: New Press, 1995.

Gerlach, Horst. *Die Russlandsmennoniten: Ein Volk Unterwegs*. Kirchheimbolanden Pfalz, self-published, GTS-Druck GmbH, 1992.

– 'Mennonites, the Molotschna, and the *Volksdeutsche Mittelstelle* in the Second World War.' Translated by John D. Thiessen. *Mennonite Life*, September 1986.

Getty, J. Arch, and Roberta T. Manning. *Stalinist Terror: New Perspectives*. Cambridge: Cambridge University Press, 1994.

Ginzburg, Eugenia. *Journey into the Whirlwind*. Translated by Paul Stevenson and Max Hayward. New York: Harcourt, Brace & World, 1967.

– *Within the Whirlwind*. Translated by Ian Boland. London: Collins & Harvill, 1981.

Goering, Jutti Epp. *Eine Familiengeschichte und Eigene Erlebnisse*. Nanaimo, BC: Goering, 2001.

Goerz, H. *Die mennonitischen Siedlungen der Krim*. Winnipeg: Echo, 1957.

– *Memrik*. Echo Verlag series. Winnipeg: Canadian Memmonite Bible College Publications, 1997.

Günther, Helmut. *Von der Hitlerjugend zur Waffen-SS*. Coburg, Germany: Nation Europa, 2001.

Harms, Wilmer A. *The Odyssey of Escapes from Russia*. Hillsboro, KS: Hearth, 1998.

Hartwig, Bernd. *Die Dinge lagen damals anders: Berichte über die Hitler-Zeit, 1933–1945*. Aachen: K. Fischer, 2002.

Hautzig, Esther. *The Endless Steppe*. Harper Keypoint edition. New York: Harper & Row, 1987.

Heimatbuch der Deutschen aus Russland, Die Landsmannschaft der Deutschen aus Russland [A journal for Germans from Russia], Stuttgart, 1966.

Hein, Gerhard, ed. *The Ufa Settlement in the Framework of the Older and Larger Mennonite Settlements in the Russia of Old; Ufa: The Mennonite Settlements, (Colonies), 1894–1938*. Translated by Mary Enns. Steinbach, MB: Derksen, 1977.

Heintzeler, Wolfgang. *Der rote Faden*. Stuttgart: Seewald, 1983.

Hildebrandt, Georg. *Wieso Lebst Du Noch: Ein Deutscher Im Gulag*. Frankfurt: Ullstein Buch, 1993.

Janzen, Marianne Heinrichs. 'The Eichenfeld Massacre, October 26, 1919.' *Preservings* 18 (June 2001): 25–31.

Joppke, Christia, and Zeev Roshenhek. 'Ethnic-Priority Immigration in Israel and Germany: Resilience versus Demise.' Working Paper no. 45, Center for Comparative Immigration Studies, University of California–San Diego, 2001.

Journal of Mennonite Studies. Edited by Royden Loewen and Al Reimer. Winnipeg: University of Winnipeg, various volumes.

Judt, Tony. 'The Longest Road to Hell.' *New York Times*, 22 December 1997.

Kapuscinski, Ryszard. *Imperium*. Translated by K. Glowczewska. Toronto: Knopf, 1994.

Kern, Erich. *Dance of Death*. Translated by Paul Findlay. London: Collins, 1951. Printed in German as *Der Grosse Rausch*.

Kershaw, Ian. *Hitler: 1889–1936: Hubris*. London: Penguin, 1998.

Kirss, Tiina A. 'Threading Ariadne's Needle: Estonian Women's Autobiographies of Siberian Deportation.' Translated by Tiina Kirss and Alliki Arroi. Ms. University of Toronto, 2004.

Klassen, Pamela. *Going by the Moon and the Stars: Stories of Two Russian Mennonite Women*. Waterloo, ON: Wilfrid Laurier University Press, 1994.

Klassen, Peter P. *Die Deutsch-Völkische Zeit in der Kolonie Fernheim 1933–1945*. Bolanden-Weierhof, Germany: Mennonitischer Geschichtsverein e.V., 1990.

– *Die Mennoniten in Paraguay: Reich Gottes Und Reich Dieser Welt*. Bolanden-Weierhof: Mennonitischer Geschichtsverein e.V., 1988.

Konrad, Anne. *And in Their Silent Beauty Speak: A Mennonite Family in Russia and Canada, 1790–1990*. Toronto, published by the author, 2004.

– *The Blue Jar*. Winnipeg: Queenston House, 1985.

– 'Translucence.' In *Family Games*, 7–16. Windsor, ON: Netherlandic, 1992.

Konrad Papers. Extensive archive of personal letters from relatives and others in USSR, Europe and South America to Peter and Luise Konrad, 1930–1980. Property of the author.

Kroeker, Abraham. *Unsere Brüder in Not: Bilder vom Leidensweg der Deutschen Kolonisten in Russland*. Striegau, Silesia, Germany: Th. Urban, 1930.

Kuromiya, Hiroaki. *Freedom and Terror in the Donbas: A Ukrainian-Russian Borderland, 1870s–1990s*. Cambridge, UK: Cambridge University Press, 1998.

– *The Voices of the Dead: Stalin's Great Terror in the 1930s*. New Haven: Yale University Press, 2007.

Letkemann, Peter. 'Den Opfern zum Gedächnis' *Bote* 78, no. 8 (2001): 7-9; no. 9 (2001): 15–16, 18.

– 'Mennonites in the Soviet Inferno, 1917–1956.' *Preservings* 13 (December 1998): 10–11.

– 'Mennonites in the Soviet Inferno 1929–1941.' *Mennonite Historian* 24, no. 4 (December 1998): 1, 6–7.

– 'Mennonite Victims of the Great Terror, 1936–1938.' *Journal of Mennonite Studies* 16 (1998): 33–58.

– 'Molochna-2004, Mennonites and Their Neighbours (1804–2004): An International Conference, Zaporizhzhia, Ukraine, June 2–5, 2004.' *Preservings* 24 (December 2004): 57–62. Also in *Mennonite Quarterly Review* 79, no. 1 (January 2005): 109–20.

Loewen, Harry. 'Can the Son Answer for the Father? Reflections on Soviet Terror (on the 60th Anniversary of His Father's Arrest).' *Journal of Mennonite Studies* 16 (1998): 76–90.

– 'A Mennonite Christian View of Suffering: The Case of Russian Mennonites in the 1930s and 1940s.' *Mennonite Quarterly Review* 77, no. 1 (January 2003): 47–68.

– ed. *Road to Freedom: Mennonites Escape the Land of Suffering*. Kitchener, ON: Pandora, 2000.

Magocsi, Paul Robert. *A History of Ukraine*. Toronto: University of Toronto Press, 1996.

Makine, Andrei. *Confessions of a Fallen Standard-Bearer*. New York: Penguin Books, 2000.

– *Dreams of My Russian Summer*. New York: Simon & Schuster, 1995.

Markova, Nina. *Nina's Journey: A Memoir of Stalin's Russia and the Second World War*. Washington, DC: Regnery Gateway, 1989.

Martin, Terry. *The Affirmative Action Empire: Nations and Nationalism in the Soviet Union, 1923–1939*. Ithaca, NY: Cornell University Press, 2001.

Medvedev, Zhores A., and Roy A. Medvedev. *A Question of Madness*. New York: Norton, 1979.

Mennoblatt: Zeitschrift für Gemeinde und Kolonie. Filadelfia, Paraguay. Bi-monthly newspaper containing letters, memoirs, and articles. Selected issues 1986–2007.

Mennonite Quarterly Review. Edited by John D. Roth. Goshen, IN: Mennonite Historical Society for Goshen College.

Mennonitische Volkswarte 9 and 12. Steinbach, MB: Warte, 1935.

The Mennonite Encyclopedia, vols. 1–5. Scottdale, PA: Mennonite Publishing House, 1959 and 1990.

Mennonitisches Jahrbuch. Newton, KS: Mennonite Publication Office, 1948.

Merridale, Catherine. *Ivan's War: The Red Army 1939–45*. London: Faber & Faber, 2006.

Montefiore, Simon Sebag. *Prince of Princes: The Life of Potemkin*. London: Phoenix, 2000.

– *Stalin: The Court of the Red Tsar*. London, Weidenfeld & Nicolson, 2003.

Moustafine, Mara. *Secrets and Spies: The Harbin Files*. Sydney: Random House Australia, 2002.

Nachtigal, Reinhard. *Die Dondeutschen, 1830 bis 1930*. Augsburg: Waldemar Weber, 2005.

Nekrich, Aleksandr. *The Punished Peoples: The Deportation and Fate of Soviet Minorities and the End of the Second World War*. Translated by George Saunders. New York: Norton, 1978.

Neufeldt, Colin, P. 'Through the Fires of Hell: The Dekulakization and Collectivization of the Soviet Mennonite Community, 1928–1933.' *Journal of Mennonite Studies* 16 (1998): 9–32.

Neufeld, Dietrich. *A Russian Dance of Death: Revolution and Civil War in Ukraine*. Translated and edited by Al Reimer. Winnipeg, Hyperion, 1977.

Neufeld, Herta. *Im Paradies … der Arbeiter und Bauern*. Hannover: Bangemann, 1986.

Neufeld, Jakob A. *Tiefenwege: Erfahrungen und Erlebnissse von Russland-Mennoniten in Zwei Jahrzehnten bis 1949*. Virgil, ON: Niagara, 1957.

Penner, Gerhard. *Mennoniten dienen in der Roten Armee*. Steinbach, MB: Carillon, 1975.

Pohl, J. Otto. *Ethnic Cleansing in the USSR 1937–1949*. Westport, CT: Greenwood, 1999.

Pörtner, Rudolf. *Heimat in der Fremde: Deutsche aus Russland Erinnern Sich*. Düsseldorf: Econ, 1992.

Preservings: Magazine/Journal of the Hanover Steinbach Historical Society Inc. Edited by Delbert Plett. Steinbach, MB. Semi-annual issues 1996–2004.

Pries, Anita. *Exiled to Siberia / Verbannung nach Sibirien*. Steinbach, MB: Derksen, 1979.

Quiring, Walter. '*Mennoniten vor Moskau*,' *Mennonitisches Jahrbuch*. Newton, KA: General Conference Mennonite Church Board of Publications, 1956.

Rahn, Peter. 'Autobiography.' Unpublished, n.d. Fernheim Colony Archives, Filadelfia, Chaco, Paraguay.Rahn, Peter [Jr]. *Mennoniten in der Umgebung von Omsk*. Winnipeg: Christian Press, 1975.

Ratzlaff, Gerhard, ed. *Auf den Spuren der Vaeter: Ein Jubilaeumsschrift der Kolonie Friesland in Ostparaguay 1937–1987*. Filadelphia, Paraguay: Cromos, 1987.

Rayfield, Donald. *Stalin and His Hangmen: The Tyrant and Those Who Killed Him*. New York: Random House, 2004.

Regehr, T.D. 'Anatomy of a Mennonite Miracle: The Berlin Rescue of 30–31 January 1947.' *Journal of Mennonite Studies* 9 (1991): 11–33.

Reger, Adina, and Delbert Plett. *Diese Steine: Die Russslandsmennoniten*. Steinbach, MB: Crossway Publications, 2001.

Reimer, Diane, and Reimer Anna. *David and Anna: My Labor of Love*. Calgary: FDM Printers, 1995.

Reimer, Johannes. *Der Verweigerer*. Bielefeld: Logos, 1991.

Rempel, David G., with Cornelia Rempel Carlson. *A Mennonite Family in Tsarist Russia and the Soviet Union, 1789–1923*. Toronto, University of Toronto Press, 2002.

Rempel, Olga. *Einer Von Vielen: Die Lebensgeschichte von Aaron P. Toews*. Winnipeg: Canadian Mennonite Bible College Publications, 1979.

Savin, A.I. *Ethno-Confession in the Soviet State: Mennonites in Siberia, 1920–1989; Annotated List of Archival Documents*. Translated by O. Shmakina and L. Kariaka. Hillsboro, KS: Russian Academy of Sciences Institute of History, Siberian Branch Source, 2008.

Schroeder, William, and Helmut T. Huebert. *Mennonite Historical Atlas*. 2nd ed. Winnipeg: Springfield Publishers, 1996.

Solzhenitsyn, Alexander. *Gulag Archipelago, 1918–1956*. New York: Harper Perennial, 1992.

– *One Day in the Life of Ivan Denisovich*. New York: Bantam Books, 1963.

Stargardt, Nicholas. *Witnesses of War: Children's Lives under the Nazis*. New York: Random House, 2005.

State Archive of Kherson Oblast, file #04-1/3, inventory #04-1/3, collection R-4033.

Toews, A.A. *Mennonitische Märtyrer*. 2 vols. Winnipeg: self-published, 1949, 1954.

Toews, J.B. *Czars, Soviets & Mennonites*. Newton, KS: Faith and Life, 1982.

– *Journeys: Mennonite Stories of Faith and Survival in Stalin's Russia*. Winnipeg: Kindred Productions, 1998.

– *Lost Fatherland: The Story of the Mennonite Emigration from Soviet Russia, 1921–1927*. Scottdale, PA: Herald, 1967.

– ed. *Selected Documents*. Winnipeg, Christian, 1975.

Topolski, Aleksander. *Without Vodka: Wartime Adventures in Russia*. Toronto: McArthur, 2000.

Ukrainian Security Service Archive (SBU), Donetsk, file no. 17/10-11752–2F; no. 3650-N-59.

Vins, Georgi. *Testament from Prison*. Translated by Jane Ellis and edited by Michael Bourdeaux. Weston, ON: Cook, 1975.

– *Wie Schafe Unter Wölfen: Erfahrungen eines Christen in sowjetischen Straflagern*. Gummersbach, Germany: Friedenstimme, 1987.

Willms, H.J., ed. *Vor den Toren Moskaus: Gottes Gnaedige Durchhilfe In Einer Schweren Zeit*. Komitee der Flüchtlinge. Yarrow, BC: Columbia, 1960.

Winter, Henry H. *Ein Hirte der Bedrängten*. Altona: Friesen Printers, 1988.

Zlezkine, Yuri. *The Jewish Century*. Princeton: Princeton University Press, 2004.

Index

265–8, 271; Andrusha Braun, 266, 268; Natasha (blond), 265–6; Natasha (dark), 265–6; Nikolai, xxi, 183, 198, 268; Tanya, 266; Vika, 266, 268; Volodya Braun, 268

'Miracle' on Amur River, 79–80

Mixed blood, 160, 168

Mixed marriage, 87, 156, 263

Molochansk (Halbstadt): Bolshevik Party, 94, 310n15; district, 311n20, 329n15; former Halbstadt, 16, 130, 301; Mennonite Centre, 249; photo, 158

Molokan, 87–8

Molotov, Viacheslav, 38, 141–2, 146, 327n4

Molotov/Ribbentrop Pact (Hitler/ Stalin non-aggression pact), 139, 141, 146, 167, 184, 186, 323n10

Montefiore, Simon Sebag, 39, 304n14, 324n20

Morozov, Pavel, 134, 264

Moscow, 11, 14, 15, 32, 39, 40, 42, 44–9, 53, 55, 57, 61, 63, 66–8, 75–6, 85, 88, 93, 95, 104, 119, 126, 147, 173, 175, 227, 233, 238–9, 250–2, 255, 269, 275, 278, 285, 293, 300

Mukhametzyanov, Massar Z., 253, 255, 283

Museums: Davlekanova, 253, 255; Margenau, 263–4; Melitopol, 249; Omsk, 260; Slavgorod, 267; Tomsk, 278; Zaporizhia, 255

NEP, *Novaya ekonomicheskaya politika* (New economic policy), 35, 37, 126

NKVD (*see also* Cheka; KGB): arrests: 1929 group, 43; 1936 group, 295–6; 1937–8 *chistka*, 97, 108; 1940 group, 186–7; police assist friends 285–6;

quotas, 105

Nansen, Fridtjof, 83–4; Nansen mission statement, 308n40; Nansen passport, 84

Nazis: administration of occupied territories, 152, 153–5, 155–6, 157–8, 160; attack USSR, 141–4; in Soviet Ukraine, xi; military (Wehrmacht), 150, 152, 154, 158, 201; (deserters) 169; retreat 1943, 166; settle refugees in Warthegau, occupied Poland, 135, 166

– German-speakers assisted in occupied Soviet Ukraine, 135, 154, 159, 244

– Jews: distribute Jewish clothing, 157; mass murders of, 153, 157, 316n10

– Poles: deport Poles as *Ostarbeiter*, 160, 167; evict Poles, 167

– religion (view of), 154, 156, 158, 318n34

– Roma, in Soviet Ukraine (kill), 143–4, 146, 152, 155, 157

– Ukrainians/*Slavs*, 136, 150–1, 152, 154–5, 160, 244; kill Soviet POWs, 316n12

Nemtsy. See Germans

Neufeld, Colin, 58

Neufeld, Heinrich, 186–7, 195–6, 323n10

Neufeld, Katya (nee Peters), 184, 186–7, 323n10

Neufeld, Jakob A., 142, 145, 157–8, 327n6

New Year's Day (Soviet holiday), 220; Father Frost, 141

Nider, Molochansk district Communist Party chair, 310n18n19n20

Nuclear tests, 69; cancer deaths, 222,